MUSE OF FIRE: *Approaches to Poetry*

MUSE OF FIRE:

Approaches to Poetry

H. Edward Richardson
UNIVERSITY OF LOUISVILLE

and

Frederick B. Shroyer
CALIFORNIA STATE COLLEGE AT LOS ANGELES

Alfred A. Knopf | NEW YORK

THIS IS A BORZOI BOOK PUBLISHED BY ALFRED A. KNOPF, INC.

Copyright © 1971 by Alfred A. Knopf, Inc.
All rights reserved under International and Pan-American Copyright Conventions.
Published in the United States by Alfred A. Knopf, Inc., New York, and simul-
taneously in Canada by Random House of Canada Limited, Toronto. Distributed
by Random House, Inc., New York.

ISBN: 0–394–31043–8

Library of Congress Catalog Card Number: 70–138319

Manufactured in the United States of America

FIRST EDITION
9876543

Since this page cannot legibly accommodate all the copyright notices, the pages
following constitute an extension of the copyright page.

Acknowledgments

FRANKLIN P. ADAMS, "Us Potes" from *The Column Book of Franklin P. Adams.* Copyright 1928 by Doubleday & Company, Inc. Reprinted by permission of Doubleday & Company, Inc.

CONRAD AIKEN, "The Morning Song of Senlin" from *Collected Poems* by Conrad Aiken. Copyright 1953 by Conrad Aiken. Reprinted by permission of Oxford University Press, Inc.

KINGSLEY AMIS, "A Dream of Fair Women" from *A Case of Samples* by Kingsley Amis. Reprinted by permission of Curtis Brown, Ltd.

W. H. AUDEN, "In Memory of W. B. Yeats" from *Collected Shorter Poems 1927–1957* by W. H. Auden. Copyright 1940 and renewed 1968 by W. H. Auden. "Paysage Moralisé" from *Collected Shorter Poems 1927–1957* by W. H. Auden. Copyright 1937 and renewed 1965 by W. H. Auden. Reprinted by permission of Random House, Inc., and Faber & Faber, Ltd.

STEPHEN VINCENT BENÉT, "Short Ode" from *The Selected Works of Stephen Vincent Benét.* Copyright, 1936, by The Curtis Publishing Company. Copyright renewed © 1964 by Thomas C. Bent, Stephanie B. Mahin, and Rachel B. Lewis. "Daniel Boone" from *A Book of Americans* by Rosemary and Stephen Vincent Benét, published by Holt, Rinehart and Winston, Inc. Copyright, 1933, by Rosemary and Stephen Vincent Benét. Copyright renewed, © 1961 by Rosemary Carr Benét. Reprinted by permission of Brandt & Brandt. "American Names," "Ghosts of a Lunatic Asylum," and "The Ballad of William Sycamore" from *Ballads and Poems* by Stephen Vincent Benét. Copyright 1931 by Stephen Vincent Benét. Copyright © 1959 by Rosemary Carr Benét. Reprinted by permission of Holt, Rinehart and Winston, Inc.

JOHN BETJEMAN, "A Subaltern's Love-Song" from *Collected Poems* by John Betjeman, published by Houghton Mifflin Company. Reprinted by permission of John Murray, Ltd.

LOUISE BOGAN, "Women" from *The Blue Estuaries* by Louise Bogan. Copyright © 1954, 1968 by Louise Bogan. Reprinted by permission of Farrar, Straus, & Giroux, Inc.

ARNA BONTEMPS, "Close Your Eyes!" from *Personals* by Arna Bontemps. Copyright © 1963 by Arna Bontemps. Reprinted by permission of Harold Ober Associates, Inc.

PHILIP BOOTH, "First Lesson" from *Letter from a Distant Land* by Philip Booth. Copyright © 1957 by Philip Booth. Reprinted by permission of The Viking Press, Inc.

RUPERT BROOKE, "The Hill," "The Great Lover," and "Heaven" from *The Collected Poems of Rupert Brooke.* Copyright 1915 by Dodd, Mead & Company, Inc. Copyright 1943 by Edward Marsh. Reprinted by permission of Dodd, Mead & Company, Inc.

GWENDOLYN BROOKS, "The Chicago Picasso" from *In the Mecca* by Gwendolyn Brooks. Copyright © 1968 by Gwendolyn Brooks Blakely. "But Can See Better There, and Laughing There" from *Selected Poems* by Gwendolyn Brooks. Copyright, 1949, by Gwendolyn Brooks Blakely. Reprinted by permission of Harper & Row, Publishers, Inc.

ROY CAMPBELL, "The Zebras" from *Adamastor* by Roy Campbell. Reprinted by permission of Curtis Brown, Ltd.

JOHN CIARDI, "The Dolls" from *In the Stoneworks* by John Ciardi. Copyright 1961 by Rutgers, The State University. "To Judith Asleep" from

Copyright 1933 and renewed 1960 by William Faulkner. Reprinted by permission of Random House, Inc.

LAWRENCE FERLINGHETTI, "The poet's eye obscenely seeing," "The pennycandystore beyond the El," "The world is a beautiful place," "'This life is not a circus where,'" and "Christ Climbed Down" from *A Coney Island of the Mind* by Lawrence Ferlinghetti. Copyright 1955, © 1958 by Lawrence Ferlinghetti. Reprinted by permission of New Directions Publishing Corporation.

DAVID FERRY, "The Milkmaid" from *On the Way to the Island* by David Ferry. Copyright © 1957 by David Ferry. Reprinted by permission of Wesleyan University Press.

F. SCOTT FITZGERALD, "Obit on Parnassus" from *The New Yorker* (June 5, 1937). Copyright © 1937, 1965 The New Yorker Magazine, Inc. Reprinted by permission of Harold Ober Associates, Inc.

ROBERT FROST, "A Soldier," "Stopping by Woods on a Snowy Evening," "West-Running Brook," "Brown's Descent," and "After Apple-Picking" from *The Poetry of Robert Frost* edited by Edward Connery Lathem. Copyright 1916, 1928, 1930, 1939, © 1969 by Holt, Rinehart and Winston, Inc. Copyright 1944, © 1956, 1958 by Robert Frost. Copyright © 1967 by Lesley Frost Ballantine. Reprinted by permission of Holt, Rinehart and Winston, Inc.

JACK GILBERT, "And She Waiting" and "The Abnormal Is Not Courage" from *Views of Jeopardy* by Jack Gilbert. Copyright © 1962 by Yale University. Reprinted by permission of Yale University Press.

ARTHUR GUITERMAN, "On the Vanity of Earthly Greatness" from *Gaily the Troubadour* by Arthur Guiterman. Reprinted by permission of Mrs. Arthur Guiterman.

THOM GUNN, "On the Move" from *The Sense of Movement* by Thom Gunn. Reprinted by permission of Faber & Faber, Ltd. "Innocence" and "Black Jackets" from *My Sad Captains* by Thom Gunn. © by Thom Gunn. Reprinted by permission of The University of Chicago Press and Faber & Faber, Ltd.

DONALD HALL, "Dr. Fatt, Instructor" published in *Harper's* (May 1960). Copyright © 1960 by Harper's Magazine, Inc. Reprinted by permission of Curtis Brown, Ltd.

THOMAS HARDY, "The Darkling Thrush," "The Man He Killed," and "The Convergence of the Twain" from *Collected Poems* by Thomas Hardy. Copyright 1925 by The Macmillan Company. Reprinted by permission of The Macmillan Company, Macmillan & Co., Ltd., London, The Macmillan Company of Canada Limited, and the Hardy Estate.

ROBERT HAYDEN, "The Diver" and "O Daedalus, Fly Away Home" from *Selected Poems* by Robert Hayden. Copyright © 1966 by Robert Hayden. "Aunt Jemima of the Ocean Waves" from *Words in the Mourning Time* by Robert Hayden. Copyright © 1970 by Robert Hayden. Reprinted by permission of October House, Inc.

ERNEST HEMINGWAY, "Champs d'Honneur." Reprinted by permission of Mary Hemingway.

GERARD MANLEY HOPKINS, "Pied Beauty" and "Windhover" from *Poems of Gerard Manley Hopkins* edited by W. H. Gardner. Copyright 1948 by Oxford University Press, Inc. Reprinted by permission of Oxford University Press, Inc.

A. E. HOUSMAN, "Oh, When I Was in Love with You," "To an Athlete Dying Young," "Terence, This Is Stupid Stuff," "When I Was One and Twenty," "The True Lover," "Is My Team Ploughing?" from "A Shropshire Lad" (Authorized Edition) from *The Collected Poems of A. E. Housman*. Copyright 1939, 1940, © 1959 by Holt, Rinehart and Winston, Inc. Copyright © 1967, 1968 by Robert E. Symons. Reprinted by permission of Holt, Rinehart and Winston, Inc., The Society of Authors as the literary representative of the Estate of A. E. Housman, and Jonathan Cape, Ltd.

LANGSTON HUGHES, "I, Too" from *Selected Poems* by Langston Hughes. Copyright 1926 by Alfred A. Knopf, Inc., and renewed 1954 by Langston Hughes. "Our Land" from *The Weary Blues* by Langston Hughes. Copyright 1926 by Alfred A. Knopf, Inc., and renewed

ARCHIBALD MACLEISH, "The End of the World" from *Collected Poems 1917–1952* by Archibald MacLeish. Copyright, 1952, by Archibald MacLeish. Reprinted by permission of Houghton Mifflin Company.

LOUIS MACNEICE, "Sunday Morning" from *The Collected Poems of Louis MacNeice* edited by E. R. Dodds. Copyright © The Estate of Louis MacNeice 1966. Reprinted by permission of Oxford University Press, Inc., and Faber & Faber, Ltd.

EDWIN MARKHAM, "The Man with the Hoe." Reprinted by permission of Virgil Markham.

JOHN MASEFIELD, "Sea Fever" from *Poems* by John Masefield. Copyright 1912 by The Macmillan Company, renewed 1940 by John Masefield. Reprinted by permission of The Macmillan Company.

EDGAR LEE MASTERS, "Harry Wilmans," "Alfonso Churchill," "Benjamin Pantier," "Mrs. Benjamin Pantier," "Editor Whedon," "Fletcher McGee," and "Lucinda Matlock." Reprinted by permission of Weissberger & Frosch, representatives of Mrs. Edgar Lee Masters.

MARCIA LEE MASTERS, "Figure." Reprinted by permission of the author.

THOMAS MERTON, "Elegy for the Monastery Barn" from *Selected Poems* by Thomas Merton. Copyright 1944 by Our Lady of Gethsemani Monastery; © 1963 by The Abbey of Gethsemani, Inc. Reprinted by permission of New Directions Publishing Corporation.

EDNA ST. VINCENT MILLAY, " 'I know I am but summer to your heart' " from *Collected Poems* by Edna St. Vincent Millay, published by Harper & Row, Inc. Copyright 1923, 1951 by Edna St. Vincent Millay and Norma Millay Ellis. Reprinted by permission of Norma Millay Ellis, Literary Executor.

VASSAR MILLER, "Reciprocity," "The Final Hunger," and "The New Icarus" from *Wage War on Silence* by Vassar Miller. Reprinted by permission of Wesleyan University Press.

MARIANNE MOORE, "Nevertheless" from *Collected Poems* by Marianne Moore. Copyright 1944 by Marianne Moore. Reprinted by permission of The Macmillan Company.

HOWARD MOSS, "The Gift to Be Simple." Copyright 1954 by Howard Moss. Reprinted by permission of the author.

OGDEN NASH, "The Turtle" from *Verses from 1929 On* by Ogden Nash. Copyright 1940 by Ogden Nash. Reprinted by permission of Little, Brown and Co.

HOWARD NEMEROV, "De Anima" from *The Next Room of the Dream.* Copyright by Howard Nemerov, 1962. Reprinted by permission of Margot Johnson Agency. "Boom!" from *The Nation* (January 25, 1958). Reprinted by permission of the publisher.

JOHN FREDERICK NIMS, "Love Poem" from *The Iron Pastoral* by John Frederick Nims, published by William Sloane Associates. Copyright 1947 by John Frederick Nims. Reprinted by permission of William Morrow and Company, Inc.

BINK NOLL, "The Picador Bit" from *The Center of the Circle* by Bink Noll. © 1962 by Bink Noll. Reprinted by permission of Harcourt Brace Jovanovich, Inc.

ONITSURA, "The World Upsidedown" from *An Introduction to Haiku* edited by Harold G. Henderson. Copyright © 1958 by Harold G. Henderson. Reprinted by permission of Doubleday & Company, Inc.

WILFRED OWEN, "Greater Love" and "Dulce et Decorum Est" from *Collected Poems* by Wilfred Owen. Copyright Chatto & Windus, Ltd., 1946, © 1963. Reprinted by permission of New Directions Publishing Corporation, Mr. Harold Owen, and Chatto & Windus, Ltd.

DOROTHY PARKER, "Résumé" from *The Portable Dorothy Parker.* Copyright 1926, renewed 1954 by Dorothy Parker. Reprinted by permission of The Viking Press, Inc.

SYLVIA PLATH, "Tulips" from *Ariel* by Sylvia Plath. Copyright © 1962 by Ted Hughes. Reprinted by permission of Harper & Row, Publishers, Inc., and Olwyn Hughes, Representative of Sylvia Plath's Estate.

EZRA POUND, "An Immorality" from *Lustra* by Ezra Pound. Copyright 1917 by Ezra Pound. All Rights Reserved. Reprinted by permission of New Directions Publishing Corporation for

renewed 1951 by Wallace Stevens. Reprinted by permission of Alfred A. Knopf, Inc.

JESSE STUART, "The Snow Lies Patched." Reprinted by permission of *American Forests*. "'I came the Womack Road from Sandy Bridge,'" "'And you, my mother, who will stack by you?,'" "'Don Davidson, you walk on earth today,'" "'Oh, Brother, come! Now let us put our hand,'" "'The stars will shine forever over you,'" and "'Maybe there is the sound of windless rain'" from *Man with a Bull-Tongue Plow*, revised edition, Dutton paperback, by Jesse Stuart. Copyright ©, 1959 by Jesse Stuart. Reprinted by permission of E. P. Dutton & Co., Inc., Publishers. "Anannis Tabor," "Pat Hennessey," "Harry Dartmore Speaks for Maitland Gray Arnett," "Royster Pennix," and "Robert Diesel" from *Album of Destiny* by Jesse Stuart. Reprinted by permission of the author.

DYLAN THOMAS, "Fern Hill," "Poem in October," "In My Craft or Sullen Art," "Incarnate Devil," and "Do Not Go Gentle into That Good Night" from *Collected Poems* by Dylan Thomas. Copyright 1939, 1946, by New Directions Publishing Corporation. Copyright 1952 by Dylan Thomas. Reprinted by permission of New Directions Publishing Corporation, J. M. Dent & Sons, Ltd., and the Trustees for the Copyrights of the late Dylan Thomas.

MELVIN B. TOLSON, "The Sea Turtle and the Shark" from *Harlem Gallery* by Melvin B. Tolson. Copyright 1965 by Twayne Publishers, Inc. Reprinted by permission of Twayne Publishers, Inc.

JEAN TOOMER, "Georgia Dusk" from *Cane* by Jean Toomer. Copyright ® 1951 by Jean Toomer. Reprinted by permission of Liveright, Publishers.

JOHN UPDIKE, "Ex-Basketball Player" from *The Carpentered Hen and Other Tame Creatures* by John Updike. Copyright © 1957 by John Updike. Originally appeared in *The New Yorker*. Reprinted by permission of Harper & Row, Publishers, Inc.

JOHN WAIN, "Reason for Not Writing Orthodox Nature Poetry" from *A Word Carved on a Sill* by John Wain. Reprinted by permission of St. Martin's Press, Inc., and Routledge & Kegan Paul, Ltd. "A Song about Major Eatherly" from *Weep Before God* by John Wain. Reprinted by permission of Curtis Brown, Ltd.

DEREK WALCOTT, "Ruins of a Great House" from *Selected Poems* by Derek Walcott. Copyright © 1962, 1963, 1964 by Derek Walcott. Reprinted by permission of Farrar, Straus & Giroux, Inc., and Jonathan Cape, Ltd.

R. B. WEBER, "Sweet Baskers and Hammerheads," originally published in *Southern Poetry Review*, IX (Fall 1968). Reprinted by permission of the author.

JOHN HALL WHEELOCK, "The Black Panther" from *The Black Panther* by John Hall Wheelock. Copyright 1922 by Charles Scribner's Sons; renewal copyright 1950 by John Hall Wheelock. Reprinted by permission of Charles Scribner's Sons.

RICHARD WILBUR, "Love Calls Us to the Things of This World" from *Things of This World* by Richard Wilbur. © 1956, by Richard Wilbur. Reprinted by permission of Harcourt Brace Jovanovich, Inc.

PETER WILD, "Death of a Cat on Rt. 84," first published in *Mica Mtn Poems* by Peter Wild, issued by Lillabulero Press, Ithaca, N. Y. Copyright 1968 by Peter Wild. Reprinted by permission of the author.

JAMES WRIGHT, "Mutterings Over the Crib of a Deaf Child" from *Collected Poems* by James Wright. Copyright © 1957 by James Wright. "Autumn Begins in Martins Ferry, Ohio" from *The Branch Will Not Break* by James Wright. Copyright © 1962 by James Wright. Reprinted by permission of Wesleyan University Press.

WILLIAM BUTLER YEATS, "The Indian Upon God" and "The Lake Isle of Innisfree" from *Collected Poems* by William Butler Yeats. Copyright 1906 by The Macmillan Company, renewed 1934 by William Butler Yeats. "A Deep Sworn Vow" from *Collected Poems* by William Butler Yeats. Copyright 1919 by The Macmillan Company, renewed 1947 by Bertha Georgie Yeats. "The Second Coming" and "Prayer for My Daughter" from *Collected*

*This book is for
Antonia and Patricia*

O for a Muse of fire, that would ascend
The brightest heaven of invention

          —Shakespeare, *Henry V, Prologue*

Preface

The two major sections of this text are an anthology of poetry—of which around 70 per cent is relatively modern, and the rest drawn from earlier twentieth-century decades and preceding centuries—and a nine-chapter presentation of major critical approaches to poetry, including a terminal essay of "synthesis" which, hopefully, demonstrates that critical schools need not necessarily be mutually exclusive.

Importantly, the poems are unaccompanied by any intervening critical apparatus. Presented in isolation, they stand unstained by any particular critical lamp. The various critical approaches presented here can thus be applied singly, in groups, or collectively to any poem in the anthology. In effect, the instructor and student are free to select *any* approach they wish—from Plato and Aristotle, say, to Cleanth Brooks and Northrop Frye.

Rather than throw the not inconsiderable number of poems presented here into one drawer, alphabetical, chronological, or otherwise, we have grouped them under fourteen thematic headings. Moreover, we have arranged the poems in each section in reverse chronological order. It occurred to us that the student might be initially reassured if he first encountered poems which spoke his own language and which in one way or another reflected his more immediate concerns. Later, delving more deeply into precedent times, he may be surprised and gratified to discover that his concerns were also those of men before him.

Substantively, we have included many poems of high quality not easily accessible to readers, some of them, surprisingly, not previously anthologized for college and university study. Many poems were painfully sacrificed to the inexorable demands of brevity, but nearly all these are easily available and often widely anthologized.

Questions arising out of the poems themselves—as well as those related to thematic relationships and the various critical approaches—are placed at the conclusions of each of the thematic groupings.

Finally, in an effort to create an essentially self-contained book, we have included a section on the basics of poetry, a glossary, and four separate indexes, the last being a pronunciation guide to poetic terms.

We hope that in *Muse of Fire* we have made a book that both student and instructor will find to be a helpful introduction to the basic techniques, criticism, and—most especially—the verities and delights of poetry.

That, certainly, was our intention.

We are especially indebted to June Fischbein of Alfred A. Knopf whose splendid, unstinting editorial assistance truly approached the collaborative; to James B. Smith whose advice and guidance were consistently helpful; and to Harold Brutlag, formerly at California State College, Los Angeles, and now at the University of Wisconsin, whose contributions to the "glossary" and "basics" sections were indeed major.

We are also greatly indebted to Harold Blythe, Belle McMaster, and Judith Hay Meador of the University of Louisville, and to Maria Sugranes of California State College, Los Angeles, for much arduous and absolutely invaluable research assistance; to Professor Robert Hayden of the University of Michigan for his advice in connection with the selection of the poems for the anthology, and to Professor Harvey Curtis Webster of the University of Louisville for his critical reading of portions of the manuscript and his subsequent recommendations. Nor is it possible to forget the ready aid of Elmer Lawson, Senior Field Representative of Alfred A. Knopf, whose good, practical suggestions were a steadying ballast.

Finally, we wish to thank all those—teachers, critics, scholars, students—who in any way, directly or indirectly, consciously or unconsciously, at one time or another entered our minds and thus, inevitably, became a part of this book.

Louisville, Kentucky   H.R.
Monterey Park, California   F.S.
August 1970

Contents

PART THREE: *The Basics of Poetry and Glossary*

PART ONE / *Approaches to Poetry*

1. Introduction

About Poetry and Its Makers

Poetry is probably the oldest and certainly, at its best, one of the highest forms of art. One theory of its origin is that it arose in primitive societies as a spontaneous expression, accompanying rhythmic movements and dances. The first poems, then, were very likely rudimentary songs and chants connected with the ritualistic observances of primitive peoples—communal and super-religious ceremonies. Such chants are still evident in American Indian dances. By 500 B.C., however, poetry had reached a distinctive literary development, especially in Greece, as evinced in the lyrics of Pindar and the dramas of Sophocles and Aeschylus.

Since poetry is so ancient it is small wonder that the genre possesses a wide variety of characteristics; its appeal may be simple or complex, commonplace or uncommon, particular or universal. Moreover, there are innumerable definitions of poetry. Here are some:

1. Coleridge—"I wish our clever young poets would remember my homely definitions of prose and poetry: that is, prose—words in their best order; poetry—the *best* words in the best order."
2. George Moore—"My definition of pure poetry, something that the poet creates out of his own personality."
3. Shelley—"Poetry is the record of the best and happiest moments of the happiest and best minds."
4. Wordsworth—"Poetry is the spontaneous overflow of powerful feelings: it takes its origin from emotion recollected in tranquility."
5. Poe—"I would define, in brief, the Poetry of

words as the Rhythmical Creation of Beauty. Its sole arbiter is taste."
6. Emerson—"The finest poetry was first experience."
7. Hazlitt—"All that is worth remembering of life is the poetry of it."
8. Dickinson—"If I read a book and it makes my whole body so cold no fire can ever warm me, I know that it is poetry. If I feel physically as if the top of my head were taken off, I know it is poetry. These are the only ways I know it. Is there any other way?"
9. Amy Lowell—"Finally most of us [imagist poets] believe that concentration is the very essence of poetry."
10. Edwin Arlington Robinson—"Poetry is a language that tells us, through a more or less emotional reaction, something that cannot be said."

These selections, most of them well known, represent only a few of the innumerable definitions of poetry. Often attitudes expressed toward both poetry and poets are in conflict or, more accurately, emphasize different aspects of the art form or the varying characteristics of the poets themselves. One early view centered on the assumption that the poet was an instrument of the gods and, when under the spell of the Muse, was indeed divinely inspired, even maddened by the experience. Plato (427–347 B.C.) stated in his *Ion* that the poet was "a light and winged and holy thing" and that he could not create until he was "out of his senses," for poetry was an "oracular gift." Such lines as these, by Shakespeare (1564–1616), "The Poets eye in a fine frenzy rolling/Doth glance from heaven to earth, from earth to heaven," from *A Midsummer-Night's Dream*, cannot be easily forgotten. Note also Shakespeare's expanded concept of the artist's humanity: "The lunatic, lover, and the poet/Are of imagination all compact." Similarly, the gift of prophecy has often been attributed to the poet, as in these lines by Henry Wadsworth Longfellow (1807–1882): "He can behold Things manifold/That have not yet been wholly told." William Wordsworth (1770–1850) believed that poets were possessed of "more than usual organic sensibility," and Henry David Thoreau (1817–1862) refused to drink or smoke because he feared such practices would dull the perception of his senses.

Consistently through the centuries, however, the idea of the poet as a "maker," as artificer of human experience, has predominated. (*Scop*, the Old English word for "poet," also meant "maker.") To Alphonse de Lamartine (1790–1869), a French poet, a poet was "whoever creates ideas in bronze, in stone, in prose, in words, or in rhymes—the poet stirs up only what is imperishable in nature and in the human heart." John Dryden (1631–1700) observed, with an emphatic assurance typical of him, that "A poet is a maker, as the word signifies; and he who cannot make, that is, invent, hath his name for nothing."

Whatever else poetry may involve (and it involves much more), its *sine qua non* is *compression*, or *intensity*. Thus Voltaire (1694–1778) wrote, "Poetry is the music of the soul, and above all of great and of feeling souls. One merit of poetry few persons will deny; it says more and in fewer words than prose." Ezra Pound (1885–) remarked that "Great literature is simply language charged with meaning to the utmost possible degree. . . . The language of prose is much less highly charged; that is perhaps the only availing distinction between prose and [poetry]."

Through comparison we may move closer to an understanding of a kind of brotherhood of the arts. A member of the "Celtic Twilight" school, Fiona MacLeod (pseudonym of William Sharp, 1855–1905), in *The Winged Destiny* (1925), referred to poetry as "the emotion of life rhythmically remembering beauty: as pictorial art and the art of verbal romance are the vision of life seen in beauty and in beauty revealed: and as music is the echo of life heard in beauty." Poetry involves human experience as other arts may. It partakes of the stuff of life, as fully, deeply, and richly as possible. Thus, although poetry communicates—whether emotions and senses or thought and reverie—it is more than communication. The English critic and editor John Middleton Murry (1889–1957) wrote, "It is the communication of an entire experience." Johann Wolfgang von Goethe (1749–1832) expressed the idea concretely: "All of my poems are 'occasional' poems—occasioned by reality and grounded in it. Poems that come out of thin air are good for nothing." Poetry embraces all experience, all things, and all life. Gustave Flaubert (1821–1880) therefore advised his fellow artists, "Let us draw it, no matter whence, for it lies everywhere, and in all things."

The creative process of great poets remains essentially a mystery. If poets are really great, we say they are "inspired." Yet this word tells us little, for the mystery of "inspiration" then remains. René Wellek and Austin Warren in their *Theory of Literature* (1942) stated that "inspiration" is a "traditional name for the unconscious factor in creation." Applied to "a shaman, prophet, or poet," it suggests that "he may be involuntarily 'possessed' by some ancestral or totemic spirit-control . . . the work seems written *through* one."[1] Such a theory may help to shed some new light on the unconscious power of a maker of poetic experiences. Many poets have commented upon their irresistible drive to give, in Shakespeare's phrase, "to airy nothing/A local habitation and a name." The Nobel laureate William Faulkner (1897–1962), who referred to himself as "a failed poet," once wrote: "If a writer has to rob his mother, he will not hesitate; the 'Ode on a Grecian Urn' is worth any number of old ladies." John Milton (1608–1674) was unable to stop writing; indeed, he declared in *Paradise Lost* that

[1] "Literature and Psychology," *Theory of Literature* (New York: Harcourt, Brace & World, 1956), p. 74. Originally published in 1942.

he would "sing with mortal voice, unchang'd To hoarse or mute, though fall'n on evil days,/ On evil days though fall'n, and evil tongues."

Poetic theories and statements diverge widely. Alexander Pope (1688–1744) demonstrated the old Latin apothegm "A poet is born, not made" (*Poeta nascitur, non fit*) in his "Epistle to Dr. Arbuthnot" as follows: "As yet a child, nor yet a fool to fame,/I lisp'd in numbers, for the numbers came." Walt Whitman (1819–1892), whose appreciation of the poet was more visceral, wrote: "I sound my barbaric yawp over the roofs of the world." American writer-critic James Branch Cabell (1879–1958) believed that "Poetry is man's rebellion against being what he is," whereas the English poet-dramatist John Drinkwater (1882–1937) thought it was "the announcement of spiritual discovery."

Whatever motivations the poet may possess or be possessed by, a yearning for immortality appears to be among them. Longfellow's lines "Distant footsteps echo/Through the corridors of Time" bespeak this desire. Ralph Waldo Emerson (1803–1882), too, recognized the time-binding quality of poetic thoughts, but in a more philosophic tone:

> We read the verses of one of the great English poets, of Chaucer, of Marvell, of Dryden, with the most modern joy,—with a pleasure, I mean, which is in great part caused by the abstraction of all *time* from their verses. There is some awe mixed with the joy of our surprise, when this poet, who lived in some past world, two or three hundred years ago, says that which lies close to my own soul, that which I also had well-nigh thought and said.

Similarly, Percy Bysshe Shelley (1792–1822) praised the immortality of John Keats in a burst of elegiac purity:

Dust to dust! but the pure spirit shall flow
Back to the burning fountain whence it came,
A portion of the Eternal, which must glow
Through time and change, unquenchably the same

. . .

He has outsoared the shadow of our night.

Unconscious powers of many kinds may provide a poet with his motivation, but he must possess the artistry with which to transmute amorphous thought, no matter how overwhelming, into consciously communicated forms of poetic expression. Various may be the tastes of men and infinite the variety of poetry; but work—the direct and conscious application of poetic skills to the flow of inspiration—is a necessary adjunct of the creative process common to all real poets. Poetry, Dylan Thomas (1914–1953) wrote, is "the rhythmic, inevitably narrative, movement from an over-clothed blindness to a naked vision that depends in its intensity on the strength of the labor put into the creation of poetry."

As abstract as poetry may seem at times, the greatest examples of the art more often than not combine homely images with lofty concepts. In his *Biographia Literaria*, Samuel Taylor Coleridge (1772–1834) said:

> The poet, described in ideal perfection, brings the whole soul of man into activity. . . . He diffuses a tone and spirit of unity, that blends, and (as it were) *fuses*, each into each by that synthetic and magical power, to which I would exclusively appropriate the name of imagination.

Carl Sandburg's laconic definition, "Poetry is the achievement of the synthesis of hyacinths and biscuits," demonstrates the point. Consider the works of Chaucer, Shakespeare, Milton, and Wordsworth, respectively. Whether the artist begins with a lowly parson on his way to Canterbury, a queen assuming the attitude of patience on a monument, an angel looking homeward, or a naked little child trailing clouds of glory—in his earthy image inheres a lofty concept. And the reader who can see and understand, though he may stand in the midst of life with the poet and feel his shoes in the dust, may also find himself in the midst of stars.

How We See and Understand Poetry

Just as the descriptions of poetry and the views of those who make it differ widely, the critical

and with conformity to established values. Actually, such an opinion is an extremist misconception. Even if we qualify our term as *literary* classicism, we must still contend with a broadly ramified and multifaceted concept.

As a term of literary thought, classicism is often employed to describe the views, methods, and aspects of a given literary production. Classical writers tended to be objective and to appeal to reason and common sense, usually in a simple and direct manner. In choice of subject they tended toward selection of items in their "known world," so to speak, and in treating such subjects, they applied traditionally accepted approaches. Intellectual and philosophical restraints were characteristic; poetry, especially, was marked by balance, dignity, and fixed forms. Stress was placed on ordered expression, indeed, on communication with clarity. Although emphasis appeared to be on philosophical content and thought—as it often was—poetic form itself was to the classic poet a thing of beauty, outlining ideality rather than describing reality. Along with this tone of formality and measured precision, then, there was a profound concern with the totality of a subject. What today we may term "realistic details" were often ignored as being of little importance in comparison to the overall form—the classical form which frequently renders to the modern eye an awesome but, nevertheless, exalted or too nearly perfect (hence, unrealistic) effect. In classical art, then, the dominant idea tended to override curiosity about the inconsistencies and mysteries of nature—especially the wild and primitive aspects of nature; the form was dominant over detail; and any tendency to experiment with both the content and form of poetry gave way to a reliance upon precedent, especially that set by the ancient Greek and Roman artists.

Classical Approaches

If one considers the father of classicism to be Aristotle, then his *Poetics* may be considered the bible of literary classicism. Certainly the work marks the first clearly delineated approach to literature, especially poetry. Through this work subsequent poets and critics can discern the meaning of much of classicism—early classicism in particular. Aristotle was concerned with descriptive principles of poetic composition, and he set out his purposes in his *Poetics* in this way:

> I propose to treat of Poetry in itself and of its various kinds, noting the essential quality of each; to inquire into the structure of the plot as requisite to a good poem; into the number and nature of the parts of which a poem is composed; and similarly into whatever else falls within the same inquiry.

Aristotle's teacher was Plato, thirty-seven years older than his pupil. Although Sir Philip Sidney (1554–1586) termed Plato "the most poetical" of all philosophers, Aristotle's teacher was most concerned with a search for truth—the meaning of life, which he found in "goodness." To Plato, ultimate realities, or absolutes, lay in an order or pattern in the universe. Just as the shadow may be mistaken for the real man who is standing between firelight and the wall of a cave, such realities are perceived only as appearances or second-hand impressions. Plato therefore questioned the value of poetry and its place in his ideal Republic, for the artist who paints a picture of a bed merely produces a result three times removed from reality (3. artist's picture; 2. carpenter's bed; 1. the idea created by God of a bed). Art was a third-rate imitation, Plato seemed to contend (*The Republic*, Bk. X), and because pleasure was its major by-product, it was hardly admissible to the ideal Republic.

Aristotle enjoyed several advantages with which to combat his teacher's arduous views. First, poetry was already tremendously popular with the Greeks of his age. Its place was high in the culture, indeed, higher than that of philosophy and other aspects of the Greek educational system. Aristotle agreed with Plato's concept of poetry as *mimesis* (an imitation of nature) up to a point, but not with his conclusion that, because it was merely third-rate imitation, it could not be related favorably to ultimate reality. Aristotle believed that poets, through their special vision, could render not only the world of nature, but could also capture the process of "becoming." That is, poets could perceive ultimate realities through nature and the imitation of nature, for the divine is mirrored in nature, and poets, by imitating it, could perceive its ever-changing manifestations. For Aristotle, if not Plato, then, the world of "becoming" was in actuality the world of reality —not merely a shadow-world of seemings.

Moreover, Aristotle felt that poetry was inherent in men, pointing out that children possessed the instinct of imitation and retained it throughout their lives. Pleasure was not an undesirable accompanying response to such imitation. In addition, man possessed an instinct for *harmonia* (harmony) and rhythm, manifested in dances. As a creature in which harmony inhered, man naturally preferred order to chaos. This meant that, in art, he desired a regular or structured form with "a beginning, a middle, and end." Much later the great German poet Goethe was to state, "What distinguishes the artist from the mere amateur is *Architectoniké* [unity and proportion in plan and technique or structure] in the highest sense; that power of execution which creates, forms, and constitutes: not the profoundness of single thoughts, not the richness of imagery, not the abundance of illustration."

Aristotle defined "tragedy," which he deemed the highest form of poetry, in these memorable terms:

> . . . an imitation of an action that is serious, complete, and of a certain magnitude; in language embellished with each kind of artistic ornament, the several kinds being found in separate parts of the play; in the form of action, not of narrative; through pity and fear effecting the proper purgation of these emotions.

The reference to "purgation" (clearing away or cleansing of undesirable elements) applies to the emotions of "pity" and "fear." Aristotle refers to fear as an agonizing awareness "of impending evil which is destructive . . ." The highest form of poetry, tragedy, deals with the corroding force of evil, which, in its various forms, is destructive to all human experience. Through the mind and heart of the spectator or reader, the poet appeals to human compassion, the sorrow felt for another's suffering—pity—and in the poet's so doing, the soul may be led out (*psychagogia*) through temporary vicarious experience and sympathetic identification, learning by emotional involvement to avoid the destructive evil of the tragic *persona*, or be freed from the tensions of pent-up emotions—ranging from our inmost frustrated hopes and demoralizing impressions to our suppressed shames and corrosive sense of sin. In so doing, *catharsis* (*katharsis*), or "the proper purgation" of emotions, is wrought. The moral effects of such literary experience, Aristotle believed, should be obvious enough.

If tragic poetry was truly great, it not only involved catharsis, but it also appealed to instinctive desires of imitation and harmony, presenting a whole action completed and filled out according to "the law of probability and necessity." Only then could it reach through the imagination, making the particular universal.

Following Plato and Aristotle, the Roman Horace (65–8 B.C.) in his *Ars Poetica* (*Art of Poetry*) reinterpreted Greek concepts of poetry for his place and time. Educated in Athens as well as Rome, he was in a position to synthesize and articulate anew the concepts of the Greek poets. One of the major effects of his work was to affirm the purposes of Aristotle's *Poetics*. Although he did not probe as deeply into the treatment of poetry, he did stress such considerations as simple clarity; unity and tempo of action; the careful arrangement of words; language usage in poetry (In "custom . . . lie the judgment, rule, and standard of speech."); suitable metrics (especially the iambic "as best fitted for dialogue" in tragedy and comedy); the history of tragedy, especially its origin with Thespis, who, in the sixth century B.C., first juxtaposed an actor with the Greek chorus; and, above all, common sense and taste—that is, "appropriateness" in dramatic action.

For example:

> Medea should not butcher her children in plain view of the audience . . . nor Procne be transformed into a bird. Whatever you try to show me openly in this way simply leaves me unbelieving and rather disgusted.

Such statements, and others in Horace's *Art of Poetry*, imply a classical emphasis on such qualities as talent, wisdom, poetic power, sensitivity, intellectual awareness, prudence, and restraint. Like Aristotle, Horace rejected Plato's concept that the poet had to be "out of his senses" in order to "invent." Indeed, Horace suggests that the poet who is "out of his senses" should be avoided: "As people avoid someone afflicted with . . . the fits, or insanity, so sensible men stay clear of a mad poet," whom children tease and only "rash fools follow. . . ." Through his refined expression and ability to synthesize classical principles of poetry, Horace was to influence later critics such as Alexander Pope, especially in Pope's *Essay on Criticism* (1711); the French neoclassicist Boileau in his *Art of Poetry* (1680); and the Italian Vida in his work of the same name (1680). More immediately, Horace anticipated such works of the English Renaissance as Sir Philip Sidney's *An Apology for Poetry* (1595).

Long before Sidney, however, the remarkable treatise *On the Sublime*, chronologically of classical origin and for years attributed to "Longinus" (213 ?–273) but possibly written by the Roman Caecilius of the first century (published in 1554 by Robortello in the original Greek), anticipated English literature as late as the so-called Romantic Age that commenced in late nineteenth-century England. Pointing to the emotion and pleasure generated by literature, Longinus was the first of the ancients to emphasize what Oscar Wilde was later to term "art for art's sake" (*l'art pour l'art*), and to do so over and above the moralistic or didactic purposes of art. As prophetic as he proved to be in some respects, however, his roots

were in classicism, just as Horace before him had seen the need of poetry "to delight" as well as "to instruct" ("*pro-desse aut delectare*").

Longinus, in articulating "the sublime," which he defined as "a certain distinction and excellence in expression," drew upon five wellsprings which nourished the poet-maker: (1) a high mind ("elevation of mind"); (2) conceptual power ("power of forming great conceptions"); (3) "vehement and inspired passion"; (4) a facility in the use of figurative language ("noble diction"); and (5) taste in style or the arrangement of words ("dignified and elevated composition"). Possibly the most striking piece of literary criticism following Aristotle's *Poetics*, the work inspired Alexander Pope to write in his *Essay on Criticism*:

> Thee, bold Longinus! . . .
> An ardent judge, who, zealous in his trust,
> With warmth gives sentence, yet is always just;
> Whose own example strengthens all his laws,
> And is himself that great Sublime he draws.

Renaissance Approaches

Sidney's *An Apology for Poetry*, first written in the early 1580s, though published after his death in battle, established him as England's first important poet-critic. The Italian philosopher-critic Boethius, in his noted *De Consolatione Philosophae* (ca. 520), echoed Plato's earlier views in his search for truth. Boethius placed Philosophy as an allegorical character above the "poetical Muses," and referred to them as "common strumpets of . . . the theatre . . ." that "will feed and nourish . . . with sweet poison." Even Music is consistent only in her inconsistency, for there is no man "that she hath not forsaken."

Dante Alighieri (1275–1321), in his *De Vulgari Eloquentia*, defined everyday speech ("the vernacular") as "that which we acquire without any rule, by imitating our nurses," and urged its literary use as being "nobler" for it was "natural to us, whereas the other is rather of an artificial kind" (that is, the Church language, Latin). One should remember that Englishmen Francis Bacon (1561–1626) and John Milton were hesitant to use ordinary language. Indeed, not until the publication of William Wordsworth's "Preface to *The Lyrical Ballads*" (1800) did the style permanently shift to what Wordsworth termed the "selection of the real language of men."

Between Longinus and Dante, the moralistic emphasis of Aristotle took on, understandably, a Christian coloring. And, as innovative as Dante was, he did little to free literature from the domination of the orthodox thought of the Middle Ages. Indeed, he subscribed to it, stating that the "aim of the whole [of his *Divine Comedy*] and of the part may be manifold" (that is, "polysemous"), but, briefly, it "is to remove those living in this life from a state of misery and to guide them to a state of happiness." This "moral philosophy or ethics . . . for practical action" had four levels of meaning: (1) *literal*, or "simple narrative"; (2) *allegorical*, or "the meaning hidden under the cloak of fables," although Dante noted, "theologians . . . take this meaning differently from the poets"; (3) *moral*, a didactic element for the benefit of "readers . . . and their descendents," which Dante related to "the Gospel of Christ"; and (4) *anagogical* (that is, "beyond sense"), an obvious relation to the classical "leading out of the soul" (Aristotle's *psychagogia*), but articulated anew in the Christian sense to which Dante was profoundly dedicated. Thus, Dante believed, a book is "spiritually expounded." A book has a necessary literal meaning, to be sure, but its ultimate and higher sense is "its spiritual meaning, which is that the soul, in forsaking its sins, becomes holy and free in its powers."

In responding to Puritan attacks on poetry, especially Stephen Gosson's *The School of Abuse* (1579); drawing directly on Horace; recapitulating Aristotle's critical principles (poetry is an imitation of nature); and infusing a portion of Plato's philosophical rather than poetical views (Plato wanted to banish only "the abuse" of poetry)—Sidney worked out, in *An Apology for Poetry*, the widest range of all Renaissance criticism. Although

he employed the views of the classicists, he went beyond them, extracting concepts of the Italian Renaissance critics and anticipating developments in later neoclassical England during the seventeenth and eighteenth centuries. Although he objected to the tendency to mix elements of tragedy and comedy in English drama and promoted the unities of time and place (whereas Aristotle had championed only the unity of action), Sidney warned against overuse of "artificial rules" and "imitative patterns." With grace and precision, Sidney reviewed the history of poetry, pointing out that it preceded history; that poetry is universal, history particular; that "Poetry is of all human learning the most ancient and of most fatherly antiquity, as from whence other learnings have taken their beginnings . . ."

Similarly, he brilliantly answered arguments against poetry, observing that man may make evil in poetry by abusing it, but never can true poetry be evil of itself. Thus, the reason poetry was not esteemed as it should have been in England was "the fault of poet-apes, not poets." Stating his own case for poetry, Sidney characterized its attackers as those having "so earth-creeping a mind that it cannot lift itself up to look to the sky of Poetry. . . ." He believed poetry transcended nature, could improve upon her, and was delightfully instructive. It was greater than philosophy, for its truth was more fully wrought and "moral"; thus, "the mathematician might draw forth a straight line with a crooked heart. . . ." He categorized poetry according to whether it applied Aristotle's basic concept of mimesis (representation of reality, or imitation) to the "inconceivable excellencies of God," or to "matters philosophical." (Poetry embodies philosophy, but is superior to it.) He also recognized "notable" categories of poetry, including heroic, lyric, tragic, comic, satiric, elegiac, and pastoral. But, like Aristotle, he did not equate differences between prose and verse modes with what makes true poetry and what does not make it. Real poetry is more than mere verse form. Finally, with imagination and refreshing boldness, he propounded the case for the superiority of the native English tongue over all other languages, and he drove his argument for poetry home, subtly leading the reader to an awareness of the witlessness of those who opposed it. There are, Sidney summarized, "many mysteries contained in Poetry, which were written darkly, lest by profane wits it should be abused."

Samuel Daniel (1562–1619), in his *Defense of Rhyme*, opposed attempts of Thomas Campion and other overzealous classicists to eliminate rhyme from English poetry and replace it with quantitative rhythmic patterns in which rhythm depended upon regularized occurrences of long and short syllables. Even Sidney and Spenser (and, later, Coleridge) wrote some quantitative verse. Along with Gabriel Harvey they organized a society based on a French Academy to promote the purpose—certainly a restricted, classical idea. In the face of such opposition, Daniel independently asserted the case for more natural accentual-syllabic English poetry with rhyme, employing

historical critical approaches to demonstrate how rhyme, "delighting the ear, and stirring the heart," characterized poetry of the past and earned the "approbation of many ages"—in short, how rhyme was naturally better suited to English.

The late Elizabethan dramatist-critic Ben Jonson (1572–1637) was strongly influenced by the ancients, both in his plays and in his collection of critical notes, *Timber; or, Discoveries* (published in 1641, after his death). Like the classicists before him, he believed the main purpose of poetry to be a presentation of goodness and happiness in living. The emphasis was on "delight" and, in form, on "proportion," which echoed Aristotle's concept of harmonia. Structurally, the work must be filled out appropriately, and contain a *"whole . . . which hath a beginning, a mid'st, and an end."* Indicating the strong influence of the ancients, he moreover insisted that action itself must be neither too great for our imagination to grasp nor too little to arouse our pleasure.

3. Neoclassicism and Emerging Romantic Approaches

Early Neoclassical Approaches

Dr. Samuel Johnson (1709–1784) called John Dryden "the father of English criticism." A liberal neoclassicist, Dryden represents a compendium of the age of "new classicism" (1660–1800). In his

work the representative qualities of taste, appropriateness, tightly unified structure, and lucidity meet. Less "theoretical" than his precursors, he was far more "descriptive," applying his criticisms in an extended fashion to analyzing the literary works of other artists. He wrote widely and well, utilizing such diverse forms as poetic drama, lyric poetry, satire, comic and heroic drama, morally instructive poetry, and literary criticism. His balance of decorum, propriety, and simple clarity resulted in an intimate ease of style. He also exhibited frequent strokes of imaginative insight anticipating Romanticism. His emphasis on proportion reflects the influence of his predecessor playwright Ben Jonson. The concept of proportion is also directly related to Aristotle's "harmonia." Dryden's careful "examen" (analytical description) of Jonson's *The Silent Woman* shows the influence of the French critics of his day, such as Pierre Corneille (1606–1684). It also points to the contextualist devices (the *explication de texte*) of the New Critics (no longer new).

Dryden's masterpiece of criticism is *An Essay of Dramatic Poesy* (1668), written in the form of a debate in the style of Plato's *Dialogues*. The four characters vigorously defend certain literary ideas of the day: (1) the superiority of the "Ancients" to the "Moderns"; (2) the obverse view, specifying the faults of the Ancients—inconsistency of form and irregularity of application of the unities of action, time, and place; (3) the superiority of the French drama over the English, akin to the second argument, in which Shakespeare is criticized for mixing comedy and tragedy as well as ignoring the three unities; and (4) the comparatively more balanced, yet still "Modern" view of Dryden himself.

He contended that English dramatists such as Shakespeare, Fletcher, and Jonson were superior to the French; indeed, he asserts, the French archpoet, Corneille, in his best play, *The Liar*, could not compete with the English in spite of his decorum and exactitude. Ultimately, he considered the best plays to be "those which best fulfill" the law of "the lively imitation of Nature," and neither the "irregularities" of English playwrights nor the "virtues" of the French "are considerable enough to place them above us." Thus, unlike Corneille, Dryden conceived of the three unities as methods to aid in structure or plotting, a means and not an end in themselves.

Dryden also emphasized the need for a naturalness of relation between action and characterization; that is, characters should arise naturally out of plot. Verisimilitude—the semblance to truth—demanded a consistency in diction, or choice and arrangement of words. All nonfunctional action, poetic lines, and characters should be avoided. Like Samuel Daniel, Dryden also defended the use of rhyme in drama, contending that if one is "to follow Nature," he should not be required to "follow her on foot," or, as he colorfully put it, be "dismounted . . . from his Pegasus." Dryden, in discerning the genius of Shakespeare, bespoke the largeness of the dramatist's soul:

> To begin, then, with Shakespeare. He was the man who of all modern, and perhaps ancient poets, has the largest and most comprehensive soul. All the images of Nature were still present to him, and he drew them, not laboriously, but luckily; when he describes anything, you more than see it, you feel it too. Those who accuse him to have wanted learning, give him the greater commendation: he was naturally learned; he needed not the spectacles of books to read Nature; he looked inwards, and found her there.

As a critic Dryden was capable of recognizing the genius of English literature from Chaucer to his age. He perceived the vibrancy of a writer's work to be not merely in its structure but in its characterization, sense of realism, gusto and verve, and, above all, "wit," which he defined as a "propriety of thoughts and words . . . elegantly adapted to the subject." He was a flexible synthesizer of classical and neoclassical views, and he could thus mediate intelligently between the views of the Ancients and those of the Moderns. He was a voice of reason standing in the midst of what Jonathan Swift later termed "the battle of the books"; he transcended his own time while absorbing the best of the past, and he anticipated the future. "It is not enough that Aristotle has said so," he wrote, "for Aristotle drew his models of tragedy from Sophocles and Euripides; *and, if he had seen ours, he might have changed his mind.*"

Alexander Pope was twelve years old when Dryden died in 1700, and it is said that Pope as a boy once saw his master in a London coffeehouse. At any rate, the older man's influence on the younger was great. Dryden believed that a major premise of classical rules was that if one could "reduce Nature into method . . . the soul of poetry" would be rendered. Pope's lines from his precocious piece *An Essay on Criticism* (published in 1711, but written when he was hardly out of his teens) paraphrase, in couplets, this central, flexible thesis of Dryden's work:

Those Rules of old discover'd, not devis'd,
Are Nature still, but Nature methodiz'd.

Other influences on Pope included Horace, who himself had absorbed much of classicism in his *Ars Poetica*. The Roman Quintilian, Vida, Boileau, and other French critics, along with the popular Longinus, made up the major sources upon whom Pope drew. Dr. Samuel Johnson's *Life of Pope* renders a portrait of a man of fluctuating contrasts —an enigmatic man of intellectual scope and miniscule jealousies; of integrity of opinion and statement and "petty artifices of parsimony"(with guests he would set "at supper a single pint upon the table" and retire). He was a man of "liberality and fidelity of friendship," and yet "He was fretful and easily displeased. . . ." This is more understandable when Johnson describes the life of this genius, housed in a dwarfed and weakened body, as one "long disease."

Pope's critical magnum opus, *An Essay on Criticism*, is a compendium of neoclassicism, embracing the entire tradition. In it he specifies general criteria of good critics and admonishes the great number of poor ones (ten bad critics for each poor writer). A foolishly applied consistency of classical rules was to him petty. With Dryden-esque liberality, he urged good judges of literature to "Survey the whole, nor seek slight faults to find," and pronounced specifically the faults of critics with limited vision. Those who emphasize metrics alone, often failing to understand the poet's content, he dramatized in subtle and scathingly epigrammatic denunciation with a remarkable union of sound and sense:

But most by Numbers★ judge a poet's song
And smooth or rough, with them, is right or wrong:
In the bright Muse, tho' thousand charms conspire,
Her voice is all these tuneful fools admire;
Who haunt Parnassus but to please their ear,
Not mend their minds; as some to church repair
Not for the doctrine, but the music there.
These equal syllables alone require,
Tho' oft' the ear the open vowels tire;
While expletives their feeble aid do★★ join,
And ten low words oft' creep in one dull line:
While they ring round the same unvar'd chimes,
With sure returns of still expected rhymes;
Where'er you find "the cooling western breeze,"
In the next line, it "whispers thro' the trees:"
If crystal streams "its pleasing murmurs creep,"
The reader's threaten'd (not in vain) with "sleep:"
Then, at the last and only couplet, fraught
With some unmeaning thing they call a thought,
A needless Alexandrine★★★ ends the song,
That, like a wounded snake, drags its slow length
   along.

★ Versification.
★★ "Do" is an expletive.
★★★ A line with twelve syllables.

Although Pope represented balance and taste in his broad application of neoclassical rules of criticism, he did warn the reader of the danger of literary sects or cults. Although he imprecated those who "reason and conclude by precedent," he deplored as well the unoriginal and unthinking critic, especially those who "catch the spreading notion of the town" and thus fail to retain the best of the past—an appropriate aloofness—in their anxiety to identify with the fads of the day. Similarly, he condemned those who "judge of authors' names, not works," as well as the lackey-critics who serve the cause of a special interest, which could apply by extension today to the servant-critics of economic, political, racial, or religious groups.

Dr. Samuel Johnson believed, as most scholars do today, that Dryden's natural genius was greater than Pope's, but he qualified his judgment in a memorable comparison of these two giants of critical aptitude: "If the flights of Dryden therefore are higher, Pope continues longer on the wing. If of Dryden's fire the blaze is brighter, of Pope's the heat is more regular and constant. . . . Dryden is read with frequent astonishment, and Pope with perpetual delight."

Neoclassicism in Transition: The Age of Dr. Samuel Johnson

The "literary dictator of London," Dr. Samuel Johnson, known also by the appellation "Dictionary Johnson" (for his great lexicon published in 1755), was the most articulate and the last of the neoclassic critics. He was broadly classical rather than narrowly neoclassical. Like Dryden, he emphasized the morally instructive dimension of art as well as its universal amplitude. This evaluation of art is rooted firmly in the Aristotelian concept of mimesis, which he interpreted, not unlike Dryden and Pope, as an imitation of wholes. This imitation was not static, but in a process of "becoming," thus enlarging first the rational, then the emotional and imaginative dimensions of human experience. Yet in this arrangement, *rationality* should be the guide to imitation, not mere emotion or mere imagination.

Living late into the eighteenth century, Johnson found his life overlapping those of the early Romantics—Goethe, Young, Thomson, Burns, Goldsmith, and Blake, to mention a few. In addition, Richardson, Fielding, Smollett, and Sterne were writing in a popular new art form—the novel. Johnson decried in these and other literary forms what he understood as an excessive preoccupation with "romantic love." He believed such an emphasis would distort and mislead; moreover, it prevented the achievement of harmonia—the propriety of parts in relation to wholistic structure. A poet should follow the well-established classical thesis of "probability and necessity" according to the demands of "the living world." Thus, it is not surprising to find that Johnson frowned upon the subjects of pastoral poetry—rustic life, vegetables, lovesick shepherds, emotions such as love and grief played out against the backdrop of sheep and the ordinary countryside—all of which he found onerous, especially in such works as Sidney's *Arcadia*, Milton's *Lycidas*, and James Thomson's *The Seasons*. Thus, in spite of the liberality of his neoclassicism, homely detail was eschewed, and this view tends to place him in opposition to such early Romantics as Wordsworth and Coleridge.

Similarly, Johnson deprecated, although he did not ignore, the metaphysical poets—Donne, Crashaw, and Herbert—believing them to be excessively "analytick": "he who dissects a sunbeam with a prism can exhibit the wide effulgence of a summer noon." Still, he observed, "To write on their plan, it was at least necessary to read and think." In such an evaluation one must realize Johnson's basic classical point: good poets first and foremost should appeal to common reason, rather than to specialized knowledge.

In opposition to the extreme neoclassicists, however, he opposed the narrow "rules" of the Augustan age (the neoclassic period of the eighteenth century). He disagreed with those who criticized Shakespeare, pointing to the overriding power of Shakespeare, who achieved "essential character" without excessive detail. A poet is like an artist who attempts to capture the whole garden, and to do so, Johnson believed, it is not necessary to "number the streaks of the tulip." As he opposed Romantic concern with what he took to be excessive detail, he similarly opposed the conservative "modern neoclassicists," such as Corneille in France, who emphasized the three unities of dramatic structure (action, time, and place), contending that "they have given more trouble to the poet, than pleasure to the auditor." Similarly, he defended Shakespeare's mingling of tragedy and comedy, averring that his work was "impregnated by genius."

Oddly enough, the French took Johnson's transcendent neoclassical views as being, in essence, "Romantic"; but Johnson would not have so contended. Despite the vigor and individuality of his critical judgment, he was essentially a man of his own Age of Reason—a classicist who was suspicious of the vast reaches of his own emotions and imaginative power. Like the more typical rationalists of his time, he feared the "hunger of imagination which preys incessantly upon life," and he perhaps best summarized his uncommon common sense in *The Rambler* (1751):

> It ought to be the first endeavor of a writer to distinguish nature from custom: or that which is right only because it is established; that he may neither violate essential principles by a desire of novelty, nor debar himself from the attainment of beauties within his view, by a needless fear of breaking rules which no literary dictator has authority to enact.

In these words, we have the gist of much of Dr. Johnson's restrained, sensible, yet flexible adaptation of the classical essence.

The Emergence of Romantic Approaches

The reaction in the arts culminating in the late eighteenth and early nineteenth centuries in England was part of a larger dynamic matrix of social, political, economic, and religious elements. The literature of an age represents not only the individual thoughts of its makers, but also, to varying extents, the society and culture in which artists function in everyday situations. We have already seen that extremely rigid neoclassical theories, such as those of Corneille, had begun to give way to more liberally evolved attitudes, such as those of Dryden, Pope, and especially Johnson. Even before Johnson, Longinus had pointed the way to literature of individuality and feeling through his emphasis on "vehement and inspired passion." He had, in short, though still a classicist, called for originality in literary endeavor and suggested what were to become Romantic directions.

Few people argued with the importance of imitating nature, but questions prevailed as to the nature of nature, and the "how" of imitation. What of human nature? What of wild, primitive nature? Under the influence of such moral philosophers as Rosseau and such doctrines as that of "the noble savage," reason and intellect gradually gave way to emotion and feeling. Pascal had earlier written, "The heart has reasons of which reason has no knowledge." In distinguishing between the poet of talent (shining like "feldspar," but crumbling with time) and the poet of genius (durable like "granite"), America's Henry David Thoreau was reflecting such earlier works as William Duff's *Essay on Original Genius* (1767), in which he emphasized in genius the union of "a plastic and comprehensive imagination," as well as "intellect" and "taste."

Dr. Johnson was not the only man of his time to find simple nature offensive. Rousseau's countryman François René de Chateaubriand stated in 1801: "I am not at all, as Mr. Rousseau, an enthusiast of savages . . . *Pure Nature*, I do not believe at all to be the most beautiful thing in the world. I have always found it quite ugly from any view, when I have had the occasion of seeing it. With the word *nature* one has lost everything."

In spite of the cultivated views of Dr. Johnson and Chateaubriand, however, the Romantic poets sensed the common man's rebellion against old customs, a corrupt society, a national church, bad laws, and the rising behemoth of economic atrocity in the onrushing Industrial Revolution. As John Middleton Murry observed in his book *The Problem of Style*,[1] "The Classical writer feels himself to be a member of an organized society, a man with duties and restrictions imposed upon him by a moral law which he deeply acknowledges. The Romantic is in rebellion against external law, and just as deeply he refuses to acknowledge its sanction. He asserts the rights of his individuality *contra mundum*." Thus, in his *The Seasons*, James Thomson (1700–1748) apostrophized the sun, celebrated the "green emerald" of nature as well

[1] John Middleton Murry, *The Problem of Style* (London: Oxford University Press, 1922); revised 1961, p. 131.

as landscapes and the domestic animals, realistically observed the "rustling . . . many-twinkling leaves/Of aspen tall," reflected upon poverty, and wrote of man ". . . whom Nature form'd of milder clay,/With every kind emotion in his heart." He appealed directly to human feeling with his *Winter* (1726), in which he depicted the freezing death of a country swain "bleaching in the northern blast" while in vain his wife waits in their cottage, the "fire fair-blazing," and while "his little children" peep out into the storm and ". . . demand their sire/With tears of artless innocence." Expressing a form of social criticism, Thomson concludes with a virtual cry for humanitarianism, for a stop to "crushed out lives" and a breaking of "legal monsters" of corrupt laws. He expresses the melioristic hope for an age with "every man within the reach of right!"

Similarly, Edward Young's "The Complaint, or Night Thoughts on Life, Death, and Immortality" (1742), Oliver Goldsmith's *The Deserted Village* (1770), *Citizen of the World* (1762), and *The Vicar of Wakefield* (1766), William Collins' "An Ode on the Popular Superstitions of the Highlands of Scotland" (1788), and Thomas Gray's much-quoted "Elegy Written in a Country Churchyard" (1751) are concerned with a profusion of so-called Romantic subjects: increasing

secular interests, especially in the common man and his affairs; new interpretations of nature, wild and primitive or violent; freedom in self-expression; opposition to literary rules and, more broadly, political and economic tyranny; exaltation of the remote past; love of far-off places; heavy reliance upon the imagination; exploration of the melancholy, death and decay, and abnormal elements; gross exaggerations of the emotionally wild "romantic hero" and the *femme fatale*; intensity of personal feeling; enthusiastic hope; the celebration, in short, of the *ideality* of man.

If one considers the Romantic age of English literature as commencing with Wordsworth and Coleridge, then the most famous of the English pre-Romantics were Robert Burns (1759–1796) and William Blake (1757–1827). Burns, a "heaven-taught" Scotsman, possessed natural genius and the romantic quality of spontaneity, "unbroke by rules of Art." Blake's *Songs of Innocence* indicate his natural gifts of spontaneity, mystical illusion, and the ability to achieve effects of simple beauty and an ingenuously wrought artistic purity. He was a visionary. To him imagination took on a sacred dimension as "the divine body in every man." Such men as these, then, seemed to have looked into the seeds of time, and foreseen the grains that would grow.

4. Basic Romantic Approaches

Like the neoclassicists before them, the major Romantics—Wordsworth, Coleridge, Byron, Shelley, and Keats—were literary critics as well as poets. At least two of them, Wordsworth and

Coleridge, were great critics. As Robert Burns had one hundred years previously, William Wordsworth chose "incidents and situations from common life" as subjects for his poetry;

unlike Burns, however, he possessed the critical ability to articulate his theories, most notably in his Preface to the *Lyrical Ballads* (1800). *Lyrical Ballads* was a book of poems which he termed to be "an experiment . . . to ascertain how far, by fitting to metrical arrangement, a selection of the real language of men in a state of vivid sensation," the "sort" and "quantity of pleasure" could be imparted. He wanted to know (1) "how far" his objective could be attained and (2) "whether it be worth attaining." Upon the answer to these two questions, he was willing to let rest his "claim to the approbation of the public."

Although Wordsworth wanted to create a kind of poetry which would be of permanent interest to mankind, he realized that his poems were different from those generally approved. He believed that the language of his poems was drawn from natural ways of thinking and speaking evident in the common man, the "humble and rustic" people, because "in that condition the essential passions of the heart find a better soil in which they can attain their maturity." He continued with a new phrasing of other general romantic concepts. One was freedom from restraint. Another was that "a plainer and more emphatic language" is less controlled by social artifice and more valid in that it arose from habitual experience and customary feelings. Still, such language was "far more philosophical" than that poets tended to use in its place, most of whom tended to "separate themselves from the sympathies of men," and instead to pander to capricious tastes in rigid but socially approved forms and expressions—mere hollow conventions.

Still, Wordsworth believed that a petty and lurid treatment in common language is worse than the most obvious kind of artifice or adherence to narrowly conceived rules. Neither did Wordsworth agree that the "language really used by men" should be unselected; rather, it should be "adopted," or "purified . . . from what appear to be its real defects, from all lasting and rational causes of dislike or disgust. . . ." Good writing should carry a "distinct purpose" if one is to be a

worthy poet. To his well-known formulation of poetry as "the spontaneous overflow of powerful feelings recollected in tranquility," he added that poems of value dealing with various subjects are created only by an individual "possessed of more than usual organic sensibility," who has "also thought long and deeply." To Wordsworth, thoughts meant the "representatives of all our past feelings."

Concerning feeling, Wordsworth was clearly Romantic, pointing out that his poetry differed from the popular poetry of his day in the initial emphasis on feeling. He was convinced that "the feeling therein developed gives importance to the action and situation, and not the action and situation to the feeling." Unlike Aristotle and even Dr. Johnson, Wordsworth believed that feeling takes precedence over action and is the dominant element in a new kind of harmonia, as it were. Thus, feeling combines with substance to form the essence of poetry, and "the subject" infusing feeling "is indeed important!" Unfortunately, Wordsworth contended, "the discriminating powers of the mind" were being blunted by a number of forces of his age—among them "great national events" (possibly a reference to the French Revolution and Napoleonic Wars); "the increasing accumulation of men in cities" (the Industrial Revolution and its accompanying social atrocities); and especially, the people's "craving for extraordinary incident," wrought by "rapid communication" (the rising journals, periodicals, and books read by the emerging middle class of the age). Wordsworth bemoaned the resulting neglect of such writers as Shakespeare and Milton and the popularity of "frantic novels, sickly and stupid German tragedies, and deluges of idle and extravagant stories in verse"—in short, the poor literature of the time.

In treating the matters of his style and purposes, Wordsworth reiterated his desire "to keep the reader in the company of flesh and blood," and thereby interest him. His pains to avoid the usual hackneyed "poetic diction" in order to bring his language nearer to "the language of men" should be recognized. Through this effort he hoped to bring a new kind of pleasure to the reader. Using a sonnet by Thomas Gray as an illustration, he averred that "the language of prose may yet be well adapted to poetry," and further stated that there is no "*essential* difference between the language of prose and metrical composition"; that, analogically, "the same human blood circulates through the veins of them both." Indeed, there is "no celestial ichor that distinguishes" the "vital juices" of poetry from those of prose. Poetry's tears are "natural and human tears."

Wordsworth defines a poet distinctively, however, as one "who rejoices more than other men in the spirit of life that is in him," and who is "affected more than other men by absent things as if they were present." Still, the poet distinguishes between art and reality, and it is desirable that he be a step removed from the "action and suffering" of real people. Although he strives to get as close as possible to reality, he must do so with taste and responsibility, employing the "principle of selection . . . for removing what would otherwise be painful or disgusting in passing." Nor will the genuine poet attempt "to elevate nature" by tricks such as sensationalism. In these ways, then, Horace's and Dryden's concepts of "decorum and propriety" are recapitulated by Wordsworth.

As romantic as Wordsworth was, he referred to Aristotle as the source of his statement that poetry "is the most philosophic of all writing," and "its object is truth, not individual and local, but general . . . carried alive into the heart by passion." Indeed, he said, "poetry is the image of man and nature," a phrase which echoes the spirit of James Thomson's famous lines (lines 246–256) from *Winter* (1726) on the robin—a plea for understanding between man and the humbler creation of nature:

The redbreast, sacred to the household gods,
Wisely regardful of the embroiling sky,
In joyless fields and thorny thickets leaves
His shivering mates, and pays to trusted man
His annual visit. Half afraid, he first

Against the window beats; then brisk alights
On the warm hearth; then, hopping o'er the floor,
Eyes all the smiling family askance,
And pecks, and starts, and wonders where he is—
Till, more familiar grown, the table-crumbs
Attract his slender feet.

The poet attempts to produce pleasure through "an acknowledgment of the beauty of the universe"; he looks at the world "in a spirit of love," and his vision is "a homage paid to the native and naked dignity of man." It is the "grand elementary principle of pleasure, by which he knows, and feels, and lives, and moves." Thus the poet looks upon "the whole complex scene of ideas and sensations," and finds "everywhere objects that immediately excite in him sympathies which, from the necessities of his nature, are accompanied by an overbalance of enjoyment." Wordsworth believed, then, that the subjects of poetry are truly universal, and he expressed his concept of poetry metaphorically as "the breath and finer spirit of all knowledge." In our age, in which the sciences and the humanities appear often to be in conflict with one another, it may seem surprising that the romantic Wordsworth looked upon poetry as "the impassioned expression which is in the countenance of all science." Further, the poet

is the rock of defence for human nature; an upholder and preserver, carrying everywhere with him relationship and love. In spite of difference of soil and climate, of language and manners, of laws and customs: in spite of things silently gone out of mind, and things violently destroyed; the poet binds together by passion and knowledge the vast empire of human society, as it is spread over the whole earth, and over all time. . . . Poetry is the first and last of all knowledge —it is as immortal as the heart of man. If the labors of men of science should ever create any material revolution, direct or indirect, in our condition, and in the impressions which we habitually receive, the poet will sleep then no more than at present; he will be ready to follow the steps of the man of science, not only in those general indirect effects, but he will be at his side, carrying sensation into the midst of the objects of the science itself. . . . If the time should ever come when what is now called science, thus familiarized to men, shall be ready to put on, as it were, a form of flesh and blood, the poet will lend his divine spirit to aid the transfiguration, and will welcome the being thus produced, as a dear and genuine inmate of the household of man.

Thus, Wordsworth fully envisioned the age of science, and transcended the ornamental and overcultivated concepts of poetry which characterized his age as it does ours.

Truly his view of poetry was a universal one, synthesizing major ideas of literary criticism of the past—Plato's transcendental faith in an absolute reality, an ultimate order of things behind the "forms" of appearance; the comparatively fluid, relativistic, and wholistic concepts of Aristotle and the classicists; and the quest for general truths to which Dr. Johnson subscribed. Yet Wordsworth, in melding these with his own views, particularized the vast scope of poetry. Emphasizing the poet's "greater promptness to think and feel" even without "immediate external excitement," and his "greater power in expressing such thoughts and feelings," he specified these thoughts and feelings in detail: our "moral sentiments" and "animal sensations"; our reactions to the "appearances of the visible universe," such as "storm and sunshine," "revolutions of the seasons," "cold and heat"; and such sensations as are precipitated by the "loss of friends and kindred," "injuries," "resentments," "gratitude and hope," and "fear and sorrow."

Yet Wordsworth was aware that particularity could be a weakness, and he emphasized the general, too (perhaps reflecting Dr. Johnson's view). He warned against his own tendency of "giving to things a false importance." He predicted the faults of third-rate Romantic poets who would choose words "incommensurate with the passion, and inadequate to raise the reader to a height of desirable excitement." He also pointed out the fault of "grossly injudicious" metrical arrangements, even though a proper "movement of metre . . . will greatly contribute to impart

passion to the words," and thus effect the poet's intention. He recognized that poetry, unlike prose, was characterized by a pleasure which he termed a "similitude in dissimilitude" (warring yet rhythmic patterns of accents and unaccents, rhyme, and related devices), and which he identified with "the direction of the sexual appetite, and all the passions connected with it. . . ." Wordsworth reflected the thought of the Age of Reason in acknowledging the view of Sir Joshua Reynolds (1723–1792) of taste as "an *acquired* talent, which can only be produced by thought and a long-continued intercourse with the best models of composition." More than his predecessors, however, Wordsworth believed that genuine poetry possessed wide and profound dimensions.

Biographia Literaria (1817), by Samuel Taylor Coleridge (1772–1834), is one of the greatest works of literary criticism in the English language. Coleridge was not a systematic thinker, but his observations are descriptively significant. He seemed to be more interested in discovering the principles of a work of art—in "describing" them—than in arriving at rules for literary criticism. In *Biographia Literaria*, Coleridge discussed his own early literary development, his relationship with Wordsworth, the background of the *Lyrical Ballads*, various critical theories, the evolution of his philosophic views, the force of one's mind actively understanding the nature of reality (not unakin to Aristotle's concept of "becoming"), the nature of imagination ("emplastic power"), and the similarities and differences between Wordsworth's approaches to poetry as expressed in the Preface to the *Lyrical Ballads* and his.

According to Coleridge, the two "cardinal points" in poetry to be implemented in the planned *Lyrical Ballads*, which he discussed in detail with Wordsworth while they were neighbors at Somerset, were (1) the "power of exciting the sympathy of the reader by a faithful adherence to the truth of nature" and (2) the "power of giving the interest of novelty by the modifying colors of imagination." These principles led to a choice of collected poems of two kinds: (1) those of a "supernatural" quality and (2) those dealing with subjects "chosen from ordinary life." Coleridge, of course, produced *The Ancient Mariner* for the collection. For him supernaturalism was akin to a kind of Platonic mystery; at any rate, he felt that supernaturalism should be related to Romanticism and that such poetry should capture human interest and appear to be true enough to produce "for these shadows of imagination that willing suspension of disbelief for the moment. . . ." Although Wordsworth had dwelled upon the commonplace rather than the supernatural aspects of poetry in his writing of the Preface, Coleridge affirms that their goals were the same in that they both desired to render "the charm of novelty to things of every day," to awaken "the mind's attention from the lethargy of custom," and to direct it toward "the loveliness and the wonders of the world before us." Coleridge looked upon that world as "an inexhaustible treasure, but for which, in consequence of the film of familiarity and selfish solicitude, we have eyes yet see not, ears that hear not, and hearts that neither feel nor understand." Inherent in such statements, of course, are Wordsworthian concerns with feeling in poetry, the individuality and originality of the choice of subject, and the freedom and integrity of the poet in dealing with them.

Coleridge reaffirms Wordsworth's "characteristic of . . . genius" while, at the same time, he calls attention to the experimental nature of the *Lyrical Ballads* and the misconception that Wordsworth rejected "as vicious and indefensible all phrases and forms of style that were not included in what he . . . called the language of *real* life." Even as he explained Wordsworth, however, Coleridge stated his own view that his friend's use of "the language of *real* life" was "unfortunately" an unclear expression. In mediating between his views and those of Wordsworth, Coleridge states his intention of explaining the differences of his own ideas from those of Wordsworth ("first, of a Poem, and secondly, of Poetry"), and diplomatically reminds the reader that "distinction is not division."

He differs with Wordsworth's concept that a poem and a prose composition are not essentially different. He explains that although a poem "contains the same elements" as prose, the difference lies in the combination of elements. Poetry is more than mere rhythmic language, or mnemonic jingles:

Thirty days hath September
April, June, and November, &c.

A "*legitimate* poem," according to Coleridge, ". . . must be one the parts of which mutually support and explain each other, all in their proportion harmonizing with and supporting the purpose and known influences of metrical arrangements." Truth, not pleasure, may be the immediate object of great poetry, as in the first chapter of *Isaiah*. In addition, poetry may exist without meter. In a sense, then, a poem, paradoxically, cannot be "all poetry." Rather, poetry "becomes" itself through its parts. Later, in his lectures on Shakespeare, Coleridge used the term "organic growth," implying a kind a mystical separate life of poetry, inextricably tied up with the meaning of *poet*:

> The poet, described in ideal perfection, brings the whole soul of man into activity, with the subordination of its faculties to each other. . . . He diffuses a tone and spirit of unity, that blends and (as it were) *fuses* each into each, by that synthetic and magical power to which we have exclusively appropriated the name of imagination . . . reveal[ing] itself in the balance or reconciliation of opposite or discordant qualities: of sameness with difference; of the general, with the concrete; the idea, with the image; the individual, with the representative; the sense of novelty and freshness, with old and familiar objects; a more than usual state of emotion, with more than usual order; judgment ever awake, and steady self-possession, with enthusiasm and feeling profound or vehement; and while it blends and harmonizes the natural and the artificial, still subordinates art to nature, the manner to the matter, and our admiration of the poet to our sympathy with the poetry.

All this is to say that the poet's genius and his

emotions—his creative *esse*, so to speak—are so interrelated that the poem becomes a kind of projected self, in which the "body of poetic genius, fancy . . . motion . . . and imagination" form "all into one graceful and intelligent whole." In his lectures on Shakespeare, Coleridge stated that this greatest of all English poets "transports himself into the very being of each personage," no matter what the nature of the character:

> The great prerogative of genius . . . is now to swell itself to the dignity of a god, and now to subdue and keep dormant some part of that lofty nature, and to descend even to the lowest character—to become everything. . . .

Coleridge also differed with Wordsworth's concept of language taken "from the mouths of men in real life," pointing out that the words of the "uneducated rustic" are not the best—indeed, are far from ideal—and that the language of certain educated men is as "real" as that of the rustic, except in its "superior number and novelty of the thoughts and relations" conveyed. The language of "low and rustic life" is not any more "real" than any other class of language, but it is ordinary, or "*lingua communis*," and this is so variable as to exist everywhere and "nowhere as a whole." In short, he exposes the generalization of Wordsworth's contention concerning "real language."

Coleridge also commented on the defects of Wordsworth's style, listing five which are as revealing of Coleridge's analytical astuteness as the six excellencies which he praised. The defects include an "*inconstancy* of the style," a "not seldom a *matter-of-factness* in certain poems," an undue emphasis on "the *dramatic* form," an "intensity of feeling disproportionate to such knowledge and value of the objects described" (a weakness Wordsworth himself recognized in the Preface, incidentally), and "thoughts and images too great for the subject."

In addition to these are the acknowledged excellencies of Wordsworth, however: "an austere purity of language both grammatically and logically" or "a perfect appropriateness of the words to the meaning"; a "correspondent weight and sanity of the Thoughts and Sentiments"; a "sinewy strength and originality of single lines and paragraphs"; the "perfect truth of nature in his images and descriptions as taken immediately from nature," a "meditative pathos, a union of deep and subtle thought with sensibility" or "a sympathy with man as man," and "pre-eminently . . . the gift of Imagination in the highest and strictest sense of the word."

In final tribute to him, Coleridge refuted the shallowness of Wordsworth's detractors and, ironically perhaps, condemned the strangely mistaken Wordsworthian admirers for praising his "*simplicity*." Having critically analyzed the poetry of his friend with impartial objectivity and perceptive skills, Coleridge observed, "His fame belongs to another age, and can neither be accelerated nor retarded. How small the proportion of the defects are to the beauties. . . ." As insightful as Coleridge's criticism is, in both *Biographia Literaria* and the various lectures of which we have records, one gathers that this poet-critic-philosopher succeeded not so much in founding a "school" or in the invention of utilitarian critical terms, but rather in describing something of the essence of the mysterious creative process of poets and poetry, with Wordsworth and Shakespeare as his object lessons.

Only the briefest space is left for comment on selected Romantic critics, all of them outstanding essayists or poets. William Hazlitt (1778–1830) concerned himself with emotional responses to art by both poet and critic; he was concerned with wit, humor, and *gusto*, which he defined as "power or passion in defining any object," generating in art an emotional excitement. His work was characterized by "sympathetic identification," or the Wordsworthian ability to identify oneself with one's fellow man, a condition out of which moral feeling is deepened. Thus, he defined poetry as "the universal language which the heart holds with nature and itself."

Thomas De Quincey (1785–1859), a Romantic

critic, produced the close contextual analysis "On the Knocking at the Gate in *Macbeth*"—a fine piece of early psychological interpretation of literature. Through it, he indicates how the murderers—Macbeth and his Lady—are, figuratively, transfigured into devils by their deed, which takes them "out of the region of human things, human purposes, human desires." He indicates how the knocking suddenly sequesters them beyond "an immeasurable gulf from the ordinary tide and succession of human affairs," and how the knocking purges the dehumanizing horror, and "the world of darkness passes away," making audible the "goings-on" of everyday life again after "the awful parenthesis that has suspended them."

Despite his early death, John Keats (1795–1821) produced a legacy of letters and notes which are not merely restatements of the essential mystery of poetry and the creative process, but which must stand among the most seriously insightful approaches to poetry and the comprehension of its origins. Although acknowledging that "it is easier to think what Poetry should be than to write it," he perceived the basic idea that a rendering of nature is essential, suggesting a liberal reading of Aristotle. And if nature is essential, naturalness is a *sine qua non*; indeed, "if Poetry comes not as naturally as the Leaves to a tree it had better not come at all." At the same time, his knowledge of his own limitations produces a touching humility that lends both balance and a tone of charm to his views: "I am . . . young, writing at random, straining at particles of light in the midst of a great darkness."

Specifically, Keats wrote that poetry should be as full and as rich and as familiar as memory itself: "Poetry should surprise by a fine excess and not by Singularity—it should strike the Reader as a wording of his own highest thoughts, and appear almost a Remembrance." Again, to some extent echoing Aristotle as well as Ben Jonson, he stated that the beauty of poetry "should never be half way," but should be complete—like the rising, hovering, declining, and setting of the sun—

leaving the reader "content" rather than merely "breathless." Like Wordsworth, he perceived a kind of common, instinctive fluidity running through man and nature. As regards man, Wordsworth had termed it an "electric fire in human nature." Keats described it as an "animal eagerness," and stated that the creature man's "eyes are bright with it" when he is possessed by a "purpose." In superior form, man's reasonings may resolve into the stuff of poetry, but the process by which this is achieved is a profound matter. Like Coleridge before him, Keats asserted the triumph of imagination in the creative process; but he believed that intensity—what Hazlitt would have termed "gusto" (that is, power and passion)—and not logic ("consequitive reasoning") is the catalyst through which the poet could become a "Man of Achievement."

All this refers to "negative capability," Keats' central critical formulation. Briefly stated, he believed that the artist, in perceiving that about which he writes, and in creating a work of "Beauty and Truth," has to get close to a kind of subverbal reality. To do so, the genuine poet is required to efface his own ego and achieve a sympathetic identification with his subject so close and so real that no secondary motivations (such as concern with abstract philosophical systems) can influence the basic honesty of his stance. Thus, at the point of greatest identity with his subject, the poet possesses no identity of his own. All his identity, as it were, has been projected into the corpus of his subject and work. Only then may a poet transmute his creative experience into a "sense of Beauty" which "obliterates all consideration." Keats himself implemented his theory with a hypothetical illustration, typical for its clarity and eloquence:

> When I am in a room with People if I ever am free from speculating on creations of my brain, then not myself goes home to myself: but the identity of every one in the room begins to press upon me [in such a way] that I am in a very little time annihilated—not only among Men; it would be the same in a Nursery of children.

In addition to his psychologically significant theory of negative capability, one of Keats' most singular insights was his awareness of the universality of great poetry and of the fact that poetry or the appreciation of it cannot be made into a narrowly restricted formula. Even a poor man of limited vision, like Cervantes' Sancho Panza, "will invent a Journey heavenward as well as anybody." Keats thus proceeded to warn both poets and readers: "We hate poetry that has a palpable design upon us—and if we do not agree, seems to put its hand in its breeches pocket." For ideal poetry "should be great and unobtrusive, a thing which enters into one's soul, and does not startle it or amaze it with itself, but with its subject."

In many ways, the critical views of Percy Bysshe Shelley reflect those of Keats, and it is hardly surprising that they should. Shelley's *Defence of Poetry* was written in 1821, a year before his death at the age of twenty-nine, and the year of Keats' death. The poets were, of course, contemporaneous Romantics, and both had been exposed to similar influences and sources, especially Wordsworth, Hazlitt, Johnson, and the ancients (foremost among these, strangely, Plato). Shelley's essay, not published until 1840, best represents his faith in poetry, especially its high social and moral value. The *Defence* also recapitulates organic theories basic to the Romantics; echoes portions and general purposes of Sir Philip Sidney's *Apology for Poetry*; harks back to the classical concepts of the wholeness of a work and the function of poetry as a means of producing moral good and enlarging the range of man's ethics, human identity, and empathy; and recapitulates basic Platonic ideals, especially in the form of ultimate absolutes and the poetic ability to perceive divine visitations and transmit them into immortal art. But unlike Plato, Shelley did not consider the poet necessarily mad, nor did he urge his exclusion from the ideal republic.

Anticipating aspects of the "New Criticism," but in a negative sense, Shelley denigrated analytical reasoning when weighed with imagination or the creative process as mental actions.

Reason simply enumerates qualities generally known, points up differences, and is "dead and spiritless." Imagination, on the other hand, perceives values "both separately and as a whole" and reveals similarities between things. "Reason is to the imagination as the instrument to the agent, as the body to the spirit, as the shadow to the substance." Shelley emphasized the totality or wholeness of imagination rather than the partial illumination of analytical reason.

Shelley perceived "Every original language near to its source" as "the chaos of a cyclic poem." This suggests Wordsworth's concept of "real language." With powerful and imaginative insights, the poet examines the heart of an "organic" universe and (like Plato) pierces through the shadows of mere seemings—the facts of history, for example, which are likened to a mirror which "obscures and distorts"—and the poet's mind becomes, in turn, a kind of "mirror which makes beautiful that which is distorted." Such is the power of imagination when exposed to "eternal truth."

Shelley stated that the view of poetry as immoral "rests upon a misconception . . . [of how] poetry acts to produce the moral improvement of man." To more specific, "Poetry lifts the veil from the hidden beauty of the world, and makes familiar objects be as if they were not familiar." Again, "the great secret of morals is love, or a going out of our nature, and an identification of ourselves with the beautiful which exists in thought, action, or person, not our own." This is sympathetic identification. Here, Shelley expands upon Aristotle's *Poetics* as well as Sidney's *Apology*, observing that poetry "enlarges the circumference of the imagination by replenishing it with thoughts of ever new delight, which have the power of attracting and assimilating to their own nature all other thoughts, and which form new intervals and interstices whose void for ever craves fresh food."

Indeed, "Poetry is . . . something divine," being at both "the centre" and "circumference of knowledge." In other words, poetry, being eternally true, coexists with the essence of things immortal; poetry pervades eternity. And in this context, one understands how Shelley could have defined poetry as "the record of the best and happiest moments of the happiest and best minds." Small wonder he could believe that "Poetry redeems from decay the visitations of the divinity in man," that "Poets are the unacknowledged legislators of the world," or that when one reads celebrated writers, he is "startled with the electric life which burns within their words."

5. Historical and Humanistic Approaches

Historical Approaches

Certainly, poetry has a historical dimension. If history is a more or less systematic account of what has happened up to the present—involving the development of peoples, countries, institutions, and cultures—it is, of course, a record of the past; we say of such things, "That is now history." The historical critic approaches poetry, as well as other genres of literature, in relation to the past, and his method is described as "historical criticism"—or sometimes, with a more specific connotation, "historicism." Horace, in his *Epistles*, nearly 2,000 years ago raised basic questions concerning the relevance of time and age to the evaluation of literature, and in England, Dryden, through the character of Eugenius in *An Essay of Dramatic Poesy*, related dramatic poetry to matters of historical age, country, and antiquity.

Although Charles Augustin Sainte-Beuve (1804–1869), the greatest literary critic of nineteenth-century France, praised classicism, he indicated the importance of a kind of universal historicism: "I am a naturalist of minds," he wrote. "What I should like to establish is the natural history of literature." He meant to do so as fully as possible, in a systematic manner, in a humanistic and basically classical sense. His systematic approaches pointed toward the comparatively more modern methods of scientific naturalism; yet Sainte-Beuve himself remained a classicist at heart, as his fifty volumes of criticism repeatedly demonstrate. It remained for Sainte-Beuve's disciple, Hippolyte-Adolphe Taine (1828–1893), through his *History of English Literature* (1863), to reduce the humanistic dimensions of his master's work and to emphasize systematically the race, or nation; the epoch, or time; and the milieu, or surroundings. He thus anticipated even more modern sociocultural approaches to literature.

As René Wellek and Austin Warren point out in *Theory of Literature* (1948),[1] "There have been

[1] René Wellek and Austin Warren, *Theory of Literature* (New York: Harcourt, Brace & World, 1956), pp. 28–29.

attempts to isolate literary history from theory and criticism," but such concepts are essentially restrictive, for even the most conservative historical reconstructionists by their very selectivity cannot record merely coldly objective or "completely neutral 'facts.'" For example, the statement "Pope was influenced by Dryden" implies not only a selection of two literary figures from countless others, but also a knowledge of the two writers and their works and an implicit, if not explicit, evaluation and interpretation of their works, even if in a limited sense.

In the broadest sense, then, we may look upon the historical approach as involving a vast range of factors. It involves more or less "objective" research concerning the "facts" of the past—especially those of the classical tradition. It also calls for informed and sensitive treatments of aspects of the life and work of the time being studied. Finally, it considers the interrelationships between these and the whole historical-cultural matrix of which they form a portion. Thus, the historical scholar-critic may be concerned with such technical matters as the basic materials and tools of research—authenticity of texts, problems in editing and dating works, and sources and influences aside from only literary ones. For example, Van Wyck Brooks, in his *The Ordeal of Mark Twain*, was concerned with the restrictive influences of his subject's wife, minister, and editor upon his thinking and attitudes, and with what he *did not* write as a result. In a technical sense, the historical approach may involve the placing of a writer and his work within a historical age, literary period, and genre study. For example, Dr. Samuel Johnson is often associated with both the Augustan Age and the Golden Age of Biography.

The historical critic may also examine the biographical details of a poet's life in an effort to explain more fully his work and his relationship to his time and culture. If necessary, he may consider the author's family and the historical period during which he lived. He may then relate this period to other periods within the country's past up to the present. By looking closely at the traits of the country and the environment in which the poet was nurtured, the critic may be enabled to explain how the poet sensed things, absorbed the ideas around him, assimilated his milieu, used his sources and influences in particular ways. The critic may thus give a larger, fuller portrait of the artist and his work than may yet have been rendered. Similarly, the reader may be enlightened in new ways as to the poet's relationship to his contemporaries or his work in contexts of literary tradition, style, genre, its similarities to and differences from them, and originality or lack of it. In the broadest sense, the historical critic, through a sympathetic and enlightened application of his tools to his subject, may produce a new vision of his subject through evaluation and interpretation of his scholarly discoveries.

Humanistic Approaches

In the broadest sense, "humanism" may be said to encompass humanity. Pursued in the spirit of humanism are those delineated studies named "humanities" languages and literatures, including, specifically, classical Greek and Latin; and other branches of learning disparate from the sciences—those involving thought and relationships—such as history, the fine arts, and philosophy. Man is the center, and philosophically, he is the measure of things humanistic. Often, humanism refers to an educational dimension in which the emphasis of study is placed upon a well-rounded cultural background, as opposed to overspecialized training, as, for example, that in a specific science which excludes a balanced curriculum based on the humanities, thus denying the scientist a broad cultural knowledge and restricting him to the singular depth of his area of study.

Traditionally, however, humanism points to the Renaissance rediscovery of the Latin and Greek classics, which was given great incentive by the invention of printing in the fifteenth century. Such humanists as the Dutch Desiderius Erasmus (1467–1536) did much to influence the establishment of sound reason and learning within an age of religious conservatism and political turmoil. In spite of the opposition of the Roman clergy to the rise of new liberal ideas (it was said of Erasmus that he laid the egg which Luther hatched), the early English humanists retained their faith. The Oxford Reformers, including Erasmus and such friends as Sir Thomas More and John Colet, were intent upon moral reform through education and especially through improving the standards of an alarmingly corrupt church. Moral training through study of the classics was emphasized, and the Oxford Reformers urged a historical approach to Biblical study. In this connection, one may observe the influence of Plato's *Republic* upon Sir Thomas More's *Utopia* (1516), especially in the theme of moral perfection in matters social and governmental.

But the devotion of humanists to man and his interests—as opposed to concerns exclusively supernatural on the one hand and scientific and naturalistic on the other—was of central importance to literary approaches extending from such antecedents as Chaucer (who was indebted to Boccaccio and Petrarch in Italy) and Sir Philip Sidney (whose *Apology* was the first distinctive synthesis of European Renaissance principles of humanism in England). The classical approaches of Plato, Aristotle, Horace, and Longinus were reasserted, and the neoclassical approaches of Jonson, Dryden, Pope, and Dr. Samuel Johnson confirmed their validity, in spite of the radical innovations of the Romantics which followed. In literary history, then, humanism reflects broad cultural examination of language and literature, thought, philosophy, and Renaissance concerns with life and morality—especially as they found their origins in Greek and Roman classicism.

Matthew Arnold (1822–1888), the son of Thomas Arnold, Headmaster of Rugby, can best be described as a reluctant neoclassicist. A perusal of his poetry reveals a man of strong emotions, which, in the main, he kept leashed in his prose.

Believing that in his time the old gods were falling, Arnold sought absolutes—intellectual and spiritual—which would hold his society together. No longer capable of believing in an anthropomorphic God, Arnold sought values which would sustain men in an increasingly neutral universe. Thus his criticism of poetry is essentially a criticism of life. Indeed, to Arnold poetry became very much identified with religion:

> The future of poetry is immense because in poetry, where it is worthy of its high destinies, our race, as time goes on, will find an ever surer and surer stay. There is not a creed which is not shaken, not an accredited dogma which is not shown to be questionable, not a received tradition which does not threaten to dissolve. Our religion has materialized itself in the fact, the supposed fact; it has attached its emotion to the fact, and now the fact is failing it. But for poetry the idea is everything; the rest is a world of illusion, of divine illusion. Poetry attaches its emotion to the idea; the idea *is* the fact. The strongest part of our religion today is its unconscious poetry. . . . More and more mankind will discover that we have to turn to poetry to interpret life for us, to console us, to sustain us. Without poetry, our science will appear incomplete; and most of what now passes with us for religion and philosophy will be replaced by poetry.

It is not our purpose here to delve into Arnold's philosophy, especially as it pertains to nonpoetical matters, but it might be helpful at this point to speculate, at least, about what he meant by "poetry" and "religion."

To begin with, Arnold suggests that great poetry contains absolute truths. To Arnold, the great poet is "poet-prophet"—one who has looked into the white, hot heart of the absolute and has then used the devices of poetry to transmit to others, through symbol, emotion, and song, what he has found there. This is, of course, essentially Platonism. What the poet has discovered is, on a literal level, essentially ineffable; but through poetry he can transcend the limitations of the informational or "scientific" word. As the poet is always transmitting the absolute, all great poets offer the same absolute substances. Thus great poetry says the same things. Form may differ, language may differ, but the essence remains the same.

From the above ideas, one can gather why Arnold identifies poetry with religion. Religion may be thought of as a many-layered entity. At the center is the Platonic truth. The next layer consists of the poet's expression of this truth through his poetry. Thus, at the core of all religions is the same truth. As man moves from barbarism to culture, this poetic core of truth is overlaid by myth, picture-book examples, anthropomorphism, and other obscuring elements. Arnold envisions that in time all of this extraneous material will be stripped away, and what will be left will be only the truth and the poetic expression of it.

This is, of course, pretty heady stuff which incorporates not a little of transcendentalist (and, of course, Emersonian) thought, but in its applicability to the world of here and now—the phenomenal world—it shows a marked, pragmatic emphasis. Indeed, we see that when Arnold speaks of poetry as the religion of the future, he does not mean that it will replace religion, but merely that it will be recognized for what it has always been—the core of religion—truth itself. Religion, on the rocks, in effect, undiluted by the waters of dogma.

Happily, at this point Arnold returns to the more concrete areas of critical approaches, and though the reader may or may not accept Arnold's metaphysical leaps, he will soon find himself at home in the charted oceans of Arnold's more mundane critical theories. But even here we find ourselves verging on some troublesome reefs, even as we traverse shallower waters. Arnold, especially in his essay *The Study of Poetry* (1880), speaks of some approaches that may interfere with a true and valid evaluation of poetry:

> Yes; constantly in reading poetry, a sense for the best, the really excellent [that poetry which contains the aforementioned absolute truth], and of the strength and joy to be drawn from it, should be present in our minds and should govern our estimate of what we read. But this real estimate, the only true one, is

liable to be superseded, if we are not watchful, by two other kinds of estimate, *the historical estimate* and *the personal estimate, both of which are fallacious* [italics added]. A poet or a poem may count to us historically, they may count to us on grounds personal to ourselves, and they may count to us really.

One of the authors of this text grew up in Indiana. When he left that state, he realized that it had been suggested to him throughout his life that among the great writers of the world were Booth Tarkington, Edward Eggleston, Gene Stratton Porter, and James Whitcomb Riley. Later he learned that their major claim to distinction lay in the fact that they all had one thing in common: they had been Hoosiers! The pride that a state or a country may have in its writers, in other words, may prevent it from judging a writer's productions objectively. Indeed, Arnold often stresses that the predominant characteristic of a good critic—one who sees the poem as it is in itself—is "disinterestedness" (that is, objectivity). Surely, one cannot argue with this. Can we doubt that all of us have been influenced by a lack of disinterestedness when we have evaluated a work of literature? Analogically, is there any father appointed a judge in a baby contest who, were his baby entered, would be capable of awarding (in all subjective honesty) the prize to any baby but his own? We think not.

Arnold continues:

> Then, again, a poet or poem may count to us on grounds personal to ourselves. Our personal affinities, likings, and circumstances have great power to sway our estimate of this or that poet's work, and to make us attach more importance to it as poetry than in itself it really possesses, because to us it is, or has been, of high importance. Here we also overrate the object of our interest, and apply to it a language of praise which is quite exaggerated.

What Arnold means here is so obvious, so universally recognizable, that it justifies little comment. Just as we tend to think that a man who holds the same opinions as we do is extremely wise, so do we often overevaluate a poem that expresses what we believe or one that is about something in which we ourselves are interested or involved. An offshoot of this idea may be called "moral" criticism, in which we judge a poem to be great because it says "good" things.

How then does Arnold suggest that we may arrive at a true estimate of a poem? He states:

> there can be no more useful help for discovering what poetry belongs to the class of the truly excellent, *and can therefor do us most good than to have always in one's mind lines and expressions of the great masters, and to apply them as a touchstone to other poetry.* Of course we are not to require this other poetry to resemble them; it may be very dissimilar. But if we have the tact we shall find them, when we have lodged them well in our minds, an *infallible* touchstone for detecting the presence or absence of high poetic quality, and also the degree of this quality, in all other poetry which we may place beside them. *Short passages, even single lines, will serve our turn quite sufficiently* [italics added].

This, then, is the formulation of Arnold's famous "touchstone" theory. Simply, if we read great poetry, we will create a measuring device in our minds with which to judge all other poetry we may subsequently encounter.

Arnold then proceeds to give some lines of great poetry which he suggests are suitable for the creation of these touchstones. As a humanist suggesting the universality of great poetry, it is hardly surprising that Arnold gives quotations in Greek and Italian as well as in English. Among the last mentioned, however, are the following:

Wilt thou upon the high and giddy mist
Seal up the ship-boy's eyes, and rock his brains
In cradle of the rude imperious surge . . .
(Shakespeare, *Henry the Fourth*—III, 1, 18–20)

If thou dids't ever hold me in thy heart,
Absent thee from felicity awhile,
And in this harsh world draw thy breath in pain
To tell my story . . .
(*Hamlet*—V, 2, 335–338)

Darken'd so, yet shown
Above them all the archangel; but his face
Deep scars of thunder had intrench'd, and care
Sat on his faded cheek . . .
(Milton, *Paradise Lost*—Bk. I, 599–602)

He continues:

> The specimens I have quoted differ widely from one another, but they have in common this: the possession of the very highest poetical quality. If we are thoroughly penetrated by their power, we shall find that we have acquired a sense enabling us, whatever poetry may be laid before us, to feel the degree in which a high poetical quality is present or wanting there. . . . It is much better simply to have recourse to concrete examples; . . . the substance and matter on the one hand, the style and manner on the other, have a mark, an accent, of high beauty, worth, and power. But if we are asked to define this mark and accent in the abstract, our answer must be: No, for we should thereby be darkening the question, not clearing it. The mark and accent are as given by the substance and matter of that poetry, by the style and manner of that poetry, and of all other poetry which is akin to it in quality.
>
> Only one thing we may add as to the substance and matter of poetry, guiding ourselves by Aristotle's profound observation that the superiority of poetry over history consists in its possessing a higher truth and a higher seriousness. . . . Let us add, therefore, to what we have said, this: that the substance and matter of the best poetry acquire their special character from *possessing, in an eminent degree, truth and seriousness.* . . . So far as *high poetic truth and seriousness are wanting to a poet's matter and substance,* so far also, we may be sure, will a high poetic stamp of diction and movement be wanting to his style and manner. In proportion as this high stamp of diction and movement, again, is absent from a poet's style and manner, we shall find, also, that high poetic truth and seriousness are absent from his substance and matter [italics added].

Although it is true that the more one is exposed to good things—poetry, music, or food, for that matter—the more he is capable of recognizing excellence, it is difficult for many to discover the absolutes in Arnold's essay, from which the pertinent lines above are quoted. Moreover, one may reasonably question whether a few lines from a poem are sufficient to demonstrate its intrinsic greatness. The quotation from *Hamlet,* for example, would seem to depend for its undoubted impact upon the reader having read all of *Hamlet* and upon his bringing that total experience with him to be again evoked by the lines.

Nonetheless, Arnold had much to say about the criticism of poetry that is demonstrably true, and if his critical vision is in places obviously limited, we can be but grateful for that which is not.

The "New Humanists" and the Resurgence of Historicism

During the first third of the twentieth century, Matthew Arnold's influence carried over into a critical movement called "The New Humanism," the major standard-bearers of which were such scholars as Irving Babbitt and Paul Elmer More. In his famous essay *The Art of Fiction* (1884), the psychological realist Henry James, while urging a freedom for the artist to write from experience, to be granted his *donnée* (generally his approach and subject), and to capture the "colour of life itself," had balanced his assertions with an admonition, contending that the naturalist Émile Zola, whose work he respected, nevertheless represented "an extraordinary effort vitiated by a spirit of pessimism on a narrow basis." James was implying, of course, the new humanist spirit in his opposition to the developing new sociocultural, naturalistic, and other related "scientific" approaches being taken toward literature. The new humanist thus found himself reasserting the importance of classical influences over the growing emphasis on newer approaches to poetry and other forms of literature.

In his "Humanism: An Essay at Definition" (1930), Irving Babbitt affirmed much of the spirit of the new humanists. He reviewed the historical background of classicism and humanism, and he noted in this connection the preferability of "the humanity of the great classical writers to . . . the excess of divinity in the mediaevalism." He noted the importance of "proportionateness," or a harmonious development of the human faculties—what he termed "nothing too much." He also pointed to humanism as *substance* rather than "a

mere veneer, something that has no deep root in the nature of things"; and to the timelessness of humanistic essences, "not of today or yesterday," but transcending the temporal process. He affirmed the importance of "intuition" (suggesting an affinity with Emersonian transcendentalism), and he discussed the humanistic emphasis on a "universal centre" of human nature, which requires "the setting up of some pattern or model for imitation," an idea which "goes even deeper than that of decorum, but is an idea that humanism shares with religion." He stressed the importance of the "right cultivation of one's humanity," inherent in the high endeavor to see life "steadily" and see it "whole," and of a recognition of the basic perversity of "the naturalistic temper," the growth of which produced the result that "the normal has come to have less appeal than the novel." He viewed man as "the measure of all things"; yet he espoused clear opposition to the Romantic assertion that man is "naturally good," the result of which has been "to discredit the traditional controls, both humanistic and religious." In such an "arcadia" of "good," one sees "humility, conversion, decorum, all go by the board in favour of unrestricted temperamental overflow," resulting in a mistaken notion of "service" evident in "all the altruists from the third Earl of Shaftesbury to John Dewey." He considers this mistaken idealism, for the historical process reveals the distinction between the "real world" and "some romantic dreamland," especially through the sad, but true, fact (evident in the "Great Wars") that "the will to power is more than a match for the will to service."

Beleaguered by the charges of being antidemocratic, proaristocratic, antiscientific, antimodern, and protradition, the new humanists appeared to be overwhelmed by the rise of the so-called New Critics (including the contextualists and formalists), the sociocultural critics, and the Marxist critics of the 1930s. But actually followers of the historical and humanist traditions, though retreating to a virtual exile, have found, especially since mid-century, many of their ideas recurring in new shapes and forms (especially historicism). Yet the worst of their ideas, particularly the extremist views of the overzealous new humanists —including cultural snobbery, hostility toward contemporaneity, hints of puritanical overtones in assertions of moral responsibility, and the complete rejection of "determinism"—have largely gone by the board. Their sound groundings in classical principles and historical methods, both interpreted with increasing flexibility since World War II, have resulted in a resurgence of the best of their ideas and a solidity of stance, which have contributed to clarifying and enriching approaches to poetry in commonsensical and illuminating ways.

6. Sociocultural Approaches

Modern sociocultural approaches to literature find their wellsprings in historical literary criticism. Author-critic Edmund Wilson thought of literary criticism as the "history of man's ideas and imaginings in the setting of the conditions which have shaped them," as he stated in his dedication of *Axel's Castle* (1931). In his essay "The Historical Interpretation of Literature" (1941), he gave a working definition of the sociocultural interpretation of literature while setting it within the context of a historical approach. He stated that it was a consideration of the "social, economic and political aspects" of a work of art.[1]

The view of literature as social commentary, however, may be considered quite apart from more traditional historical views. Although an overlapping is present, the sociocultural critic emphasizes different factors. For example, he places less importance on the text, its authenticity, various editions, and editorial changes—

in short, on the historical tracing of just how a work of art comes down to us. Again, the sociocultural critic is less interested in the biography of the poet and such intrinsic matters as the literary context of the work—its relationship to literary periods, purely literary influences and sources, style, technical analysis of poetic images, and rhetoric. Neither is he interested in the aesthetic concerns of *l'art pour l'art*.

The sociocultural critic gets away from textual matters, but like Dr. Johnson and the classicists before him, he is still interested in the moral implications of a poem. Under "society" and "culture" he subsumes not only social, political, and economic concerns, but also moral, philosophical, and other broadly cultural ones. True, such historical humanists as Sainte-Beuve and Arnold also emphasized the intellectual, moral, social, and educational aspects of what we call "culture" —and with universal implications transcending national boundaries—but their emphasis remained essentially Platonic. Their approach was thus an aesthetic historicism rooted in classicism. Arnold

[1] Edmond Wilson, "The Historical Interpretation of Literature," *The Triple Thinkers* (New York: Harcourt, Brace & Co., 1948), p. 257.

believed the idea of a poem to be a world unto itself: "for poetry the idea is everything; the rest is a world of illusion, of divine illusion. Poetry attaches its emotion to the idea; the idea *is* the fact."

The socioculturalist's method suggests more of Taine's approach, in which the stress is placed on "scientific," causative inquiries into—let us consider, for example—"the moral condition" which produces a "literature, philosophy, society, art, group of arts"; and on the question of what may be the "conditions of race, epoch, circumstance," which are most fitted to produce this moral condition. As Taine sought to develop "the recondite mechanism" for approaching English literature as early as 1863, the modern socioculturalists' approaches suggest those of naturalism, with their emphasis on objective examination of a cultural complex—the total environmental causes presumed to lead to a certain result. Fictional history based on social realities was emphasized by Henry James, and its validity was confirmed by the early realist William Dean Howells in *Criticism and Fiction* (1891). Both were echoing Emerson's concept of the poet as a filter of nature, society, and moral transfiguration. This concept was further elaborated upon by Walt Whitman in his "Preface to the 1855 Edition of *Leaves of Grass*":

> The United States themselves are essentially the greatest poem. . . . [The poet] is the equalizer of his age and land. . . . An individual is as superb as a nation when he has the qualities which make a superb nation. . . . The proof of a poet is that his country absorbs him as affectionately as he has absorbed it.

The effect of egalitarianism was to point the way to an increasing awareness of social science.

The sociological critics found that poetry and prose were inspired by the economic atrocities, political upheavals, and social shiftings and "implosions" which seemed everywhere to accompany the Industrial Revolution and the increasing urbanization of great masses of people. For example, the urging for better industrial conditions and reform in child labor gave Sarah N. Cleghorn incentive to write such a purely sociocultural poem as "The Golflinks Lie So Near the Mill" (1917):

> The golflinks lie so near the mill
>   That almost every day
> The laboring children can look out
>   And see the men at play.[2]

Among the earliest publications devoted exclusively to liberal and radical concerns, particularly Socialist criticism, was the periodical *Comrade* (published in New York, 1901–1905), which featured approaches to poetry based on social and libertarian, as well as literary, values. The literary critics most obviously concerned with politically extrinsic (nonliterary) matters were, perhaps, the Marxists. Bernard Smith, in his *Forces in American Criticism*, stated this general description of the Marxist thesis:

> a work of literature reflects its author's society. To determine the character and value of the work we must therefore, among other things, understand and have an opinion about the social forces that produced the ideology it expresses as an attitude toward life. Marxism enables us to understand those forces by explaining the dialectical relationship of a culture to an economy and of that culture to the classes which exist in that economy. At the same time, by revealing the creative role of the proletariat in establishing a communist society, which alone can realize universal peace and well-being. Marxism offers a *scale* of value. Moral as well as political judgments follow from that thesis—and they include a condemnation of the bourgeois sexual code, of woman's traditional place in the community, and of the accepted relative prestige of labor and unproductive leisure. Of immediate significance to the critic is the conception of reality from which the thesis is evolved and which the thesis defines.[3]

Alick West, in his *Crisis and Criticism* (1937), takes as his thesis the questionable assertion con-

---

[2] Sarah N. Cleghorn, *Portraits and Protests* (New York: Henry Holt & Co., 1917).
[3] Bernard Smith, *Forces in American Criticism* (New York: Harcourt, Brace & Co., 1939), pp. 287–288.

cerning the origin of language (a complex linguistic riddle of nearly hopeless proportions)—that language "grew as a form of social organization"—and proceeds to the conclusion that "literature as art continues that growth." But the implication of the delineation of the function of literature as a concomitant of social growth is clear enough. Christopher Caudwell (pseudonym of Christopher St. John Sprigg, 1907–1937), in his *Illusion and Reality* subtitled "A Study of the Sources of Poetry" (1937), perhaps came closest to working out the earliest comprehensive theory of Marxist approaches to literary art. Caudwell's view of the artistic process, as one may expect, is deeply rooted in sociocultural soil, as the poet experiences

a tension between tradition and experience . . . in his heart. Just as the scientist is the explorer of new realms of outer reality; the artist continually discovers new kingdoms of the heart. Both therefore are explorers, and necessarily therefore share a certain loneliness. But if they are individualists, it is not because they are non-social, but precisely because they are performing a social task. They are non-social only in this sense, that they are engaged in dragging into the social world realms at present non-social and must therefore have a foot in both worlds.[4]

Raymond Williams, in *Culture and Society*, distinguished between nineteenth- and twentieth-century views of society and culture in this way: it was not only Marx, but others as well, who insisted that "basic economic organization" could no longer be separated from "moral and intellectual concerns"—that "industrialism," with its constantly changing techniques and methods of production, indeed affected and influenced in subtle and obvious ways the *donnée* of the writer (and ultimately his moral responsibility), as well as the individual and society as a whole. And yet Williams questions a basic point of Marxist criticism, "whether the economic element is in fact *determining*" [italics added], concluding that the controversy is "an unanswerable question."

Still, he does not deny other sociocultural saliencies: "the shaping influences of economic change can of course be distinguished. . . . But the difficulty lies in estimating the final importance of a factor which never, in practice, appears in isolation."[5]

Although he admitted the limitations of Marxist critics, Malcolm Cowley did mention the advantages of such extrinsic approaches to literature. He maintained that previous critics for a century had been looking at poetry and fiction "purely in terms of literature," relying on rarefied phrases when abstractions failed them, being "traditional" until "criticism in our times has advanced scarcely farther than in those of Aristotle. . . ." Literature, he felt, had to be tested by extrinsic disciplines, such as "philosophy, psychology, sociology, medicine, and by history most of all," and "that explains the importance of the Marxist critics."[6] Earlier, in *Exile's Return* (1934), he had treated the "gentlemen volunteers" of World War I—the uprooted poets and artists who gravitated to post-Versailles Paris during the 1920s—within the social, political, moral, and aesthetic context of American disillusionment and subsequent disaffiliation.

Van Wyck Brooks, too, emphasized historical and social values in his work, especially criticizing what he felt to be the destructive moral force of America's "Puritan morality." But portions of his *Sketches in Criticism* bear a tone of radical urgency: "Who can count indeed the impulses which, in history, poets have stirred to life, unlocked, as it were, and liberated into the sphere of action?" Concerning the Irish Rebellion, "of this generation," he observed:

Ireland . . . awakened to the desire to become itself, to direct its own destinies; and what was the fountainhead of that desire but the poets of Ireland? The conditions were ripe, the people had become susceptible, the poets spoke. To what extent was not the character of the Russian Revolution, of the French

---

[4] Christopher Caudwell, *Further Studies in a Dying Culture*, ed. and with a Preface by Edgell Rickword (London: Bodley Head, 1949), p. 109.

[5] Raymond Williams, *Culture and Society* (London: Chatto & Windus, 1958), p. 280.
[6] Malcolm Cowley, "Yeats and O'Faolain," *The New Republic*, 98 (February 15, 1939), 49–50.

Revolution, determined by the characters of poets, novelists and philosophers?[7]

Similarly, although the label fits loosely, at one time or another and in varying degrees, Edmund Wilson, Granville Hicks, and Newton Arvin related their ideas to Marxist approaches to literature. Hicks was at once the most systematic and radical of these prominent critics. For a time, Kenneth Burke and Malcolm Cowley were sympathetic with Marxist approaches, but by the time of World War II and the Russo-German Pact (August 1939), even the most extreme of the group underwent disillusionment. The enthusiasm of most Marxist critics, as well as that of many who had been sympathetic with Marxist views during the depression years of the 1930s, waned quickly. René Wellek and Austin Warren in their *Theory of Literature*,[8] when evaluating Marxist and other sociocultural criticism, raised objections against "too crude short cuts from economics to literature." Neither do expansions of profit necessarily "elicit great poets." Such approaches easily tend to become overzealous, and what may appear to be causal elements in the development of art may not necessarily be causal at all.

Take, for example, the assumption that England demonstrated a certain slackening of literary vitality during the seventeenth century compared to the preceding century. Under Queen Elizabeth the English had just experienced the richest and most phenomenal literary period in English history. Still, the great names of the following seventeenth century, even though their luster may be dimmed somewhat by that of Elizabethan illuminaries, should be evident. John Milton is considered by many English scholars second in poetic genius only to Shakespeare; and Jonson, Donne, Crashaw, Herbert, Dryden, and the Restoration dramatists are by no means inglorious. Moreover, the seventeenth century was one of Newtonian glory—a

singular period in science. Yet England's overall cultural efforts may have been diluted by a number of schismatic factors. She was preoccupied with religious dissension, Archbishop Laud's oppressive measures having played havoc with the potential contributions that the Separatists could have made to the country. The fervor of the Roundheads also tended to suppress artistic growth and cast a shadow over the land. The jubilant artists of Charles II's liking were French as often as English; and, finally, the people themselves were devoting much of their energy to a Parliament-Monarch feud culminating with the Glorious Revolution of 1688.

The general sociocultural examination obviously is not without merit, especially if one desires to go beyond the poem itself—to understand related aspects of a civilization's development which may in turn illuminate the poem. It is useful if one is aware of the limitations of the method, and if one can relate one's findings accurately to an increased understanding of the art (its meanings) and the artist (his motivations)—in short, if one seeks answers to the seemingly mysterious "what?" "why?" and "how?" of a poet and his work.

With the decline of the Marxist influence, different and new liberal approaches developed, although some had been developing before. For example, John Dewey, in his general views, and particularly in *Democracy and Education* (1926), had expounded upon meanings of education beyond considerations of the intellectual process, the school and related institutions, the teacher, and the student. His emphasis was, to some extent, deterministic; he believed that learning depends upon the individual in relation to all possible impacts upon him—not only intellectual, but social, physical, economic, and spiritual. Man is the end result of all such impacts. He especially placed the emphasis on social experience as a means of education. Education and democracy are inextricably interwoven, because democracy offers "associated living, of conjoint, communicated experience." Through communication, whole groups of people can participate in the educative

---

[7] Van Wyck Brooks, *Sketches in Criticism* (New York: E. P. Dutton, 1932), p. 303.

[8] René Wellek and Austin Warren, *Theory of Literature* (New York: Harcourt, Brace & World, 1956), p. 95.

social process which inheres in the essence of democratic societies. Educating for democracy means educating for all pertinent social needs including the economic—job training for factory work. automobile mechanics, police science, driving, cooking and food services—in short, education for *any* need of society. In such a scheme of things, the place of poetry, or any other form of art, becomes important mainly for its value as *communication*—that is, *as a means to learning* through interpenetrating the social complex. Concerning Dewey's views of the arts as tools of education, views which reached their apex of popularity in the 1930s and are still functional in the theories of many public-school educators today, Mortimer J. Adler wrote:

> Dewey's point about the arts as educative through being instruments of *communication* in society, establishes a *social* meaning of education, which must be clearly distinguished from the didactic sense in which the arts are viewed by Plato as instruments of moral and intellectual *instruction*, and from the *aesthetic* sense in which Aristotle views the arts as satisfying man's desire to learn by providing him with objects of *contemplation*. The value of communication follows properly from the nature of art as imitation, or, as Dewey says, "representation," in the same way that the values of contemplation, purgation, and recreation do. Dewey's analysis here is in the Aristotelian manner. It should be clear, furthermore, that this *social education* concerns the whole population, children and adults alike. When a democrat talks about the educational value of the arts he is not thinking exclusively about the training of the young but rather about the effects of the arts in binding all members of the community more closely together through the sharing, actual or vicarious, of experiences.[9]

With such a concept of poetry, one may well imagine using a poem as a convenient springboard for the development of social conversation in such an educational course as, say, group dynamics. The important thing would not be the poem itself,

of course, but rather, its function as a means of getting people to talk, to share ideas, to understand others better, and to express themselves more readily and effectively. The poem would serve as a "reference point" for the group, and to a considerable extent its success would be determined by its popularity, the breadth and depth of its appeal for whatever the *social* purpose might be—communication or whatever.

Finally, in recognizing that sociocultural approaches to poetry, important as they are, make up only pieces of the great mosaic representing life and art, Adler further observes, "Few relations are more complicated and delicate than that of a poet and society." Sociocultural critics are concerned with certain basic questions, and at their best, they may sometimes offer valuable insights into them. They consider such questions as: "What is the poet's obligation to his fellow man?" "Is art merely a cultural or social ornament, or does it proceed from the very fountainhead of the cultural life of man?" Ultimately, they consider a question piercing the very core of sociocultural approaches to poetry: "if poetry is central to human culture, what are the proper criteria for criticizing and evaluating it?"

The student who arduously desires to relate his study of poetry or any other form of culture to the issues of society today or yesterday cannot fulfill his wishes without viewing poetry within a sociocultural context, of course. But he should be aware of the total historical vision of such an approach, from Plato and Aristotle through the Marxist critics. He should be aware of the inherent limitations of the method, of its sometimes misleading assumptions, and of the tenuous nature of sociocultural interpretations of a poet's motivations and intentions. Above all, perhaps, he should be keenly aware of the fact that the sociocultural method is *extrinsic* by nature, and he should be especially conscious of the need to refer repeatedly to the text of the poem itself—in short, to give *intrinsic* balance to his views by knowing the poem well.

---

[9] Mortimer J. Adler, *Poetry and Politics* (Pittsburgh: Duquesne University Press, 1966), p. 204.

7. "New Critical" Approaches

First, it would be best to point out that there is really no specific and definable approach known as "The New Criticism" for analyzing poetry and other literary genres. Furthermore, there is no easily identifiable school of criticism whose adherents are known as "The New Critics." The term "New Criticism" is, at best, a useful generalization indicating a whole range of basically *intrinsic* literary approaches based upon the contention that poetry is worthy of study in itself, as poetry. Such approaches are sometimes known by other names, too, such as "formalist," "contextualist," "objective," "analytical," and "explicative." From them, especially since the 1940s, new directions have continued to emerge. This has resulted in broader and more flexible approaches than those suggested by these earlier terms.

A description of work done by individuals who may be identified with comparatively recent (especially twentieth-century) intrinsic approaches may tend to clarify what is meant by "The New Criticism" or "The New Critics." Whenever we use these verbal labels their use should be understood to lie within the general context of intrinsic approaches to poetry. The terms should not be avoided, for students of poetry will often hear them and should be able to understand and use them as the handy, though sometimes vague, generalizations that they are.

Among the examples of New Critical approaches are those brilliantly espoused in I. A. Richards' *The Principles of Literary Criticism* and *Practical Criticism*.[1] Because of Richards' profound influence

[1] I. A. Richards, *The Principles of Literary Criticism*, 2nd ed. (London: Kegan Paul, Trench, Trubner & Co., 1924; New York: Harcourt, Brace & Co., 1926) and *Practical Criticism* (London: Kegan Paul, Trench, Trubner & Co., 1929; New York: Harcourt, Brace & Co., 1935).

on most poetic analysis today, and because of the heavy reliance of many English teachers upon his methods of using semantic devices in close examens of poetry (some have actually produced highly popular poetry anthologies based largely upon his ideas), he deserves our closest attention.

Working from the basic thesis that even poetic language should be as *extensional* as possible (that is, as close to objective reality as possible), he attempted to analyze the language of poetry concretely. In doing so, he developed a list of ten difficulties in understanding poetry: (1) realizing its plain meaning on the level of communicating information; (2) apprehending the sensuous dimension of poetic language; (3) developing the capacity to transmute sense responses, especially the visual, through emotional levels and into a meaningful imaginative dimension; (4) responding privately to poetry, what Richards terms "mnemonic irrelevances"; (5) giving "stock responses" to poetry, or responding emotionally to key phrases or clichés, such as "mother love," "home sweet home," or "God and country," which trigger automatic responses not legitimately worked out in the poem; (6) reacting with "sentimentality," that is, wearing one's heart on one's sleeve, or responding with more emotion than is inherent in the poem; for the poet, this means demanding too much, thus often producing a grotesque or even comic effect rather than a genuine one; (7) reacting with "inhibition," or wearing one's heart *up* one's sleeve rather than letting it beat normally—the reverse of "sentimentality"; (8) failing to be objective, especially where "doctrinal adhesions" are concerned, as when one's responses are consistent with one's own religious beliefs, political convictions, or preconceived notions, and the "truth-value" of such views is allowed to bear upon the worth of the poetry; (9) permitting technical aspects of poetry to dominate our response to the poem— what Richards terms "technical presuppositions"; (10) blocking appreciation of poetry through "general critical preconceptions," or placing evaluative criteria upon poetry through the application of critical theories learned before the poetic experience.[2] For example, one might foolishly object to *Hamlet* because it does not follow Corneille's concept of the unity of time, claim it is a bad play, and deny himself the knowledge and pleasure to be derived from a masterpiece.

Richards admitted other difficulties in perceiving poetry, but he contended that these ten probably covered most problems of fairly well-balanced personalities, "blinding narcissism," "groveling self-abasement," and other "aberrations" of one's self-image excepted. Richards believed that if the reader were aware of these problems, he could begin to deal more effectively with them as obstacles to genuine poetic experience.[3]

In *Practical Criticism*, by explicating several poems, Richards demonstrated four kinds of analytical meaning from which one can synthesize a more accurate understanding of poetry. Again, because of the fairly wide use of Richards' New Critical approach, we believe the "meanings" should be at least briefly outlined, as they may aid readers of poetry here:

1. The meaning of "sense." This refers to the communication of poetry on the basic denotative (dictionary) level through language of information such as we encounter in science books, newspapers, and journals. Each poem may be paraphrased (put into one's own words) and understood at least on this basic level of sense by most readers. Indeed, it is a desirable first step in arriving at a meaning of a poem which most readers can share.
2. The meaning of "feeling." Once the poet's basic subject is understood, even tentatively, on the level of sense, the reader can begin to perceive the poet's mental posture, or attitudes toward his subject—his emotions, moods, opinions, dispositions. This feeling should be described with thoughtfully selected adjectives consistent with the sense of the poem previously worked out.
3. The meaning of "tone." Literally, the word suggests the modulation, pitch, or intonation of the voice of the speaker, which expresses a special meaning or feeling. Richards applied "tone" to the poet to mean the poet's attitude toward the reader and his relationship with his audience. Although one thinks of feeling and tone as being conscious, either or both may, to some extent, be unconscious.
4. The meaning of "intention." Aside from the poet's (or speaker's) basic level of meaning or information which can be paraphrased in one's own words (sense), the poet's complex of attitudes toward his subject (feeling), and that toward his audience or readers (tone), ideally he is endeavoring to fulfill an aim through the artistic medium of poetry, an idea or group of ideas, a *theme*, one might say, which is more or less conscious but sometimes unconscious. He may merely wish to express his meanings and vague feelings (despair, hope, exhilaration, for example), but most often his intention is a composite of his sense, feeling, and tone. A careful examination of these three kinds of meaning can help to elucidate the fourth— the poet's intention itself, although Richards pointed out that intention tends to dominate the other kinds of meaning in a poem, that intention is, indeed, an additional influence separable from sense, feeling, and tone.[4]

With all the limitations of Richards' approaches to poetry considered, one can readily see how his methods tend to remove the poem from abstract areas and to place it into an analytical context in which students of the art form may examine poetry *as poetry*. In this connection, I. A. Richards is very

[2] Richards, *Practical Criticism*, ibid., pp. 13–17.
[3] *Ibid.*, p. 17.

[4] *Ibid.*, pp. 181–183.

meaning, each intensifying and lending strength to the other. Ransom put it another way. After diagraming the relationship between meter and meaning in a poem, he pointed out that meter may at first appear to interfere with the actual progress of the content, "till presently it works a radical innovation: it induces the provision of icons [sudden wider associations] among the symbols (words). This launches poetry upon its career." Thus the form of poetry combines with its substance to form its peculiar essence—an ontological dimension of artistic language transcending the language of science or information, saying something that cannot be said on any other level of language, or in any other way.

In concluding, Ransom related his ideas to an explanatory summary of modernist poetry, especially that of poets like Pound, Eliot, Tate, Stevens, and Auden, suggesting possible answers to questions students of poetry invariably raise about such poets and their work, which has become widely anthologized. The following points are in no way intended as a summary of Ransom's observations. Rather, they are liberally interpreted and, in some instances, augmented compressions of some of his ideas and amplifications of others, which may prove useful to the student:

1. A relationship to traditionalists, but mainly one of reaction, as well as culmination.
2. A heavy emphasis on the texture of poetry. He advocated careful choice of words, with consideration of their connotative values, and attention to its details rather than general meanings. All of this often leads to startlingly original images, but it frequently leads to intellectualized and, paradoxically perhaps, obscure poetry, reflective of fragmented thought.
3. Experiments with new forms and apparent formlessness. This indicated his restlessness and his rebellion against the forms of the past. Dissatisfaction with "transparently artful" poetic devices.
4. A distaste for an age of science and a consequent quest for a "greater ontological competence," or a kind of original poetic achievement not expressible in any way other than the poem itself.
5. Approval of the conscious use of verbal "icons" (words and forms of words which exceed definition outside the poetic context in which they are used).
6. General lack of enthusiasm for regularized meters as a reaction to traditional substance or content as well as to form; for the adaptations of meter to meaning are direct, though the meanings themselves often "antiscientific" or apparently illogical.
7. Enthusiasm for juxtapositions of poetic images without clearly logical relationships or grammatical connectives; the desire is to achieve "an ontological density," but the apparent result is "logical obscurity."
8. View of the world as "more mysterious than intelligible," perhaps "more evil than good," evident in thematic oppositions to the workaday world of "business, science, and positivism."
9. Frequent skepticism of feeling and tone in poetry, related perhaps to literary decadence, with an emphasis on indirection and subtlety; generally, the context remains indeterminate, leaving modernist poets open to charges of obscurantism.
10. A nostalgia not inconsistent with a love of and respect for traditional poetry of high quality, but accompanied by a conscious quest for a "real ontological efficacy," a new poetry achieved with new critical insights and applications.[13]

Much remains to be said about the approaches of other New Critics—T. E. Hulme, Ezra Pound, and R. P. Blackmur to mention a few—but space remains for only the briefest remarks about selected aspects. Ezra Pound was in the avant-garde and probably had the greatest influence. Eliot's

[13] *Ibid.*, pp. 279–336. See especially pp. 291, 295, 316, 331.

"The Waste Land" (1922) is dedicated "For Ezra Pound," and just as Pound blue-penciled the young Hemingway's works and helped him to learn a clean forcefulness of language he also revised and edited Eliot's masterpiece, cutting out large sections and tightening the structure. This ultimately led to the stylistic mastery which brought both Eliot and Hemingway the Nobel Prize. Such poets as Amy Lowell, "H. D." (Hilda Doolittle), Carl Sandburg, William Carlos Williams, and other imagists shared the opinions expressed by Pound in an important essay entitled "Vorticism,"[14] in which he listed three of the tenets of imagist poetry:

1. Direct treatment of the "thing," whether subjective or objective.
2. To use absolutely no word that does not contribute to the presentation.
3. As regarding rhythm: to compose in sequence of the musical phrase, not in sequence of the metronome.[15]

In this essay Pound implemented his definitions of vorticism and imagism in relating how he came to write, and revise into its final form, his famous "hokku-like" poem "In a Station of the Metro." He emphasized in the process the importance of the functional (absolute necessity for the whole) rather than the merely utilitarian (merely decorative or incidentally useful) nature of the image, the importance of the past (or a knowledge of the classics), and the absolute need for intensity (not mere formulization, for though mathematics may state facts, "It Makes No Picture," and "it does not grip hold of Heaven"). In short, the vorticist evades mere "shells of thought," for his is a deeper need. To the vorticist, "every concept, every emotion, presents itself to the vivid consciousness in some primary form," what one may term the

deepest essence of thought and feeling. The imagist "does not use images as ornaments," Pound writes. "The image is itself the speech." Thus, Pound seems to conceive of vorticism as the dynamic core of imagism itself.

Of the remaining approaches of the New Critics (and there are many more), some involve important current concepts while others are basically descriptive and general. Some involve analyzing and synthesizing older concepts. For example, Allen Tate investigated the moral dimensions of poetry in his major critical works *The Man of Letters in the Modern World* (1955) and *Collected Essays* (1959). In his essay "Our Cousin, Mr. Poe,"[16] he explores the kinship Americans feel for Poe as man and artist, in spite of his "moral indifference." Many of Poe's famous critical formulations are contained in "The Poetic Principle" (1850) and "The Philosophy of Composition" (1846). In these works he demonstrated the necessity for conscious artistry in the creative process—the importance of setting a tone appropriate to the effect to be wrought, making available an *"excess of suggested meaning."* He pointed out the "richness" of the aesthetic symbolism of Poe's poetry, noting how the raven in "The Raven" becomes "emblematical of *Mournful and Neverending Remembrance"* (Poe's own words). The essays also contain his criticism of the transcendentalists, and they stress the importance of technical aspects such as unity, intensity, and brevity of structure so as to create the desired effect.

All of this had, to some extent, attracted the New Critics, although not as much as they had entranced the French Symbolists of the nineteenth century such as Baudelaire, Mallarmé, and Verlaine. Baudelaire translated Poe's works into French, and all of these Symbolist poets were so deeply influenced by him that they attempted consciously to apply his techniques (particularly the use of suggestion rather than literal statement

---

[14] Ezra Pound, "Vorticism," *Fortnightly Review*, XCVI (September 1, 1914), 461–471; reprinted in Sutton and Foster (eds.), *Modern Criticism* (New York: Odyssey Press, 1963), pp. 132–138, from which page references are taken.
[15] *Ibid.*, p. 133.

[16] Allen Tate, "Our Cousin, Mr. Poe," *Partisan Review*, XVI (December, 1949), 1207–1219; reprinted in Sutton and Foster (eds.), *Modern Criticism, op. cit.*, pp. 383–390, from which page references are taken.

and the blurred distinctions between abstract and concrete expressions).

As Poe had rejected didacticism (obvious moral instruction) as a goal of poetry, so did the New Critics, finding in Poe an ally against the new humanists such as Irving Babbitt and Paul Elmer More, who had rested their case against Poe upon his "limited moral range." Yet as Tate points out, Poe's efficacy, though somehow deeply rooted in our culture, was tragically disaffiliated from the kind of "sensibility" which "keeps us in the world." Poe's "sensation locks us into the self, feeding upon the disintegration of its objects and absorbing them into the void of the ego."[17]

To summarize, then, Poe is generally admired by the New Critics for his critical style, his "lucid and dispassionate" exposition, his "clear and rigorous logic," and his all-too-rare "restraint." He is also frequently condemned by them for his "Gothic glooms," "glutinous prose," and "flummery" and for his thematic absorption with death rather than life, his metronomic rhythms often unrelated to meaning, and his general tendency to be "all appetite without sensibility." Despite his many failures, though, Poe managed to combine "the primitive with the decadent: primitive, because he had neither history nor the historical sense; decadent, because he was the conscious artist of an intensity which lacked moral perspective."[18] Thus, he had broken, frantically perhaps, with the traditional critical temper of his age. In spite of the jagged deep valleys and the uneven heights he traced, and because of his general direction toward New Critical approaches, Poe is looked upon as a poet-critic who remains both an attraction and an anathema for many twentieth-century critics.

T. S. Eliot's criticism appears to be that of a poet writing about his poetry—consciously reflecting upon what it is, what he thought it was, what it could be. Even though his approaches to poetry seem often to be attitudes of the moment, even though his work is highly individualistic—and certainly his criticism is more austerely religious in tone than that of Babbitt and Arnold before him —he is considered a New Critic for numerous reasons. First, he is part of that clustering of twentieth-century thinkers who broke radically from the humanistic, historical traditions directly before them, even though he had mastered historical approaches early in his career, as evinced in his first collection of essays, *The Sacred Wood*. In the "Preface" to the 1928 edition, he stated:

> It will not do to talk of "emotion recollected in tranquility," which is only one poet's account of his recollection of his own methods; or to call it a "criticism of life," than which no phrase can sound more frigid to anyone who has felt the full surprise and elevation of a new experience of poetry. And certainly poetry is not the inculcation of morals, or the direction of politics; and no more is it religion or an equivalent of religion, except by some monstrous abuse of words. And certainly poetry is something over and above, and something quite different from, a collection of psychological data about the minds of poets, or about the history of an epoch; for we could not take it even as that unless we had already assigned to it a value merely as poetry. . . . We can only say that a poem, in some sense, has its own life; that its parts form something quite different from a body of neatly ordered biographical data; that the feeling, or emotion, or vision, resulting from the poem is something different from the feeling or emotion or vision in the mind of the poet.[19]

The perceptive student will note that in this statement Eliot summarizes historically, cutting across various approaches to poetry, condemning those of Wordsworth, Arnold, the early realists and sociocultural critics, and the new humanists (especially Babbitt and More). He does this even as he condemns the historical methods of such critics as Taine and Edmund Wilson, who believed in relating the work of a poet to his life or the epoch in which he lived, including pertinent biographical and historical data.

Indeed, Eliot's mastery of historicism was so complete that he performed new syntheses of

[17] *Ibid.*, p. 386.
[18] *Ibid.*, p. 389.

[19] T. S. Eliot, *The Sacred Wood* (New York: Barnes & Noble, 1928), pp. ix–x.

ideas in relation to literature. For example, in his essay "The Metaphysical Poets" (1921) he observed distinctions between "intellectual" poets and "reflective" poets. Tennyson and Browning are typical of the former, for "they do not feel their thought as immediately as the odour of a rose," whereas "a thought to Donne was an experience" which "modified his sensibility." Eliot further states, "When a poet's mind is perfectly equipped for its work, it is constantly amalgamating disparate experience." Ordinary men experience life piecemeal and fail to associate falling in love, reading philosophy, typewriting, and cooking. All of these experiences are dissimilar, to be sure; but the minds of the best poets are perpetually "forming new wholes" out of such materials. Eliot believed that the poets of the sixteenth century "possessed a mechanism of sensibility which could devour any kind of experience." However, by the seventeenth century, "a *dissociation of sensibility* set in, from which we have never recovered; and this dissociation, as is natural, was aggravated by the influence of the two most powerful poets of the century, Milton and Dryden" [italics added]. Their great artistry tended to conceal the lack of the kind of "sensibility" possessed by such poets as John Donne. The Romantic poets such as Shelley and Keats are deficient in another respect. They failed to transcend their "sentimental age," which was in such abandoned rebellion against rationalistic neoclassicism that self-expression became a sort of blur. Even the best of the Romantics exhausted themselves; "they thought and felt by fits, unbalanced," and both Shelley and Keats died before they could bring about a "unification of sensibility" in any complete sense.[20]

Despite Eliot's general antipathy for Romantic poets and their poetry (Coleridge is an exception), his statement in "Tradition and Individual Talent," written early in his career, echoes Keats' concept of "negative capability":

What happens is a continual surrender of himself [the poet] as he is at the moment to something which is more valuable. The progress of an artist is a continual self-sacrifice, a continual extinction of the personality. . . . Poetry is not a turning loose of emotion, but an escape from emotion; it is not the expression of personality, but an escape from personality.[21]

Yet a major distinction between Eliot's and Keats' ideas on the essential impersonality of poetry is Eliot's insistence that the poet have the ability to assimilate the past. To use Eliot's own words, "What is to be insisted upon is that the poet must develop or procure the consciousness of the past and that he should continue to develop this consciousness throughout his career." With such an awareness, the poet not only has more to say, but also becomes "a more finely perfected medium in which special, or very varied, feelings are at liberty to enter into new combinations."

Through various "floating feelings," Eliot believed, such a poet may develop a "new art emotion," related both to the literature and culture of the past and to his individual talent. The poet does not seek "new human emotions to express," for such a quest would bring him to the sensational and perverse. Rather, his proper business is to use "ordinary" emotions, and in transmitting them to poetry, "to express feelings which are not in actual emotions at all." For Eliot, then, the emotions of the past, or those which one may never have experienced at all, are sources as effective as those familiar to him. Eliot emphasized the *objective theory of art*, treating the poem as an object in itself. He felt that "*significant* emotion . . . has its life in the poem and not in the history of the poet." But a poet is a compendium of the living past, too—a product of all that has been, as well as a conscious artist of the present. The poet is a master of tradition as well as one embodying an individual talent. To summarize, Eliot believed that the poet "is not likely to know what is to be done unless he lives in what is not merely the present, but the present moment of the past, unless

[20] T. S. Eliot, "The Metaphysical Poets," *Selected Essays of T. S. Eliot* (New York: Harcourt, Brace & World, 1960), pp. 247–248. Originally published in 1932.

[21] Eliot, "Tradition and Individual Talent," *The Sacred Wood, op. cit.*, pp. 52–53, 58.

he is conscious, not of what is dead, but of what is already living."[22]

Inherent in Eliot's concepts of impersonality and "*significant* emotion" is the meaning of the figurative expression "objective correlative," which was to him the "only way of expressing emotion in the form of art." It is:

a set of objects, a situation, a chain of events which shall be the formula of that *particular* emotion, such that when the external facts, which must terminate in sensory experience, are given, the emotion is immediately evoked.

In escaping emotion, the poet finds the formula for dealing with it—a kind of impersonal symbol in which the emotion inheres, especially for the poet, but clearly, in a more universal sense, for readers too.

Perhaps the most important common characteristic of Eliot's approaches to poetry and those of other New Critics, especially those treated earlier in this chapter, is a basically intrinsic consideration of the work of art—what might be termed "aesthetic distance," or, again, the "objective theory of art." For example, one finds a strong correlation between the thesis of Cleanth Brooks and Robert Penn Warren's introduction to their college text, *Understanding Poetry* (1938) and that of Eliot's Preface to the 1928 edition of *The Sacred Wood*. Eliot made a "repeated assertion that when we are considering poetry we must consider it primarily as poetry and not another thing."[23] Brooks and Warren echoed Eliot in their statement "that if poetry is worth teaching at all it is worth teaching as poetry." In amplification of the idea, they emphasized the importance of grasping poetry as a "literary construct." They felt that this was a first step in understanding it. Implied in this concept is that the nature of poetry is "autotelic"—"self-bearing" and "self-existing." It is certainly not meant to be reduced to dominant extrinsic purposes, such as didacticism, whether the instruction be moral, political,

religious, or whatever. The critical approach should be "concrete and inductive," the kind implied by the French term *explication de texte* and typical of most *contextualist* criticism. Finally, the poem should be approached "as an organic system of relationships," not isolated in bits and pieces.[24]

Eliot stated, "Honest criticism and sensitive appreciation is directed not upon the poet, but upon the poetry," pointing out that if the poem is an organic whole all else is irrelevant. W. K. Wimsatt and Monroe Beardsley defined and described the "intentional fallacy" in an essay of that name[25] as the mistake of evaluating a poem in the light of what the poet himself may say about his "intention." This is a mistake because, if a poem is an objective unit out of which all meaning radiates, then the poet's ideas about the poem, imposed from the outside, may not be relevant. One should scrutinize such external judgments with care, and they should by no means be considered automatically valid, for "Critical inquiries are not settled by consulting the oracle" (the poet himself). Wimsatt and Beardsley also warned against the "affective fallacy." This refers to the confusion between the *being* of the poem and the *result* of the poem—what the poem *is* and the *effect the poem produces* in one's thought processes, particularly one's emotional responses.

Later in his career, particularly in the volume *After Strange Gods* (1934), Eliot identified more fully with those American critics known as "Agrarians" or "Fugitives," most of whom were, at one time or another, associated with Vanderbilt University. The group consisted of such men as Brooks, Davidson, Ransom, Tate, and Warren. It was characterized by an interest in an established

[22] *Ibid.*, pp. 52–54, 57–59.
[23] *Ibid.*, p. viii.

[24] Cleanth Brooks and Robert Penn Warren, "Letter to the Teacher (1938)," *Understanding Poetry* (New York: Henry Holt & Co., 1953), pp. xi–xv. Originally published in 1938.
[25] W. K. Wimsatt and Monroe Beardsley, "The Intentional Fallacy," *The Verbal Icon* (Lexington: University of Kentucky Press, 1954), pp. 3–18. For a treatment of "The Affective Fallacy," see pp. 21–39.

culture (the ante-bellum South), a quest for stability, and generally conservative and orthodox religious views. All of this, along with an intrinsic and formalist approach to poetry, attracted Eliot's interest. After all, Eliot had earlier declared himself "a classicist in literature, an Anglo-Catholic in religion, and a royalist in politics." But even at this time, Eliot refused to be pinned down. In his *Frontiers of Criticism* (1956), he even went so far as to deny his own profound influence: "I fail to see any critical movement which can be said to derive from myself,"[26] he wrote. In retrospect, he seems to have been a kind of peripatetic poet-

[26] "A Lecture by T. S. Eliot Delivered at the University of Minnesota Williams Arena, April 30, 1956" (Minneapolis: University of Minnesota Press, 1956), p. 6.

critic; a keenly perceptive commentator upon the literature of the past; a critic who could focus on the best in our best poets while remaining an insightful observer of their shortcomings; an exploratory maker of critical phrases (more often, a remaker of them, giving them new meanings); a champion of formalist poetry (the intrinsic study of it); a man deeply concerned with baffling aspects of culture and religion; an intuitive and original synthesizer of the best of the past; and a bardic chronicler of that past in its *living* sense. He possessed at once the ability to perceive it, to relate it to the living moments of the present, to articulate it in critical approaches for his contemporaries and posterity, and to transmute his finest discoveries into enduring poetry.

8. Psychological, Archetypal, and Mythopoeic Approaches

We wonder how genius creates. Even when we understand the basics of poetry—such matters as meter, rhyme, and figurative language—and how they are used in the poet's craft, there remains the riddle of how a poem becomes a poem— how it germinates in the poet's core, develops, and emerges as immortal art. It is a mystery into which we can only glimpse insights, for the bright illumination eludes us. Down through time and into our own age poets and other artists have

occasionally expressed themselves on clues to the mystery.

D. H. Lawrence spoke of the strange inner formulation of art. He emphasized the poet's "awareness of forms and figures," which he equated with memory, while cryptically taking exception to his own statement by noting, "but it is more than memory." The emotional dimension of poetry—the effect the creation of poetry has upon the emotions of the poet himself—was of prime significance to William Butler Yeats, for, as he stated in his essay "The Thinking of the Body" (1924), art "could not move us at all, if our thought did not rush out to the edges of our flesh." Furthermore, there is no way of reducing the creative process to a mathematical formula: "art shrinks from . . . every abstract thing, from all that is of the brain only, from all that is not a fountain jetting from the entire hopes, memories, and sensations of the body."[1]

Henry James looked upon literary art as an effort toward making clarity out of chaos. Rudyard Kipling emphasized the problem of identity—of attempting to "think in another man's skin"—and the problem of the artist's "personal daemon." He suggested motivations to which the poet's consciousness must subordinate itself: "When your Daemon is in charge, do not try to think consciously. Drift, wait, and obey. . . ."

Some modern writers have moved closer to psychological acknowledgments in commenting upon artistic creation. Gertrude Stein, for example, stated that "creation must take place between the pen and the paper, not before in a statement or afterwards in a recasting." But she meticulously qualified the statement thus: "Yes, before in a thought, but not in careful thinking. It will come if it is there and if you will let it come, and if you have anything you will get a sudden *creative recognition*. You won't *know* how it was . . ." [italics added]. Her theory of the importance of creative recognition, expressed in sexual, procreative terms, was suggestive of Freudian theories:

> You cannot go into the womb to form the child; it is there and makes itself and comes forth whole— and there it is and you have made it and have felt it, but it has come itself—and that is creative recognition. Of course you have a little more control over your writing than that; you have to know what you want to get; but when you know that, let it take you and

if it seems to take you off the track don't hold back, because that is perhaps where *instinctively* you want to be and if you hold back and try to be always where you have been before, you will go dry.[2]

Amy Lowell, in her *Poetry and Poets* mentioned some contemporaneous views of the poetic process: "the fusion of contradictory ideas" (Robert Graves); the "result and relief of emotional irritation and tension" (Sara Teasdale); and a "yielding to a psychical state verging on daydream" (Professor Prescott). At the same time, she indicated her own view that she knew very little ("only a millionth part"). She met poems "where they touch consciousness, and that is already a considerable distance along the road of evolution." She stated: "the truth is that there is a little mystery here, and no one is more conscious of it than the poet himself."[3]

The creative power of the unconscious mind is evinced in the famous passage in Coleridge's "Prefatory Note to 'Kubla Khan,'" written in the fall of 1797, in which he contended he had been reading "Purchas's Pilgrimage," in which Kubla Khan was mentioned, along with other details that were to appear in the poem—when, after taking an anodyne, he fell asleep for three hours:

> at least [a sleep] of the external senses, during which time [I] had the most vivid confidence, that [I] could not have composed less than from two to three hundred lines; if that indeed can be called composition in which all the images rose up before [me] as things, with a parallel production of the correspondent expressions, without any sensation or consciousness of effort. On awaking [I] appeared to [myself] to have a distinct recollection of the whole, and taking [my] pen, ink, and paper, instantly and eagerly wrote down the lines that are here preserved."

The rest is well known, too—how Coleridge was interrupted by a person on business, and how when the poet returned to his work, he could recall only a few scattered lines, for "all the rest had

[1] W. B. Yeats, "The Thinking of the Body," *Essays*, rev. ed. (New York: Macmillan, 1924); reprinted in Brewster Ghiselin, *The Creative Process* (New York: New American Library, 1955), pp. 106–107.

[2] John Hyde Preston, "A Conversation," *The Atlantic*, 56 (August 1935), 188.
[3] Amy Lowell, *Poetry and Poets* (Boston: Houghton Mifflin, 1930), p. 24.

passed away like the images on the surface of a stream into which a stone has been cast."

Modern poets have noted other relationships between the creative process and unconscious factors—even those arising out of individual pressures, difficulties, and illnesses, such as anxieties, fears, and even neuroses. T. S. Eliot, in his *The Use of Poetry*, stated that much of the creative process is not conscious. Indeed,

> writing gives the impression of having undergone a long incubation, though we do not know until the shell breaks what kind of egg we have been sitting on. To me it seems that at these moments, which are characterised by the sudden lifting of the burden of anxiety and fear which presses upon our daily life so steadily that we are unaware of it, what happens is something *negative*: that is to say, not "inspiration" as we commonly think of it, but the breaking down of strong habitual barriers—which tend to re-form very quickly.[4]

A. E. Housman, in *The Name and Nature of Poetry*, stated that he had seldom "composed from the wish rather than the impulse," and that when he had, he had not been successful. He stated that the production of poetry, at least initially, "*is less an active than a passive process*" [italics added]:

> if I were obliged, not to define poetry, but to name the class of things to which it belongs, I should call it a secretion: whether a natural secretion, like turpentine in the fir, or a morbid secretion, like the pearl in the oyster. I think that . . . I may not deal with the material so cleverly as the oyster does . . . because I have seldom written poetry unless I was rather out of health, and the experience, though pleasurable, was generally agitating and exhausting.[5]

[4] T. S. Eliot, *The Use of Poetry* (London: Faber & Faber, 1933), p. 144. As an interesting sidelight, it has recently been noted that Eliot, having overworked as bank clerk, book reviewer, and editor of *Criterion*, suffered a breakdown and was required medically to take a rest cure at Margate and in a Swiss sanatorium in late 1921. It was during this period of enforced rest that he wrote *The Waste Land*. For further details see Donald Gallup, "T. S. Eliot & Ezra Pound: Collaborators in Letters," *The Atlantic*, 225 (January 1970), 54.

[5] A. E. Housman, *The Name and Nature of Poetry* (New

Since the creative process remains a mystery, we who are curious can only endeavor to understand more, to describe the mental processes by which art becomes itself. The study can move from complex individual men to the recipient universal man. Recent developments in literary criticism and associated fields of inquiry—especially in psychological, archetypal, and mythopoeic approaches to poetry—may aid us in this endeavor.

Psychology is often thought of as a natural science dealing with the human mind and its functions, the emotions or feelings, and desires. It is sometimes called a "biosocial" science, and it utilizes experimental, clinical, and statistical techniques, although it remains far from an exact and classified body of knowledge. Many psychological fields exist today, among them general psychology, differential psychology, abnormal psychology, animal psychology, child psychology, and social psychology. However, we are concerned with the "psychology of literature"—a subject so broad and deep that only something of its early adumbrations, origins in Freudian psychoanalysis, archetypal and mythopoeic associations, and ever-widening paths of study can be indicated in these pages.

From Chapter 2 of this book, "Basic Elements: Classical and Renaissance Approaches," the student may recall Plato's concept of ultimate realities or absolutes, which were distorted in man's perception into mere shadows cast upon the wall of a cave. Plato felt that poets compose not out of art, but rather out of "inspiration"—a "*divine afflatus*" in the original sense of the expression. They are "possessed . . . not in their right mind . . . out of [their] senses," and they are impelled or driven by the "Muse" to create their works. Aristotle's emphasis was different from Plato's, for Aristotle approached art in a way similar to the way in which the formalists do today. He approached the poem rather than the poet, systematically exploring, in his *Poetics*, the conscious elements of

York: Macmillan, 1933); reprinted in A. E. Housman, *Selected Prose*, ed. John Carter (Cambridge, Eng.: Cambridge University Press, 1962), p. 194.

making poetry. Yet even such a champion of cognitive artistry as Aristotle noted certain mysteries in what may be termed the "artisanship of poetry." At best he described them memorably, although he left much unexplained. He felt that poetry involves not only mimesis (an imitation of nature), but also a *becoming* (a perception of ultimate, though active and ever-changing, realities gotten through the process of mirroring nature). He felt that poetry is inherent in man from childhood, accompanied by a sense of pleasure and harmonia (a sense of order as in rhythm in dancing). Tragedy is also inherent, accompanied by the need for catharsis (a purgation of the emotions of pity and fear and their corrosive forces, suggesting the lifting of tensional burdens). Also natural to man is a capacity for (sympathetic identification with) the tragic human condition of the persona or hero-character, which is often followed by a leading-out of the soul—the shaping and patterning force (psychagogia).

To give the impression that Plato and Aristotle displayed a curiosity about the creative process not shared by other poets or philosophers until Coleridge and the moderns would be unfair. Numerous artists, from Longinus to the neo-classicists, made reference to the complex aspects of how poetry is made. For example, John Dryden, in his "Dedication of the Rival-Ladies" (1664), observed something of the dim origins of art, emphasizing the formulative period prior to its actual, or physical, writing. As dedicator, he noted that the work was "designed" within him

> long before it was a play; *when it was only a confused mass of thoughts, tumbling over one another in the dark; when the fancy was yet in its first work, moving the sleeping images of things towards the light,* there to be distinguished, and then either chosen or rejected by [my conscious] judgment [italics added].

Dryden's statement of how this particular work emerged is typical of many more, all of which bear a direct relationship to modern psychological, archetypal, and mythopoeic approaches to poetry.

Not until the late nineteenth century, however, with the emergence of the psychoanalytical movement, did such approaches really begin to produce meaningful insights into the creative process—how it works; the poet's state of mind at creative moments; the relationships between the poet's life and his work (the work reflecting the life, and the life the work); the often subtle but sometimes obvious connections between art and neuroses (mental disorders resulting in partial disorganization of the personality, less serious than psychoses) —and into striking patterns of recurring myths, as well as the emergence of *archetypes* (original patterns or models) in literary art. Although numerous writers have been interested in the mental processes of poets and other artists, the major credit for the discovery, development, and application of specific new tools of psychology is justifiably given to Sigmund Freud (1856–1939) and to Carl Gustav Jung (1875–1961). Subsequent developments in psychology, of course, have resulted in new approaches, enlarging our understanding of the artist and the nature of his work. Literary specialists have employed psychological tools with which to illuminate the complex of man-artist-work, as William Phillips in his collection of essays *Art and Psychoanalysis* (1957), to which such scholars and artists as Thomas Mann, Kenneth Burke, Leslie Fiedler, and Lionel Trilling contributed. Let us consider some of Freud's basic psychoanalytical approaches to literary processes.

In his essay "One of the Difficulties of Psycho-Analysis" (1917), Freud distinguished between "self-preservative or ego-instincts" and "sexual instincts" (the "libido"). He proceeded to develop his theory that some neuroses emerge from "a conflict between ego-instincts and sexual instincts." The self-controlling ego (the *conscious* mind) forces the sexual instincts into "by-paths of sub-stitutive gratification which become manifest as symptoms of a neurosis." Psychoanalysis is the method by which the repressed desires are brought into the open and consciously examined in talks with the analyst. It is hoped that a solution to the neurosis will be found. Strangely enough, it is found merely through the conscious recognition of the problem by the sufferer himself. Both the conscious and unconscious minds, having been made aware of the conflict, form a kind of alliance that is usually strong enough to overwhelm any neurosis which tends to break down the personality, if we can assume that the problem is not organic (physical) in origin.

However, if the individual's libidinal problem remains suppressed within his ego, he remains neurotic, and his condition is known as "narcissism"—a word taken from the name of the youth in the Greek myth who fell in love with his own reflection. Most children are excessively narcissistic. Normally, they learn to grow "outside themselves," we say. Simply, in Freudian terms, they move from "narcissism to object-love" as they mature, although "a certain amount of libido is always retained in the ego. . . . Object-libido was at first ego-libido and can be again transformed into ego-libido." Thus, Freud believed that good health necessitated a "full mobility" of the libido between the ego and externalized objects (people, concepts). This is the essence of Freud's libido-theory of neuroses, by which he explained morbid self-absorptions of man and offered his possible cure, which involved keeping the ego open to external objects.

Recognizing that primitive, childlike man was for a long time comfortable with his "self-love," Freud then linked the theory to what he termed "three severe wounds of man's self-love":

1. The great discovery of Copernicus (earlier, Aristarchus of Samos) that the earth was not the center of the universe but merely a small celestial body that moved around the sun. At this time, "the self-love of humanity suffered its first blow, the *cosmological* one."
2. The publication in 1859 of *Origin of Species*, by Charles Darwin, which struck at man's "arrogance" in separating himself from the animal kingdom and attributing to himself "an immortal soul," claiming "a divine descent." At this point in time, the second

blow was dealt: the "*biological* blow to human narcissism."

3. New insights gained from psychoanalysis. Man develops "somewhere in the core of his ego" an "organ of observation to keep a watch on his impulses and actions." "Eerie disorders" develop when a part of one's mind is withdrawn from conscious knowledge. The impulses are repressed through unconscious mental processes. Psychoanalysis wishes to educate the ego with two discoveries: "that the life of the sexual instincts cannot be totally restrained, and that mental processes are in themselves unconscious and only reach the ego and come under its control through incomplete and untrustworthy perceptions . . ." These two discoveries "amount to a statement that *the ego is not master in its own house.* Together they represent the third wound inflicted on man's self-love . . . the *psychological* one."

Following this statement of the final wound, Freud observed what all of us at times must have thought, "No wonder, therefore, that the ego shows no favour to psycho-analysis and persistently refuses to believe in it."[6]

The deep "psychological wound" dealt to man by Freud has been related in various ways to creative artists and their works, but one should be keenly aware of the fact that Freud himself used literary sources with which to amplify, if not always explain, his own psychological views. Notably, he used the Sophoclean tragedy *Oedipus Rex* in formulating his so-called "Oedipus Complex," demonstrating the universality of the legend in the dreams of people today, as in those of the ancient Greeks. Upon many occasions Freud was fascinated by the imaginative processes of the artist and sought no easy explanations for their complexity. A summary of and commentary upon

[6] Sigmund Freud, "One of the Difficulties of Psycho-Analysis," trans. Joan Riviere, in *On Creativity and the Unconscious*, selected and with introduction and annotations by Benjamin Nelson (New York: Harper & Brothers, 1958), pp. 1–10. First published (in Hungarian) in the *Nyugat*, 1917.

Freud's "The Relation of the Poet to Day-Dreaming" may serve to give us a more substantive grasp of how psychological approaches may be used to illuminate and describe in new ways the elusive mysteries of the creative process.

A genuine curiosity exists, Freud began, concerning just how the poet is "able to carry us with him in such a way and to arouse emotions in us of which we thought ourselves perhaps not even capable." The enigma remains—even poets themselves cannot explain clearly the creative process. Although answers to such questions may never make us writers, we would like to "find some activity in ourselves . . . akin to the writing of imaginative works." After all, poets do "assure us that every man is at heart a poet, and that the last poet will not die until the last human being does." Here Freud expressed a tone clearly of praise, if not of envy, of the poet—an expressed hope that "the distance between" poets and "ordinary human beings" might be lessened. Those who continue to think that Freud's view of the artist was that he is merely a talented neurotic would do well to note praise.

Freud proceeded to relate children's play—that pretend world in which the child selects what he wishes from reality and arranges things in new ways that please him more—to the imaginative writer. Children's play, in turn, is related to "day-dreaming," and Freud observes that language preserves the "relationship between children's play and poetic creation." But in the products of creative imagination there are added ironies and complexities:

> The unreality of this poetical world of imagination . . . has very important consequences for literary technique; for many things which if they happened in real life could produce no pleasure can nevertheless give enjoyment in a play—many emotions which are essentially painful may become a source of enjoyment to the spectators and hearers of a poet's work.[7]

[7] Sigmund Freud, "The Relation of the Poet to Day-Dreaming," trans. I. F. Grant Duff, in *On Creativity and the Unconscious, ibid.*, p. 45. First published in *Neue Revue,* I, 1908.

As people grow up, they exchange the "play-world" for the creation of fantasies. Freud states, "I believe that the greater number of human beings create fantasies at times as long as they live." The child often reveals his fantasies, but the adult—like Walter Mitty of James Thurber's creation—supresses his, for he is ashamed of them. Moreover, he often cherishes them as if they were a kind of private craft, he the sole creator and spectator, and in a rapture of narcissism he holds them in secret. However, neurotics often suffer the necessity of "giving an account of what they suffer and what they enjoy." Perhaps they feel that it is the only way in which they can retain their mental health. Everybody else has daydreams, too.

The major source of fantasies is a search for wish fulfillment—the desire to improve upon a reality which often is unsatisfactory. Frequently, these wishes concern the ambitions of the dreamer (usually men). The wishes may also be erotic (usually women, "for their ambition is generally comprised in their erotic longings"). These two classes are often united, however. For example, heroes from Lancelot at Camelot to Rostand's Cyrano de Bergerac, and from Balzac's Père Goriot to F. Scott Fitzgerald's "Great Gatsby," performed their ambitious deeds for a woman, "at whose feet all . . . triumphs are . . . laid."

Fantasies have three dimensions of time—"memory of an early experience," "some event in the present," and "a situation which is to emerge in the future, representing the fulfilment of the wish"—but the fantasy simultaneously "hovers between" these three dimensions of time. To illustrate, one may conceive of a kind of Horatio Alger story: a hard-working orphan boy who sells newspapers on a busy corner, daydreaming of the family life in which he once felt warm and secure, imagines himself rescuing the daughter of his employer, an editor, from an accident. For his daring and heroic part in sweeping her out of the pathway of a team of berserk horses, the orphan boy is rewarded with money and a better newspaper job. Soon, the daughter falls in love with him, her father dies, and he inherits the family business with the proviso that he marry the daughter. The two are in love anyway; they marry and have a family of their own, out of which is created a warm, secure life. "So," as Freud summarized, "past, present and future are threaded, as it were, on the string of the wish that runs through them all."

Freud noted that fantasies may become "overpowerful" and compulsive. If so, they may constitute the basis for an outbreak of neurosis or psychosis, and they also may be symptomatic first steps for various pathologies. More important, and pertinent to the analysis of literature, fantasies and dreams are closely interrelated. Shame and repression are even more obvious in dreams of nocturnal origin, but both are based on wish fulfillments.

Freud narrowed his presentation of poets to those who "seem to create their material spontaneously," rather than including those whose works are based on epics and tragedies (readymade legends and myths). Here Freud sheds his controversial light upon versifiers of sentimental poems and upon domestic-sentimental novelists and writers. What he has to say, of course, is logically applicable to many present-day counterparts in radio, cinematic, and television soap operas. The hero sets out as the "centre of interest," winning our sympathy by incredible means. He is at times charismatic—indeed, at times virtually haloed under some divine protection. "Nothing can happen to me!" he seems to declare, in action if not outrightly. He is "his Majesty the Ego, the hero of all day-dreams and all novels," Freud notes. Such heroes fulfill the reader's image of self-love. To illustrate, many women fall in love with the indomitable James Bond, who is magnificently virile, intellectually brilliant, heroically decisive, scintillating in his wit, and devilishly *good*. By comparison, other characters are perversely *bad*—his enemies—and they are "flat" characters, obsessed with evil intentions.

Of course, many imaginative works transcend

such simplistic relationships with the "original naïve day-dream," and Freud admitted as much. In psychological works, in which the persona-hero is described "from within," peculiarities and inconsistencies may perhaps be explained by the "tendency of modern writers to split up their ego by self-observation into many component-egos, and in this way to personify the conflicting trends in their own mental life in many heroes." In naturalistic works, such as Zola's novels and Stephen Crane's poems, "the ego contents itself with the role of spectator."

Freud then moved into one of his most meaningful theories concerning the creative process. He related his concept of the three periods of the day-dream (past, present, and future), as well as the nocturnal dream, to the artistic rendering of wish-fulfillment:

> Some actual experience which made a strong impression on the writer had stirred up a memory of an earlier experience, generally belonging to childhood, which then arouses a wish that finds a fulfilment in the work in question, and in which elements of the recent event and the old memory should be discernible.[8]

Admitting that his formula may have been "too schematic," Freud nevertheless treated it as a tentative approach for psychological analysis, contending that "the stress laid on the writer's memories of his childhood . . . is ultimately derived from the hypothesis that imaginative creation, like day-dreaming, is a continuation of and substitute for the play of childhood." As examples (and there are many more) Wordsworth's "Ode on Intimations of Immortality," Whitman's "Out of the Cradle Endlessly Rocking," Yeats' "The Lake Isle of Innisfree," or Frost's "Stopping by Woods on a Snowy Evening," all illustrate the past-present-future phenomenon, set within the matrix of wish fulfillment. Such creativity is not to be confused with works fashioned from "readymade material," which, Freud seemed to believe, are treated with a greater objectivity and cognition

[8] *Ibid.*, p. 52.

by the poet. Yet they, too, seem to reflect "wish-phantasies," though of a universal scope:

> As far as it goes, this material is derived from the racial treasure-house of myths, legends, and fairy-tales. The study of these creations of racial psychology is in no way complete, but it seems extremely probable that *myths*, for example are distorted vestiges of the wish-phantasies of whole nations—the age-long dreams of young humanity [italics added].

At this point in his essay, Freud noted that he had not yet treated the means by which poets produce "emotional reactions in us" with their works. He then reminds us of the shame or guilt one feels in one's daydreaming and nocturnal dreaming—so much shame and guilt that he hides them from others, for even if we heard such fantasies told, they would either "repel us," or "leave us cold." Yet when the literary artist presents us with his poem or play—what in the Freudian sense we may take to be the product of the poet's transmuted dreams—we react to it as art, sensing pleasure, as Horace observed in his *Ars Poetica*. Freud then articulated his hypotheses with psychological tools. He specifically hypothesized that the writer employs at least two methods in his *modus operandi*:

1. He "softens the egotistical character of the day-dream by changes and disguises, and he bribes us by the offer of a purely formal, that is, aesthetic, pleasure in the presentation of his phantasies," this "increment of pleasure" releasing in us a "yet greater pleasure," which Freud terms an "incitement premium" or "forepleasure."

2. Recognizing that the pleasure we experience in reading a poem "proceeds from the release of tensions in our minds," the poet manages to structure art within the context of an aesthetic distance, thereby creating a kind of illusion in which we lose ourselves while simultaneously identifying its details, and in which "we can enjoy our own day-dreams without reproach or shame."[9]

[9] *Ibid.*, p. 54.

It remained for Freud's colleague Carl Gustav Jung to carry further the theories of myths. Freud had referred to myths as the "distorted vestiges of the wish-phantasies of whole nations," although he admitted that the study of them was not complete. Perhaps it would be well to point out that these two great explorers of the unconscious parted company on various ideas. For example, unlike Freud, Jung insisted that the unconscious was not entirely without morality. Jung thought that it indeed contained evidences of a religious dimension, and that although it could be "personal" (individual), it was also "super-personal" or "collective," for some fantasies and dreams have "no foundation of personal memory," and appear to be "transcendent." The "collective unconscious," then, evinces itself through "certain legends and themes" that "repeat themselves the whole world over in identical *forms*" [italics added], and are "manifestations of the deeper layers of the unconscious where sleep the primordial images common to humanity." Jung stated, "To these images I also apply the term *archetypes* (*Urbilder*)" [first italics added]. Jung further observed, "The archetype is . . . operative always and everywhere." Archetypes are described as "the psychic residua of numberless experiences of the same type," occasioned by ancestors rather than the individual, but the tendencies toward the patterns and forms of which the individual retains strong intuitive predispositions.[10]

Of archetypes, Gilbert Murray, in *The Classical Tradition in Poetry*, wrote lyrically and memorably, noting that the motifs of such stories as those Freud and Jung had in mind are "deeply implanted in the memory of the race," and though they may seem "strange," there is yet "that within us which leaps at the sight of them, a cry of the blood which tells us we have known them always." *Hamlet*, *Agamemnon*, and *Electra* are "well-wrought," and the poets are in "full command of the technical instruments"—in short, artistic

[10] Carl Gustav Jung, *Two Essays on Analytical Psychology*, trans. H. G. and C. F. Baynes (London: Baillière, Tindall & Cox, 1928), pp. 66–72, 81, 103–104, 115, 118–119, 139.

mastery is clearly evident. But to explain what is the essence of profundity and power in these works, Murray suspects

> a strange, unanalyzed vibration below the surface, an undercurrent of desires and fears and passions, long slumbering yet eternally familiar, which have for thousands of years lain near the root of our most intimate emotions and been wrought into the fabric of our most magical dreams. How far into past ages this stream may reach back, I dare not even surmise; but it seems as if the power of stirring it or moving with it were one of the last secrets of genius.[11]

More recently, Jolande Jacobi, in *Complex/Archetype/Symbol in the Psychology of C. G. Jung*, observed that Jung used the word "archetype" to refer both to images of which we are actually aware, and to those "still latent and nonperceptible." Jacobi also noted similarities between the archetype and the Platonic "Idea," but distinguishes Plato's immutable concept of the immutability of absolutes from the Jungian view of the archetype as a dynamic and living part of the unconscious, "endowed with generative force." Archetypes are not inherited as images in the usual sense, but rather they are "primordial images," similar in pattern and form, which act as "hidden organizers of representations . . . underlying the *invisible order* of the unconscious psyche."[12] Archetypal images, then, would appear to have a more subtle and amorphous origin within the unconscious than the words "image" or "figure" suggest. We may understand from this that not the image or the figure, but the patterning tendency, with which we are enabled to interpret archetypal images, figures, and forms, is what inheres within our collective unconscious.

Jung advocated not only human understanding of the transcendent creative force of the unconscious, including archetypes and the relationship

of them to what we often term "instincts," but a conscious quest for understanding them, in order, among other reasons, to gain a beneficial harmony with them:

> The unconscious can indeed give us all the furtherance and help that bountiful nature holds in store for man in overflowing abundance. The unconscious has possibilities that are quite shut off from the conscious; for the unconscious commands not only all the subliminal psychic contents, all that has been forgotten and overlooked, but also the wisdom and experience of uncounted centuries, a wisdom that is deposited and lying potential in the human brain.[13]

Archetypal approaches to poetry are subtle enough that they are usually avoided by those who prefer more definite, analyzable techniques. The archetypal critic holds that the geniune poet writes out of his unconscious while he applies conscious artistic skills. As T. S. Eliot observed, "organisation is necessary as well as 'inspiration.'" The poet consciously shapes the unconscious shadows which give energy and life to his cognition, and in writing out of the unconscious wellspring, the poet transmutes archetypal sources, let us say, into consciously communicated lyrical forms or into characters in a poetic drama. Although the techniques change in the poem, novel, story, and essay, the archetypal process is virtually the same for all. The most powerful renderings often take the form of poetry. Eliot also noted, "The pre-logical mentality persists in civilized man, but becomes available only to or through the poet."

It would be well to emphasize that responses of readers of poetry involve a kind of creativity, too, as Eliot may have indicated in his Introduction to *The Use of Poetry*:

> The poem's existence is somewhere between the writer and the reader; it has a reality which is not simply the reality the writer is trying to "express", or of his experience of writing it, or of the experience of the reader or of the writer as reader. Consequently the

[11] Gilbert Murray, *The Classical Tradition in Poetry*, 2nd ed. (Cambridge, Mass.: Harvard University Press, 1930), pp. 239–240. Originally published in 1927.

[12] Jolande Jacobi, *Complex/Archetype/Symbol in the Psychology of C. G. Jung*, trans. Ralph Manheim (London: Routledge & Kegan Paul, 1959), pp. 33–35, 49–52.

[13] Jung, *op. cit.*, p. 118.

problem of what a poem "means" is a good deal more difficult than it at first appears.[14]

The reader's creative role in the poetic experience can be fulfilled successfully only if the responses to the poem are effectively produced in his mind, emotions, and—above all—his imagination. If the archetypes are transmuted with artistic skill, the reader's responses should be in kind. The reader should know, sense, and live imaginatively with such patterns or motifs, and his *esse* (self or being) should be open to absorb them with the power with which they are charged.

Those who would limit sources for archetypal approaches to psychology alone take a narrow road to understanding the complexities of poetic art, as Maud Bodkin observed in her still basic *Archetypal Patterns in Poetry*. Added insights may be gained through anthropological study of primitive cultures. For example, in developing the term "cultural pattern," anthropologists worked out a cluster of ideas bearing marked relationships to the Jungian archetype—the preexisting "configuration." Such shaping forms or patterns may have significant power even when they are assimilated from the environment "upon slight contact only," if they are absorbed in such a manner as to strike "predisposing factors in mind and brain." If ideas of "intimate and emotional character" are to be assimilated, the predisposition must be there. In order to perceive the essence of archetypal experience, the reader must feel, as he gleans the work before him, the "stir within" him of "larger systems of feeling, of memory, of ideas, of aspirations."[15]

In using archetypes, the poet enriches the old legends or communal forms, and the traditional story or vague memory becomes an aesthetic entity—with deep cultural roots—that has been intensified and illuminated. The singular value of the representation, especially for the "archetypal-ist," is that what was a legend, tall tale, myth, or fantasy hovering on the peripheries of conscious awareness, is placed into the context of recoverable experience. Substance that was deeply rooted in the past, perhaps crudely told over and over and vaguely swept with undefined emotion, becomes more precise and effectual in its sensuous detail, more powerful in its emotional impact, and more artistic in its imaginative dimension. The language of poetry, and more broadly, art, can capture all of this more fully.

Whatever else archetypes may denote, they also involve universal symbols mysteriously concealed and treated in such a way that they inhere embryonically in the artistic process. The stranger the unconscious drive and the higher the cognitive artistry, the greater the artistic purity. As Leslie Fiedler noted in *An End to Innocence* (1955), only later may the mystery of the archetype be revealed, thus availing itself to analytical and allegorical interpretations, varying even then with the language of the age.

Mythopoeic, psychological, and archetypal approaches are interwoven to form a fabric in which all three threads are discernible but, nevertheless, part of the whole cloth. It should come as no surprise then, that mythopoeists developed the mass of their critical approaches to poetry after Freud's work on the unconscious and dreams and after Jung's introduction of the concept of the "collective" or "racial unconscious," out of which archetypal concepts were developed. Many archetypes, however, are embedded in myths. The word "myth" is derived from the Greek *mythos*, originally meaning "speech," or

[14] Eliot, *op. cit.*, p. 30.
[15] Maud Bodkin, *Archetypal Patterns in Poetry* (London: Oxford University Press, 1934); reprinted (Cleveland and New York: World, 1965), pp. 1–5. The seminal importance of this book, because of its synthesis of psychological, archetypal, and mythopoeic approaches to poetry, would seem to make a summary of its basic contents of much value to the student. The book makes the concept of archetypes concrete and demonstrates their close interrelationship with psychological and mythopoeic approaches. Included in the author's discussion of archetypal patterns are these: archetypal patterns in tragic

poetry; rebirth archetype, archetype of Paradise-Hades, Heaven and Hell; archetypal images of woman; archetypal images of the devil, hero, God; archetypal patterns in sacred and contemporary literature.

"story," and used by Aristotle in his *Poetics* to mean "plot" or "narrative structure." The word now connotes a cluster of meanings. Myths may be traditional stories rooted in the folklores of nations. They are often representative or explanatory of phenomena in nature and often nonliterary and irrational in formulation. They frequently embody religious rites, imaginary persons, representative (symbolical) concepts, and gods and heroes.

Sir James Frazer's *The Golden Bough* (1890)—anthropological at its base—has proved a virtually inexhaustible source of myths, rituals, symbols, and archetypes for twentieth-century poets. Critic John B. Vickery, in his "*The Golden Bough*: Impact and Archetype," pointed to poetic treatments of "rationality, fertility, irrationality, sterility, sex, superstition, and survival," and equated in importance Frazer's "dialectic of myth and reality," Marx's socioeconomic manifestoes, Darwin's biological explorations and evolutionary theories, and Freud's psychological discoveries.

Substantively like Jung, Philip Wheelwright, in *The Burning Fountain*, interpreted archetypes as "preconsciously rooted symbols ... from 'the dark backward and abysm of time'; equipping our thought and imagination with an ancestral dimension without which true reverence, and therefore the very substance of our conscious life, would go dry and dead." Wheelwright employed Gottfried Herder's term "mythologems"—a term which Jung himself had first appropriated from Herder—meaning great, recurrent themes of mythology, and he treated them archetypally as "persistent patterns of human thought and expression," which have emerged as "story-elements in the literature of many distinct races." Each myth "embodies an archetypal idea—a set of depth-meanings of perduring significance within a widely shared perspective, and transcending the limits" of the language of information. Myth is dynamic, not an imposed fiction; it is a method of seeing, a visionary approach ultimately shaped into myth, but "genuine

myth is a matter of perspective first, invention second."[16]

Northrop Frye, in *Fables of Identity: Studies in Poetic Mythology*, stated that music moves in the dimension of time, and painting moves in that of space. Just as music and art have such dimensions, as well as "rhythm" and "pattern," respectively, literature also possesses *a rhythm of narrative* and *a pattern of meaning*: "The myth is the central informing power that gives archetypal significance to the ritual and archetypal narrative to the oracle. Hence *the myth is the archetype*, though it might be convenient to say *myth only when referring to the narrative*, and *archetype when speaking of the significance* [motif or theme]" [italics added].[17] In his stimulating *Anatomy of Criticism*, Frye referred to myth as "a structural organizing principle of literary form." In order to perceive an artistic work, one may, of course, study it analytically, or inductively, as the formalists do, but the result will be piecemeal. In order to understand the essential archetypal and mythic organization, one must "stand back" and view the whole, the "organizing design."[18]

In summary, we venture to say that mythopoeic criticism offers one of the most far-reaching approaches to poetry employed today. As critical movements go, it seems to occupy an avant-garde

[16] Philip Wheelwright, *The Burning Fountain* (Bloomington: Indiana University Press, 1954), pp. 91–92, 159. *Mythologems* mentioned in this context by Wheelwright are "the Divine Father, the Earth Mother, the World Tree, the satyr or centaur or other man-animal monster, the descent into Hell, the Purgatorial stair, the washing away of sin, the castle of attainment, the culture-hero such as Prometheus bringing fire or other basic gift to mankind, the treacherous betrayal of the hero, the sacrificial death of the god, the god in disguise or the prince under enchantment." Also see Wheelwright's sixth chapter, "The Archetypal Symbol," in *Metaphor and Reality* (Bloomington: Indiana University Press, 1962), pp. 111–128.

[17] Northrop Frye, *Fables of Identity: Studies in Poetic Mythology* (New York: Harcourt, Brace & World, 1963), pp. 14–15.

[18] Northrop Frye, *Anatomy of Criticism* (Princeton, N.J.: Princeton University Press, 1957), p. 140.

position similar to that held by the New Criticism in the 1940s, in spite of the controversy which surrounds it. As the leading mythopoeist, Northrop Frye has thrown down the gauntlet to the whole phalanx of literary specialists, even to literary psychologists. To illustrate, while admitting that Freud's view of the Oedipus complex has helped us to understand literature in new ways (note, for example, Dr. Ernest Jones' *The Problem of Hamlet and the Oedipus-Complex*, 1947), Frye could not help but wonder if it was the Oedipus myth that was the generative force that shaped the psychological insights. The question has a kind of revolutionary merit, but perhaps it was intended to be an ironic expression of the need for a synthesis of various approaches to poetry, rather than divisive and contradictory challenges.

Erich Fromm, in *The Forgotten Language*, pointed out the limitations of psychological approaches—the tendency toward "a certain dogmatism and rigidity" resulting from intensive self-absorption with a single viewpoint, narrowly confused with "the only true" viewpoint. Too often we ignore "the many-sidedness of symbolic language and try to force it into the Procrustean bed of one, and only one, kind of meaning."[19]

[19] Erich Fromm, *The Forgotten Language* (New York: Rinehart & Co., 1951), p. 9.

In spite of the catholicity and depth of the mythopoeic approach—with its synthesis of history, fine arts, the history of ideas, literary anthropology, rhetoric, philosophy, religion, philology, sociology, and the counterparts of psychological and archetypal techniques, which often lead to the enrichment of pluralistic insights—it remains dominated by a centrality of principle. As potentially rewarding as this approach may be, its exclusive emphasis tends often to leave out too much of the poet's conscious artistry—the techniques and skills of which he is *consciously* aware. At times, the mythopoeist may even give the impression that the experience of literature has little to do with the poem itself, and he may appear to treat the poet as a virtual reflection of the Platonic concept of him as a "light and winged and holy thing" uttering "his oracles." Thus, the picture of the poet given to us is distorted. Mythopoeically, we see him producing not so much poems of conscious artistry as transmuted dreams of his visions of a remote and mythic past, emerging out of archetypal patterns buried in the deep recesses of the collective unconscious.

And yet, but for this frequent lack of balance and formalistic substructure, the approach is powerful, it offers much that the term "extrinsic" cannot explain away, and it takes us toward the larger view.

9. A Synthesis of Approaches

The final approach we offer is a synthesis of approaches. Let us apply what seems appropriate from each of the previous approaches to an example. Any poem will do, but perhaps we should, for illustrative purposes, choose one which challenges specific insights from each of the approaches, while, at the same time, it offers difficulties to new readers of poetry. For ease of reference throughout this chapter, we include the poem below with numbered lines and a suggested scansion:

William Butler Yeats

The Second Coming

	Line Number
Turning and turning in the widening gyre	1
The falcon cannot hear the falconer;	2
Things fall apart; the centre cannot hold;	3
Mere anarchy is loosed upon the world,	4
The blood-dimmed tide is loosed, and everywhere	5
The ceremony of innocence is drowned;	6
The best lack all conviction, while the worst	7
Are full of passionate intensity.	8
Surely some revelation is at hand;	9
Surely the Second Coming is at hand.	10
The Second Coming! Hardly are those words out	11
When a vast image out of *Spiritus Mundi*	12
Troubles my sight: somewhere in sands of the desert	13
A shape with lion body and the head of a man,	14
A gaze blank and pitiless as the sun,	15
Is moving its slow thighs, while all about it	16
Reel shadows of the indignant desert birds.	17
The darkness drops again; but now I know	18
That twenty centuries of stony sleep	19
Were vexed to nightmare by a rocking cradle,	20
And what rough beast, its hour come round at last,	21
Slouches towards Bethlehem to be born?	22

(1920)

Even a first reading of the poem suggests that it lends itself broadly to classical, Renaissance, and Romantic approaches. For example, the general form of the poem is blank verse. But there are many variations on the basic blank-verse pattern. The lines are not uniformly iambic pentameter. Fourteen of the twenty-two lines consist of more or less than ten syllables. The unusual thought groupings are indicated by at least eight run-on lines (enjambment) and eight pauses within lines (caesuras). Finally, the poem employs unusual sound devices (for example, the three accents in line 21, "what rough beast"), subtle partial rhymes, and repetitious sound units. All of this suggests that the blank verse is not typically "classical," but original and subjectively experimental.

Though the poem appears to have a religious subject, one perceives, upon a closer reading, that the context is heavily ironic, even harshly so; certainly there is not the customary solemn treatment of a religious subject in a "rational" sense. To be sure, there are, expressed in the poem, traditional values, aspects of conformity, and a sense of comfort in the past and the known world. But there are also clashes. Religion and tradition give way to historical and sociocultural shiftings. There is an evident despair at the apparent inevitability of change and an unmistakable sense of fear in the face of an unknown future.

Ancient classicism would consider the whole matter of form to be dominant over details (as it was in Greek statues), but this is not true of "The Second Coming." Here, form and substance work together, yet in such a way that the details stand out. Although a philosophical system may be at work in Yeats' poem (the historical critic, we suggest, would find it of interest), the basic appeal of the poem, it would seem, is romantic, for it appeals to the emotions rather than to reason or to things known. The plethora of images and symbols would tend to undergird this concept. Indeed, if one reads closely, one may experience a kind of effusion of undefined emotion.

To be sure, Yeats, in his original way, was practicing a kind of mimesis, or imitation of nature, although much remains to be said about the way in which he conceived of "nature." The poem makes up a whole (it has harmonia)—a beginning, middle, and end. It has a design and structure (architectoniké); and yet it is highly symbolic in nature—so much so that the design would tend to elude the classicist. The poem reveals a kind of classic restraint, though, especially when one considers how much more blatantly violent it could be in arousing emotions of pity and fear. Yeats' skill is classic in its precision, too. John Unterecker has noted in the Introduction to a collection of critical essays, *Yeats*, the conscious aspects of Yeats' artistry—his contempt for "the sloppy expressionist who values his emotion more than the shaping of it," his conviction that poorly crafted or "bastard art" is "symptomatic of our chaotic world," and his practice of "absolute integrity of craft."[1]

One can easily find Longinus' sources of the sublime in the poem. For example, there is a facility in the use of figurative language. There also appear to be moralistic purposes, even a Christian coloring suggestive of the anagogy

[1] John Unterecker (ed.), *Yeats* (Englewood Cliffs, N.J.: Prentice-Hall, 1963), p. 5.

(elements beyond sense) of Dante, which itself reflected Aristotle's psychagogia (leading out the soul). However, one soon discovers that despite its title and despite the moral implications it raises, the poem is not a Christian poem in the sense that Dante's poetry was, with anagogy prevailing in it.

Consistent with Sidney's recommended approaches, Yeats makes no effort to adhere to artificial rules or excessively imitative patterns. Inherent in his poem is a flavor of antiquity precedent to history itself. It embodies philosophy, one senses, but is somehow beyond it, as all good poetry must be. And there seem to be mysteries in the poem "darkly written," as Sidney would have noted. However, whether purposes of the poem relate to goodness, happiness, or delight, as Ben Jonson would have desired, is clearly arguable.

Sainte-Beuve, in his influential essay "What Is a Classic?" (1850) answered his titular question in this way:

> A true classic, as I should like to hear it defined, is an author who has enriched the human mind, who has really augmented its treasures, who has made it take one more step forward, who has discovered some unequivocal moral truth, or has once more seized hold of some eternal passion in that heart where all seemed known and explored; who has rendered his thought, his observation, or his discovery under no matter what form, but broad and large, refined, sensible, sane, and beautiful in itself; who has spoken to all in a style of his own which yet belongs to all the world, in a style which is new without neologisms, new and ancient, easily contemporaneous with every age.

This is a broad, though rational, attempt to grasp an author's classicism. To the neoclassicist the poem would likely have appeared vague and imprecise. It would have indicated, to the rationalistic mind, a suspension of consciousness. Alluding to twenty centuries, and symbolically, to even more time, within the microcosm of twenty-two lines would doubtless have met with a skeptical eye from Corneille and perhaps even from Dryden. One suspects that Dryden, as he transcended the narrow rules of his age (imposed by the radically atavistic "moderns"), could have anticipated the magnitude of another age and experienced visions of it; but he might have taken Yeats to task for endeavoring to paint too broad a canvas with only twenty-two lines. As Dryden did with Shakespeare, though, he would certainly have sought evidence of "the largest and most comprehensive soul," and he might have glimpsed more in Yeats' poem than would normally meet the neoclassical eye. Similarly, one imagines Pope might have caught something of the unity of sound and meaning in "The Second Coming," although he might have resented, in this curiously cryptic poem, something foreign to his conservative religious views—an aura of cultism.

Dr. Johnson might well have declared the poem repugnant to his sense of lucidity and rationality. He might have looked upon it as being overburdened with obscure particularities, for he felt that to paint a garden one need not "number the streaks of the tulip." In its subjectivity and obscurantism, the poem might have appeared hopelessly romantic—the ultimate insult to the Augustan mind. The fear and shock generated by the ending of "The Second Coming" might well have alienated Dr. Johnson upon first reading, for, one recalls, he was suspicious even of his own emotions and imaginative power.

In her book on Yeats, *Divided Image*, Margaret Rudd referred to the Romantic visionary poet William Blake as "Yeats's master," stating that both shared an important likeness in their concern with "the drama of the inner life" and that whereas Blake was preoccupied with "prophecy," Yeats "categorically equated [poetry] with magic."[2] George Fraser noted in *W. B. Yeats*, "He was the last great poet in the English romantic tradition; and the only poet in that tradition, except Byron, with a genuine sense of humour and gift of wit."[3]

Certainly one may observe in "The Second Coming" an interest in original, subjective, and mythic concerns; a concern over freedom of self-expression; a seeking of comfort through, if not an exaltation of, the past and its traditions; an exploration of decay, abnormality, and gloom; an exaggeration of ancient mythic elements; and an intensity of personal feeling. But, on the other hand, the ideality of man seems to be placed within a realistic context—even one of tragic disillusionment. Hope (if there is, indeed, hope), is never, even by implication, enthusiastic. It may not be going too far to state that an indication of hope seems deliberately suppressed—cut off. Thus, Edmund Wilson, in *Axel's Castle*, tells us that Yeats, by the time he wrote "The Second Coming," had made a conscious decision to "eliminate from his poetry both Romantic rhetoric and Symbolistic mistiness."[4]

Similarly, Arthur Mizener calls attention to Yeats' often-stated desire to achieve, in Yeats' word, "reality"—what Mizener, in his essay "The Romanticism of W. B. Yeats," interprets as "simplicity, order and concreteness." And yet one sees in the poem qualities that Wordsworth emphasized: a "greater promptness to think and feel," and the treatment of such subjects as "animal sensations" and "fear and sorrow." Again, Yeats' absorption with supernatural matters reminds one of Coleridge's guiding principle for his choices of poetry in the *Lyrical Ballads*—that poetry should be true enough to produce for the "shadows of imagination that willing suspension of disbelief for the moment. . . ." Coleridge would consider whether or not Yeats' "The Second Coming" is a *"legitimate* poem" made up of "parts which mutually support and explain each other," and whether or not the work possesses "imagination in the highest and strictest sense of the word."

[2] Margaret Rudd, *Divided Image* (London: Routledge & Kegan Paul, 1953), pp. 188–189.

[3] George S. Fraser, *W. B. Yeats* (London, New York, Toronto: Longmans, Green & Co., 1954), p. 29.

[4] Edmund Wilson, *Axel's Castle* (New York: Scribner's, 1931).

[5] Arthur Mizener, "The Romanticism of W. B. Yeats," in *The Permanence of Yeats*, ed. by James Hall and Martin Steinmann (New York: Macmillan, 1950), p. 144. Originally published in *The Southern Review*, VII, 3 (Winter 1942), 601–623.

One imagines that Hazlitt would have been concerned with the "gusto" of the work—its "power or passion," a necessary prerequisite for "sympathetic identification." Keats would have sought to perceive a "negative capability" in the poet through his work and to determine the basic honesty of the poet's stance. If the poem is great, he would have queried, is it also "unobtrusive"—subtle enough that the reader is amazed not so much with the poem as with its subject? Shelley would have looked for the triumph of imagination over "analytical reasoning," or the perception of values "both separately and as a whole," revealing similarities between things—say, the interrelationships between apparently disparate images in "The Second Coming." Shelley would have observed with interest "the circumference of knowledge" indicated by the poem, and especially, whether or not it contains "something divine" —whether it pervades eternity itself.

How well does "The Second Coming" lend itself to a historical approach? In *Vision and Revision in Yeats's "Last Poems,"* Jon Stallworthy demonstrated just how well it does: "In Yeats' cyclic view of history one religion rises as another falls. Apollo and Dionysus prefigure Buddha, who prefigures Christ, who prefigures the 'rough beast' of 'The Second Coming', 'slouching toward Bethlehem to be born.'"[6] More basically, in *Between the Lines: Yeats's Poetry in the Making* (1963), Stallworthy dated the composition of the poem (January 1919) and traced Yeats' various revisions of it.

Critics employing the historical approach reveal that the earliest forms of the lines were but pale hints of what was to come. For example, "falcon" was initially "hawk." Stallworthy agreed with Richard Ellmann's stimulating examination of the poem in *The Identity of Yeats* (1954):

The image of the falcon who is out of the falconer's control should not be localized, as some have suggested, as an image of man loose from Christ; Yeats would

not have cluttered the poem by referring to Christ both as falconer and as rocking cradle further on. Essentially the falcon's loss of contact implies man's separation from every ideal of himself that has enabled him to control his life, whether this comes from religion or philosophy or poetry. It is also, in more general terms, his break with every traditional tie.[7]

The Variorum Edition of the Poems of W. B. Yeats revealed eight changes in wording or spatial arrangements.[8] Stallworthy noted Yeats' original uses of such early word groupings as "intellectual gyre," which is growing "wider and more wide," and he indicates through such historical methods possible meanings and interpretations of later forms. According to the *Variorum*, "gyre" is to be related to a "mathematical movement" as inevitable as the pattern of growth found in a willow, which develops "evenly," or in a bamboo shoot, which grows "from joint to joint," or in the order of an animal's development "peculiar to it." Similarly,

The mind, whether expressed in history or in the individual life, has a precise movement, which can be quickened or slackened but cannot be fundamentally altered. The gyre, then, is really two gyres, representing conflict. Both circle about a centre, spiraling upward or downward, either widening to an open circle or narrowing to a point in the center of a circle, illustrated thusly:[9]

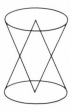

---

[6] Jon Stallworthy, *Vision and Revision in Yeats's "Last Poems"* (Oxford: Clarendon Press, 1969), p. 151.

[7] Richard Ellmann, *The Identity of Yeats*, 2nd ed. (New York: Oxford University Press, 1964), pp. 258–259.
[8] Peter Allt and Russell Alspach (eds.), *The Variorum Edition of the Poems of W. B. Yeats* (New York: Macmillan, 1957), pp. 401–402. Further references will be indicated by *Variorum*.
[9] *Ibid.*, pp. 823–824.

On the spiraling movement can be represented the suffering in life, various emotions, subjective life, and objective life. But the movement, whether of the individual or of history, is either outward or inward, widening or narrowing; the individual or historical force, as the case may be, becomes stronger as it moves closer to or farther away from the center.

More will be said of the psychological dimension of the gyral concept, but at this point it would seem more appropriate to emphasize its historical significance. Vivienne Koch observed, in *W. B. Yeats: The Tragic Phase*, that "The Second Coming" marked one of Yeats' earliest uses of gyral imagery and that the complexity of "the gyres as the symbolic centre of Yeats's cosmology" aside, the *general* uses of these "interlocking gyres represent process; they are the characteristic movement or dynamic of the universe. As such, they explain the career of individual human experience, as well as that of civilizations and universes."[10] Stallworthy also places the conflicting gyres into a concrete historical context. To illustrate, he expands upon a later-abandoned first-draft line, "the germans are ( ) [*sic*] now to Russia come," drawing further internal evidence from external events:

> By the end of July 1917 the Russian front had crumbled in face of the enemy. In October of that year the Bolsheviks brought off their revolution, and at the Treaty of Brest-Litvosk, on 3 March 1918, Lenin had surrendered to the Germans; Finland, Esthonia, Courland, Lithuania, and tracts of Russian Poland. The Germans had indeed come to Russia, and I think it not impossible that Yeats, with his reverence for the aristocratic virtues epitomized by Castiglione, had in mind the fate of the Russian Royal House, as he wrote: "Though every day some innocent has died."[11]

In support of Stallworthy's historical interpretation of "The Second Coming," Alex Zwerdling, in *Yeats and the Heroic Ideal*, remarked that the poem "deals with the process of history."[12] Austin Warren, in his essay "William Butler Yeats: The Religion of a Poet," eschews an orthodox religious interpretation, perceiving "an unflinching view of world history which moves characteristically not by smooth progressions but by revolutions, reversals, and brutalities."[13] In short, he sees in Yeats' work a poetic comprehension of realism. Further, T. S. Eliot wrote in his essay of 1940, "The Poetry of W. B. Yeats,"

> There are some poets whose poems can be considered more or less in isolation, for experience and delight. There are others whose poetry, though giving equally experience and delight, *has a larger historical importance. Yeats was one of the latter.* He was one of the few whose history was the history of our own time, who are part of the consciousness of our age, which cannot be understood without them.[14] [italics added].

Although we cannot cover all aspects of the historical approach as they might be applied to "The Second Coming" within these pages, we have suggested some of them, varying from the examination of revisions to the examination of broad relationships of the poem to the events of the age. Something remains to be said about a third aspect of this approach—an examination of Yeats' life, especially during the period in which the poem evolved. To illustrate another kind of detail the historical critic would note, we might examine a few of Yeats' major sources and influences. The major literary source obviously is the King James Bible. Glancing at the poem, one notes such obvious

---

[10] Vivienne Koch, *W. B. Yeats: The Tragic Phase* (Baltimore: Johns Hopkins Press, 1951), pp. 93–94.

[11] Jon Stallworthy, *Between the Lines: Yeats's Poetry in the Making* (Oxford: Clarendon Press, 1963), pp. 18–19.

[12] Alex Zwerdling, *Yeats and the Heroic Ideal* (New York: New York University Press, 1965), p. 160.

[13] Austin Warren, "William Butler Yeats: The Religion of a Poet," in *The Permanence of Yeats, op. cit.*, p. 236. Originally published in *The Southern Review*, VII, 3 (Winter 1942), 624–638.

[14] T. S. Eliot, "The Poetry of W. B. Yeats," in *The Permanence of Yeats, op. cit.*, p. 343. An address to Friends of the Irish Academy at the Abbey Theatre, June 1940, it was originally published in *The Southern Review*, VII, 3 (Winter 1942), 442–454.

allusions to Biblical material as the title, "The Second Coming." There are specific Biblical images, such as that of a force unleashing a flood, indicated by the phrase, "The . . . tide is loosed." Note also the choice of "revelation" with its Biblical connotations, the use of the Latin "Spiritus" rather than the usual *Anima*, the tone of mystery in "somewhere in sands of the desert," the vague "shape with lion body and the head of man," the anatomical designation in "moving its slow thighs," the time allusion "twenty centuries," the eschatology perhaps inherent in "stony sleep," the obvious "rocking cradle," the "rough beast" which "slouches," and "Bethlehem"—the birthplace of Christ. All these correlate with Biblical sources. Matthew 24 suggests the characteristics of the age of The Second Coming—wars and rumors of wars, international conflicts, famines, pestilences, persecutions, great iniquities, love waxing cold, the beginnings of sorrow, each and all gathering into an awful intensity at the end. Revelation 4:7 reads, "And the first beast was like a lion . . . and the third beast had a face as a man. . . ." Daniel 7:4 refers to a lion-eagle-man-man's heart image in much the same general way. Ezekiel 1:10 alludes to the face-of-man-face-of-lion description of the beast. And Revelation 19:11-16 proclaims Christ's Second Coming in an apocalyptic vision, "And he hath on his . . . thigh a name written, KING OF KINGS, AND LORD OF LORDS," but (unlike Yeats' treatment) followed by the doom of the antagonist—the false prophet, or Antichrist, and his cohorts.

In addition, Stallworthy cites Shelley's "Ozymandias" and *Prometheus Unbound* (lines 625-628) as influences. Margaret Rudd saw echoes of Blake's prophetic "The First Book of Urizen," especially of his line "In stony sleep ages roll'd over him," but more generally of the Urizen image as a whole. The historical critic would recognize Yeats as a modern, chronologically, but such sources and influences as these would raise the question of the influence of Romanticism on his work. Part of the historical concern would be Yeats' place in a literary tradition. Was Yeats a late Romantic,

and, if so, to what extent do his works derive from Romantic sources?

The historical approach may demand that the student of the poem go into the poet's family background. To illustrate, George Fraser called attention to Yeats' "Irish Protestant Ascendancy" —to the Irish view of his family as "minor gentry" and the London view of them as "shabby-genteel bohemians." He noted Yeats' Pre-Raphaelite influences as well as his traditional values, which were seasoned with a "religion of beauty." Both of these had been transmitted by his father. Fraser saw Yeats as a "dreamy, solitary youth" with a "lack of formal education," and he observed the early French Symbolist influences which were introduced by his friend Arthur Symons, his slow growth as a poet, and his early friendships with such "decadents" as Lionel Johnson and Ernest Dowson.[15] Such a background sketch might shed light on Yeats' formulative heritage, attitudes, and ways of thinking, which in turn may have a bearing on the meaning of such phrases as "Things fall apart," "The best," "passionate intensity," and "The darkness drops again," as well, indeed, as the meaning of the whole of "The Second Coming."

The determination of whether or not "The Second Coming" is concerned with such matters as philosophy and morality—especially as they stem from classical sources in Greek and Roman literature—would be essential in humanistic approaches. Like Matthew Arnold, the head spokesman for humanism in the nineteenth century, Yeats was aware that the old gods were falling. In Zwerdling's phrase, Yeats possessed a "constant nostalgia for a 'Romantic Ireland' in which heroism was still valued highly," but he sang in his refrain to "September 1913":

Romantic Ireland's dead and gone,
It's with O'Leary in the grave.

Not unlike Arnold, Yeats had witnessed the changing of a traditional, aristocratic culture; consequently, he experienced a conflict between

[15] Fraser, *op. cit.*, pp. 10-12.

the desire to cling to old myths of Ireland, the dream of the hero, and the familiar comforts of his dreamy youth—and the necessity of conforming to the sudden rise of a shifting middle class and proletariat. Reacting to disillusionment over the conflict between religion materializing itself in supposed facts, and consequently attaching emotions to facts that failed it, Arnold identified poetry with religion. For him, poetry became the idea: "Poetry attaches its emotion to the idea; the idea *is* the fact." In *The Trembling of the Veil* (1922), Yeats echoed Arnold, even to the point of naming the scientific culprit with whom Arnold had crossed swords:

> . . . deprived by [Thomas] Huxley . . . of the simple-minded religion of my childhood, I had made a new religion, almost an infallible church of poetic tradition, of a fardel of stories, and of personages, and of emotions, inseparable from their first expression, passed on from generation to generation by poets and painters with some help from philosophers and theologians.[16]

Yeats did not come nearly as close to Plato as Arnold had, although Yeats did attempt to strike through extraneous material and to make poetic expression "count to us *really*," to use Arnold's phrase. Yeats wished to treat poetry as the core of religion. Concerning "The Second Coming," Arnold would have asked, "Are there any touchstones for detecting the presence of high poetic quality?" Again, he would have asked himself and others whether, in reading the poem, one sensed a kind of "measuring device" which rendered the lines comparable to those of classic origin ("classic" in the sense of poetry of the highest order). We can imagine him asking if the poem possesses "in any eminent degree, truth and seriousness." Arnold stated that readers may discover in certain lines memorable "touchstones," as he called them, with which another poem may be evaluated. Does

one see, or even begin to sense, such lines in "The Second Coming"?

Concerning the new humanism, one can immediately note certain correspondences between Yeats' poem and selected points from Irving Babbitt's ten-point formulation of a definition of humanism and its functions. Among the characteristics of "The Second Coming" of which the new humanists would approve are the theme of "divinity in mediaevalism," proportionateness in treatment of subject, acknowledgment of the importance of "intuition" and feelings, the typical humanistic emphasis on a "universal centre" of human nature shared with religion, an effort to see life "steadily" and "whole," a recognition of the chaotic and unstructured nature of modern "naturalistic" man—whose poetry reflects a kind of outrage of disorder (in short, a lack of classical restraint)—the perception of man as "the measure of things," and a clear opposition to the Romantic assertion that mankind is "naturally good."

Most Yeatsian scholars agree that Yeats' fame will rest upon the poetry of his last twenty years, from 1919 to 1939. With more experience and increasing skill came a "sharpening and hardening of his attitudes," as George Fraser stated, and "the development of the tough, complex, and ironical 'later style.'"[17] Whether this new attitude was a "realism," as Yeats insisted, or something different —a simple winnowing of the chaff from the seeds of talent—it was clearly a movement away from Romanticism.

Although the sociocultural approach to poetry involves a consideration of the social, economic, and political conditions surrounding it—and therefore overlaps, in some ways, with the historical approach—the major emphasis of the sociocultural approach is on social commentary rather than historical method, the nature of the text, and other more traditional literary matters. A major question would be: What are the *social* implications of the work? Inherent in the word "social" would be moral, philosophical, and other broadly cultural

[16] William Butler Yeats, *The Trembling of the Veil* (London: T. Werner Laurie, 1922); reprinted in *The Autobiography of William Butler Yeats* (New York: Macmillan, 1938), p. 101.

[17] Fraser, *op. cit.*, p. 18.

interests. What are the social realities of the work? What social, economic, and political forces gave incentive to the creation of "The Second Coming," and how closely is it related to them?

The Marxist would want to know how the poem reflects society—specifically, the "dialectical relationship" between the culture and the classes of people within it. Reflecting Christopher Caudwell's view, he would want to know as much as possible about Yeats' "tension between tradition and experience," and thus gain insights into Yeats' performance of a "social task" through the poem. One is reminded of Van Wyck Brooks' statement, noted earlier, concerning the Irish Rebellion—its "conditions" predisposed the people to rebellion, and, consequently, poetic "impulses" were unlocked by those conditions.

To answer these and similar questions, one should first recognize the kinships they suggest with historical approaches. Examples of topical events preceding the composition of "The Second Coming" were international in scope—the Germans had invaded Russia, the Royal House had been overthrown, and Lenin had capitulated to the Germans. It is not at all impossible that the violence and atrocities accompanying World War I, including the Bolshevik Revolution and the cold-blooded murdering of the Royal Family already alluded to, were part of the historical matrix out of which the poet wrote.[18]

Yeats, to be sure, was earlier shaken by the Easter (or Irish) Rebellion in 1916, although he was not an extreme nationalist. The woman foremost in his life up to the war, the beautiful Maud Gonne, was an anti-English political activist. She had urged Yeats to become involved in movements for Irish freedom. He loved her deeply, as his drama *Countess Cathleen* and his "Rose" poems attest. But after her marriage to the radical Major John MacBride and his subsequent martyrdom as one of the executed leaders of the bloody Irish Rebellion, Yeats lost contact with the men of Ireland,

[18] Stallworthy, *Between the Lines, op. cit.,* pp. 18–19, supports this general view in his tracing of the poem's growth.

those from the towns and country, and "became more unaware of the forces working for Ireland's freedom," as Maud Gonne noted in *Scattering Branches* (1940). True, Yeats never shared her political fanaticism; even though he admired her fiery spirit and dedication, he often found himself in opposition to her views. A. N. Jeffares, in his *W. B. Yeats: Man and Poet* (1949), observes that in December 1918, when Maud returned to Ireland in defiance of the English ban against her, Yeats refused to take her in. There is more to the story than can or should be indicated here. Yeats' own wife, the former Miss Hyde-Lees (whom he had married just over a year before) was ill with severe flu and expecting a child—the daughter to be born in February 1919. Aware of possible investigations and searches by the authorities as well as likely disturbances to his sick wife and, perhaps, anticipated domestic repercussions, Yeats at first refused to take Maud in, or even to tell his wife about her request to enter their home. Although this whole area is possibly more relevant to psychological approaches, it may, nevertheless, be worth pursuing briefly within a sociocultural context, too. Maud's presence at this time in Yeats' life may have represented a kind of symbolical center for him—a phase of the "realism" which he had entered and with which he was deeply concerned. Inevitably, Yeats and Maud quarreled. But he relented, and both he and his wife invited her into the house by Christmas.

Although it would be overzealous as well as illogical to relate "The Second Coming" to Maud Gonne MacBride's sudden return and virtual intrusion, the sudden occurrence of all these events—their intensified convergence close to the period of composition—may possibly lend sociocultural insights into the poem. Therefore, the socioculturalist would examine the following as they relate to his purposes: Maud's presence during the poet's experience of divided feelings, the recency of his marriage, his wife's condition, the expectation of his child's birth into a world about which he was despondent, Maud's triggering of old memories such as the haunting Easter Rebellion and MacBride's martyrdom, perhaps the stirring of old political interests, a resulting conflict in his sense of responsibility toward Irish freedom, a sense of new-found identity with the old Irish yearning for independence, and the innumerable current political upheavals surrounding him (for example, the hegemony of the Sinn Fein or Separatist party in the 1918 elections, their policy of noncooperation with the English, the armed resistence and guerrilla warfare which had broken out with retaliation on both sides, and the terror and daily outrages just prior to the rise of the Irish Free State). All of this followed closely upon the world-wide tragedy of the Great War and the general aura of disillusionment of post-Versailles Europe and the Western world, in which Yeats' world was already becoming immersed.

Yet one wonders, with Dylan Thomas, whether war can produce poetry at all. Fraser's summary of Yeats' attitudes in this whole area seems pertinent:

> His own personal dream had been of a free Ireland that would be a kind of replica, without the tensions or troubles, without the injustice to the majority. . . . He hoped that the "Big Houses" would survive, that the Protestant Ascendancy would still, because of their wealth, their wit, and their manners, constitute a dominant group. He thought of the local grandees patronizing poets and the peasants touching their hats. He was romantically innocent about politics. He found, of course, what had come into existence was not a Protestant-dominated aristocratic Republic but a Roman Catholic farmers' democracy; and the farmers did not want to touch their hats to anybody. Yeats had hoped that Dublin, as the capital of a free Ireland, would become a great cultural centre; he saw the "blind, bitter town" becoming more rather than less provincial.[19]

Even so, Stephen Spender, in *The Destructive Element*, maintained that "The Second Coming" refers to the coming of fascism. Louis MacNeice doubts the precision of Spender's view in *The Poetry of W. B. Yeats*, but he notes that the "blood-dimmed tide"

does represent that upsurge of instinctive violence which, other outlets being barred, finds a natural outlet in fascist mob-mania. That the rise of this tide is heralded with a certain relish is attributable to the fact that Yeats had a budding fascist inside himself. With a fatalism parallel to that of the Marxists he felt that the world was ripe for the rule of "the worst." Paradoxically, perhaps, he felt that this would give the individual freedom as prison has been known to give it to prisoners and the Roman Catholic Church to Catholics; he never made the idea of freedom contingent on democracy.[20]

Some socioculturalists consider the aim of literature to be social education—the communication of social purposes. Such purposes may be related to a critic's concept of what a poet's obligation to his fellow man should be. Yeats himself noted that the "widening gyre" image bears a relationship to "our scientific, democratic, fact-accumulating, heterogeneous civilization" and to the "revelation as in a lightning flash . . . of the civilization that must slowly take its place . . ." (*Variorum*, p. 825). In "William Butler Yeats: The Religion of a Poet" Austin Warren called attention to Yeats' having absorbed Darwin and Huxley as authorities but having refused to implement their assumptions in both his philosophy and work because they "contravened his imagination." Thus, Yeats spurned their scientific "progress" and turned instead to a "kind of traditionary primitivism"—to those insights gained from myth in early civilization rather than at the end of it.[21] Margaret Rudd saw the whole image of the falcon's flight, the falconer and gyre as representative of "a period of anarchy and violence" following one "of innocence and beauty."[22] Louis MacNeice compared the poem with T. S. Eliot's "The Waste Land," observing that both poets are "anti-Bolshevik" and "obsessed" with the "decay of eastern Europe" and the "enervation of the general European tradition,"

---

[19] Fraser, *op. cit.*, pp. 18–19.

[20] Louis MacNeice, *The Poetry of W. B. Yeats* (London and New York: Oxford University Press, 1941), pp. 132–133.
[21] Warren, *op. cit.*, p. 224.
[22] Rudd, *op. cit.*, p. 166.

although the "passionate intensity" of the "worst" holds no encouragement for Yeats.[23] Richard Ellmann wrote of Yeats' personal horror at the events in Europe and his troubled attitude, revealed in his *Autobiographies* (1922), toward the "growing murderousness of the world." Ellmann cited the eloquent disillusionment of Yeats' concluding sentence of the autobiographical fragment *The Trembling of the Veil* (1922): "After us the Savage God."[24] Morton I. Seiden is more general, commenting on the sociocultural setting of the poem in troubled Ireland, Yeats' role as an interpreter with a "private myth," and the emergence of modern Ireland as a symbol of universal twentieth-century confusion in politics, society, and religion.[25]

Such brief summaries of selected views of literary scholars and Yeatsian specialists may help us to see that sociocultural approaches to poetry may represent at least *pieces* of the mosaic which make up the living art of "The Second Coming." They may also hint at its broader outlines of intention.

The balance wrought by a closer view of the poem as art worthy of study in itself may help us to see "The Second Coming" in a more accurate perspective. We remember Eliot's emphasis on the intrinsic approaches of the so-called New Critics—the importance of considering poetry "primarily as poetry and not another thing."[26] Such an approach is consistent with the objective theory of art and with Ransom's insistence on an "ontological view" of poetry. That is, Ransom felt that a poem should be "self-existing" or "autotelic," and not dominated by extrinsic purposes.

Certainly it would be good to remind ourselves

again that there are many New Critical approaches —so many that the label is misleading—and that although there is no single school or movement to which the term exclusively applies, most New Critical ideas seem to cluster rightly together in their distinction from earlier humanistic approaches. Here we can but draw from a few of the New Critical approaches as they apply to and illuminate Yeats' "The Second Coming."

Glancing over the list which Richards developed of ten difficulties in understanding poetry, the perceptive student will immediately see Richards' contention of the need for understanding the poem on the basic level of information, temporarily deferring any attempt to interpret it. One should endeavor to perceive the sensuous elements of the poem (that is, the appeal to the five senses); to transmit these to emotional and imaginative dimensions of understanding; to avoid excessively "private" responses to the poem, including "stock responses" (for example, jumping to the conclusion that the poem is religious because of its title and Biblical allusions); to avoid overreacting with "sentimentality," an excessive emotional response not generated by the poem itself; to avoid underreacting through "inhibition," thereby denying oneself an honest experience; to avoid preconceived notions ("Doctrinal Adhesions") as they may tend to bear upon "The Second Coming"; to avoid "technical presuppositions," such as metrical preconceptions of "what form poetry should be written in"; and to avoid permitting "general critical preconceptions" to block one's appreciation of the poem before one can enjoy the experience of it.

Applying Richards' four kinds of analytical meaning, we should now proceed to an explication of the poem (*explication de texte*). First, an explication of the *sense* of the poem may be achieved through a paraphrase, or a rephrasing in the student's own words. This should be concerned with the basic level of the language of information; there should be no attempt to interpret the poem in this stage of analysis. Such a paraphrase would be:

[23] MacNeice, *op. cit.*
[24] Ellmann, *op. cit.*, p. 258. See W. B. Yeats, *Autobiographies* (New York: Macmillan, 1927), pp. 238–239.
[25] Morton I. Seiden, *William Butler Yeats: The Poet as Mythmaker* (East Lansing: Michigan State University Press, 1962).
[26] T. S. Eliot, *The Sacred Wood* (New York: Barnes & Noble, 1928), p. viii.

Stanza 1

As a falcon repeatedly turns in an ever-enlarging spiraling motion, it cannot respond to its master. All matters seem to come loose from each other; there is no central force to hold them together. The theory that government interferes unjustly with individual liberty becomes a reality as the world becomes subtly governmentless. A flood, the color of which is darkened with blood, occurs—perhaps the result of some causal agent implied by the passive voice "is loosed"—and in all places the established ritual of noncorruption and freedom from guile and evil is "drowned." It seems that the finest and most outstanding men have no profound beliefs or principles, while the bad or the most harmful and destructive are filled with zealous dedication.

Stanza 2

Of course, some significant revelation is about to take place. Of course, the Second Advent—the return of Christ to earth and all implied by this—is about to take place. Yet even as the "I" (persona) of the poem expresses "The Second Coming!" in verbal symbols, he is disturbed by a visual impression emerging from a life principle of the world (the soul of the world). Its general form is that of a lion's body with man's head. The expression is an empty stare, as devoid of mercy as the sun itself. Its thighs move slowly as, all about the beast, birds of the desert recoil and fly round and round as if in shock and scorn. Night comes suddenly once more; but now the persona realizes that two thousand years of rocklike sleep were tormented into a frightening dream by the rocking of a cradle. And the question arises: What crude beast, its time having arrived, moves in a drooping, slovenly gait toward the place where Christ was born—there to be brought into life itself?

The poet's subject tentatively would seem to be, as the title indicates, the apocalyptic "Second Coming" of Christ. Upon further examination, however, one notes repeated references to world disintegration, anarchy, the loss of ceremony and order in life, and the loss of innocence itself. The poet is aware that the apathy of the best people and the agitation of the worst are preconditions of the revelatory Second Advent. All this relates to the poet's *feeling* toward his subject, becoming a matter of deep concern, a disturbing confrontation—even a kind of hallucinatory preoccupation. With sudden insight, the poet's persona seems to sense that all that for two millennia was inevitable and doomed to happen has come to pass. Another time with other values has come which will end traditional values developed in the Christian world of Western civilization. The poet's feeling toward his subject is therefore one of confusion and awe. He makes reevaluations that lead to further horror, approaching his subject as one might be expected to approach events beyond one's ken such as the Hebrew Armageddon itself, or wars or rumors of wars. The feeling is dichotomous, for the poet reveals a sorrow at the passing of the known world, the traditional world, even as he experiences a sense of resignation to the cyclical certitude of that passing. The poet's feeling clearly reveals a conflict between the intellect and the human heart.

The poet's relationship to his audience—his tone—is indirect, ironic, and subtle. It is also ambiguous, for the image that comes to his persona's mind arises both from Biblical sources (Matthew 24; Revelation 4:7, 19:11-16; Ezekiel 1:10; and Daniel 7:4), as was noted in the application of historical approaches, and from the life principle of the world (*Spiritus Mundi*)—a non-Christian concept. An added paradox, then, lies in the poet's suggestion that the Antichrist may displace Christ, even though in Revelation 19:11-20, a heroic Christ upon a white horse (suggesting the age of knighthood), declaring his authority with the sign "KING OF KINGS, AND LORD OF LORDS both on his vesture and *on his thigh*" [italics added], defeats the beast and his cohorts and casts them "alive into a lake of fire burning with brimstone." Yet, if the subject of the poem is, indeed, "The Second Coming," there is no tone of victory or joy at the "good news," but rather, paradoxically, there is one of resigned sorrow at the passing of an age and anticipatory horror of what the future may hold for humanity.

Apparently, then, the *intention* of the poet is that the subject consist only partly of the Biblical Second Coming. Indeed, more persistent as subjects are the trouble of the world preceding the Advent and the disillusionment at the demise of an age and its traditions. In this passing age, not only the persona, but, by implication, Yeats himself had found comfort, marred only by the visionary foreknowledge of its inevitable disintegration. Such an intention is consistent with Seiden's analysis. Seiden noted a twofold interpretation of Yeats' symbol of the falcon. He felt that it both paved "the way to a cultural rebirth," and "savagely extinguish[ed] the past." And he extended the "rough beast" more particularly, contending, "The Sphinx will bring with it a better time; but it must violently destroy whatever precedes its reign."[27] Anticipating such views as those of Seiden, Ransom, in "Yeats and His Symbols," stated that the second stanza

> sounds Christian in the beginning, but develops an image whose source is not Scripture but Spiritus Mundi, and which concerns something like an Egyptian Sphinx, and the passing of Christ in his favor. The language is worthy of the matter. The matter is valid enough if it is reasonable to say: Twenty centuries have passed, and the ideal they professed has come to perfect ineptitude and impotence; a new millennium will dawn, and we cannot tell what ideal it will obey; very likely, a monstrous ideal of abstract animal power.[28]

Contextually, Ellmann stated that the "rocking cradle" (line 20) is the cradle of Christianity, and that "While Yeats is not fond of Christianity, and regards its suppression of individual personality as having led to the present anarchy, yet at the end of the poem he envisages something far worse." The final irony, that the new god is born in Bethlehem, "which Christianity associates with passive infancy and the tenderness of maternal love," results in a "brutishness" which is "particularly frightful."[29] The qualification of the slouching beast as a "shape" (line 14) engenders a portentous and

awesome feeling, and here Yeats' intention seems clearly to partake of his feeling.

An analysis of *sense*, *feeling*, and *tone* leads one necessarily toward the meaning of the poet's *intention*, as we have endeavored to show. Although some contextualists would insist on keeping sense, feeling, and tone separated from intention and from external interpretations, we have rather chosen to interweave aspects of the poet's intention with feeling and tone (since each complements the other two). We have also chosen to share with the reader important, though varying, insights of other critics of the poem. However, we do agree with contextualists that the sense or paraphrase of the poem requires a deliberate withholding of the tendencies to make interpretive responses until feeling and tone naturally lead into an exploration of the poet's intention. How can we generalize about the poem? In summary, Yeats seems to have experienced the tragedy of his own time and caught a vision of his own age as being on a great outward-moving spiral of human history. He blended this vision with Christian allusions and symbols, and he imparted, in the imaginative language of poetry, something of his feeling toward the experience, sharing his startling impressions in sensuous lyrics, producing emotional responses, and ultimately rendering the whole in an artistic *experience*. The poem fits the belief of most New Critics that, as Archibald MacLeish wrote in "Ars Poetica,"

A poem should not mean
But be.

Concerned with the intrinsic "being" of a poem, one incisive New Critical approach would involve close textual analysis of the *prosody* of "The Second Coming." Modern contextualists would scan the poem (and there are more scansions of the poem than the one we offer), but they would not be satisfied with a simple, structural treatment. Rather, they would want to know the relationship between the devices of sound in Yeats' poem and its meaning. A possible area for analysis, we suggest, would be the relationship between the

[27] Seiden, *op. cit.*
[28] John Crowe Ransom, "Yeats and His Symbols," *The Kenyon Review*, I, 3 (Summer 1939), 309–322. Later published in *The Permanence of Yeats*, *op. cit.*, pp. 103–104.
[29] Ellmann, *op. cit.*, pp. 259–260.

frequent series of accents, which break the usual iambic pattern, and ultimate intention. Note those series of accents: "Things fáll" (line 3); "blood-dimmed tíde" (line 5); "bést láck áll" (line 7); "Súrely" (lines 9, 10); "thóse wórds óut" (line 11); "sómewhére" (line 13); "ás the sún" (line 15); "slów thíghs" (line 16); "réel shádows" (line 17); "twénty" (line 19); "níghtmáre" (line 20); and "whát róugh béast" (line 21). By using such metrical devices, what meaning does Yeats wish to stress? Similar prosodic questions could be raised concerning the use of time (suspended rhythm) within and at the ends of lines (caesuras and examples of enjambment). Also, one should note the subtle sound devices located especially at the ends of lines, although they do not constitute rhyme. In the first stanza, for example, the ends of lines 1, 2, and 5 may be associated with an "r" sound, lines 3, 4, and 6 with a "d" sound. Such patterns of repetitive sounds run all through the poem, even linking sounds in the first and second stanzas. How may such sound devices, even when they do not constitute pure rhyme, tend to unify lines, strengthen their associations in subtle ways which may act as a flash upon the mind, producing sensuous responses linked to meanings that might otherwise be lost? Such matters are legitimate areas of interest for the contextualist, and they may shed much intrinsic light upon nuances of meaning in the poem. Modern poets such as Robert Frost (and John Crowe Ransom) have commented upon the pull and tug going on between the meaning of a poem and its metrical devices. How does the sound add to the argument? How does each tend to control each? How do both meld into a more intensely meaningful whole? A synthesis of the mechanics of a poem with its meaning reflects the need, as William Empson emphasized, of avoiding pure analysis of either one without the other. Shelley saw the matter whole, too, and commented upon the desirability of bringing individual parts together for a totalistic experience. One danger of the contextualist's approach is that it may tend to leave the poem dissected into pieces, and thus to deaden it rather than to bring it to life as a whole existing force.

Questions that Ransom as well as other New Critics would want to answer in explicating "The Second Coming" would include these: Does Yeats' poem evoke an ontological dimension of artistic language transcending the language of science or information? Does it say something that cannot be said on any other level of language or in any other way? There are several other frames of reference within which "The Second Coming" may be analyzed. From our examination of New Critical approaches in Chapter 7 of this book, we would point to Ransom's explanation of modern poetry and how it differs from traditional types (see p. 40); Ezra Pound's tenets concerning imagist poetry and Vorticism (p. 41); and Allen Tate's moralistic investigations, including his treatment of Poe's experimental emphasis on unity, intensity, brevity, effect, and aesthetic symbolism (pp. 41–42). Note that this emphasis was characteristic of French Symbolism, which, of course, was later to influence William Butler Yeats, especially through his friendship with Arthur Symonds. Finally, we point to the wide-ranging critical attitudes of T. S. Eliot (pp. 42–45).

Finally, how would the so-called New Critics evaluate "The Second Coming" and Yeats' ability as a poet? Ransom observed that in Yeats' later poetry, of which "The Second Coming" is a part, we see him at his best. Specifically, in "Yeats and His Symbols," Ransom stated, "I concur as instantly as any other critic in the judgment that he had by nature the finest poetic gift in our time, and by technical discipline one of the subtlest and surest instruments in the history of English poetry."[30]

However, I. A. Richards, in *Science and Poetry*, noting Yeats' absorption with the occult tradition, wrote,

[30] Ransom, *op. cit.*, p. 95.

Now he turns to a world of symbolic phantas-magoria about which he is desperately uncertain. He is uncertain because he has adopted as a technique of inspiration the use of trance, of dissociated phases of consciousness, and the revelations given in these dissociated states are insufficiently connected with normal experience.[31]

Such a view puts us in mind of Tate's contention that Poe was, while deeply rooted in uniquely American culture, somehow dissociated from the kind of sensibility which "keeps us in the world." Donald Davidson, in his "Yeats and the Centaur," praises Yeats for his use of myth and legend (Yeats had declared, "all art should be a Centaur finding in the popular lore its back and strong legs"). Yet Davidson reluctantly reaches the conclusion that, as helpful as Yeats' use and development of such lore may be, it often fails in the literary dimension because it is too delicate and, one would assume, too often obscure to be functionally absorbed by readers.[32] Yet if the function of criticism is to "promote the understanding and enjoyment of literature,"[33] as Eliot remarked as late as 1956, then we must assume that Yeats' faults do not necessarily preclude his merits, but rather, they challenge our efforts to understand them and to discriminate between them and his more obvious merits. In this way we find what is truly praiseworthy.

Through "The Second Coming," we can see that Yeats was a master of his tradition as well as a kind of "poet-seer" who endeavored to look into the future. If his interest was, indeed, in the past, perhaps this was because he desired to be aware of not what is dead, to paraphrase Eliot again, but of what is still living. Yeats, then, synthesized the past, present, and future in his work. Small wonder that he was not always completely successful—and what poet is? Any assessment of his value must involve the height of his achievement as well as the depth of his failures, and the vague outlines of his gyres, myths, beasts, demons, and gods, and the riddle of what they mean.

Psychological, archetypal, and mythopoeic approaches, as we have seen in Chapter 8, may be brought to bear upon the work and the artist. The mythopoeist, as well as the psychologist and archetypalist, sees the poet and his production wholistically; hence, he considers divisions between the two to be artificial barriers. One of Yeats' biographers, A. N. Jeffares, in his Foreword to *W. B. Yeats: Man and Poet*, wrote,

> He drew much of his material from his life; his emotions coloured all that he read; and almost all that he wrote was subjective. *The man and the artist cannot be separated*; his life and his writings are complementary and interwoven to an unusual degree. His life throws light on his works and his works reflect that life. Therefore, some knowledge of his life and background is necessary for the better understanding of his poetry [italics added].[34]

In this statement may lie insights into how a poetic genius such as Yeats creates—one of the major concerns of the literary psychologist.

We recall from the previous chapter that much of the creative process is not conscious. Indeed, a poem may arise out of some "burden of anxiety and fear . . . something *negative*."[35] It can be likened to "a morbid secretion, like the pearl in the oyster," and it may come into being when one is "rather out of health"[36] Remarking on Yeats' philosophy of the occult as a kind of "necessary plaything," Fraser observed that Yeats possessed "a powerful and distressed creative mind."[37] Suggesting an inner conflict, Austin Warren, in

---

[31] I. A. Richards, *Science and Poetry* (New York: W. W. Norton, 1926), pp. 86–87.
[32] Donald Davidson, "Yeats and the Centaur," *The Southern Review*, VII, 3 (Winter 1942), 510–615. Later published in *The Permanence of Yeats, op. cit.*, pp. 284–285.
[33] Eliot, *The Frontiers of Criticism* (1956), p. 16.

[34] A. N. Jeffares, *W. B. Yeats: Man and Poet* (London: Routledge and Kegan Paul, 1949), p. vii.
[35] T. S. Eliot, *The Use of Poetry* (London: Faber & Faber, 1933), p. 144.
[36] A. E. Housman, *The Name and Nature of Poetry* (New York: Macmillan, 1933), reprinted in A. E. Housman, *Selected Prose*, ed. John Carter (Cambridge, Eng.: Cambridge University Press, 1962), p. 194.
[37] Fraser, *op. cit.*, p. 17.

"William Butler Yeats: The Religion of a Poet," stated that Yeats, after he had absorbed Darwin and Huxley, underwent a kind of "Pascalian antithesis"—a continuing argument between the "head" and the "heart."[38]

What of Yeats' concepts and uses of archetypal patterns? Kenneth Burke, in his essay "On Motivations in Yeats," wrote that Yeats utilizes "traditional psychoanalytic lore."[39] He assumed that Yeatsian symbolism, as Yeats himself wrote numerous times, "is derived from the Great Memory that is the common pool of all mankind." In "The Second Coming," Yeats converted the term "Great Memory" to "*Spiritus Mundi*," otherwise known as "*Anima Mundi*" (the latter term attributed to Henry More), which Yeats defined as "a general storehouse of images which have ceased to be a property of any personality or spirit."[40] In a 1901 essay entitled "Magic," Yeats stated that our memories shift along their outer edges, so to speak, but that they are part of one Great Memory—the memory of Nature. All this reflects the essence of what we earlier examined in our study of archetypes, and it may partially explain how Yeats, to use Freud's early expression, is able "to carry us with him in such a way to arouse emotions in us of which we thought ourselves perhaps not even capable."[41]

In the light of one of the basic Freudian psychoanalytical theories, the "libido-theory of neuroses," let us examine a Yeatsian commentary upon the "gyre":

the circling is always narrowing or spreading, because one movement or other is always the stronger. In other words, *the human soul is always moving outward into the objective* world or inward into itself. . . . The

man, in whom the movement inward is stronger than the movement outward, the man who sees all reflected within himself, the subjective man, reaches the narrow end of a gyre at death [compare Freud's mortido theory]. . . . The objective man on the other hand, whose gyre moves outward, receives at this moment the revelation, not of himself seen from within for that is impossible to objective man, but of himself as if he were somebody else [perhaps the projection of ego into the libido-object of creative art?]. [Italics added.][42]

Relating Freud's 1917 essay "One of the Difficulties of Psycho-Analysis" to Yeats' gyral vision, the literary psychologist might say that the spiraling inward of the subjective man as conceived by Yeats is akin to narcissism as conceived by Freud, whereas the movement outward in gyral imagery is related to the ego-libido progression from ego to object love. Just as Yeats sees both ideas of outward widening motion or inward narrowing motion—with intensity of consciousnesses themselves dependent upon the degree of contrast—Freud observed, "A certain amount of libido is always retained in the ego"[43] (ego-libido), although much may go out (object-libido). Freud also believed in the necessity of a "full mobility" of the libido between the ego and externalized objects, people, or concepts. Both theories are dynamic analogies with generally similar end results. The inward, narrowing motion suggests narcissistic self-absorption, which is self-destructive. The outward, widening motion suggests keeping the ego open to external objects—allowing it to exert creative, rather than destructive, energies, and produce in the process constructive accomplishments of various forms.[44]

Similarly, one may find many kinships between one of Freud's earlier essays, "The Relation of the Poet to Day-Dreaming" (1908), and Yeats' admitted methods of composition. Yeats believed,

[38] Warren, *op. cit.*, p. 233.
[39] Kenneth Burke, "On Motivations in Yeats," *The Southern Review*, VII, 3 (Winter 1942), 547–561. Later published in *The Permanence of Yeats, op. cit.*, pp. 254–255.
[40] *Variorum, op. cit.*, p. 822; Jeffares, *op. cit.*, p. 209.
[41] Sigmund Freud, "The Relation of the Poet to Day-Dreaming," trans. I. F. Grant Duff, in *On Creativity and the Unconscious*, selected and with introduction and annotations by Benjamin Nelson (New York: Harper & Brothers, 1958), p. 44.

[42] *Variorum, op. cit.*, p. 824.
[43] Freud, "One of the Difficulties of Psycho-Analysis," trans. Joan Riviere, in *On Creativity and the Unconscious, op. cit.*, pp. 3–4.
[44] Students interested in this thesis may enjoy reading Erich Fromm's essay "The Creators and the Destroyers," *Saturday Review*, 47 (January 4, 1964), 22–25.

like Blake, that the world of dreams possessed a reality of its own—perhaps more genuine than the objective world of workaday reality. We know that Yeats deliberately attempted to suspend his conscious faculties to make himself more susceptible to the "subconscious."[45]

Wish-fulfillment, Freud believed, is the major theme of fantasies. He believed that man's dreams tend to be ambitious, women's erotic, but that both kinds of fantasies are often united. Many men have performed their ambitious deeds for a woman, "at whose feet" they lay their "triumphs." Thus, the literary psychologist may search for such a generative force in Yeats poetry as Maud Gonne, the beautiful woman whom he loved deeply and long, even turning to political activity, at least partly to win her praise. She was the inspiration of many of his poems. A sketch of her history has already been treated in a sociocultural context, including her identification with the "Rose" poems and the play *The Countess Cathleen* (1892). But Yeats alluded to her as late as 1939 in "The Circus Animals' Desertion," in which a "Lion and woman" image appears, along with an "embittered heart" and a first-person reference to

I, starved for the bosom of his faery bride?

And then a counter truth filled out its play,
The Countess Cathleen was the name I gave it;
She, pity-crazed, had given her soul away,
But masterful Heaven had intervened to save it.
I thought my dear must her own soul destroy,
So did fanaticism and hate enslave it,
And this brought forth a dream and soon enough
This dream itself had all my thought and love.[46]

Here we have, then, early and late artistic productions inspired by Maud Gonne or, at least, alluding to her. Applying another Freudian principle—wish-fulfillment—the literary psychologist may see an application to "The Second Coming" of

past, present, and future "threaded as it were, on the string of the wish that runs through them all."[47] Recapitulating Yeats' circumstances just prior to the composition of "The Second Coming" in 1919, one may see something of the "present" out of which the poem emerged. Though we cannot know all of Yeats' actual movements and motivations at the time, we may well know enough to see a tension between his ego and libido-object. The literary psychologist would see Maud Gonne as the "woman in some corner of the picture,"[48] to use Freud's term.

Thus, the background of his long romance with Maud Gonne and related matters would be pertinent source materials for a psychological study of the poem. The conditions surrounding its composition extended far back in time. He had met the famed beauty in Dublin in 1888 when he was twenty-three, and in 1919, when he was fifty-four, he published these lines in *The Wild Swans at Coole*:

Young men no longer suddenly catch their breath
When you are passing.[49]

He first proposed to her in 1891 in Dublin. Caught up in violent anti-English hatred and Irish movements for nationalism, she desired Yeats' friendship, and for a time she converted him into a kind of political activist, although he could not share her radical views. Much to his disappointment, she married, in 1903, John MacBride—an Irish hero against the English in the Boer War. Yeats thought the marriage a poor match, and although she later separated from MacBride, her Roman Catholic faith would not permit her to divorce him and marry Yeats, even if she had wanted to. After MacBride's execution in 1916, Yeats went to Normandy, where Maud was living out of the range of English authority, and there, he proposed again. She refused. Then, strangely, Yeats found himself falling in love with Maud's attractive

---

45 W. B. Yeats, *Essays* (New York: Macmillan, 1924). See also Jeffares, *op. cit.*, p. 209; Freud, *op. cit.*

46 William Butler Yeats, "The Circus Animals' Desertion," *Last Poems and Two Plays* (Dublin: Cuala Press, 1939); *Variorum*, pp. 629–630. Also see Jeffares, *op. cit.* p. 71.

47 Freud, "The Relation of the Poet to Day-Dreaming," *op. cit.*, pp. 47–49.

48 *Ibid.*, p. 48.

49 In "Broken Dreams," *Variorum, op. cit.*, p. 355.

young daughter by adoption, Iseult. The next year, in 1917, after receiving Maud's permission, he proposed to Iseult, who (as Maud had warned him she might) had difficulty making up her mind. Even so, Yeats managed to get the family back to England, but he could not secure clearance from the authorities for Maud to return to Ireland. In September 1917, Yeats experienced a crisis on the boat when Iseult would not make her decision. The strain was nearly too much for a bachelor in his fifties who was about to change his whole way of life. But marriage he was determined upon. He informed Iseult he knew another lovely girl who would marry him, and the next month, in October 1917, he did marry Miss Hyde-Lees. Yeats' feverish quest for marriage may suggest, on a broad level, a search for some kind of stability, or for love and wisdom, but its frantic circumstances indicate a desperate grasping for order within a life of chaos.[50] In psychological terms, this would indicate a loss of ego control and an anarchy of the libido, which must have always been especially strong in Yeats.

If we accept Freud's thesis of an event of the present making "a strong impression on the writer," it would seem that Maud Gonne's "second coming" into Yeats' life would have been a sufficient causal agent to have "stirred up a memory of an earlier experience."[51] If Yeats' had indeed retreated far enough into his old memories, he may have stirred up a sexual fantasy for the Maud Gonne about whom, projecting his ego outward, he had often dreamed, and he may have then transmitted those dreams into poetry.

Within such a Freudian context, several images in "The Second Coming" take on sexual overtones. For example, the title may indicate, on one level, a significant "second" meeting, or on another, sexual orgasm; line 1, possibly, sexual intercourse; line 2, the lack of personal control or mastery of the ego over powerful unconscious desires; lines 3–5, a freely associated identity with the disintegrating world of order and propriety; line 6, a conscious awareness of guilt, the source of which may still be disguised, representing either the "ceremony" of his recent marriage, or his child about to be born, or both; lines 7–8, castigation of himself as "the best," perhaps a condemnation of Madame MacBride in the role of temptress as "the worst," although she still exudes for him her typical "passionate intensity." Note that in *The Countess Cathleen* the thinly disguised Irish heroine had bartered her soul to Satan, only to conquer even him, thus becoming a kind of mythic Irish savior.

Although this line of development represents, at best, only a caricature of Freudian analysis, the remaining part of the poem may be treated in much the same way. If we pursue the approach further, the final wish-fulfillment may be easy to explain in psychological terms, if one can imagine that Yeats' guilt and disillusionment in himself and in Madame MacBride were deep enough. The "rocking cradle" (perhaps the as-yet-unborn and innocent child) is an antipode to the probable consequences of this loss of control, this trammeling on innocence, this identity with disorder, chaos, and Dionysian revelry, and finally, to the ultimate destruction of the world. Why would Yeats choose such an antithetical image within the context of such annihilative violence? The answer may indicate Yeats' Protestant fear of breaking the Mosaic law—a real fear, deep in his unconscious, but functioning in such a way as to dominate his ego. Only the traditional summoning to judgment at the end of the world can lift the burden of what the ego can interpret only as tormenting shame. At this point, then, libido gives way to mortido, and life to death.

Of course, the Freudian theory suffers, as Freud himself noted, from being "too schematic."[52] In addition, it leaves out too much that is known, and it consists of projections with insubstantial support. An artist functions consciously, too—

---

[50] For these and further details, see Jeffares' eighth chapter, *op. cit.*, "The Married Philosopher," pp. 186–213 *passim*.
[51] Freud, "The Relation of the Poet to Day-Dreaming," *op. cit.*, p. 52.

[52] *Ibid.*, p. 52.

in his daily problem solving, in his relations with his family and friends, and in meeting reality situations. Nevertheless, the example may serve as an illustration of the Freudian principle of the past-present-future phenomenon, culminating in wish-fulfillment, applied to "The Second Coming."

But the literary psychologist would not stop here. In the effort to understand formative forces in a poet's work, he would not hesitate to go beyond that work, into others. Several Yeatsian specialists have noted similarities between "The Second Coming" and "A Prayer for my Daughter." In *Between the Lines*, Jon Stallworthy observed the following:

> Only two or three months elapsed between the writing of "The Second Coming" and "A Prayer for my Daughter", *and not for nothing did Yeats have them printed next to each other.* Both, it will be seen, stem from a mood of depression brought on by the First World War. . . . The two poems have also a "cradle" and a theme in common. "The ceremony of innocence is drowned" is an idea explored at greater length in "A Prayer for my Daughter"[53] [italics added].

In the phrase "ceremony of innocence," Ellmann also saw a relationship to the subsequent poem, "A Prayer for my Daughter." Ellmann felt that a common theme was that ceremony is the soul's way of "protecting itself against the vulgarity of the streets; once ceremony is obliterated, the best men have nothing to hold them above the tide."[54]

On February 26, 1919, Yeats' daughter, Anne Butler Yeats, was born. Not long after, perhaps motivated by his daughter's aura of innocence in addition to the weight of responsibility and the magic joy that such an event can bring to a father, he saw the world anew. In June he composed "A Prayer for my Daughter." A summary of pertinent lines from the poem and of comments upon it such as the literary psychologist might tend to make may offer further insights into feelings, ideas, and themes in "The Second Coming."

[53] Stallworthy, *Between the Lines*, op. cit., pp. 24–25.
[54] Ellmann, op. cit., p. 259.

After "praying for an hour," Yeats' persona sees into the future—a time which, for his persona of "The Second Coming," was blocked with a beast and a problematical birth and immersed in fear and prophetic destruction. This time, the persona is

Imagining in excited reverie
That the future years had come,
Dancing to a frenzied drum
Out of the murderous innocence of the sea.

He prays that his daughter may be lovely, but not "beautiful overmuch." Then follow allusions to Helen of Troy and the foolish marriage of Venus to Vulcan, as well as thoughts about the folly of some women in marrying into poverty and sorrow, the virtues of courtesy, the nature of charm and real love, and the balance that must be maintained between merriment and the inevitable quarrels in the relationships of lovers. Then, perhaps reflecting upon himself and his own marriage, Yeats writes,

Yet many, that have played the fool
For beauty's very self, has charm made wise,
And many a poor man that has roved,
Loved and thought himself beloved,
From a glad kindness cannot take his eyes.

His own "sort of beauty," he notes, "has dried up of late," though, and behind the following lines, perhaps, are thoughts of Maud Gonne—his arguments with her and his relationship to her:

If there's no hatred in a mind
Assault and battery of the wind
Can never tear the linnet from the leaf.

An intellectual hatred is the worst,
So let her think opinions are accursed.
Have I not seen the loveliest woman born
Out of the mouth of Plenty's horn,
Because of her opinionated mind
Barter that horn and every good
By quiet natures understood
For an old bellows full of angry wind?

The soul may recover "radical innocence" when "all hatred" is "driven hence." One may find happiness through enlightened self-discovery, ful-fillment, and personal responsibility. He prays for his daughter's marriage to be "accustomed" and "ceremonious," for

> . . . arrogance and hatred are the wares
> Peddled in the thoroughfares.
> How but in custom and in ceremony
> Are innocence and beauty born?[55]

The intentional and affective fallacies considered under New Critical approaches aside, the literary psychologist will probe the whole man-artist-production matrix to illuminate ultimate meanings. Here, for example, he may well interpret the latter poem as a thematic sequel to "The Second Coming," and while the New Critic may con-clude that the organic unity of the earlier poem is an "ontological" entity, self-contained and worthy unto itself, the psychological approach demands a larger view. While the *intrinsic* approach would emphasize the pessimism of the earlier poem, the *extrinsic* may well point to the affirmation of the latter.

Archetypal and mythopoeic aspects of Yeats' work are profound and, like psychological approaches, could easily form the basis of a whole book. Alex Zwerdling, in *Yeats and the Heroic Ideal*, conjectures that Yeats "took upon himself what he considered the all-important task of re-educating the world in appreciation of the heroic individual, so that the broken circle could be closed once again." Such a theme is evident in "The Second Coming," for in it he depicts a world without a mythic and heroic ideal—a world in which God is dead and the fear of death is metaphorically represented as a "rough beast" that "Slouches towards Bethlehem to be born." According to Zwerdling, Yeats desired to establish once again "an icon now tarnished and all but forgotten: the icon of the hero."[56] A mythopoeic interpretation of "The Second Coming," then, would seem to indicate that a coherent world is

impossible without heroes—in individual life, religion, or government. The "centre" of such existence "cannot hold," but will end in a bloody tide of destruction and "mere anarchy." Yeats found his heroes in such myths as those of Cuchulain (the Irish warrior), Oedipus, and Antigone.

William York Tindall, in *W. B. Yeats*, stated that the gyral movement, historically spiraling for two millennia, has its base in mythos—specifically, in the classic narrative of Leda and the Swan, a union of "girl and bird [god]," and also in the Christian story of "Mary and the pigeon [Holy Ghost] for our cycle."[57]

Northrop Frye, in *Fables of Identity*, examined traditional mythology and folklore in Yeats' poetry as well as the poet's use of systems of metaphysical spiritualism. Glancing once again at "The Second Coming," one can see archetypes, embedded in myths, functioning in cycles. The archetypes include blood, ceremony, revelation, rebirth, conflict between generations and between ages, heaven-hell patterns, Edenic innocence, the loss of innocence, the devil, and God. But there seems to be no functional hero. Why? Perhaps the mythopoeist, along with the literary psychol-ogist and archetypalist, would suggest that Yeats meant to have no hero—that in this segment of his poetry he desired to dramatize the prospect of a world without a hero and only hint at the vague outlines of an antihero. And, as has been suggested, all three would sense that the poem is an incomplete one. The mythopoeist might presume that the hero is merely "offstage," about to appear in another poem. Like the historical critic, yet on another level and with other intentions, the mythopoeist would go on to seek out a larger context consistent with a mythic perspective into which he could fit the poem.

Plutarch tells the story of the ancient King Scilurus who, on his deathbed, was preparing to

---

[55] *Variorum*, *op. cit.*, pp. 403–406. Note Jeffares' treatment of the poem, *op. cit.*, p. 213.

[56] Zwerdling, *op. cit.*, pp. 22–23.

[57] William York Tindall, *W. B. Yeats* (New York: Columbia University Press, 1966), p. 28.

leave "four-score" sons surviving him. He asked his sons to gather around him, which they did. He gave them a bundle of arrows, requesting each to break the bundle. Not a one could break the whole bundle, though all tried. When the bundle of arrows was returned, the father drew out the arrows one by one, easily breaking each one, although his strength was that of a dying man. Thus, he taught his sons that if they remained united in their stance they would be strong; but if they allowed themselves to be divided, they would fall.

In the Introduction to this book, we commented upon the reasons that so many critical approaches to poetry have developed—the search for order, for example, or the illusion of critical exactitude. The analogy of the critic-reader to a prism, the poem to the sun, and the resulting spectrum of colors to human experiences varying in depth, hue, and meaning, seems appropriate to repeat here. For the ultimate meaning of a poem is totalistic—at times clear, at times subtle—just as the light streaming through the prism fans out into a whole spectrum of colors at times clearly perceptible, but at times subtle, as, for example, when the violet edges blend into the orange. Approaches to poetry, too, are at times distinctive and at times overlapping.

Three or two or even one approach will be helpful in getting at the being and meaning of poetry. When we say that a critic-reader is narrow or has a limited vision, what we mean is that he overzealously follows a single approach or rigidly adheres to only two or three approaches, creating for himself not real understanding, but a partial comprehension, and, to that extent, his knowledge is self-deluding. In mistaking the part for the whole, he denies himself the fullest understanding and enjoyment of poetry.

In *Muse of Fire: Approaches to Poetry*, we have endeavored to introduce the reader to at least eight colors of the critical spectrum: classical and Renaissance approaches; neoclassical and early Romantic approaches; basic Romantic approaches; historical and humanistic approaches; socio-cultural approaches; New Critical approaches; psychological, archetypal, and mythopoeic approaches; and a synthesis of approaches. In doing so, we have attempted to describe something of the depth, varying hues, texture, and nuances of each color of the spectrum. We have approached poetry, moving historically from Plato to the present, with a pronounced emphasis on nineteenth- and twentieth-century contributions to literary criticism, and the heaviest emphasis, certainly, upon a synthesis, or a unity of all approaches—the last implemented in the analysis of a specific poem.

PART TWO / *The Poetry*

1. Childhood and Loss of Innocence

My green, graceful bones fill the air
With sleeping birds. Alone, alone
And with them I move gently.
I move at the heart of the world.

[James Dickey, *In the Tree House at Night*]

Laurence Josephs

Children in the Park

". . . said the Gryphon: "I went to the classical master,
though. He was an old crab, he was."
"I never went to him," the Mock Turtle said with a sigh.
"He taught Laughing and Grief, they used to say."
"So he did, so he did," said the Gryphon, sighing in his
turn; and both creatures hid their faces in their paws."

Lewis Carroll

Behind the meaning of each day, not meaning
    day,
Some live whose every element is sunny;
Whose smooth vocation grows, out-branching
    play,
Whose victories are kind, whose losses funny.

True to the seed they hold, they spring from
    children;
The whole sky sings around them like a lyre.
The flashing light of their transplanted acumen
Contains the cognate ratio of spark to fire.

They learn by learning while their mothers sit
Inweaving daytime placidly about their lives;   10
They watch their children change; they never
    think of it
As an especial good, but since it gives

Its growth to praise, they welcome their own
    peace.
Now in the world beyond them, see their boys
Who never turn to need them, but increase
In bravery and wisdom, move from toys

To girls, to money, houses, weapons, charts;
Who then forget the pleasure park they had to
    love,
Correctly substituting mirrors for their hearts,
Who learn to prove, but never to improve;   20

Forgetting there were times when to their
    clouded eyes
The gravel of the paths seemed gold or silver.
That once they glimpsed a running friend and
    felt surprise
At what they felt, and wept when it was over.

(*1963*)

Arna Bontemps

Close Your Eyes!

Go through the gates with closed eyes.
Stand erect and let your black face front the west.
Drop the axe and leave the timber where it lies;
A woodman on the hill must have his rest.

Go where leaves are lying brown and wet.
Forget her warm arms and her breast who
 mothered you,
And every face you ever loved forget.
Close your eyes; walk bravely through.
(1963)

Jack Gilbert

And She Waiting

Always I have been afraid
of this moment:
of the return to love
with perspective.

I see these breasts
with the others.
I touch this mouth
and the others.
I command this heart
as the others.   10
I know exactly
what to say.

Innocence has gone
out of me.
The song.
The song, suddenly,
has gone out
of me.
(1962)

John Ciardi

The Dolls

Night after night forever the dolls lay stiff
by the children's dreams. On the goose-feathers
 of the rich,
on the straw of the poor, on the gypsy ground—

wherever the children slept, dolls have been
 found
in the subsoil of the small loves stirred again
by the Finders After Everything. Down lay
the children by their hanks and twists. Night
 after night
grew over imagination. The fuzzies shed, the
 bright
buttons fell out of the heads, arms ripped, and
 down
through goose-feathers, straw, and the gypsy
 ground   10
the dolls sank, and some—the fuzziest and most
 loved—
changed back to string and dust, and the dust
 moved
dream-puffs round the Finders' boots as they dug,
sieved, brushed, and came on a little clay dog,
and a little stone man, and a little bone girl, that
 had kept
their eyes wide open forever, while all the
 children slept.
(1961)

James Dickey

In the Tree House at Night

And now the green household is dark.
The half-moon completely is shining
On the earth-lighted tops of the trees.
To be dead, a house must be still.
The floor and the walls wave me slowly;
I am deep in them over my head.
The needles and pine cones about me

Are full of small birds at their roundest,
Their fists without mercy gripping
Hard down through the tree to the roots 10
To sing back at light when they feel it.
We lie here like angels in bodies,
My brothers and I, one dead,
The other asleep from much living,

In mid-air huddled beside me.
Dark climbed to us here as we climbed
Up the nails I have hammered all day
Through the sprained, comic rungs of the ladder
Of broom handles, crate slats, and laths
Foot by foot up the trunk to the branches   20
Where we came out at last over lakes

Of leaves, of fields disencumbered of earth
That move with the moves of the spirit.
Each nail that sustains us I set here;
Each nail in the house is now steadied
By my dead brother's huge, freckled hand.
Through the years, he has pointed his hammer
Up into these limbs, and told us

That we must ascend, and all lie here.
Step after step he has brought me,   30
Embracing the trunk as his body,
Shaking its limbs with my heartbeat,
Till the pine cones danced without wind
And fell from the branches like apples.
In the arm-slender forks of our dwelling

I breathe my live brother's light hair.
The blanket around us becomes
As solid as stone, and it sways.
With all my heart, I close
The blue, timeless eye of my mind.   40
Wind springs, as my dead brother smiles
And touches the tree at the root;

A shudder of joy runs up
The trunk; the needles tingle;
One bird uncontrollably cries.
The wind changes round, and I stir
Within another's life. Whose life?
Who is dead? Whose presence is living?
When may I fall strangely to earth,

Who am nailed to this branch by a spirit?   50
Can two bodies make up a third?
To sing, must I feel the world's light?
My green, graceful bones fill the air
With sleeping birds. Alone, alone
And with them I move gently.
I move at the heart of the world.
                                    (1961)

Thom Gunn

Innocence

for Tony White

He ran the course and as he ran he grew,
And smelt his fragrance in the field. Already,
Running he knew the most he ever knew,
The egotism of a healthy body.

Ran into manhood, ignorant of the past:
Culture of guilt and guilt's vague heritage,
Self-pity and the soul; what he possessed
Was rich, potential, like the bud's tipped rage.

The Corps developed, it was plain to see,
Courage, endurance, loyalty and skill   10
To a morale firm as morality,
Hardening him to an instrument, until

The finitude of virtues that were there
Bodied within the swarthy uniform
A compact innocence, child-like and clear,
No doubt could penetrate, no act could harm.
                                    (1961)

John Ciardi

In Ego with Us All

In ego with us all, behind the world and Mother,
in the woods behind the house, where the old
          well is
for everyone to remember, I remember
the stone-green water's far-down breathing over
the lead-gold-emerald frog that shines there
when the light goes high enough to find him.

It was the Secret Place. Jesse James came there,
Babe Ruth, Charlie Chaplin, Captain Nemo.
And when the light fell deepest, Pa came smiling:
"See, I'm not dead: show me what's in the well."
Then how the frog sang up from the stones and
       water,   11
sweet as canaries, and golden in our look!

Till a bell clanged it to lead. "All right, I'm
       coming!"
It was The Lonely Place, bell-emptied in a wink,
even the Frog gone, which was again only
the round stone I had dropped, both arms
       extended
over the center to aim it true and forever.
And counted all my nights to the sound of the
       splash.

And never heard it. In ego with us all
I think there is no hearing it. It is dropped,   20
it lies there, it changes when the light lets it.
But no one hears it hit. Is it forever
the bell clangs just at that instant?
Are the clang and the splash one sound neither

Father nor Mother, but both? I do not know
what there is of us in that well that dreamed me
through light and dark. The thought is years
       from the thought,
and our lives are not a thing chosen but a thing
that happens to us. Out of that well, perhaps.
Out of it or another impossibility, certainly.   30

I have let go my tears for less than this.
Even at movies, damning myself for a fool,
I have leaked sentiment for dead dolls.
Who are you? Have you a drier eye?—
In ego with us all, I confess all:
there is no world but what falls in that well,

sings out when the light goes high enough,
       sinks off
to slime and stone between. And the thought
lies years from the thought. The Lonely Place

is the ruins of The Secret Place. The True is
       quiet: 40
leaves nudge it, grasshoppers fizz in it, water
       laps it,
the singing comes up from the well—the voice
       of Quiet.

And years from all, in ego with us all, as I have
       shed
with all of us, damning for all of us, the wrong
tears for not-enough reason, I will sit tending
the silence coldly told of what tears are true
in ego with us all, in the secret place
a noise can shatter, and a life not mend.

             (*1959*)

Denise Levertov

The Quarry Pool

Between town and the
old house, an inn—
the Half-Way House.
So far one could ride, I remember,

the rest was an uphill walk,
a mountain lane with
steep banks and sweet
hedges, half walls of

gray rock. Looking
again at this looking-glass face   10
unaccountably changed in a week,
three weeks, a month,

I think without thinking of
Half-Way House. Is it
the thought that this far
I've driven at ease, as in a bus,

a country bus where one could talk to the driver?
Now on foot towards the village;
the dust clears, silence
draws in around one. I hear 20
the rustle and hum of the fields: alone.

It must be the sense
of essential solitude that chills me
looking into my eyes.
I should remember

the old house at the walk's ending,
a square place with a courtyard,
granaries, netted strawberry-beds,
a garden that was many

gardens, each one 30
a world hidden from the
next by leaves, enlaced trees,
fern-hairy walls, gilly-flowers.

I should see, making
a strange face at myself,
nothing to fear in the thought of
Half-Way House—

the place one got down
to walk—. What is
this shudder, this 40
dry mouth?

Think, please, of the quarry pool,
the garden's furthest
garden, of your childhood's
joy in its solitude.

(*1958*)

David Ferry

The Milkmaid

A practised gesture of her practised hand,
So ivory, and so bejeweled with finger tip,
Made all our party put on her livery,
Seeking to pay her lip service, singing her
Songs she had no mind to hear from us.

All brilliant baldheads in our row gave back
Her radiance, so that her motions were our wit,
Reflections of the notions in our skulls,
Which beat with poems to her practised skills.
We made a lady of her in our poems. 10

She was a milkmaid once, whose head we'd
        turned,
That, turning, in the mirror saw itself
Under its truest guise, faithfullest aspect.
We brought her to the city in our songs,
Mistress most wise of the city we brought her to.

Alone, released from us, her mirror told
The same tale twice, the lesson she'd learned well.
She glittered in her eye, her buttery skin
Turned satin, silk, or damask, ivory, pearl,
All that we'd sung of her in our amorous songs. 20

O brave milkmaid, we cried, as she stepped out,
Dressed in her borrowed finery, flouting us,
The nose turned high that country suns had
        peeled,
O brave milkmaid, be brave when finery tatters!
You are not wise as us in these city matters!

(*1957*)

Lawrence Ferlinghetti

"The pennycandystore beyond the El"

The pennycandystore beyond the El
is where I first
           fell in love
                  with unreality
Jellybeans glowed in the semi-gloom
of that september afternoon
A cat upon the counter moved among
                  the licorice sticks
        and tootsie rolls
    and Oh Boy Gum   10

Outside the leaves were falling as they died

A wind had blown away the sun

A girl ran in
Her hair was rainy
Her breasts were breathless in the little room

Outside the leaves were falling
        and they cried
             Too soon! too soon!
                (*1955*)

Dylan Thomas

Fern Hill

Now as I was young and easy under the apple
    boughs
About the lilting house and happy as the grass
    was green,
    The night above the dingle starry,
      Time let me hail and climb
    Golden in the heydays of his eyes,
And honoured among wagons I was prince
    of the apple towns
And once below a time I lordly had the trees
    and leaves
      Trail with daisies and barley
    Down the rivers of the windfall light.

And as I was green and carefree, famous among
    the barns   10
About the happy yard and singing as the farm
    was home,
    In the sun that is young once only,
      Time let me play and be
    Golden in the mercy of his means,
And green and golden I was huntsman and
    herdsman, the calves
Sang to my horn, the foxes on the hills barked
    clear and cold,
      And the sabbath rang slowly
    In the pebbles of the holy streams.

All the sun long it was running, it was lovely,
    the hay
Fields high as the house, the tunes from the
    chimneys, it was air   20
  And playing, lovely and watery
      And fire green as grass.
  And nightly under the simple stars
As I rode to sleep the owls were bearing the
    farm away,
All the moon long I heard, blessed among stables,
    the night-jars
  Flying with the ricks, and the horses
    Flashing into the dark.

And then to awake, and the farm, like a
    wanderer white
With the dew, come back, the cock on his
    shoulder: it was all
  Shining, it was Adam and maiden,   30
    The sky gathered again
  And the sun grew round that very day.
So it must have been after the birth of the simple
    light
In the first, spinning place, the spellbound horses
    walking warm
  Out of the whinnying green stable
    On to the fields of praise.

And honoured among foxes and pheasants by
    the gay house
Under the new made clouds and happy as the
    heart was long,
  In the sun born over and over,
    I ran my heedless ways,   40
  My wishes raced through the house high hay
And nothing I cared, at my sky blue trades, that
    time allows
In all his tuneful turning so few and such
    morning songs
  Before the children green and golden
    Follow him out of grace,

Nothing I cared, in the lamb white days, that
    time would take me
Up to the swallow thronged loft by the shadow
    of my hand,

In the moon that is always rising,
    Nor that riding to sleep
  I should hear him fly with the high fields   50
And wake to the farm forever fled from the
    childless land.
Oh as I was young and easy in the mercy of his
    means,
    Time held me green and dying
    Though I sang in my chains like the sea.

                        (1946)

Richard Eberhart

The Soul Longs to Return Whence It Came

I drove up to the graveyard, which
Used to frighten me as a boy,
When I walked down the river past it,
And evening was coming on. I'd make sure
I came home from the woods early enough.
I drove in, I found the place, I
Left the motor running. My eyes hurried,
To recognize the great oak tree
On the little slope, among the stones.
It was a high day, a crisp day,   10
The cleanest kind of Autumn day,
With brisk intoxicating air, a
Little wind that frisked, yet there was
Old age in the atmosphere, nostalgia,
The subtle heaviness of the Fall.
I stilled the motor. I walked a few paces;
It was good, the tree; the friendliness of it.
I touched it, I thought of the roots;
They would have pierced her seven years.
O all peoples! O mighty shadows!   20
My eyes opened along the avenue
Of tombstones, the common land of death.
Humiliation of all loves lost,
That might have had full meaning in any
Plot of ground, come, hear the silence,
See the quivering light. My mind worked
Almost imperceptibly, I

In the command, I the wilful ponderer.
I must have stood silent and thoughtful
There. A host of dry leaves   30
Danced on the ground in the wind.
They startled, they curved up from the ground,
There was a dry rustling, rattling.
The sun was motionless and brittle.
I felt the blood darken in my cheeks
And burn. Like running. My eyes
Telescoped on decay, I out of command.
Fear, tenderness, they seized me.
My eyes were hot, I dared not look
At the leaves. A pagan urge swept me.   40
Multitudes, O multitudes in one.
The urge of the earth, the titan
Wild and primitive lust, fused
On the ground of her grave.
I was a being of feeling alone.
I flung myself down on the earth
Full length on the great earth, full length,
I wept out the dark load of human love,
In pagan adoration I adored her.
I felt the actual earth of her.   50
Victor and victim of humility,
I closed in the wordless ecstasy
Of mystery: where there is no thought
But feeling lost in itself forever,
Profound, remote, immediate, and calm.
Frightened, I stood up, I looked about
Suspiciously, hurriedly (a rustling),
As if the sun, the air, the trees
Were human, might not understand.
I drew breath, it made a sound,   60
I stepped gingerly away. Then
The mind came like a fire, it
Tortured man, I thought of madness.
The mind will not accept the blood.
The sun and sky, the trees and grasses,
And the whispering leaves, took on
Their usual characters. I went away,
Slowly, tingling, elated, saying, saying,
Mother, Great Being, O Source of Life
To whom in wisdom we return,   70
Accept this humble servant evermore.

(*1940*)

D. H. Lawrence

Piano

Softly, in the dusk, a woman is singing to me;
Taking me back down the vista of years, till I see
A child sitting under the piano, in the boom of
      the tingling strings
And pressing the small, poised feet of a mother
      who smiles as she sings.

In spite of myself, the insidious mastery of song
Betrays me back, till the heart of me weeps to
      belong
To the old Sunday evenings at home, with
      winter outside
And hymns in the cozy parlor, the tinkling
      piano our guide.

So now it is vain for the singer to burst into
      clamor
With the great black piano appassionato. The
      glamour   10
Of childish days is upon me, my manhood is cast
Down in the flood of remembrance, I weep like
      a child for the past.

(*1934*)

John Crowe Ransom

Janet Waking

Beautifully Janet slept
Till it was deeply morning. She woke then
And thought about her dainty-feathered hen,
To see how it had kept.

One kiss she gave her mother,
Only a small one gave she to her daddy
Who would have kissed each curl of his shining
      baby;
No kiss at all for her brother.

"Old Chucky, old Chucky!" she cried,
Running across the world upon the grass   10
To Chucky's house, and listening. But alas,
Her Chucky had died.

It was a transmogrifying bee
Came droning down on Chucky's old bald head
And sat and put the poison. It scarcely bled,
But how exceedingly

And purply did the knot
Swell with the venom and communicate
Its rigor! Now the poor comb stood up straight   20
But Chucky did not.

So there was Janet
Kneeling on the wet grass, crying her brown hen
(Translated far beyond the daughters of men)
To rise and walk upon it.

And weeping fast as she had breath
Janet implored us, "Wake her from her sleep!"
And would not be instructed in how deep
Was the forgetful kingdom of death.

    (1927)

William Wordsworth

Ode on Intimations of Immortality from Recollections of Early Childhood

The Child is Father of the Man;
And I could wish my days to be
Bound each to each by natural piety.

I

There was a time when meadow, grove, and
    stream,
The earth, and every common sight,
    To me did seem
    Apparelled in celestial light,

The glory and the freshness of a dream.
It is not now as it hath been of yore;—
    Turn wheresoe'er I may,
    By night or day,
The things which I have seen I now can see no
    more.

II

    The Rainbow comes and goes,   10
    And lovely is the Rose.
    The Moon doth with delight
Look round her when the heavens are bare.
    Waters on a starry night
    Are beautiful and fair;
    The sunshine is a glorious birth;
    But yet I know, where'er I go,
That there hath past away a glory from the earth.

III

Now, while the birds thus sing a joyous song,
    And while the young lambs bound   20
    As to the tabor's sound,
To me alone there came a thought of grief:
A timely utterance gave that thought relief,
    And I again am strong:
The cataracts blow their trumpets from the
    steep;
No more shall grief of mine the season wrong;
I hear the Echoes through the mountains throng,
The Winds come to me from the fields of sleep,
    And all the earth is gay;
    Land and sea   30
    Give themselves up to jollity,
    And with the heart of May
    Doth every Beast keep holiday;—
    Thou Child of Joy,
Shout round me, let me hear thy shouts, thou
    happy Shepherd-boy!

IV

Ye blessèd Creatures, I have heard the call
    Ye to each other make; I see
The heavens laugh with you in your jubilee;
    My heart is at your festival,
    My head hath its coronal,   40

The fulness of your bliss, I feel—I feel it all.
    Oh evil day! if I were sullen
    While Earth herself is adorning,
        This sweet May-morning
    And the Children are culling
        On every side,
    In a thousand valleys far and wide,
    Fresh flowers; while the sun shines warm,
And the Babe leaps up on his Mother's arm:—
    I hear, I hear, with joy I hear!   50
    —But there's a Tree, of many, one,
A single Field which I have looked upon,
Both of them speak of something that is gone:
        The Pansy at my feet
        Doth the same tale repeat:
Whither is fled the visionary gleam?
Where is it now, the glory and the dream?

V

Our birth is but a sleep and a forgetting:
The Soul that rises with us, our life's Star,
    Hath had elsewhere its setting,   60
        And cometh from afar:
    Not in entire forgetfulness,
    And not in utter nakedness,
But trailing clouds of glory do we come
        From God, who is our home:
Heaven lies about us in our infancy!
Shades of the prison-house begin to close
        Upon the growing Boy
But He beholds the light, and whence it flows,
        He sees it in his joy;   70
The Youth, who daily farther from the east
    Must travel, still is Nature's Priest,
        And by the vision splendid
        Is on his way attended;
At length the Man perceives it die away,
And fade into the light of common day.

VI

Earth fills her lap with pleasures of her own;
Yearnings she hath in her own natural kind,
And, even with something of a Mother's mind,
        And no unworthy aim,   80
        The homely Nurse doth all she can

To make her Foster-child, her Inmate Man,
        Forget the glories he hath known,
And that imperial palace whence he came.

VII

Behold the Child among his new-born blisses,
A six years' Darling of a pigmy size!
See, where 'mid work of his own hand he lies,
Fretted by sallies of his mother's kisses,
With light upon him from his father's eyes!
See, at his feet, some little plan or chart,   90
Some fragment from his dream of human life,
Shaped by himself with newly-learned art;
        A wedding or a festival,
        A mourning or a funeral;
            And this hath now his heart,
        And unto this he frames his song:
            Then will he fit his tongue
To dialogues of business, love, or strife;
        But it will not be long
        Ere this be thrown aside,   100
        And with new joy and pride
The little Actor cons another part;
Filling from time to time his 'humorous stage'
With all the Persons, down to palsied Age,
That Life brings with her in her equipage;
        As if his whole vocation
        Were endless imitation.

VIII

Thou, whose exterior semblance doth belie
        Thy Soul's immensity;
Thou best Philosopher, who yet dost keep   110
Thy heritage, thou Eye among the blind,
That, deaf and silent, read'st the eternal deep,
Haunted for ever by the eternal mind,—
        Mighty Prophet! Seer blest!
        On whom those truths do rest,
Which we are toiling all our lives to find,
In darkness lost, the darkness of the grave;
Thou, over whom thy Immortality
Broods like the Day, a Master o'er a Slave,
A Presence which is not to be put by;   120
Thou little Child, yet glorious in the might
Of heaven-born freedom on thy being's height,

Why with such earnest pains dost thou provoke
The years to bring the inevitable yoke,
Thus blindly with thy blessedness at strife?
Full soon thy Soul shall have her earthly freight,
And custom lie upon thee with a weight,
Heavy as frost, and deep almost as life!

IX

    O joy! that in our embers
    Is something that doth live,   130
    That nature yet remembers
    What was so fugitive!
The thought of our past years in me doth breed
Perpetual benediction: not indeed
For that which is most worthy to be blest;
Delight and liberty, the simple creed
Of Childhood, whether busy or at rest,
With new-fledged hope still fluttering in his
      breast:—
    Not for these I raise
    The song of thanks and praise;   140
  But for those obstinate questionings
  Of sense and outward things,
  Fallings from us, vanishings;
  Blank misgivings of a Creature
Moving about in worlds not realised,
High instincts before which our mortal Nature
Did tremble like a guilty Thing surprised:
    But for those first affections,
    Those shadowy recollections,
    Which, be they what they may,   150
Are yet the fountain-light of all our day,
Are yet a master-light of all our seeing;
  Uphold us, cherish, and have power to make
Our noisy years seem moments in the being
Of the eternal Silence: truths that wake,
    To perish never:
Which neither listlessness, nor mad endeavour,
    Nor Man nor Boy,
Nor all that is at enmity with joy,
Can utterly abolish or destroy!   160
  Hence in a season of calm weather
    Though inland far we be,
Our Souls have sight of that immortal sea
    Which brought us hither,
    Can in a moment travel thither,

And see the Children sport upon the shore,
And hear the mighty waters rolling evermore.

X

Then sing, ye Birds, sing, sing a joyous song!
    And let the young Lambs bound
    As to the tabor's sound!   170
We in thought will join your throng,
    Ye that pipe and ye that play,
    Ye that through your hearts today
    Feel the gladness of the May!
What though the radiance which was once so
      bright
Be now for ever taken from my sight,
  Though nothing can bring back the hour
Of splendour in the grass, of glory in the flower;
    We will grieve not, rather find
    Strength in what remains behind;   180
    In the primal sympathy
    Which having been must ever be;
    In the soothing thoughts that spring
    Out of human suffering;
    In the faith that looks through death,
In years that bring the philosophic mind.

XI

And O, ye Fountains, Meadows, Hills, and
    Groves,
Forbode not any severing of our loves!
Yet in my heart of hearts I feel your might;
I only have relinquished one delight   190
To live beneath your more habitual sway.
I love the Brooks which down their channels fret,
Even more than when I tripped lightly as they;
The innocent brightness of a new-born Day
    Is lovely yet;
The Clouds that gather round the setting sun
Do take a sober colouring from an eye
That hath kept watch o'er man's mortality;
Another race hath been, and other palms are won.
Thanks to the human heart by which we live.   200
Thanks to its tenderness, its joys, and fears,
To me the meanest flower that blows can give
Thoughts that do often lie too deep for tears.
          (*1807*)

William Blake

The Lamb

Little Lamb, who made thee?
  Dost thou know who made thee?
Gave thee life, & bid thee feed
By the stream & o'er the mead;
Gave thee clothing of delight,
Softest clothing, wooly, bright;
Gave thee such a tender voice,
Making all the vales rejoice?
  Little Lamb, who made thee?
  Dost thou know who made thee?   10

Little Lamb, I'll tell thee,
  Little Lamb, I'll tell thee:
He is called by thy name,
For he calls himself a Lamb.
He is meek, & he is mild;
He became a little child.
I a child, & thou a lamb,
We are called by his name.
  Little Lamb, God bless thee!
  Little Lamb, God bless thee!   20

(*1789*)

William Blake

Piping Down the Valleys Wild

Piping down the valleys wild,
Piping songs of pleasant glee,
On a cloud I saw a child,
And he laughing said to me:

'Pipe a song about a Lamb!'
So I piped with merry chear.
'Piper, pipe that song again;'
So I piped: he wept to hear.

'Drop thy pipe, thy happy pipe;
Sing thy songs of happy chear:'   10
So I sung the same again,
While he wept with joy to hear.

'Piper, sit thee down and write
In a book, that all may read.'
So he vanish'd from my sight,
And I pluck'd a hollow reed,

And I made a rural pen,
And I stain'd the water clear,
And I wrote my happy songs
Every child may joy to hear.   20

(*1789*)

EXERCISES

"Children in the Park" [Josephs]

1. How is Laurence Josephs' poem related to the theme of this section, "Childhood and Loss of Innocence"? What does the poet have to say about the differences between the worlds of childhood and adulthood? How does he make fresh those differences? Point out specific images to support your answer.

2. Consider the last four stanzas closely. In what ways does Josephs manage to create condensed, vivid impressions of the passage of time as children move from childhood to adulthood? Does the park itself symbolize something different from nature and escape from workaday reality? Discuss.

3. What does the poet mean by stating that children, as they grow up and "move from toys" (line 16) to other matters, begin to ". . . forget the pleasure park they had to love,/Correctly substituting mirrors for their hearts,/Who learn to prove, but never to improve" (lines 18–20)? Is his attitude satirical? Discuss.

"The Dolls" [Ciardi]

5. Consider all the images of dolls in the poem. How do they represent different civilizations and various periods of history? Discuss.

6. Who are the "Finders After Everything" (line 6)?

7. Discuss the irony of the ". . . little clay dog,/and a little stone man, and a little bone girl . . ." (lines 14–15) having "their eyes wide open forever, while all the children slept" (line 16)? Is sleep a euphemism? What

4. Examine the final stanza. How does the poet manage to project the reader from the language of information into sensuous response, emotional reaction, and, ultimately, imagination? Discuss.

statement does this poem make about the significance of life and death as they relate to childhood and loss of innocence? Discuss.

8. Apply T. S. Eliot's term "objective correlative" (see p. 44) to this poem in as many ways as you can. What is the most obvious objective correlative in the poem?

"In the Tree House at Night" [Dickey]

9. Relate to this poem as many Romantic approaches to poetry as you can. For example, consider John Keats' term "negative capability" (p. 23). In what ways does James Dickey evince negative capability in his poem? In considering this question, decide whether it

is possible for a poet to become so completely identified with his subject that the reader is caught up with such a strong consciousness of it that the poetic result (the poem) effaces all other considerations, including the name of the poet who wrote the poem? Discuss.

"Janet Waking" [Ransom]

10. In your reading of this poem, consider how Dr. Samuel Johnson as a typical neoclassicist (15–16) might have responded to it. Would he have found in the poem a definite metrical and stanzaic form which would have appealed to him?

11. Is the poem completely lucid and rational, or are parts of it unclear and difficult to understand? Do you find any peculiar constructions of language—for example, "deeply morning" (How can a morning be deep?); "transmogrifying bee" (How did the bee "change" Chucky?); "Janet,/ . . . crying her brown hen/ . . . To rise and walk"?

12. Briefly summarize what happens in the poem. Who is the narrator of the poem? Does the poem lend itself to humanistic approaches—that is, do you find the poet concerned with such matters as philosophy, life,

and morality? the permanent as opposed to the transitory, the real as opposed to the illusory, life as opposed to death, reality as opposed to myth? Discuss. In this connection, does the poem suggest to you a questioning of simple religious views of childhood? the ideals of childhood? Discuss Janet's concept of death in relation to her pet rooster, Chucky.

13. In Matthew Arnold's phrase is the poem classic in the sense of being "poetry of the highest order," or does it possess "in any eminent degree, truth and seriousness"?

14. Consider the last stanza closely. Concerning the New Humanism, represented by Irving Babbitt (see pp. 30–31), do you find in this poem an emphasis on what could be termed a "universal centre"? Explain.

"*Innocence*" [Gunn]

15. Read the poem, noting the themes of childhood and innocence. Then paraphrase the poem. Is it possible that one can grow up without losing his innocence, at least to a large extent?

16. We sometimes speak of people as being in "another world." When this idea is applied to the poem, what is especially ironic about Tony White's retention of innocence in his other world (if indeed he is the persona of the poem)? What is that world?

17. Is there a paradox in this poem? Examine closely the final stanza. What does the poet mean by the phrase "The finitude of virtues . . ." (line 13)? How can a soldier be innocent? Discuss.

"*In Ego with Us All*" [Ciardi]

This poem requires a working definition of the term "ego." In psychoanalytic theory, ego may be conceived of as an aspect of mind made up of memory, conscious defensive mechanisms, and perception. Its function is to act as a mediator between the id (primordial instinctive urges) and the superego (learned social and parental prohibitions). So-called intrapsychic conflicts may develop between the ego and the forces of the id and superego between which it mediates. With these basically Freudian observations in mind, carefully discuss the poem.

18. Using psychological approaches, discuss pertinent images and phrases in the poem, including ". . . the world and Mother" (line 1) and "the old well" (line 2). Discuss also the various color images, the image of the "Secret Place" (line 7), the significance of the proper names, the appearance of "Pa" (line 9), later "Father" (line 25), the dropping of the stone into the well, the lack of a splashing sound, the sound of "bell clangs" (line 23) instead, references to "The Lonely Place" (line 14), "The True" (line 40), ". . . the voice of Quiet" (line 42), and references to sentimental tears.

19. Is the sixth stanza meant to be purely sentimental? Is it antisentimental? Discuss the term "sentimentality" and its relationship to this poem. Then discuss the function of the stanza within the context of the whole poem.

20. Relate Denise Levertov's "The Quarry Pool" to the discussion of Ciardi's poem. Do you see relationships between these poems, Richard Eberhart's "The Soul Longs to Return Whence It Came" and D. H. Lawrence's "Piano"? Discuss these relationships, whether they be general (the use of memory in all these poems), or specific (the use of sentimentality in Ciardi's and Lawrence's poems). Contrast any of these poems with Arna Bontemps' "Close Your Eyes!"

"*The Milkmaid*" [Ferry] and "*The pennycandystore beyond the El*" [Ferlinghetti]

21. How are these two poems related to the theme of childhood and loss of innocence?

22. A poet's feeling is his attitude toward his subject. After reading these two poems carefully, define each poet's subject. Make a list of four or five adjectives which describe Ferry's feeling. Ferlinghetti's feeling. Discuss.

"*Fern Hill*" [Thomas]

23. Few poets possess Dylan Thomas' ability to combine the sights and sounds of nature with the musicality of great poetry. Discuss the sense images in the poem "Fern Hill." Does the poem also possess images of movement and kinesthesia that contribute to a driving rhythm, a powerful energy?

24. Discuss irony as it relates to the poem—particularly the final stanza. How do lines 53–54, "Time held me green and dying/Though I sang in my chains like the sea," relate to the theme of childhood and loss of innocence? Discuss. Do you see a relationship between this poem and John Crowe Ransom's "Janet Waking"? Discuss.

"*Ode on Intimations of Immortality from Recollections of Early Childhood*" [Wordsworth]

25. This is one of the great poems of the Romantic period in English literature. Applying any critical approaches you wish, point out special lines, images, and ideas of the poem which appeal to you. What Romantic aspects of the poem are evident to you?

26. To use Wordsworth's own verbiage about what poetry should be, do you find in the poem any "grossly injudicious" metrical arrangements? If so, discuss. Do you find he has chosen words which are "incommensurate with the passion, and inadequate to raise the reader to a height of desirable excitement"? Discuss both aspects as you perceive them.

27. Does the movement of the meter "greatly contribute to impart passion to the words"? Discuss.

28. In Coleridge's terms, does the poem possess the "power of giving the interest of novelty by the modifying colours of imagination"? Discuss. Similarly, does the poem capture human interest and appear to be true enough to produce "for . . . shadows of imagination that willing suspension of disbelief for the moment..."?

29. Finally, in your reading of Wordsworth's famous "Ode," do you discover any often-quoted or especially memorable lines? Are any of these lines significant enough, in your judgment, to merit the application of Matthew Arnold's term, "touchstone"? Discuss.

"*The Lamb*" and "*Piping Down the Valleys Wild*" [Blake]

30. Read these two poems. Blake's poetry is highly musical. With this thought in mind, examine both poems and determine their general meter and rhyme schemes. Discuss his metrical techniques.

31. Although metrics alone may be interesting to contextualists, most New Critics feel there should be a relationship between the sound of poetry and its meaning. Just as you have examined the rhyme and meter of these poems, now consider their meanings. Do you see relationships between Blake's devices of sound and meaning in each poem? Discuss.

2. Nature and the Human Spirit

Sweet is the lore which Nature brings;
Our meddling intellect
Mis-shapes the beauteous forms of things:—
We murder to dissect.

[William Wordsworth, *The Tables Turned*]

Denise Levertov

To the Snake

Green Snake, when I hung you round my neck
and stroked your cold, pulsing throat
      as you hissed to me, glinting
arrowy gold scales, and I felt
      the weight of you on my shoulders,
and the whispering silver of your dryness
      sounded close at my ears—

Green Snake—I swore to my companions that
      certainly
         you were harmless! But truly
I had no certainty, and no hope, only desiring   10
      to hold you, for that joy,
            which left
a long wake of pleasure, as the leaves moved
and you faded into the pattern
of grass and shadows, and I returned
smiling and haunted, to a dark morning.

                (*1958*)

Ted Hughes

The Jaguar

The apes yawn and adore their fleas in the sun.
The parrots shriek as if they were on fire, or strut
Like cheap tarts to attract the stroller with the nut.
Fatigued with indolence, tiger and lion

Lie still as the sun. The boa-constrictor's coil
Is a fossil. Cage after cage seems empty, or
Stinks of sleepers from the breathing straw.
It might be painted on a nursery wall.

But who runs like the rest past these arrives
At a cage where the crowd stands, stares,
      mesmerized,   10
As a child at a dream, at a jaguar hurrying
      enraged
Through prison darkness after the drills of his
      eyes

On a short fierce fuse. Not in boredom—
The eye satisfied to be blind in fire,
By the bang of blood in the brain deaf the ear—
He spins from the bars, but there's no cage to
      him

More than to the visionary his cell:
His stride is wildernesses of freedom:
The world rolls under the long thrust of his heel.
Over the cage floor the horizons come.   20

                (*1957*)

Jesse Stuart

The Snow Lies Patched

The snow lies patched on our enduring hills
Where surfaces first face the morning sun;
Snow-water mumbles down slow winter rills
But stops when sunset freezing has begun.

And winter birds seek shelter for the night
In fodder shocks and in the frozen grass
And shadows of owls' wings in pale moonlight
Frighten the timid rabbits when they pass.
And then to see an evening silhouette
Of snow-patched crazy quilt against the moon, 10
Enduring beauty one cannot forget
That cannot come too often or too soon.
On cone-shaped northside slopes the snow lies
    deep
Where weakened winter suns can't penetrate
And barren oaks wind-creak in frozen sleep
Unmindful night is long when spring is late.

(*1957*)

John Wain

Reason for Not Writing Orthodox Nature Poetry

The January sky is deep and calm.
The mountain sprawls in comfort, and the sea
Sleeps in the crook of that enormous arm.

And Nature from a simple recipe—
Rocks, water, mist, a sunlit winter's day—
Has brewed a cup whose strength has dizzied me.

So little beauty is enough to pay;
The heart so soon yields up its store of love,
And where you love you cannot break away.

So sages never found it hard to prove 10
Nor prophets to declare in metaphor
That God and Nature must be hand in glove.

And this became the basis of their lore.
Then later poets found it easy going
To give the public what they bargained for,

And like a spectacled curator showing
The wares of his museum to the crowd,
They yearly waxed more eloquent and knowing

More slick, more photographic, and more proud:
From Tennyson with notebook in his hand 20
(His truth to Nature fits him like a shroud)

To moderns who devoutly hymn the land.
So be it: each is welcome to his voice;
They are a gentle, if a useless, band.

But leave me free to make a sterner choice;
Content, without embellishment, to note
How little beauty bids the heart rejoice,

How little beauty catches at the throat,
Simply, I love this mountain and this bay
With love that I can never speak by rote, 30

And where you love you cannot break away.

(*1956*)

Richard Eberhart

The Horse Chestnut Tree

Boys in sporadic but tenacious droves
Come with sticks, as certainly as Autumn,
To assault the great horse chestnut tree.

There is a law governs their lawlessness.
Desire is in them for a shining amulet
And the best are those that are highest up.

They will not pick them easily from the ground.
With shrill arms they fling to the higher branches,
To hurry the work of nature for their pleasure.

I have seen them trooping down the street 10
Their pockets stuffed with chestnuts shucked,
    unshucked.
It is only evening keeps them from their wish.

Sometimes I run out in a kind of rage
To chase the boys away: I catch an arm,
Maybe, and laugh to think of being the
　　　lawgiver.

I was once such a young sprout myself
And fingered in my pocket the prize and trophy.
But still I moralize upon the day

And see that we, outlaws on God's property,
Fling out imagination beyond the skies,　　　　20
Wishing a tangible good from the unknown.

And likewise death will drive us from the scene
With the great flowering world unbroken yet,
Which we held in idea, a little handful.

　　　　　　　　　　　　　　(1951)

William Everson

August

Smoke color:
Haze thinly over the hills, low hanging,
But the sky steel, the sky shiny as steel, and the
　　　sun shouting.
The vineyard: in August the green-deep and
　　　heat-loving vines
Without motion grow heavy with grapes.
And he in the shining, on the turned earth,
　　　loose-lying,
The muscles clean and the limbs golden, turns to
　　　the sun the lips and the eyes;
As the virgin yields, impersonally passionate,
From the bone core and the aching flesh, the
　　　offering.

He has found the power and come to the glory. 10
He has turned clean-hearted to the last god, the
　　　symbolic sun.
With earth on his hands, bearing shoulder and
　　　arm the light's touch, he has come.

And having seen, the mind loosens, the nerve
　　　lengthens,
All the haunting abstractions slip free and are
　　　gone;
And the peace is enormous.

　　　　　　　　　　　　　　(1948)

Jesse Stuart

Anannis Tabor

The words of earth turn over from my plow.
I notice every shining mellow word
As it rolls over from the white mould-board.
You'd laugh to see the chattering blackbirds
Follow the furrows, picking at my words.
They understand the mellow words somehow.
Dirt words are words no printer sets to print
For they will never lie on the clean page.
Dirt words will never be the people's rage.
Dirt words will lie on pages of the world　　　10
And speak through tender blossoms first
　　　unfurled
About the last of March or first of April . . .
When men go forth to plow the greening
　　　tendril
Green words of earth are speaking to the world.

　　　　　　　　　　　　　　(1944)

Jesse Stuart

"I came the Womack Road from Sandy Bridge"

I came the Womack Road from Sandy Bridge.
When red sumacs were nodding with the dew,
The sun rose even with the Seaton Ridge;
Under the leaves a golden ray came through.
A man with horse and buggy passed me by,
A jar-fly sang upon the weedy hill;
A mallard duck flew over with a cry,

A crow flew by with something in its bill.
I went the Womack Road from Sandy Bridge
When red sumacs were drinking back the dew. 10
The moon rose even with the Seaton Ridge;
Under the leaves a silver ray came through.
I could pick blackberries along the way,
For moonlight on the fields was bright as day.

(*1934*)

Carl Sandburg

Grass

Pile the bodies high at Austerlitz and Waterloo.
Shovel them under and let me work—
    I am the grass; I cover all.

And pile them high at Gettysburg
And pile them high at Ypres and Verdun.
Shovel them under and let me work.
Two years, ten years, and passengers ask the
    conductor:
      What place is this?
      Where are we now?

    I am the grass. 10
    Let me work.

(*1932*)

Robert Frost

Stopping by Woods on a Snowy Evening

Whose woods these are I think I know.
His house is in the village though;
He will not see me stopping here
To watch his woods fill up with snow.

My little horse must think it queer
To stop without a farmhouse near
Between the woods and frozen lake
The darkest evening of the year.

He gives his harness bells a shake
To ask if there is some mistake. 10
The only other sound's the sweep
Of easy wind and downy flake.

The woods are lovely, dark and deep,
But I have promises to keep,
And miles to go before I sleep,
And miles to go before I sleep.

(*1923*)

Wallace Stevens

The Snow Man

One must have a mind of winter
To regard the frost and the boughs
Of the pine-trees crusted with snow;

And have been cold a long time
To behold the junipers shagged with ice,
The spruces rough in the distant glitter

Of the January sun; and not to think
Of any misery in the sound of the wind,
In the sound of a few leaves,

Which is the sound of the land 10
Full of the same wind
That is blowing in the same bare place

For the listener, who listens in the snow,
And, nothing himself, beholds
Nothing that is not there and the nothing that is.

(*1923*)

Jean Toomer

Georgia Dusk

The sky, lazily disdaining to pursue
   The setting sun, too indolent to hold
   A lengthened tournament for flashing gold,
Passively darkens for night's barbecue,

A feast of moon and men and barking hounds,
   An orgy for some genius of the South
   With blood-shot eyes and cane-lipped scented
      mouth,
Surprised in making folk-songs from soul sounds.

The sawmill blows its whistle, buzz-saws stop,
   And silence breaks the bud of knoll and hill, 10
   Soft settling pollen where plowed lands fulfill
Their early promise of a bumper crop.

Smoke from the pyramidal sawdust pile
   Curls up, blue ghosts of trees, tarrying low
   Where only chips and stumps are left to show
The solid proof of former domicile.

Meanwhile, the men, with vestiges of pomp,
   Race memories of king and caravan,
   High-priests, an ostrich, and a juju-man,
Go singing through the footpaths of the
      swamp.   20

Their voices rise . . . the pine trees are guitars,
   Strumming, pine-needles fall like sheets of
      rain . . .
   Their voices rise . . . the chorus of the cane
Is caroling a vesper to the stars . . .

O singers, resinous and soft your songs
   Above the sacred whisper of the pines,
   Give virgin lips to cornfield concubines,
Bring dreams of Christ to dusky cane-lipped
      throngs.

                        (1923)

Walter de la Mare

Silver

Slowly, silently, now the moon
Walks the night in her silver shoon;
This way, and that, she peers, and sees
Silver fruit upon silver trees;
One by one the casements catch
Her beams beneath the silvery thatch;
Couched in his kennel, like a log,
With paws of silver sleeps the dog;
From their shadowy cote the white breasts peep
Of doves in a silver-feathered sleep;   10
A harvest mouse goes scampering by,
With silver claws and a silver eye;
And moveless fish in the water gleam,
By silver reeds in a silver stream.

                     (1913)

Emily Dickinson

I Heard a Fly Buzz

I heard a Fly buzz—when I died—
The Stillness in the Room
Was like the Stillness in the Air—
Between the Heaves of Storm—

The Eyes around—had wrung them dry—
And Breaths were gathering firm
For that last Onset—when the King
Be witnessed—in the Room—

I willed my Keepsakes—Signed away
What portion of me be   10
Assignable—and then it was
There interposed a Fly—

With Blue—uncertain stumbling Buzz—
Between the light—and me—
And then the Windows failed—and then
I could not see to see—

                    (1896)

Emily Dickinson

These Are the Days When Birds Come Back

These are the days when Birds come back—
A very few—a Bird or two—
To take a backward look.

These are the days when skies resume
The old—old sophistries of June—
A blue and gold mistake.

Oh fraud that cannot cheat the Bee—
Almost thy plausibility
Induces my belief.

Till ranks of seeds their witness bear—   10
And softly thro' the altered air
Hurries a timid leaf.

Oh Sacrament of summer days,
Oh Last Communion in the Haze—
Permit a child to join.

Thy sacred emblems to partake—
Thy consecrated bread to take
And thine immortal wine!

(1890)

Emily Dickinson

I Taste a Liquor Never Brewed

I taste a liquor never brewed—
From Tankards scooped in Pearl—
Not all the Frankfort Berries
Yield such an Alcohol!

Inebriate of Air—am I—
And Debauchee of Dew—
Reeling—thro endless summer days—
From inns of Molten Blue—

When "Landlords" turn the drunken Bee
Out of the Foxglove's door—   10
When Butterflies—renounce their "drams"—
I shall but drink the more!

Till Seraphs swing their snowy Hats—
And Saints—to windows run—
To see the little Tippler
From Manzanilla come!

(1861)

Walt Whitman

Grass

A child said *What is the grass?* fetching it to me
　　with full hands;
How could I answer the child? I do not know
　　what it is any more than he.

I guess it must be the flag of my disposition, out
　　of hopeful green stuff woven.
Or I guess it is the handkerchief of the Lord,
A scented gift and remembrancer designedly
　　dropt,
Bearing the owner's name some way in the
　　corners, that we may see and remark, and
　　say *Whose?*
Or I guess the grass is itself a child, the produced
　　babe of the vegetation.
Or I guess it is a uniform hieroglyphic,
And it means, Sprouting alike in broad zones and
　　narrow zones,
Growing among black folks as among white,   10
Kanuck, Tuckahoe, Congressman, Cuff, I
　　give them the same, I receive them the
　　same.

And now it seems to me the beautiful uncut hair
    of graves.

Tenderly will I use you curling grass,
It may be you transpire from the breasts of
    young men,
It may be if I had known them I would have
    loved them,
It may be you are from old people, or from
    offspring taken soon out of their mothers'
    laps.
And here you are the mothers' laps.

This grass is very dark to be from the white
    heads of old mothers,
Darker than the colorless beards of old men,
Dark to come from under the faint red roofs of
    mouths.   20

O I perceive after all so many uttering tongues,
And I perceive they do not come from the roofs
    of mouths for nothing.
I wish I could translate the hints about the dead
    young men and women,
And the hints about old men and mothers, and
    the off-spring taken soon out of their laps.

What do you think has become of the young
    and old men?
And what do you think has become of the
    women and children?

They are alive and well somewhere,
The smallest sprout shows there is really no
    death,
And if ever there was it led forward life, and does
    not wait at the end to arrest it,
And ceas'd the moment life appear'd.   30
All goes onward and outward, nothing collapses,
And to die is different from what any one
    supposed, and luckier.

                 (*1855*)

Percy Bysshe Shelley
Ode to the West Wind

I

O, wild West Wind, thou breath of Autumn's
    being,
Thou, from whose unseen presence the leaves
    dead
Are driven, like ghosts from an enchanter
    fleeing,

Yellow, and black, and pale, and hectic red,
Pestilence-stricken multitudes: O, thou,
Who chariotest to their dark wintry bed

The wingèd seeds, where they lie cold and low,
Each like a corpse within its grave, until
Thine azure sister of the spring shall blow

Her clarion o'er the dreaming earth, and fill   10
(Driving sweet buds like flocks to feed in air)
With living hues and odours plain and hill:

Wild Spirit, which art moving everywhere;
Destroyer and preserver; hear, oh, hear!

II

Thou on whose stream, 'mid the steep sky's
    commotion,
Loose clouds like earth's decaying leaves are
    shed,
Shook from the tangled boughs of Heaven and
    Ocean,

Angels of rain and lightning: there are spread
On the blue surface of thine aëry surge,
Like the bright hair uplifted from the head   20

Of some fierce Mænad, even from the dim verge
Of the horizon to the zenith's height
The locks of the approaching storm. Thou dirge

Of the dying year, to which this closing night
Will be the dome of a vast sepulchre,
Vaulted with all thy congregated might

Of vapors, from whose solid atmosphere
Black rain, and fire, and hail will burst: oh, hear!

III

Thou who didst waken from his summer dreams
The blue Mediterranean, where he lay,   30
Lulled by the coil of his crystalline streams,

Beside a pumice isle in Baiæ's bay,
And saw in sleep old palaces and towers
Quivering within the wave's intenser day,

All overgrown with azure moss and flowers
So sweet, the sense faints picturing them! Thou
For whose path the Atlantic's level powers

Cleave themselves into chasms, while far below
The sea-blooms and the oozy woods which wear
The sapless foliage of the ocean, know   40

Thy voice, and suddenly grow grey with fear,
And tremble and despoil themselves: oh, hear!

IV

If I were a dead leaf thou mightest bear;
If I were a swift cloud to fly with thee;
A wave to pant beneath thy power, and share

The impulse of thy strength, only less free
Than thou, O, uncontrollable! If even
I were as in my boyhood, and could be

The comrade of thy wanderings over heaven,
As then, when to outstrip thy skiey speed   50
Scarce seemed a vision; I would ne'er have
        striven

As thus with thee in prayer in my sore need,
Oh! lift me as a wave, a leaf, a cloud!
I fall upon the thorns of life! I bleed!

A heavy weight of hours has chained and bowed
One too like thee: tameless, and swift, and proud.

V

Make me thy lyre, even as the forest is:
What if my leaves are falling like its own!
The tumult of thy mighty harmonies

Will take from both a deep, autumnal tone,   60
Sweet though in sadness. Be thou, Spirit fierce,
My spirit! Be thou me, impetuous one!

Drive my dead thoughts over the universe
Like withered leaves to quicken a new birth!
And, by the incantation of this verse,

Scatter, as from an unextinguished hearth
Ashes and sparks, my words among mankind!
Be through my lips to unawakened earth

The trumpet of a prophecy! O, wind,
If Winter comes, can Spring be far behind?   70
                                    (*1820*)

William Wordsworth

I Wandered Lonely as a Cloud

I wandered lonely as a cloud
That floats on high o'er vales and hills,
When all at once I saw a crowd,
A host, of golden daffodils;
Beside the lake, beneath the trees,
Fluttering and dancing in the breeze.

Continuous as the stars that shine
And twinkle on the milky way,
They stretched in never-ending line
Along the margin of a bay: 10
Ten thousand saw I at a glance,
Tossing their heads in sprightly dance.

The waves beside them danced; but they
Out-did the sparkling waves in glee:
A poet could not but be gay,
In such a jocund company:
I gazed—and gazed—but little thought
What wealth the show to me had brought:

For oft, when on my couch I lie
In vacant or in pensive mood,   20
They flash upon that inward eye
Which is the bliss of solitude;
And then my heart with pleasure fills,
And dances with the daffodils.

(*1807*)

William Wordsworth

The Tables Turned

Up! up! my Friend, and quit your books;
Or surely you'll grow double:
Up! up! my Friend, and clear your looks;
Why all this toil and trouble?

The sun, above the mountain's head,
A freshening lustre mellow
Through all the long green fields has spread,
His first sweet evening yellow.

Books! 'tis a dull and endless strife:
Come, hear the woodland linnet,   10
How sweet his music! on my life,
There's more of wisdom in it.

And hark! how blithe the throstle sings!
He, too, is no mean preacher:
Come forth into the light of things,
Let Nature be your Teacher.

She has a world of ready wealth,
Our minds and hearts to bless—
Spontaneous wisdom breathed by health,
Truth breathed by cheerfulness.   20

One impulse from a vernal wood
May teach you more of man,
Of moral evil and of good,
Than all the sages can.

Sweet is the lore which Nature brings;
Our meddling intellect
Mis-shapes the beauteous forms of things:—
We murder to dissect.

Enough of Science and of Art;
Close up those barren leaves;   30
Come forth, and bring with you a heart
That watches and receives.

(*1798*)

William Collins

Ode to Evening

If ought of Oaten Stop, or Pastoral Song,
May hope, O pensive *Eve*, to sooth thine Ear,
    Like thy own brawling Springs,
    Thy Springs, and dying Gales,
O *Nymph* reserv'd, while now the bright-hair'd
        Sun
Sits in yon western Tent, whose cloudy Skirts,
    With Brede ethereal wove,
    O'erhang his wavy Bed:
Now Air is hush'd, save where the weak-ey'd
        Bat,
With short shrill Shriek flits by on leathern Wing,
    Or where the Beetle winds   11
    His small but sullen Horn,
As oft he rises 'midst the twilight Path,
Against the Pilgrim born in heedless Hum:
    Now teach me, *Maid* compos'd,
    To breathe some soften'd Strain,
Whose Numbers stealing thro' thy darkning
        Vale,
May not unseemly with its Stillness suit,
    As musing slow, I hail
    Thy genial lov'd Return!   20

For when thy folding Star arising shews
His paly Circlet, at his warning Lamp
   The fragrant *Hours*, and *Elves*
   Who slept in Buds the Day,
And many a *Nymph* who wreaths her Brows with
     Sedge,
And sheds the fresh'ning Dew, and lovelier
     still,
   The *Pensive Pleasures* sweet
   Prepare thy shadowy Car.
Then let me rove some wild and heathy Scene,
Or find some Ruin 'midst its dreary Dells,   30
   Whose Walls more awful nod
   By thy religious Gleams.
Or if chill blustring Winds, or driving Rain,
Prevent my willing Feet, be mine the Hut,
   That from the Mountain's Side,
   Views Wilds, and swelling Floods,
And Hamlets brown, and dim-discover'd Spires,

And hears their simple Bell, and marks o'er
     all
   Thy Dewy Fingers draw
   The gradual dusky Veil.   40

While *Spring* shall pour his Show'rs, as oft he
     wont,
And bathe thy breathing Tresses, meekest *Eve*!
   While *Summer* loves to sport,
   Beneath thy ling'ring Light:
While sallow *Autumn* fills thy Lap with Leaves,
Or *Winter* yelling thro' the troublous Air,
   Affrights thy shrinking Train,
   And rudely rends thy Robes.
So long regardful of thy quiet Rule,
Shall *Fancy*, *Friendship*, *Science*, smiling *Peace*,   50
   Thy gentlest Influence own,
   And love thy fav'rite Name!

                   (*1746*)

EXERCISES

"*To the Snake*" [Levertov] and "*The Jaguar*" [Hughes]

1. Do these poems seem to be concerned primarily with nature (animals) as disparate from the human spirit, with human attitudes, or with both? Discuss. Whatever your answer, do the animals become more representative of human attitudes than of animalic nature?

2. What is each poet's attitude (feeling) toward his subject? In discussing the two poems, apply the following terms: "irony," "paradox," and "symbol."

"*The Snow Lies Patched*" [Stuart] and "*Stopping by Woods on a Snowy Evening*" [Frost]

3. In your reading of Stuart's poem, notice the images of nature as they appeal to the five senses. What are the various forms of life Stuart mentions, and do they seem to fit the context of the poem?

4. In what ways does the poem lend itself to classical approaches? Romantic approaches? In framing your answer, consider whether the form of this poem is

dominant over the details or the details dominant over the form. Discuss.

5. How does the last line of the poem, "Unmindful night is long when spring is late," summarize the poet's attitude (feeling) toward his subject?

6. Relate Stuart's poem to Robert Frost's "Stopping by Woods on a Snowy Evening" in as many ways as you

can. Discuss the similarities of and differences between the two poems. Do both poems contain themes other than "nature and the human spirit"? Do both lend themselves to a variety of approaches to poetry?

Consider, for example, sociocultural approaches (social responsibility), humanistic approaches (moral responsibility), and any other approaches that may occur to you.

"The Snow Lies Patched" [Stuart] and *"Reason for Not Writing Orthodox Nature Poetry"* [Wain]

7. Is Stuart's poem more or less classical in nature than Wain's poem? Discuss. In what ways could you compare the first two stanzas of Wain's poem with Stuart's poem? Discuss. Wain's fourth and fifth stanzas include generalizations about what he considers to be "orthodox nature poetry." What are they? The sixth, seventh, and eighth stanzas echo and extend Wain's earlier contentions. How would the classicists and neoclassicists (see pp. 7–10; pp. 12–16) react to Wain's views of poets who relate truth to nature? In answering this question, consider the Aristotelian concept of mimesis

(imitation of nature) as a major purpose of poetry well up into the eighteenth century.

8. Do Wain's last three stanzas in any way indicate a Romantic approach to poetry? Explain. Does Wain seem open, in Wordsworth's phrasing, to a "promptness to think and feel"? If so, specify lines indicating that he does. Is Wain's poetry characterized by what Hazlitt called "gusto" as it strives for "power or passion"? Compare and contrast Wain's poem with Stuart's poem for these and other Romantic elements.

"The Horse Chestnut Tree" [Eberhart]

9. Briefly paraphrase the poem. Strictly speaking, is this poem about nature, or is it about nature plus much more? How does the nature motif serve to introduce other themes? Among other possibilities, consider in your answer the following themes: childhood and loss of innocence, wisdom and beauty, the shadow world, humor and folly, and death and affirmation.

10. Examine the poem contextually, relating to portions of the poem the following poetic terms: hyperbole, as in ". . . the great horse chestnut tree" (line 3), ". . . run out in a kind of rage" (line 13), ". . . outlaws on God's property,/Fling out imagination beyond the skies" (lines 19–20), and ". . . the great flowering world . . ." (line 23); metaphor, as in "shining amulet"

(line 5) and "prize and trophy" (line 17); connotation, as in "assault" (line 3) and ". . . trooping down the street" (line 10); and litotes, or understatement, as in "a little handful" (line 24). Now examine the entire poem as an extended metaphor—especially the final two stanzas as further extensions of the basic metaphor. Discuss.

11. Finally, interpret the poem in your own words. Has the poet said what cannot be stated in any other way or stated as well in any other way? What does your answer tell you about the language of poetry in comparison to the language of information or general communication?

"August" [Everson] and *"Anannis Tabor"* [Stuart]

12. Why is Everson's poem included in this thematic section? Could it possibly be interpreted as a love poem instead of a nature poem? Discuss.

13. The apparent ambiguity of the poem lies in the fact that it is an extended metaphor. Relate the indirectly compared items. For example, "sun shouting" (line 3)

demonstrates a linkage between the sun and a shouting person, and if the sun metaphorically "shouts," then it must do so with its bright light and intense heat. With what may the ". . . green-deep and heat-loving vines" (line 4) growing "heavy with grapes" (line 5) be compared? To what may the "muscles clean," "limbs golden" (line 7) and yielding virgin figures be likened? 14. How does such a metaphorical interpretation lead us to an understanding of the poet's feeling? Is this feeling toward the August earth passionate? profoundly loving? inspiring? luminously peaceful? Discuss. Are Everson's feeling and tone legitimately achieved through the use of love imagery? Discuss, giving specific reasons for your answers.

15. The poem by Jesse Stuart is also an extended metaphor, but with different aspects of nature compared. Discuss the poem and its effectiveness within this context. If Stuart appears to be saying that nature is more eloquent than the words of poets, then determine the methods by which Stuart achieves his intention. Compare and contrast the effectiveness of the two extended metaphors—Everson's and Stuart's—giving specific reasons for your opinions.

"I came the Womack Road from Sandy Bridge" [Stuart]

16. Is this a Shakespearean sonnet? Such a sonnet has three quatrains and a concluding couplet. Usually, an idea is developed in each of the quatrains, and a resolution or conclusion is reached in the couplet. What time of day does the poet treat in the first quatrain? What aspects of life—animal life in particular—in the second? What time of day in the third? Even though the poem concludes with night imagery, in what way does the poet achieve a cyclical unity with the first quatrain? Discuss.

17. Is the poet's feeling toward his subject an infectious composite of freshness toward life, ingenuousness, spontaneity, and invigoration—in brief, a simple joy of nature? How would you describe his feeling, and do you identify with it? Discuss.

"Grass" [Sandburg] and *"Grass"* [Whitman]

18. Why is Sandburg's poem included in this section rather than, say, "War"? Relate the two poems in as many ways as you can. Does grass in both poems serve a symbolical function, representing the eternal force of nature? If so, what does each poet have to say about the enormousness of nature and the contrasting limitation of man's part in it? Discuss. What of man as human spirit rather than biological entity? Does either poet make a distinction? Discuss.

"Georgia Dusk" [Toomer]

19. One quality of first-rate poetry is the ability to combine homely images with lofty concepts. To what extent does Toomer achieve this combination in his poem? Discuss. What does his poem have to say about nature and the human spirit? about sociocultural issues of the recent American past? about the desire of man, as one American writer has phrased it, to be better than he knows he can be; or, as another has put it, to reach out to the stars? Discuss.

General

20. Choose any one of the remaining poems in this section and relate to it as many critical approaches as possible. Here are some suggested beginnings: Wallace Stevens' "The Snow Man" (Hazlitt's concept of "sympathetic identification"); Walter de la Mare's "Silver" (contextualist devices of repetition, alliteration); Emily Dickinson's "I Heard a Fly Buzz" (New Critical emphasis on intense irony); Dickinson's "I Taste a Liquor Never Brewed" (New Critical emphasis on the relationship between devices of sound and meaning. Note especially the use of *slant rhyme*); Shelley's "Ode to the West Wind" (Shelley's own

Romantic approaches, especially his perception of values "both separately and as a whole"); Wordsworth's "I Wandered Lonely as a Cloud" and "The Tables Turned" (Wordsworth's own Romantic criteria, especially the application of what he termed "language really used by men"); and William Collins' "Ode to Evening" (general Romantic aspects, such as subjec-tivity, experimental treatment of the subject, the appeal to the senses and feeling rather than to rationality, imaginative appeal, a concern with the strange and immeasurable, the wild and primitive aspects of nature, and an intention of stirring the imagination and mystic powers associated with it).

3. Struggle for Identity

In goggles, donned impersonality,
In gleaming jackets trophied with the dust,
They strap in doubt—by hiding it, robust—
And almost hear a meaning in their noise.

[Thom Gunn, *On the Move*]

Robert Hayden

The Diver

Sank through easeful
azure. Flower
creatures flashed and
shimmered there—
lost images
fadingly remembered.
Swiftly descended
into canyon of cold
nightgreen emptiness.

Freefalling, weightless   10
as in dreams of
wingless flight,
plunged through infra-
space and came to
the dead ship,
carcass that swarmed with
voracious life.
Angelfish, their
lively blue and
yellow prised from   20
darkness by the
flashlight's beam,
thronged her portholes.
Moss of bryozoans

blurred, obscured her
metal. Snappers,
gold groupers explored her,
fearless of bubbling
manfish. I entered
the wreck, awed by her silence,   30
feeling more keenly
the iron cold.
With flashlight probing
fogs of water
saw the sad slow
dance of gilded
chairs, the ectoplasmic
swirl of garments,
drowned instruments
of buoyancy,   40
drunken shoes. Then
livid gesturings,
eldritch hide and
seek of laughing
faces. I yearned to
find those hidden
ones, to fling aside
the mask and call to them,
yield to rapturous
whisperings, have   50
done with self and
every dinning
vain complexity.
Yet in languid
frenzy strove, as
one freezing fights off
sleep desiring sleep;
strove against the
cancelling arms that
suddenly surrounded   60
me, fled the numbing
kisses that I craved.
Reflex of life-wish?
Respirator's brittle
belling? Swam from
the ship somehow;
somehow began the
measured rise.

(1962)

Theodore Roethke

In a Dark Time

In a dark time, the eye begins to see.
I meet my shadow in the deepening shade;
I hear my echo in the echoing wood—
A lord of nature weeping to a tree.
I live between the heron and the wren,
Beasts of the hill and serpents of the den.

What's madness but nobility of soul
At odds with circumstance? The day's on fire!
I know the purity of pure despair,
My shadow pinned against a sweating wall.   10
That place among the rocks—is it a cave,
Or winding path? The edge is what I have.

A steady storm of correspondences!
A night flowing with birds, a ragged moon,
And in broad day the midnight comes again!
A man goes far to find out what he is—
Death of the self in a long, tearless night,
All natural shapes blazing unnatural light.

Dark, dark my light, and darker my desire.
My soul, like some heat-maddened summer fly,   20
Keeps buzzing at the sill. Which I is *I*?
A fallen man, I climb out of my fear.
The mind enters itself, and God the mind,
And one is One, free in the tearing wind.

(1960)

W. D. Snodgrass

Home Town

I go out like a ghost,
nights, to walk the streets
I walked fifteen years younger—
seeking my old defeats,
devoured by the old hunger;
I had supposed

this longing and upheaval
had left me with my youth.
Fifteen years gone; once more,
the old lies are the truth:
I must prove I dare,
and the world, and love, is evil.

I have had loves, had such
honors as freely came;
it does not seem to matter.
Boys swagger just the same
along the curbs, or mutter
among themselves and watch.

They're out for the same prize.
And, as the evening grows,
the young girls take the street,
hard, in harlequin clothes,
with black shells on their feet
and challenge in their eyes.

Like a young bitch in her season
she walked the carnival
tonight, trailed by boys;
then, stopped at a penny stall
for me; by glittering toys
the pitchman called the reason

to come and take a chance,
try my hand, my skill.
I could not look; bereft
of breath, against my will,
I walked ahead and left
her there without one glance.

Pale soul, consumed by fear
of the living world you haunt,
have you learned what habits lead you
to hunt what you don't want;
learned who does not need you;
learned you are no one here?

(1959)

Thom Gunn

On the Move

'*Man, you gotta Go.*'

The blue jay scuffling in the bushes follows
Some hidden purpose, and the gust of birds
That spurts across the field, the wheeling
    swallows,
Have nested in the trees and undergrowth.
Seeking their instinct, or their poise, or both,
One moves with an uncertain violence
Under the dust thrown by a baffled sense
Or the dull thunder of approximate words.

On motorcycles, up the road, they come:
Small, black, as flies hanging in heat, the Boys,
Until the distance throws them forth, their hum
Bulges to thunder held by calf and thigh.
In goggles, donned impersonality,
In gleaming jackets trophied with the dust,
They strap in doubt—by hiding it, robust—
And almost hear a meaning in their noise.

Exact conclusion of their hardiness
Has no shape yet, but from known whereabouts
They ride, direction where the tires press.
They scare a flight of birds across the field:
Much that is natural, to the will must yield.
Men manufacture both machine and soul,
And use what they imperfectly control
To dare a future from the taken routes.

It is a part solution, after all.
One is not necessarily discord
On earth; or damned because, half animal,
One lacks direct instinct, because one wakes
Afloat on movement that divides and breaks.
One joins the movement in a valueless world,
Choosing it, till, both hurler and the hurled,
One moves as well, always toward, toward.

A minute holds them, who have come to go:
The self-defined, astride the created will

They burst away; the towns they travel through
Are home for neither bird nor holiness,
For birds and saints complete their purposes.
At worst, one is in motion; and at best,
Reaching no absolute, in which to rest,
One is always nearer by not keeping still.　　40

Vigour within the discipline of shape.
Come here, friend, yearly, till you've carved the
　　bark
With all the old virtues, young in fibre, names
　　That swell with time and tree, no dreams,
No ornaments, but tallies for your work.
　　　　　　　　　　　　　　(1957)

He never learned a trade, he just sells gas,
Checks oil, and changes flats. Once in a while,　　20
As a gag, he dribbles an inner tube,
But most of us remember anyway.
His hands are fine and nervous on the lug
　　wrench.
It makes no difference to the lug wrench, though.

Off work, he hangs around Mae's Luncheonette.
Grease-grey and kind of coiled, he plays pinball,
Sips lemon cokes, and smokes those thin cigars;
Flick seldom speaks to Mae, just sits and nods
Beyond her face towards bright applauding tiers
Of Necco Wafers, Nibs, and Juju Beads.　　30
　　　　　　　　　　　　　　(1957)

John Updike

Ex-Basketball Player

Pearl Avenue runs past the high-school lot,
Bends with the trolley tracks, and stops, cut off
Before it has a chance to go two blocks,
At Colonel McComsky Plaza. Berth's Garage
Is on the corner facing west, and there,
Most days, you'll find Flick Webb, who helps
　　Berth out.

Flick stands tall among the idiot pumps—
Five on a side, the old bubble-head style,
Their rubber elbows hanging loose and low.
One's nostrils are two S's, and his eyes　　10
An E and O. And one is squat, without
A head at all—more of a football type.

Once Flick played for the high-school team,
　　the Wizards.
He was good: in fact, the best. In '46
He bucketed three hundred ninety points,
A county record still. The ball loved Flick.
I saw him rack up thirty-eight or forty
In one home game. His hands were like wild
　　birds.

Vassar Miller

The New Icarus

Slip off the husk of gravity to lie
Bedded with wind; float on a whimsy, lift
Upon a wish: your bow's own arrow, rift
Newton's decorum—only when you fly.
But naked. No false-feathered fool, you try
Dalliance with heights, nor, plumed with metal,
　　shift
And shear the clouds, imperiling lark and swift
And all birds bridal-bowered in the sky.

Your wreck of bone, barred their delight's
　　dominions,
Lacking their formula for flight, holds imaged　　10
Those alps of air no eagle's wing can quell.
With arms flung crosswise, pinioned to wooden
　　pinions,
You, in one motion plucked and crimson-
　　plumaged,
Outsoar all Heaven, plummeting all Hell.
　　　　　　　　　　　　　　(1956)

Lawrence Ferlinghetti

"The world is a beautiful place"

The world is a beautiful place
                    to be born into
if you don't mind happiness
                    not always being
                              so very much fun
        if you don't mind a touch of hell
                              now and then
            just when everything is fine
                              because even in heaven
                    they don't sing   10
                    all the time

        The world is a beautiful place
                              to be born into
        if you don't mind some people dying
                              all the time
                or maybe only starving
                              some of the time
                which isn't half so bad
                              if it isn't you

    Oh the world is a beautiful place   20
                              to be born into
        if you don't much mind
                    a few dead minds
            in the higher places
                        or a bomb or two
                now and then
                        in your upturned faces
        or such other improprieties
                        as our Name Brand society
                is prey to   30
                        with its men of distinction
        and its men of extinction
                        and its priests
            and other patrolmen
                        and its various segregations

and congressional investigations

and other constipations

that our fool flesh

is heir to

Yes the world is the best place of all   40

for a lot of such things as

making the fun scene

and making the love scene

and making the sad scene

and singing low songs and having inspirations

and walking around

looking at everything

and smelling flowers

and goosing statues

and even thinking   50

and kissing people and

making babies and wearing pants

and waving hats and

dancing

and going swimming in rivers

on picnics

in the middle of the summer

and just generally

'living it up'

Yes   60

but then right in the middle of it

comes the smiling

mortician   (1955)

Richard Eberhart

The Tobacconist of Eighth Street

I saw a querulous old man, the tobacconist of
    Eighth Street.
Scales he had, and he would mix tobacco with
    his hands

And pour the fragrance in a paper bag.
You walked out selfishly upon the city.

Some ten years I watched him. Fields of Eire
Or of Arabia were in his voice. He strove to
    please.
The weights of age, of fear were in his eyes,
And on his neck time's cutting edge.

One year I crossed his door. Time had crossed
    before.
Collapse had come upon him, the collapse of
    affairs.   10
He was sick with revolution,
Crepitant with revelation.

And I went howling into the crooked streets,
Smashed with recognition: for him I flayed the
    air,
For him cried out, and sent a useless prayer
To the disjointed stones that were his only name:

Such insight is one's own death rattling past.
(1953)

William Everson

The Stranger

Pity this girl.
At callow sixteen,
Glib in the press of rapt companions,
She bruits her smatter,
Her bed-lore brag.
She prattles the lip-learned, light-love list.
In the new itch and squirm of sex,
How can she foresee?

How can she foresee the thick stranger,
Over the hills from Omaha,   10
Who will break her across a hired bed,
Open the loins,
Rive the breach,
And set the foetus wailing within the womb,
To hunch toward the knowledge of its disease,
And shamble down time to doomsday?
(1948)

Gwendolyn Brooks

But Can See Better There, and Laughing There

pygmies are pygmies still, though percht on Alps.
Edward Young

But can see better there, and laughing there
Pity the giants wallowing on the plain.
Giants who bleat and chafe in their small grass,
Seldom to spread the palm; to spit; come clean.

Pygmies expand in cold impossible air,
Cry fie on giantshine, poor glory which
Pounds breast-bone punily, screeches, and has
Reached no Alps: or, knows no Alps to reach.
(1945)

Dylan Thomas

Poem in October

    It was my thirtieth year to heaven
Woke to my hearing from harbour and
        neighbour wood
    And the mussel pooled and the heron
        Priested shore
        The morning beckon
With water praying and call of seagull and rook
And the knock of sailing boats on the net
        webbed wall
        Myself to set foot
        That second
In the still sleeping town and set forth.   10

    My birthday began with the water-
Birds and the birds of the winged trees flying
        my name
    Above the farms and the white horses
        And I rose
        In rainy autumn

And walked abroad in a shower of all my days.
High tide and the heron dived when I took the
    road
      Over the border
      And the gates
Of the town closed as the town awoke.   20

A springful of larks in a rolling
Cloud and the roadside bushes brimming with
    whistling
    Blackbirds and the sun of October
      Summery
      On the hill's shoulder,
Here were fond climates and sweet singers
    suddenly
Come in the morning where I wandered and
    listened
    To the rain wringing
      Wind blow cold
In the wood faraway under me.   30

Pale rain over the dwindling harbour
And over the sea wet church the size of a snail
    With its horns through mist and the castle
      Brown as owls
    But all the gardens
Of spring and summer were blooming in the
    tall tales
Beyond the border and under the lark full
    cloud.
    There could I marvel
      My birthday
Away but the weather turned around.   40

It turned away from the blithe country
And down the other air and the blue altered sky
    Streamed again a wonder of summer
      With apples
      Pears and red currants
And I saw in the turning so clearly a child's
Forgotten mornings when he walked with his
    mother
    Through the parables
      Of sun light
And the legends of the green chapels   50

And the twice told fields of infancy
That his tears burned my cheeks and his heart
    moved in mine.
    These were the woods the river and sea
      Where a boy
    In the listening
Summertime of the dead whispered the truth of
    his joy
To the trees and the stones and the fish in the
    tide.
    And the mystery
      Sang alive
Still in the water and singingbirds.   60

And there could I marvel my birthday
Away but the weather turned around. And the
    true
    Joy of the long dead child sang burning
      In the sun.
    It was my thirtieth
Year to heaven stood there then in the summer
    noon
Though the town below lay leaved with October
    blood.
    O may my heart's truth
      Still be sung
On this high hill in a year's turning.   70

           (1945)

Jesse Stuart

Pat Hennessey

When I was young, I never understood
How women were the builders of a dream . . .
Something there was . . . a passion in my blood
To dig down deep and find a living thing.
I did not know of life; I felt for life.
It was mysterious then as it is still.
Just think to dig for life down in a hill!
When I was walking in the big earth room

One April when the trees were white with
    bloom,
I dreamed of fruit the slender twigs would
    bear.   10
The apple tree was maker of a dream . . .
An apple coming through such slender stem !
And when my mother came, I stood beside her.
She was the tree and I was fruit born of her.

                            (*1944*)

Langston Hughes

I, Too

I, too, sing America.

I am the darker brother.
They send me to eat in the kitchen
When company comes,
But I laugh,
And eat well,
And grow strong.

Tomorrow,
I'll be at the table
When company comes.   10
Nobody'll dare
Say to me,
"Eat in the kitchen,"
Then.

Besides,
They'll see how beautiful I am
And be ashamed—

I, too, am America.

                            (*1926*)

William Butler Yeats

The Lake Isle of Innisfree

I will arise and go now, and go to Innisfree,
And a small cabin build there, of clay and wattles
    made :
Nine bean-rows will I have there, a hive for the
    honeybee,
And live alone in the bee-loud glade.

And I shall have some peace there, for peace
    comes dropping slow,
Dropping from the veils of the morning to
    where the cricket sings;
There midnight's all a glimmer, and noon a
    purple glow,
And evening full of the linnet's wings.

I will arise and go now, for always night and day
I hear lake water lapping with low sounds by
    the shore;   10
While I stand on the roadway, or on the
    pavements grey,
I hear it in the deep heart's core.

                            (*1890*)

Innisfree: Symbolical of aspiration, Yeats knew the name
of the little island in Lough Gill from boyhood. He wished
to live there in imitation of Thoreau, an ambition from
his teens, and years later the name of Innisfree haunted
him to return.

Walt Whitman

Out of the Cradle Endlessly Rocking

Out of the cradle endlessly rocking,
Out of the mocking-bird's throat, the musical
    shuttle,
Out of the Ninth-month midnight,

Over the sterile sands and the fields beyond,
    where the child leaving his bed wandered
    alone, bareheaded, barefoot,
Down from the showered halo,
Up from the mystic play of shadows twining
    and twisting as if they were alive,
Out from the patches of briers and blackberries,
From the memories of the bird that chanted to
    me,
From your memories, sad brother, from the fitful
    risings and fallings I heard,
From under that yellow half-moon late-risen
    and swollen as if with tears,   10
From those beginning notes of yearning and
    love there in the mist,
From the thousand responses of my heart never
    to cease,
From the myriad thence-aroused words,
From the word stronger and more delicious
    than any,
From such as now they start the scene revisiting,
As a flock, twittering, rising, or overhead
    passing,
Borne hither, ere all eludes me, hurriedly,
A man, yet by these tears a little boy again,
Throwing myself on the sand, confronting the
    waves,
I, chanter of pains and joys, uniter of here and
    hereafter,   20
Taking all hints to use them, but swiftly leaping
    beyond them,
A reminiscence sing.

Once Paumanok,
When the lilac-scent was in the air and Fifth-
    month grass was growing,
Up this seashore in some briers,
Two feathered guests from Alabama, two
    together,
And their nest, and four light-green eggs spotted
    with brown,
And every day the he-bird to and fro near at
    hand,
And every day the she-bird crouched on her
    nest, silent, with bright eyes,

And every day I, a curious boy, never too close,
    never disturbing them,   30
Cautiously peering, absorbing, translating.

Shine! shine! shine!
Pour down your warmth, great sun!
While we bask, we two together.
Two together!
Winds blow south, or winds blow north,
Day come white, or night come black,
Home, or rivers and mountains from home,
Singing all time, minding no time,
While we two keep together.   40

Till of a sudden,
Maybe killed, unknown to her mate,
One forenoon the she-bird crouched not on the
    nest,
Nor returned that afternoon, nor the next,
Nor ever appeared again.
And thenceforward all summer in the sound of
    the sea,
And at night under the full of the moon in
    calmer weather,
Over the hoarse surging of the sea,
Or flitting from brier to brier by day,
I saw, I heard at intervals the remaining one,
    the he-bird,   50
The solitary guest from Alabama.

Blow! blow! blow!
Blow up sea-winds along Paumanok's shore;
I wait and I wait till you blow my mate to me.

Yes, when the stars glistened,
All night long on the prong of a moss-scalloped
    stake,
Down almost amid the slapping waves,
Sat the lone singer wonderful causing tears.

He called on his mate,
He poured forth the meanings which I of all men
    know.   60
Yes, my brother, I know,—

The rest might not, but I have treasured every
    note,
For more than once dimly down to the beach
    gliding,
Silent, avoiding the moonbeams, blending
    myself with the shadows,
Recalling now the obscure shapes, the echoes,
    the sounds and sights after their sorts,
The white arms out in the breakers tirelessly
    tossing,
I, with bare feet, a child, the wind wafting my
    hair,
Listened long and long.
Listened to keep, to sing, now translating the
    notes,
Following you, my brother.   70

Soothe! soothe! soothe!
Close on its wave soothes the wave behind,
And again another behind embracing and lapping,
    every one close,
But my love soothes not me, not me.

Low hangs the moon, it rose late,
It is lagging—O I think it is heavy with love, with
    love.

O madly the sea pushes upon the land,
With love, with love.

O night! do I not see my love fluttering out among
    the breakers?
What is that little black thing I see there in the white?

Loud! loud! loud!   81
Loud I call to you, my love!

High and clear I shoot my voice over the waves,
Surely you must know who is here, is here,
You must know who I am, my love.

Low-hanging moon!
What is that dusky spot in your brown yellow?
O it is the shape, the shape of my mate!
O moon, do not keep her from me any longer.

Land! land! O land!   90
Whichever way I turn, O I think you could give
    me my mate back again if you only would,
For I am almost sure I see her dimly whichever way
    I look.
O rising stars!
Perhaps the one I want so much will rise, will rise
    with some of you.
O throat! O trembling throat!
Sound clearer through the atmosphere!
Pierce the woods, the earth,
Somewhere listening to catch you must be the one
    I want.

Shake out carols!
Solitary here, the night's carols!   100
Carols of lonesome love! death's carols!
Carols under that lagging, yellow, waning moon!
O under that moon where she droops almost down
    into the sea!
O reckless despairing carols!

But soft! sink low!
Soft! let me just murmur,
And do you wait a moment, you husky-noised sea,
For somewhere I believe I heard my mate responding
    to me,
So faint, I must be still, be still to listen,
But not altogether still, for then she might not come
    immediately to me.   110

Hither, my love!
Here I am! here!
With this just-sustained note I announce myself to you,
This gentle call is for you my love, for you.

Do not be decoyed elsewhere:
That is the whistle of the wind, it is not my voice,
That is the fluttering, the fluttering of the spray,
Those are the shadows of leaves.

O darkness! O in vain!
O I am very sick and sorrowful.   120
O brown halo in the sky near the moon, drooping
    upon the sea!

O troubled reflection in the sea!
O throat! O throbbing heart!
And I singing uselessly, uselessly all the night.

O past! O happy life! O songs of joy!
In the air, in the woods, over fields,
Loved! loved! loved! loved! loved!
But my mate no more, no more with me!
We two together no more.

The aria sinking.   130
All else continuing, the stars shining,
The winds blowing, the notes of the bird
        continuous echoing.
With angry moans the fierce old mother
        incessantly moaning.
On the sands of Paumanok's shore gray and
        rustling,
The yellow half-moon enlarged, sagging down,
        drooping, the face of the sea almost
        touching,
The boy ecstatic, with his bare feet the waves,
        with his hair the atmosphere dallying,
The love in the heart long pent, now loose, now
        at last tumultuously bursting,
The aria's meaning, the ears, the soul, swiftly
        depositing,
The strange tears down the cheeks coursing,
The colloquy there, the trio, each uttering,   140
The undertone, the savage old mother incessantly
        crying,
To the boy's soul's questions sullenly timing,
        some drowned secret hissing,
To the outsetting bard.

Demon or bird (said the boy's soul)
Is it indeed toward your mate you sing? or is
        it really to me?
For I, that was a child, my tongue's use sleeping,
        now I have heard you,
Now in a moment I know what I am for, I
        awake,
And already a thousand singers, a thousand songs,
        clearer, louder and more sorrowful than
        yours,

A thousand warbling echoes have started to life
        within me, never to die.

O you singer solitary, singing by yourself,
        projecting me,   150
O solitary me listening, never more shall I
        cease perpetuating you,
Never more shall I escape, never more the
        reverberations,
Never more the cries of unsatisfied love be
        absent from me.
Never again leave me to be the peaceful child
        I was before what there in the night,
By the sea under the yellow and sagging moon,
The messenger there aroused, the fire, the sweet
        hell within,
The unknown want, the destiny of me.
O give me the clew! (It lurks in the night here
        somewhere)
O if I am to have so much, let me have more!
A word then, (for I will conquer it)   160
The word final, superior to all,
Subtle, sent up—what is it?—I listen;
Are you whispering it, and have been all the
        time, you sea-waves?
Is that it from your liquid rims and wet sands?

Whereto answering, the sea,
Delaying not, hurrying not,
Whispered me through the night, and very
        plainly before daybreak,
Lisped to me the low and delicious word death,
And again death, death, death, death,
Hissing melodious, neither like the bird nor like
        my aroused child's heart,   170
But edging near as privately for me, rustling
        at my feet,
Creeping thence steadily up to my ears and
        laving me softly all over,
Death, death, death, death, death.

Which I do not forget,
But fuse the song of my dusky demon and
        brother.

That he sang to me in the moonlight on
     Paumanok's gray beach,
With the thousand responsive songs at random,
My own songs awaked from that hour,
And with them the key, the word up from the
     waves,
The word of the sweetest song and all songs,   180
That strong and delicious word which, creeping
     to my feet,
(Or like some old crone rocking the cradle,
     swathed in sweet garments, bending aside)
The sea whispered me.

                     (*1859*)

John Keats

When I Have Fears That I May Cease to Be

When I have fears that I may cease to be
Before my pen has glean'd my teeming brain,
Before high pilèd books, in charact'ry,
Hold like rich garners the full-ripen'd grain;
When I behold, upon the night's starr'd face,
Huge cloudy symbols of a high romance,
And think that I may never live to trace
Their shadows, with the magic hand of chance;
And when I feel, fair creature of an hour!
That I shall never look upon thee more,   10
Never have relish in the faery power
Of unreflecting love!—then on the shore
Of the wide world I stand alone, and think
Till Love and Fame to nothingness do sink.

                     (*1848*)

Anonymous

Edward, Edward

'Why dois your brand sae drap wi bluid,
     Edward, Edward,
Why dois your brand sae drap wi bluid,
   And why sae sad gang yee O?'

l. 1. *dois:* does; *brand:* blade; *sae:* so.
l. 4. *gang:* go.

'O I hae killed my hauke sae guid,
     Mither, mither,
O I hae killed my hauke sae guid,
   And I had nae mair bot hee O.'

'Your haukis bluid was nevir sae reid,
     Edward, Edward,   10
Your haukis bluid was nevir sae reid,
   My deir son I tell thee O.'
'O I hae killed my reid-roan steid,
     Mither, mither,
O I hae killed my reid-roan steid,
   That erst was sae fair and frie O.'

'Your steid was auld, and ye hae got mair,
     Edward, Edward,
Your steid was auld, and ye hae got mair,
   Sum other dule ye drie O.'   20
'O I hae killed my fadir deir,
     Mither, mither,
O I hae killed my fadir deir,
   Alas, and wae is mee O!'

'And whatten penance wul ye drie for that,
     Edward, Edward?
And whatten penance will ye drie for that?
   My deir son, now tell me O.'
'Ile set my feit in yonder boat,
     Mither, mither,   30
Ile set my feit in yonder boat,
   And Ile fare ovir the sea O.'

'And what wul ye doe wi your towirs and your
     ha,
     Edward, Edward?
And what wul ye doe wi your towirs and your
     ha,
   That were sae fair to see O?'

l. 8. *nae mair:* no more.
l. 9. *reid:* red.
l. 16. *erst:* before.
l. 17. *mair:* more.
l. 20. *dule:* dolor, grief; *drie:* grieve, suffer.
l. 24. *wae:* woe.
l. 29. *feit:* feet.

'Ile let thame stand tul they doun fa,
    Mither, mither,
Ile let thame stand tul they doun fa,
    For here nevir mair maun I bee O.'   40

'And what wul ye leive to your bairns and your
    wife,
    Edward, Edward?
And what wul ye leive to your bairns and your
    wife,
    Whan ye gang ovir the sea O?'
'The warldis room, late them beg thrae life,
    Mither, mither,
The warldis room, late them beg thrae life,
    For thame nevir mair wul I see O.'

'And what wul ye leive to your ain mither deir,
    Edward, Edward?   50
And what wul ye leive to your ain mither deir?
    My deir son, now tell me O.'
'The curse of hell frae me sall ye beir,
    Mither, mither,
The curse of hell frae me sall ye beir,
    Sic counseils ye gave to me O.'

        (*ca. 18th century in English*)

l. 40. *maun:* must.
l. 41. *bairns:* children.
l. 45. *The warldis room:* the world has room; *thrae:* through.
l. 53. *frae:* from; *beir:* bear.
l. 56. *Sic:* such.

Thomas Campion

Fain Would I Wed

Fain would I wed a fair young man that night
    and day could please me,
When my mind or body grieved that had the
    power to ease me.
Maids are full of longing thoughts that breed a
    bloodless sickness,
And that, oft I hear men say, is only cured by
    quickness.
Oft I have been wooed and praised, but never
    could be movëd;
Many for a day or so I have most dearly lovëd,
But this foolish mind of mine straight loathes the
    thing resolvëd;
If to love be sin in me, that sin is soon absolvëd.
Sure I think I shall at last fly to some holy order;
When I once am settled there, then can I fly no
    farther.   10
Yet I would not die a maid, because I had a
    mother,
As I was by one brought forth, I would bring
    forth another.

        (*1617*)

EXERCISES

1. The struggle for identity is known psychologically as "individuation." It is the continuing process by which an individual fulfills his singular given dispositions; it is the evolution of the self into what each person feels himself to be. It is not to be confused with egotism, but rather, it is the making up of a composite of all of the peculiarities which must take expression in the form of the individual personality (*esse*). This journey to self-discovery, or this struggle for identity, is itself an archetype. Carl G. Jung defined archetypes as "the psychic residua of numberless experiences of the same type"—themes and images "deeply implanted in the memory of the race" of man. They may seem strange because they lie below the consciousness of man. We often sense them or feel them, rather than understand them. But we can perceive them in poetry—through

allegory and symbol—which stir our emotions with the shock of recognition. Briefly review *psychological*, *archetypal*, and *mythopoeic* approaches. Then, as accurately as possible, give definitions of these italicized terms.

"The Diver" [Hayden]

2. Equipped with this review and your definitions, consider the first poem of this section. First, paraphrase Hayden's poem, noting especially these lines and phrases: "lost images/fadingly remembered" (lines 5–6), the ". . . canyon of cold/nightgreen emptiness" (lines 8–9), "Freefalling, weightless" (line 10). Specifically determine the meaning of "infra-/space" (lines 13–14), "bryozoans" (line 24), "bubbling/manfish" (lines 28–29), "ectoplasmic/swirl of garments" (lines 37–38), "drunken shoes" (line 41), "eldritch hide" (line 43), "laughing/faces" (lines 44–45), "those hidden/ones, to fling aside/the mask and call to them" (lines 46–48), "have/done with self and/every dinning/vain complexity" (lines 50–53), "fights off/sleep desiring sleep" (lines 56–57), "kisses that I craved" (line 63), "Reflex of life-wish" (line 64), and "measured rise" (line 68).

3. Water, of course, is an archetypal symbol of life; it may also indicate rituals or ceremonies. Within the dreamlike matrix of Hayden's poem, for what is the persona searching? (This is a complex question with many possible answers.) Discuss. Could you describe the search as one for the biological history of man— hence, as evolutionary? Could you describe it as self-abnegating? fugitive? frightening? mystical? awesome? hesitant? fantasy-stippled? sexual? self-revealing? devoted toward one's fellowman? desirous of escaping loud, artificial, even meaningless existence? suppressive of desire that is socially and personally unaccepted? reluctantly affirmative of human existence? On the surface, of course, the poem deals with a diver who enters a sunken ship; but on deeper archetypal levels, may the poem be said to deal with a different kind of "diving": the more complex descent into one's self? To what extent may the poem justifiably be placed within the thematic unit of "Struggle for Identity"? With what other approaches may this poem be treated? Discuss.

"In a Dark Time" [Roethke]

4. What archetypes do you find in this poem? Choose those images most pertinent to the question and discuss them. Especially consider the line in the third stanza, "A man goes far to find out what he is" (line 16).

Through the symbol of darkness, what archetypes are revealed? Discuss. In what ways is the poem related thematically to "Struggle for Identity"? Discuss.

"Home Town" [Snodgrass], *"Ex-Basketball Player"* [Updike], and *"The Stranger"* [Everson]

5. Part of the process of discovering one's identity involves struggling through (and surviving) that phase of life we call adolescence. These three poems emphasize the failure to find one's identity within the context of adolescence. Briefly paraphrase each poem, noting that each poet features a persona who, in some way, identifies with aspects of life emphasized during the period of adolescence. In sequential order, consider the specific failures of each. Snodgrass' persona returns to his hometown and momentarily retrogresses to adolescent preoccupations. Updike's Flick Webb, once a fine basketball player, ". . . never learned a trade" (line 19) but is a helper in a gas station, and sometimes as a joke ". . . dribbles an inner tube" (line 21). Everson's sixteen-year-old girl, somewhat flippant about her discovery of sex, cannot see into her doomed future.

6. Each of these personae is, to varying degrees, tragic. Which is, perhaps, the most hopeful? the most hopeless?

7. In what indirect ways do all three poets make a commentary upon the demoralization which often accompanies the failure of a human being to discover his identity? Discuss.

"On the Move" [Gunn]

8. Notice the progression of ideas in this poem. Summarize each stanza in your own words, and then comment on the lines which seem to you to be most significant in relation to the theme of quest for identity. For example, in the second stanza, note that those who ride the motorcycles are dressed in a certain way. They are compared to ". . . flies hanging in heat . . ." (line 10). The noise of their motors is likened to ". . . thunder held by calf and thigh" (line 12), and, by wearing goggles, they have "donned impersonality" (line 13). Gunn writes, "They strap in doubt—by hiding it, robust—/ And almost hear a meaning in their noise" (lines 15–16). Does he all but state his dominant theme with these lines?

9. It is a well-known fact that one may escape one's problems of identity in a variety of ways: retreating into a world of childhood, wearing emblems meant to represent an identity (everything from badges to clothes which are, in effect, a kind of uniform substituted for an identity), or migrating or traveling—moving about from place to place. More than one psychologist has noted that the American pioneer, rather than subjecting himself to the rules of others, often migrated farther west. Do the black-jacketed boys with the motorcycles appear to be identifying with their frontier forebears or struggling to affiliate themselves with a new age in which the machine may become a goal within itself rather than a means to achieve a more meaningful life? Is this a timely poem? Discuss.

10. Does the poet feel that the cyclists, in their travels, wearing their ". . . gleaming jackets trophied with the dust" (line 14) have, in a sense, found a partial solution to the problem of identity? In considering your answer, examine closely the fourth stanza. Does the poet suggest that there may be some progress even within the fury of an apparently meaningless motion, a movement "always toward, toward" (line 32)?

11. What points would the sociocultural critic have to make about the problems of identity faced by robust young male adolescents in a machine age? What other criticisms of modern society are implied by the poet? Mention specific lines and images which support your observations.

"The New Icarus" [Miller] and "The Tobacconist of Eighth Street" [Eberhart]

12. Examine Miller's poem. The myth of Icarus is well known. Daedalus, a skilled artificer who had designed a labyrinth on the island of Crete for King Minos later earned the regent's wrath and was placed in the prison of his own making with his young son, Icarus. He contrived wings of beeswax and feathers to effect their escape. The impulsive young Icarus failed to heed his father's advice to fly midway between the ocean and the sun so as to preserve the wings on their long flight to Sicily. Instead he flew too close to the sun, and he plunged into the ocean—what later became known as the Icarian Sea. The saddened father, Daedalus, survived the ordeal.

The desire of man to fly, free, is both mythopoeic and archetypal. The story we call myth, the theme archetype. What relationships do you find between Vassar Miller's poem and the myth (story)? the archetype (theme)? In a metaphorical sense, may one fly toward his own self-discovery or individuation? The historical critic would be interested in the poet as well as the poem. He would discover, perhaps, that Vassar Miller has suffered in life with a physical affliction. Does such a historical approach, or biographical knowledge, help you in understanding the poem, especially the significance of the title? Discuss. What special problems of identity may be created by physical debilities, human suffering, disease, crippling, and other handicaps? Discuss.

13. Now read Eberhart's poem. Do you find any images akin to flight in the poem, particularly in the fourth stanza? Just as the flight of Icarus ended in tragedy and frustration, do you sense an archetypal parallel in the circumstances of the ". . . querulous old man, the tobacconist of Eighth Street" (line 1)? Compare and contrast the two poems. How do they both fit into the theme of the struggle for identity?

"*The world is a beautiful place*" [Ferlinghetti]

14. Sociocultural approaches to poetry may be brought to bear upon this poem. Read the poem, noting carefully the sardonic, irreverent, and heavily ironic feeling and tone. What social, economic, and political aspects of this poem are evident? Assuming that literature may be considered as social commentary, what are some of the aspects of modern culture which Ferlinghetti questions and imprecates? Discuss. Does Ferlinghetti reveal a "tension between tradition and experience . . . in his heart" consistent with the Marxist critic Christopher Caudwell's observations about poets? Point out specific lines of the poem which lend validity to your answer. Do you sense social, political, moral, and aesthetic disillusionment in the poet's work? The question becomes important in determining whether his feeling develops naturally out of his poetry, or whether it is imposed from without upon his poetry, thus placing the result—whether we call it a poem or not—somewhere between true literature and polemical writing. Discuss.

"*But Can See Better There, and Laughing There*" [Brooks] and "*I, Too*" [Hughes]

15. Read these two poems. Psychologists have admonished us that the two extremes one may experience in the struggle for identity may be represented by sedentary conservatism (rigidity), on the one hand, and excessive migratory habits (confusion and disorder), on the other. Both, of course, are illusory substitutes for truly satisfying individual fulfillment—what psychologists call "ego integrity," and what most of us call, simply, "self-respect." With each of these poems in mind, define some of the major problems of the American Negro child in his effort to achieve personal identity or integrity of self. What problems has the American Negro shared in common with the American frontiersman? What varying forms of autocracy tended to "fence in" both? Do both Brooks and Hughes indicate that their people may achieve an American identity, too? Point to specific lines which support your views. Although both poems are ultimately optimistic and affirmative, do they differ in feeling and tone? Discuss.

"*Poem in October*" [Thomas] and "*Pat Hennessey*" [Stuart]

16. Both Dylan Thomas' "Poem in October" and Jesse Stuart's "Pat Hennessey" are replete with nature imagery. Compare and contrast the lines dealing with these images, especially in the early portions of the poems. Other specific parallels may be followed throughout the poems, including such details as the mention of fruit—both use apples. Strangely, the poems seem to run in parallel streams as both poets reflect upon their childhoods and the poignant memories of their mothers. Both conclude in a kind of paean of joy, in which the protagonists recognize the miracle of their own lives, as well as the continuity of life from parent to child. In what ways does each poem eloquently bespeak a kind of fulfillment of the individual search for self-discovery? Point to specific lines and images which you think most effectively express the theme.

"*The Lake Isle of Innisfree*" [Yeats] and "*Out of the Cradle Endlessly Rocking*" [Whitman]

17. Consistent with the theme of this section of poetry, what do these two poems have in common? In what ways does each poet demonstrate that one must get back to essences—nature, water, childhood—in order to refresh himself in his journey toward self-discovery? Discuss. Do you see relationships between these poems and other poems in the section? Comment.

4. Love of Many Kinds

And I would rather have my sweet,
Though rose-leaves die of grieving,

Than do high deeds in Hungary
To pass all men's believing.

[Ezra Pound, *An Immorality*]

R. B. Weber

Sweet Baskers and Hammerheads

"Your wild eyes looked green on mine"

never fish   my rising head
swam greenly so   took swimming strokes
into my sea—   in the channel of
shook stare.   love's openness:
Your finsharp swish your soft intent
came quick to cut   caught fin's caress,
my reef of fear: relentless knife
hot tearing run   that ran your sheath
you salted tail—   for rare and saving   10

      springs of yes.

    Frail Sharpers Greet
    All Skins Replete,
    Your Bright-Boned Meat.   (*1969*)

Roger Shattuck

The Future of Romance

A Texas Pastoral

In air-locked housecars
flank to flank they sit deprived of nothing
munching gum in shiftless splendor
stuck to the seat and to each other.
Public lovers on a rear-vision roadbed
god knows what they do in private
except crawl inside each other's skin
or separate just far and long enough
to telephone for another date.

After seven months of steady going   10
with a transistor set to keep them warm
at last they reach the drive-in marriage lot
and park.

They never wrote a love letter
nor saw the reason to.

(*1964*)

Laurence Josephs

My Father Playing Golf

Sorrowfully, softly swearing
Between egg-sandwiches and
Waiting: time out for sun worship,
My gallant father on the links,
Whose initialed ball with speed
Carries his eye like a blue bird.

All, always with love, he speeds
As a flag the wind, a swift, linnet,
The light above small flowers
And time's dearness from damp dawn   10
And prayed-for day (the sunset),
While weather news he eats as if from kitchens.

Whose wrists the sinews navigate I love,
And love attending on those mysteries
He tells: how like a dragon-
Hunter to the awful grove he comes;
How beats his way beyond, engreaved with
          lightfern
And the cumbrous roots,

At last upon the open where a princess-
Banner flies. Alas then, my poor father falls   20
Into the dry moat of his favorite game:
The death trap of his Sunday life
He fights, but, fighting, loves.
And whence he casts up to the waiting air
Such brilliant fountains of irradiate sand
As sway his battle to their lovely sight!

                                        (*1963*)

Howard Nemerov

De Anima

Now it is night, now in the brilliant room
A girl stands at the window looking out,
But sees, in the darkness of the frame,
Only her own image.

And there is a young man across the street
Who looks at the girl and into the brilliant
          room.
They might be in love, might be about to meet,
If this were a romance.

In looking at herself, she tries to look
Beyond herself, and half become another,   10
Admiring and resenting, maybe dreaming
Her lover might see her so.

The other, the stranger standing in cold and
          dark,
Looks at the young girl in her crystalline room.
He sees clearly, and hopelessly desires,
A life that is not his.

Given the blindness of her self-possession,
The luminous vision revealed to his despair,
We look to both sides of the glass at once
And see no future in it.   20

These pure divisions hurt us in some realm
Of parable beyond belief, beyond
The temporal mind. Why is it sorrowful?
Why do we want them together?

Is it the spirit, ransacking through the earth
After its image, its being, its begetting?
The spirit sorrows, for what lovers bring
Into the world is death,

The most exclusive romance, after all,
The sort that lords and ladies listen to   30
With selfish tears, when she draws down the
          shade,
When he has turned away,

When the blind embryo with his bow of bees,
His candied arrows tipped with flower heads,
Turns from them too, for mercy or for grief
Refusing to be, refusing to die.

                                        (*1962*)

Vassar Miller

Reciprocity

You who would sorrow even for a token
Of hurt in me no less than you would grieve
For seeing me with my whole body broken
And long no less to solace and relieve;
You who, as though you wished me mere Good
     Morning,
Would smash your heart upon the hardest stones
Of my distress as when you once, unscorning,
Would sleep upon the margin of my moans—
I yield my want, this house of gutted portals,
All to your want, I yield this ravaged stack,   10
In testimony that between two mortals
No gift may be except a giving back.
What present could I make you from what skill
When your one need is me to need you still?

                           (*1960*)

Philip Booth

First Lesson

Lie back, daughter, let your head
be tipped back in the cup of my hand.
Gently, and I will hold you. Spread
your arms wide, lie out on the stream
and look high at the gulls. A dead-
man's float is face down. You will dive
and swim soon enough where this tidewater
ebbs to the sea. Daughter, believe
me, when you tire on the long thrash
to your island, lie up, and survive.   10
As you float now, where I held you
and let go, remember when fear
cramps your heart what I told you:
lie gently and wide to the light-year
stars, lie back, and the sea will hold you.

                           (*1957*)

Richard Wilbur

Love Calls Us to the Things of This World

    The eyes open to a cry of pulleys,
And spirited from sleep, the astounded soul
Hangs for a moment bodiless and simple
As false dawn.
                   Outside the open window
The morning air is all awash with angels.

    Some are in bed-sheets, some are in blouses,
Some are in smocks: but truly there they are.
Now they are rising together in calm swells
Of halcyon feeling, filling whatever they wear
With the deep joy of their impersonal breathing;

    Now they are flying in place, conveying   11
The terrible speed of their omnipresence, moving
And staying like white water; and now of a
    sudden
They swoon down into so rapt a quiet
That nobody seems to be there.
                      The soul shrinks

    From all that it is about to remember,
From the punctual rape of every blessèd day,
And cries,
          "Oh, let there be nothing on earth
                      but laundry,
Nothing but rosy hands in the rising steam
And clear dances done in the sight of heaven."   20

    Yet, as the sun acknowledges
With a warm look the world's hunks and colors,
The soul descends once more in bitter love
To accept the waking body, saying now
In a changed voice as the man yawns and rises,

"Bring them down from their ruddy gallows;
Let there be clean linen for the backs of thieves;
Let lovers go fresh and sweet to be undone,
And the heaviest nuns walk in a pure floating
Of dark habits,
                    keeping their difficult balance." 30
                                        (*1956*)

David Ignatow

The Complex

My father's madness is to own himself,
for what he gives is taken. He is
a single son of God. He is mad
to know the loves he owns are for his keeping,
so if he does not love he is without himself,
for God has said, Of love you are a man.
You are yourself, apart from me.
And madly my father seeks his loves,
with whom there is no standing,
for as he would own himself   10
he is the measuring rod,
and slowly owes himself to God,
giving of himself with forced breath.
                                        (*1955*)

Theodore Roethke

I Knew a Woman

I knew a woman, lovely in her bones,
When small birds sighed, she would sigh back
        at them;
Ah, when she moved, she moved more ways
        than one:
The shapes a bright container can contain!
Of her choice virtues only gods should speak,
Or English poets who grew up on Greek
(I'd have them sing in chorus, cheek to cheek).

How well her wishes went! She stroked my chin,
She taught me Turn, and Counter-turn, and
        Stand;
She taught me Touch, that undulant white skin;
I nibbled meekly from her proffered hand;   11
She was the sickle; I, poor I, the rake,
Coming behind her for her pretty sake
(But what prodigious mowing we did make).

Love likes a gander, and adores a goose:
Her full lips pursed, the errant note to seize;
She played it quick, she played it light and
        loose;
My eyes, they dazzled at her flowing knees;
Her several parts could keep a pure repose,
Or one hip quiver with a mobile nose   20
(She moved in circles, and those circles moved).

Let seed be grass, and grass turn into hay:
I'm martyr to a motion not my own;
What's freedom for? To know eternity.
I swear she cast a shadow white as stone.
But who would count eternity in days?
These old bones live to learn her wanton ways:
(I measure time by how a body sways).
                                        (*1954*)

Vassar Miller

The Final Hunger

Hurl down the nerve-gnarled body hurtling
        head-
Long into sworls of shade-hush. Plummeting,
        keep
The latch of eyelids shut to so outleap
Care's claws. Arms, legs, abandon grace and
        spread
Your spent sprawl—glutton ravening to be fed
With fats, creams, fruits, meats, spice that heavy-
        heap
The hands, that golden-gloss the flesh, of sleep,
Sleep, the sole lover that I take to bed.

But they couch crouching in the darkness, city
Of wakefulness uncaptured by assaulting— 10
Senses by sleep unravished and unwon.
Sun-sword night-sheathed, lie never between
    (have pity!)
Between me and my love, between me and the
    vaulting
Down the dense sweetness of oblivion.
                     (1951)

John Ciardi

To Judith Asleep

My dear, darkened in sleep, turned from the
    moon
that riots on curtain stir with every breeze,
leaping in moths of light across your back . . .
far off, then soft and sudden as petals shower
down from wired roses—silently, all at once—
you turn, abandoned and naked, all let down
in ferny streams of sleep and petaled thighs
rippling into my flesh's buzzing garden.

Far and familiar your body's myth-map lights,
traveled by moon and dapple. Sagas were
    curved 10
like scimitars to your hips. The raiders' ships
all sailed to your one port. And watchfires
    burned
your image on the hills. Sweetly you drown
male centuries in your chiaroscuro tide
of breast and breath. And all my memory's shores
you frighten perfectly, washed familiar and far.

Ritual wars have climbed your shadowed flank
where bravos dreaming of fair women tore
rock out of rock to have your cities down
in loot of hearths and trophies of desire. 20
And desert monks have fought your image back
in a hysteria of mad skeletons.
Bravo and monk (the heads and tails of love)
I stand, a spinning coin of wish and dread,

counting our life, our chairs, our books and walls,
our clock whose radium eye and insect voice
owns all our light and shade, and your white
    shell
spiraled in moonlight on the bed's white beach;
thinking, I might press you to my ear
and all your coils fall out in sounds of surf 30
washing a mystery sudden as you are
a light on light in light beyond the light.

Child, child, and making legend of my wish
fastened alive into your naked sprawl—
stir once to stop my fear and miser's panic
that time shall have you last and legendry
undress to old bones from its moon brocade.
Yet sleep and keep our prime of time alive
before that death of legend. My dear of all

saga and century, sleep in familiar-far. 40
Time still must tick *this is, I am, we are.*
                     (1949)

John Frederick Nims

Love Poem

My clumsiest dear, whose hands shipwreck vases,
At whose quick touch all glasses chip and ring,
Whose palms are bulls in china, burs in linen,
And have no cunning with any soft thing

Except all ill at ease fidgeting people:
The refugee uncertain at the door
You make at home; deftly you steady
The drunk clambering on his undulant floor.

Unpredictable dear, the taxi drivers' terror,
Shrinking from far headlights pale as a dime 10
Yet leaping before red apoplectic streetcars—
Misfit in any space. And never on time.

A wrench in clocks and the solar system. Only
With words and people and love you move at
 ease.
In traffic of wit expertly manoeuvre
And keep us, all devotion, at your knees.

Forgetting your coffee spreading on our flannel,
Your lipstick grinning on our coat,
So gayly in love's unbreakable heaven
Our souls on glory of spilt bourbon float. 20

Be with me darling early and late. Smash glasses—
I will study wry music for your sake.
For should your hands drop white and empty
All the toys of the world would break.

      (1947)

Jesse Stuart

Harry Dartmore Speaks for Maitland Gray Arnett

This cedar stands a lone bewildered ghost
For one I loved in life, respect in death;
Her lichened stone reads that she is not lost,
It heralds Paradise with angel breath.
I cannot say it was my fault she died,
She who has borne a child for one of us;
Loved more by me but was another's bride.
Gray seeded grass and wind now weep for her
And dead phlox stems weep winter rain-drop
 tears.
I pass her cedar without words to say 10
Since Maitland has slept here for many years,
Married to Bill through vows, her precious clay,
Married to me through love, devotion, kiss . . .
She died for one of us in her child-birth!
'Love's more than marriage vows, man should
 know this,'
Whispers the shaggy cedar from its earth.

      (1944)

Richard Eberhart

' When Doris Danced '

When Doris danced under the oak tree
The sun himself might wish to see,
Might bend beneath those lovers, leaves,
While her her virgin step she weaves
And envious cast his famous hue
To make her daft, yet win her too.

When Doris danced under the oak tree
Slow John, so stormed in heart, at sea
Gone all his store, a wreck he lay.
But on the ground the sun-beams play. 10
They lit his face in such degree
Doris lay down, all out of pity.

      (1940)

Jesse Stuart

" And you, my mother, who will stack by you?"

And you, my mother, who will stack by you?
In beauty—yes—others are beautiful
And you are not in flesh and fancy guise.
But you have lived a life so rich and full,
Few worldly beauties stack beside of you.
If they'd gone through with all you have gone
 through,
Their eyes would blear and blue fade from the
 blue,
Their flesh would be as rugged as yours too.
You've asked no man the odds of work to do,
You've done your share—you've done it with
 a will, 10
You've done it with the solidness of hill.
And unafraid you've met your life, my mother—

Now unafraid, I say there is no other
That after all can stack beside of you—
The tree in you, flower in you, the hill,
Color of autumn leaf, the twisted grape-vine
    will.

                (1934)

Stephen Vincent Benét

American Names

I have fallen in love with American names,
The sharp names that never get fat,
The snakeskin-titles of mining-claims,
The plumed war-bonnet of Medicine Hat,
Tucson and Deadwood and Lost Mule Flat.

Seine and Piave are silver spoons,
But the spoonbowl-metal is thin and worn,
There are English counties like hunting-tunes
Played on the keys of a postboy's horn,
But I will remember where I was born.   10

I will remember Carquinez Straits,
Little French Lick and Lundy's Lane,
The Yankee ships and the Yankee dates
And the bullet-towns of Calamity Jane.
I will remember Skunktown Plain.

I will fall in love with a Salem tree
And a rawhide quirt from Santa Cruz,
I will get me a bottle of Boston sea
And a blue-gum nigger to sing me blues
I am tired of loving a foreign muse.   20

Rue des Martyrs and Bleeding-Heart-Yard,
Senlis, Pisa, and Blindman's Oast,
It is a magic ghost you guard
But I am sick for a newer ghost,
Harrisburg, Spartanburg, Painted Post.

Henry and John were never so
And Henry and John were always right?
Granted, but when it was time to go
And the tea and the laurels had stood all night,
Did they never watch for Nantucket Light?   30

I shall not rest quiet in Montparnasse.
I shall not lie easy at Winchelsea.
You may bury my body in Sussex grass,
You may bury my tongue at Champmédy.
I shall not be there. I shall rise and pass.
Bury my heart at Wounded Knee.

                (1927)

Louise Bogan

Women

Women have no wilderness in them,
They are provident instead,
Content in the tight hot cell of their hearts
To eat dusty bread.

They do not see cattle cropping red winter grass,
They do not hear
Snow water going down under culverts
Shallow and clear.

They wait, when they should turn to journeys,
They stiffen, when they should bend.   10
They use against themselves that benevolence
To which no man is friend.

They cannot think of so many crops to a field
Or of clean wood cleft by an axe.
Their love is an eager meaninglessness
Too tense, or too lax.

They hear in every whisper that speaks to them
A shout and a cry.
As like as not, when they take life over their
    door-sills
They should let it go by.   20

                (1922)

Edna St. Vincent Millay

" *I know I am but summer to your heart* "

I know I am but summer to your heart,
And not the full four seasons of the year;
And you must welcome from another part
Such noble moods as are not mine, my dear.
No gracious weight of golden fruits to sell
Have I, nor any wise and wintry thing;
And I have loved you all too long and well
To carry still the high sweet breast of Spring.
Wherefore I say: O love, as summer goes,
I must be gone, steal forth with silent drums,   10
That you may hail anew the bird and rose
When I come back to you, as summer comes.
Else will you seek, at some not distant time,
Even your summer in another clime.

(1920)

William Butler Yeats

A Prayer for My Daughter

Once more the storm is howling, and half hid
Under this cradle-hood and coverlid
My child sleeps on. There is no obstacle
But Gregory's wood and one bare hill
Whereby the haystack- and roof-levelling wind,
Bred on the Atlantic, can be stayed;
And for an hour I have walked and prayed
Because of the great gloom that is in my mind.

I have walked and prayed for this young child
            an hour
And heard the sea-wind scream upon the tower,[10]
And under the arches of the bridge, and scream
In the elms above the flooded stream;
Imagining in excited reverie
That the future years had come,
Dancing to a frenzied drum,
Out of the murderous innocence of the sea.

May she be granted beauty and yet not
Beauty to make a stranger's eye distraught,
Or hers before a looking-glass, for such,
Being made beautiful overmuch,   20
Consider beauty a sufficient end,
Lose natural kindness and maybe
The heart-revealing intimacy
That chooses right, and never find a friend.

Helen being chosen found life flat and dull
And later had much trouble from a fool,
While that great Queen, that rose out of the
            spray,
Being fatherless could have her way
Yet chose a bandy-leggèd smith for man.
It's certain that fine women eat   30
A crazy salad with their meat
Whereby the Horn of Plenty is undone.

In courtesy I'd have her chiefly learned;
Hearts are not had as a gift but hearts are earned
By those that are not entirely beautiful;
Yet many, that have played the fool
For beauty's very self, has charm made wise,
And many a poor man that has roved,
Loved and thought himself beloved,
From a glad kindness cannot take his eyes.   40

May she become a flourishing hidden tree
That all her thoughts may like the linnet be,
And have no business but dispensing round
Their magnanimities of sound,
Nor but in merriment begin a chase,
Nor but in merriment a quarrel.
O may she live like some green laurel
Rooted in one dear perpetual place.

My mind, because the minds that I have loved,
The sort of beauty that I have approved,   50
Prosper but little, has dried up of late,
Yet knows that to be choked with hate
May well be of all evil chances chief.
If there's no hatred in a mind
Assault and battery of the wind
Can never tear the linnet from the leaf.

An intellectual hatred is the worst,
So let her think opinions are accursed.
Have I not seen the loveliest woman born
Out of the mouth of Plenty's horn,   60
Because of her opinionated mind
Barter that horn and every good
By quiet natures understood
For an old bellows full of angry wind?

Considering that, all hatred driven hence,
The soul recovers radical innocence
And learns at last that it is self-delighting,
Self-appeasing, self-affrighting,
And that its own sweet will is Heaven's will;
She can, though every face should scowl   70
And every windy quarter howl
Or every bellows burst, be happy still.

And may her bridegroom bring her to a house
Where all's accustomed, ceremonious;
For arrogance and hatred are the wares
Peddled in the thoroughfares.
How but in custom and in ceremony
Are innocence and beauty born?
Ceremony's a name for the rich horn,
And custom for the spreading laurel tree.   80

(*1919*)

Rupert Brooke

The Hill

Breathless, we flung us on the windy hill,
    Laughed in the sun, and kissed the lovely grass.
    You said, "Through glory and ecstasy we pass;
Wind, sun, and earth remain, the birds sing still,
When we are old, are old. . . ." "And when we
    die
    All's over that is ours; and life burns on
Through other lovers, other lips," said I,
—"Heart of my heart, our heaven is now, is
    won!"

"We are Earth's best, that learnt her lesson here.
    Life is our cry. We have kept the faith!" we
        said;   10
    "We shall go down with unreluctant tread
Rose-crowned into the darkness!" . . . Proud we
    were,
And laughed, that had such brave true things
    to say.
—And then you suddenly cried, and turned
    away.

(*1915*)

Scharmel Iris

April

I loved her more than moon or sun—
    There is no moon or sun for me;
Of lovely things to look upon,
    The loveliest was she.

She does not hear me, though I sing—
    And, oh, my heart is like to break!
The world awakens with the Spring,
    But she—she does not wake!

(*1914*)

Ezra Pound

An Immorality

Sing we for love and idleness,
Naught else is worth having.

Though I have been in many a land,
There is naught else in living.

And I would rather have my sweet,
Though rose-leaves die of grieving,

Than do high deeds in Hungary
To pass all men's believing.

(*1912*)

Ernest Dowson

Non Sum Qualis Eram Bonae Sub Regno Cynarae

Last night, ah, yesternight, betwixt her lips and
    mine
There fell thy shadow, Cynara! thy breath was
    shed
Upon my soul between the kisses and the wine;
And I was desolate and sick of an old passion,
    Yea, I was desolate and bowed my head—
I have been faithful to thee, Cynara! in my
    fashion.

All night upon mine heart I felt her warm heart
    beat,
Night-long within mine arms in love and sleep
    she lay;
Surely the kisses of her bought red mouth were
    sweet;
But I was desolate and sick of an old passion,   10
    When I awoke and found the dawn was gray—
I have been faithful to thee, Cynara! in my
    fashion.

I have forgot much, Cynara! gone with the wind,
Flung roses, roses riotously with the throng,
Dancing, to put thy pale, lost lilies out of mind;
But I was desolate and sick of an old passion,
    Yea, all the time, because the dance was long—
I have been faithful to thee, Cynara! in my
    fashion.

I cried for madder music and for stronger wine,
But when the feast is finished and the lamps
    expire,   20
Then falls thy shadow, Cynara! the night is thine;
And I am desolate and sick of an old passion,
    Yea, hungry for the lips of my desire—
I have been faithful to thee, Cynara! in my
    fashion.

                (1896)

A. E. Housman

Oh, When I Was in Love with You

Oh, when I was in love with you,
    Then I was clean and brave,
And miles around the wonder grew
    How well did I behave.

And now the fancy passes by,
    And nothing will remain,
And miles around they'll say that I
    Am quite myself again.

                (1896)

Percy Bysshe Shelley

Love's Philosophy

The fountains mingle with the river
    And the rivers with the ocean,
The winds of heaven mix for ever
    With a sweet emotion;
Nothing in the world is single,
    All things by a law divine
In one another's being mingle—
    Why not I with thine?

See the mountains kiss high heaven
    And the waves clasp one another;   10
No sister-flower would be forgiven
    If it disdain'd its brother:
And the sunlight clasps the earth,
    And the moonbeams kiss the sea—
What are all these kissings worth,
    If thou kiss not me?

                (1819)

Robert Burns

O, My Luve Is Like a Red, Red Rose

O, my luve is like a red, red rose,
   That's newly sprung in June.
O my luve is like the melodie
   That's sweetly played in tune.

As fair art thou, my bonnie lass,
   So deep in luve am I,
And I will luve thee still, my dear,
   Till a' the seas gang dry.

Till a' the seas gang dry, my dear,
   And the rocks melt wi' the sun!   10
And I will luve thee still, my dear,
   While the sands o' life shall run.

And fare thee weel, my only luve,
   And fare thee weel awhile!
And I will come again, my luve,
   Though it were ten thousand mile!

                          (*1796*)

Anonymous

Lord Randal

'O where hae ye been, Lord Randal, my son?
O where hae ye been, my handsome young
    man?'
'I hae been to the wild wood; mother, make my
    bed soon,
For I'm weary wi hunting, and fain wald lie
    down.'

'Where gat ye your dinner, Lord Randal, my son?

l. 4. *fain:* would be glad.

Where gat ye your dinner, my handsome young
    man?'
'I din'd wi my true-love; mother, make my bed
    soon,
For I'm weary wi hunting, and fain wald lie
    down.'

'What gat ye to your dinner, Lord Randal,
    my son?
What gat ye to your dinner, my handsome young
    man?'   10
'I gat eels boiled in broo; mother, make my
    bed soon,
For I'm weary wi hunting, and fain wald lie
    down.'

'What became of your bloodhounds, Lord
    Randal, my son?
What became of your bloodhounds, my hand-
    some young man?'
'O they swelld and they died; mother, make my
    bed soon,
For I'm weary wi hunting, and fain wald lie
    down.'

'O I fear ye are poisond, Lord Randal, my son!
O I fear ye are poisond, my handsome young
    man!'
'O yes! I am poisond; mother, make my bed
    soon,
For I'm sick at the heart and I fain wald lie
    down.'   20

              (*ca. 18th century in English*)

l. 6. *gat ye:* got you.

Andrew Marvell

To His Coy Mistress

Had we but world enough, and time,
This coyness, lady, were no crime.
We would sit down, and think which way
To walk, and pass our long love's day.

Thou by the Indian Ganges' side
Should'st rubies find: I by the tide
Of Humber would complain. I would
Love you ten years before the Flood,
And you should, if you please, refuse
Till the conversion of the Jews.   10
My vegetable love should grow
Vaster than empires, and more slow.
An hundred years should go to praise
Thine eyes, and on thy forehead gaze:
Two hundred to adore each breast:
But thirty thousand to the rest;
An age at least to every part,
And the last age should show your heart.
For, lady, you deserve this state,
Nor would I love at lower rate.   20
   But at my back I always hear
Time's wingèd chariot hurrying near:
And yonder all before us lie
Deserts of vast eternity.
Thy beauty shall no more be found;
Nor, in thy marble vault, shall sound
My echoing song: then worms shall try
That long-preserved virginity,
And your quaint honour turn to dust,
And into ashes all my lust.   30
The grave's a fine and private place,
But none, I think, do there embrace.
   Now, therefore, while the youthful hue
Sits on thy skin like morning dew,
And while thy willing soul transpires
At every pore with instant fires,
Now let us sport us while we may;
And now, like amorous birds of prey,
Rather at once our Time devour,
Than languish in his slow-chapt power.   40
Let us roll all our strength and all
Our sweetness up into one ball,
And tear our pleasures with rough strife
Thorough the iron gates of life.
Thus, though we cannot make our sun
Stand still, yet we will make him run.

                                  (*1681*)

Sir John Suckling

The Constant Lover

Out upon it, I have loved
   Three whole days together!
And am like to love three more,
   If it prove fair weather.

Time shall moult away his wings
   Ere he shall discover
In the whole wide world again
   Such a constant lover.

But the spite on't is, no praise
   Is due at all to me: 10
Love with me had made no stays,
   Had it any been but she.

Had it any been but she,
   And that very face,
There had been at least ere this
   A dozen dozen in her place.

                          (*1659*)

Robert Herrick

Upon Julia's Clothes

Whenas in silks my Julia goes,
Then, then, methinks, how sweetly flows
That liquefaction of her clothes!

Next, when I cast mine eyes, and see
That brave vibration each way free,
O, how that glittering taketh me!

                          (*1648*)

Robert Herrick

To the Virgins, to Make Much of Time

Gather ye rosebuds while ye may,
  Old Time is still a-flying:
And this same flower that smiles today
  Tomorrow will be dying.

The glorious lamp of heaven, the sun,
  The higher he's a-getting,
The sooner will his race be run,
  And nearer he's to setting.

That age is best which is the first,
  When youth and blood are warmer;   10
But being spent, the worse, and worst
  Times still succeed the former.

Then be not coy, but use your time,
  And while ye may, go marry;
For, having lost but once your prime,
  You may for ever tarry.

                (1648)

Edmund Waller

On a Girdle

  That which her slender waist confined,
Shall now my joyful temples bind;
No monarch but would give his crown,
His arms might do what this has done.

  It was my heaven's extremest sphere,
The pale which held that lovely deer,
My joy, my grief, my hope, my love,
Did all within this circle move!

  A narrow compass! and yet there
Dwelt all that's good, and all that's fair!   10
Give me but what this ribband bound,
Take all the rest the sun goes round!

                (1645)

William Shakespeare

Sonnet 130

My mistress' eyes are nothing like the sun,
Coral is far more red than her lips' red.
If snow be white, why then her breasts are dun,
If hairs be wires, black wires grow on her head.
I have seen roses damasked, red and white,
But no such roses see I in her cheeks.
And in some perfumes is there more delight
Than in the breath that from my mistress reeks.
I love to hear her speak, yet well I know
That music hath a far more pleasing sound.   10
I grant I never saw a goddess go,
My mistress, when she walks, treads on the
    ground.
  And yet, by Heaven, I think my love as rare
  As any she belied with false compare.

                (1609)

William Shakespeare

Sonnet 73

That time of year thou mayst in me behold
When yellow leaves, or none, or few, do hang
Upon those boughs which shake against the
    cold,
Bare ruin'd choirs, where late the sweet birds
    sang.
In me thou see'st the twilight of such day
As after sunset fadeth in the west,
Which by and by black night doth take away,
Death's second self, that seals up all in rest.

In me thou see'st the glowing of such fire
That on the ashes of his youth doth lie,   10
As the death-bed whereon it must expire
Consum'd with that which it was nourish'd by.
  This thou perceivest, which makes thy love
    more strong,
  To love that well which thou must leave ere
    long.

                              (1609)

Christopher Marlowe

The Passionate Shepherd to His Love

Come live with me and be my love,
And we will all the pleasures prove
That hills and valleys, dales and fields,
Or woods, or steepy mountain yields.

And we will sit upon the rocks,
And see the shepherds feed their flocks
By shallow rivers, to whose falls
Melodious birds sing madrigals.

And I will make thee beds of roses
And a thousand fragrant posies;   10
A cap of flowers, and a kirtle
Embroidered all with leaves of myrtle;

A gown made of the finest wool
Which from our pretty lambs we pull;
Fair lined slippers for the cold,
With buckles of the purest gold;

A belt of straw and ivy buds,
With coral clasps and amber studs;
And if these pleasures may thee move,
Come live with me, and be my love.   20

The shepherd swains shall dance and sing
For thy delight each May morning;
If these delights thy mind may move,
Then live with me and be my love.

                              (1599)

Sir Walter Raleigh

The Nymph's Reply to the Shepherd

If all the world and love were young
And truth in every shepherd's tongue,
These pretty pleasures might me move
To live with thee and be thy love.

Time drives the flocks from field to fold
When rivers rage and rocks grow cold,
And Philomel becometh dumb;
The rest complain of cares to come.

The flowers do fade, and wanton fields
To wayward winter reckoning yields;   10
A honey tongue, a heart of gall,
Is fancy's spring, but sorrow's fall.

Thy gowns, thy shoes, thy beds of roses,
Thy cap, thy kirtle, and thy posies
Soon break, soon wither, soon forgotten,
In folly ripe, in reason rotten.

Thy belt of straw and ivy buds,
Thy coral clasps and amber studs,
All these in me no means can move
To come to thee and be thy love.   20

But could youth last and love still breed,
Had joys no date nor age no need,
Then these delights my mind might move
To live with thee and be thy love.

                              (1599)

EXERCISES

After reading the poems of this section, you may experience an increased awareness of the multitude of meanings, as well as the subtle nuances, of love. Following are ten somewhat arbitrary groupings of kinds of love suggested by the poems of this section. Doubtless, there are other possible groupings, too. Using whatever approaches to poetry which you think most suitable, select at least one poem in addition to the one we have categorized under each heading, and relate both, as substantively as possible, to their particular category. Do you see relationships between the paired poems significant enough that you can comment upon them? Discuss. Do you see relationships between poems placed in different categories? Do some poems seem to fit several categories? In your treatment of these questions, utilize references to lines and phrases of the poems, and demonstrate how the poet sheds new light upon old ideas or states old ideas in such a way that they seem new and freshly meaningful:

1. *Familial love* (father, mother, son, daughter)
   a. Philip Booth's "First Lesson"
   b. Your choice(s)

2. *Sensitive and tenderly sensuous love between the sexes*
   a. Andrew Marvell's "To His Coy Mistress"
   b. Your choice(s)

3. *Physical love between the sexes (lust, seduction, sexual intercourse)*
   a. R. B. Weber's "Sweet Baskers and Hammerheads"
   b. Your choice(s)

4. *Exaltation of the sexual opposite as the highest form of love*
   a Ezra Pound's "An Immorality"
   b. Your choice(s)

5. *Love of life, earthly existence, places*
   a. Stephen Vincent Benét's "American Names"
   b. Your choice(s)

6. *Romantic love with mixed emotions (for example, joy and grief)*
   a. Rupert Brooke's "The Hill"
   b. Your choice(s)

7. *Strange forms of love* (compulsion; impulse; incomplete and unfulfilled love; perversions, such as voyeurism, fetishism, fanaticism, and masochism)
   a. "Lord Randal"
   b. Your choice(s)

8. *Love between the sexes viewed analogically* (that is, seen through analogies, similes, and indirect comparisons)
   a. Scharmel Iris' "April"
   b. Your choice(s)

9. *Uniquely individual love*
   a. Ernest Dowson's "Non Sum Qualis Eram Bonae Sub Regno Cynarae"
   b. Your choice(s)

10. *Transcendent love* (placing of personhood above physical appearance)
    a. William Shakespeare's Sonnet 130
    b. Your choice(s)

5. War

And though your hand be pale,
Paler are all which trail
Your cross through flame and hail:
Weep, you may weep, for you may touch them not.
[Wilfred Owen, *Greater Love*]

LeRoi Jones

Audubon, Drafted

(For Linda)

It does not happen. That love, removes
itself. (I am leaving, Goodbye!

                                        Removes

itself, as rain, hard iron rain
comes down, then stops. All those
eyes opened for morning, close with
what few hours given them. With tears,
or at a stone wall, shadows drag down.

I am what I think I am. You are what
I think you are. The world is the   10
one thing, that will not move. It is
made of stone, round, and very ugly.

                                        (1964)

John Wain

A Song about Major Eatherly

The book (Fernard Gigon's Formula for Death—The
Atom Bombs and After) *also describes how Major
Claude R. Eatherly, pilot of the aircraft which carried the*
second bomb to Nagasaki, later started having nightmares.
His wife is quoted as saying: 'He often jumps up in the middle
of the night and screams out in an inhuman voice which
makes me feel ill: "Release it, release it."'

Major Eatherly began to suffer brief periods of madness,
says Gigon. The doctors diagnosed extreme nervous depression
and Eatherly was awarded a pension of 237 dollars a month.

This he appears to have regarded 'as a premium for
murder, as a payment for what had been done to the two
Japanese cities'. He never touched the money, and took to
petty thievery, for which he was committed to Fort Worth
prison.
[Report in *The Observer*, August 1958]

I

Good news. It seems he loved them after all.
His orders were to fry their bones to ash.
He carried up the bomb and let it fall.
And then his orders were to take the cash,

A hero's pension. But he let it lie.
It was in vain to ask him for the cause.
Simply that if he touched it he would die.
He fought his own, and not his country's wars.

His orders told him he was not a man:
An instrument, fine-tempered, clear of stain,   10
All fears and passions closed up like a fan:
No more volition than his aeroplane.

But now he fought to win his manhood back.
Steep from the sunset of his pain he flew
Against the darkness in that last attack.
It was for love he fought, to make that true.

II

To take life is always to die a little: to stop
any feeling and moving contrivance, however
    ugly,
unnecessary, or hateful, is to reduce by so much
    the total
of life there is. And that is to die a little.   20

To take the life of an enemy is to help him,
a little, towards destroying your own. Indeed,
    that is why
we hate our enemies: because they force us to
    kill them.
A murderer hides the dead man in the ground:
but his crime rears up and topples on to the living,
for it is they who now must hunt the murderer,
murder him, and hide him in the ground: it is
    they
who now feel the touch of death cold in their
    bones.

Animals hate death. A trapped fox will gnaw
through his own leg: it is so important to live   30
that he forgives himself the agony,
consenting, for life's sake, to the desperate teeth
grating through bone and pulp, the gasping yelps.

That is the reason the trapper hates the fox.
You think the trapper doesn't hate the fox?
But he does, and the fox can tell how much.
It is not the fox's teeth that grind his bones,
It is the trapper's. It is the trapper, there,
Who keeps his head down, gnawing, hour after
    hour.

And the people the trapper works for, they are
    there too,   40
heads down beside the trap, gnawing away.
Why shouldn't they hate the fox? Their cheeks
    are smeared
with his rank blood, and on their tongues his
    bone
being splintered, feels uncomfortably sharp.

So once Major Eatherly hated the Japanese.

III

Hell is a furnace, so the wise men taught.
The punishment for sin is to be broiled.
A glowing coal for every sinful thought.

The heat of God's great furnace ate up sin,
Which whispered up in smoke or fell in ash: 50
So that each hour a new hour could begin.

So fire was holy, though it tortured souls,
The sinners' anguish never ceased, but still
Their sin was burnt from them by shining coals.

Hell fried the criminal but burnt the crime,
Purged where it punished, healed where it
    destroyed:
It was a stove that warmed the rooms of time.

No man begrudged the flames their appetite.
All were afraid of fire, yet none rebelled.
The wise men taught that hell was just and
    right.   60

'The soul desires its necessary dread:
Only among the thorns can patience weave
A bower where the mind can make its bed.'

Even the holy saints whose patient jaws
Chewed bitter rind and hands raised up the dead
Were chestnuts roasted at God's furnace doors.

The wise men passed. The clever men appeared.
They ruled that hell be called a pumpkin face.
They robbed the soul of what it justly feared.

Coal after coal the fires of hell went out.   70
Their heat no longer warmed the rooms of time,
Which glistened now with fluorescent doubt.

The chilly saints went striding up and down
To warm their blood with useful exercise.
They rolled like conkers through the draughty
    town.

Those emblematic flames sank down to rest,
But metaphysical fire can not go out:
Men ran from devils they had dispossessed,

And felt within their skulls the dancing heat
No longer stored in God's deep boiler-room.   80
Fire scorched their temples, frostbite chewed their
          feet.

That parasitic fire could race and climb
More swiftly than the stately flames of hell.
Its fuel gone, it licked the beams of time.

So time dried out and youngest hearts grew old.
The smoky minutes cracked and broke apart.
The world was roasting but the men were cold.

Now from this pain worse pain was brought to
          birth,
More hate, more anguish, till at last they cried,
'Release this fire to gnaw the crusty earth: 90

Make it a flame that's obvious to sight
And let us say we kindled it ourselves,
To split the skulls of men and let in light.

Since death is camped among us, wish him joy,
Invite him to our table and our games.
We cannot judge, but we can still destroy'.

And so the curtains of the mind were drawn.
Men conjured hell a first, a second time:
And Major Eatherly took off at dawn.

IV

Suppose a sea-bird,   100
its wings stuck down with oil, riding the waves
in no direction, under the storm-clouds, helpless,
lifted for an instant by each moving billow
to scan the meaningless horizon, helpless,
helpless, and the storms coming, and its wings
          dead,
its bird–nature dead:
                              Imagine this castaway,

loved, perhaps, by the Creator, and yet
          abandoned,
mocked by the flashing scales of the fish beneath
          it,
who leap, twist, dive, as free of the wide sea
as formerly the bird of the wide sky,   110
now helpless, starving, a prisoner of the surface,
unable to dive or rise:
                              this is your emblem.
Take away the bird, let it be drowned
in the steep black waves of the storm, let it be
          broken
against rocks in the morning light, too faint to
          swim:
take away the bird, but keep the emblem.

It is the emblem of Major Eatherly,
who looked round quickly from the height of
          each wave,
but saw no land, only the rim of the sky
into which he was not free to rise, or the silver   120
gleam of the mocking scales of the fish diving
where he was not free to dive.

Men have clung always to emblems,
to tokens of absolution from their sins.
Once it was the scapegoat driven out, bearing
its load of guilt under the empty sky
until its shape was lost, merged in the scrub.

Now we are civilized, there is no wild heath.
Instead of the nimble scapegoat running out
to be lost under the wild and empty sky,   130
the load of guilt is packed into prison walls,
and men file inward through the heavy doors.

But now that image, too, is obsolete.
The Major entering prison is no scapegoat.
His penitence will not take away our guilt,
nor sort with any consoling ritual:
this is penitence for its own sake, beautiful,
uncomprehending, inconsolable, unforeseen.
He is not in prison for his penitence:
it is no outrage to our law that he wakes   140

with cries of pity on his parching lips.
We do not punish him for cries or nightmares.
We punish him for stealing things from stores.

O, give his pension to the storekeeper.
Tell him it is the price of all our souls.
But do not trouble to unlock the door
and bring the Major out into the sun.
Leave him: it is all one: perhaps his nightmares
grow cooler in the twilight of the prison.
Leave him; if he is sleeping, come away.   150
But lay a folded paper by his head,
nothing official or embossed, a page
torn from your notebook, and the words in
          pencil.
Say nothing of love, or thanks, or penitence:
say only 'Eatherly, we have your message.'

                                        (*1960*)

Joseph Langland
War

When my young brother was killed
By a mute and dusty shell in the thorny brush
Crowning the boulders of the Villa Verde Trail
On the island of Luzon,

I laid my whole dry body down,
Dropping my face like a stone in a green park
On the east banks of the Rhine;

On an airstrip skirting the Seine
His sergeant brother sat like a stick in his barracks
While cracks of fading sunlight   10
Caged the dusty air;

In the rocky rolling hills west of the Mississippi
His father and mother sat in a simple Norwegian
          parlor
With a photograph smiling between them on
          the table
And their hands fallen into their laps
Like sticks and dust;

And still other brothers and sisters,
Linking their arms together,
Walked down the dusty road where once he ran
And into the deep green valley   20
To sit on the stony banks of the stream he loved
And let the murmuring waters
Wash over their blood-hot feet with a springing
          crown of tears.

                                        (*1955*)

Randall Jarrell
The Death of the Ball Turret Gunner

From my mother's sleep I fell into the State,
And I hunched in its belly till my wet fur froze.
Six miles from earth, loosed from its dream of
          life,
I woke to black flak and the nightmare fighters.
When I died they washed me out of the turret
          with a hose.

                                        (*1945*)

Stephen Vincent Benét
Short Ode

It is time to speak of these
Who took the long, strange journey overseas,
Who fell through the air in flames.
Their names are many. I will not name their
          names
Though some were people I knew;
After some years the ghost itself dies, too,
And that is my son's picture on the wall
But his girl has been long married and that is all.

They died in mud, they died in camps of the flu.
They are dead. Let us leave it so.   10
The ones I speak of were not forced, I know.
They were men of my age and country, they
      were young men
At Belleau, at the seaports, by the Aisne.
They went where their passion took them and
      are not.
They do not answer mockery or praise.

You may restore the days
They lived beneath and you may well restore
The painted image of that fabled war,
But not those faces, not the living ones
Drowned in the water, blown before the guns   20
In France or Belgium or the bitter sea
(And the foreign grave is far, and men use the
      name,
But they did not go for votes or the pay they
      got
Or the brave memorial speech by the D.A.R.).
It is far, the foreign grave. It is very far
And the time is not the same.
But certain things are true
Despite the time, and these were men that I
      knew,
Sat beside, walked beside,
In the first running of June, in the careless
      pride.   30
It is hard to think back, to find them, to see
      their eyes
And none born since shall see those, and the
      books are lies,
Being either praise or blame.
But they were in their first youth. It is not the
      same.
You, who are young, remember that youth
      dies.
Go, stranger, and to Lacedemon tell,
They were shot and rotted, they fell
Burning, on flimsy wings.
And yet it was their thought that they did well.
And yet there are still the tyrants and the kings.   40

(*1936*)

Robert Frost

A Soldier

He is that fallen lance that lies as hurled,
That lies unlifted now, come dew, come rust,
But still lies pointed as it plowed the dust.
If we who sight along it round the world,
See nothing worthy to have been its mark,
It is because like men we look too near,
Forgetting that as fitted to the sphere,
Our missiles always make too short an arc.
They fall, they rip the grass, they intersect
The curve of earth, and striking, break their own;
They make us cringe for metal-point on stone.   11
But this we know, the obstacle that checked
And tripped the body, shot the spirit on
Further than target ever showed or shone.

(*1928*)

Ernest Hemingway

Champs d'Honneur

Soldiers never do die well;
   Crosses mark the places—
Wooden crosses where they fell,
   Stuck above their faces.
Soldiers pitch and cough and twitch—
   All the world roars red and black;
Soldiers smother in a ditch,
   Choking through the whole attack.

(*1923*)

Wilfred Owen

Dulce et Decorum Est

Bent double, like old beggars under sacks,
Knock-kneed, coughing like hags, we cursed
      through sludge,

Till on the haunting flares we turned our backs,
And towards our distant rest began to trudge.
Men marched asleep. Many had lost their boots,
But limped on, blood-shod. All went lame, all
    blind;
Drunk with fatigue; deaf even to the hoots
Of gas-shells dropping softly behind.

Gas! GAS! Quick, boys!—An ecstasy of
    fumbling,
Fitting the clumsy helmets just in time,   10
But someone still was yelling out and stumbling
And floundering like a man in fire or lime.—
Dim through the misty panes and thick green
    light,
As under a green sea, I saw him drowning.

In all my dreams before my helpless sight
He plunges at me, guttering, choking, drowning.

If in some smothering dreams, you too could pace
Behind the wagon that we flung him in,
And watch the white eyes writhing in his face,
His hanging face, like a devil's sick of sin;   20
If you could hear, at every jolt, the blood
Come gargling from the froth-corrupted lungs,
Bitter as the cud
Of vile, incurable sores on innocent tongues,—
My friend, you would not tell with such high zest
To children ardent for some desperate glory,
The old Lie: *Dulce et decorum est*
Pro patria mori.

                          (1920)

Wilfred Owen

Greater Love

Red lips are not so red
   As the stained stones kissed by the English
    dead.
Kindness of wooed and wooer
Seems shame to their love pure.

O Love, your eyes lose lure
   When I behold eyes blinded in my stead!

Your slender attitude
   Trembles not exquisite like limbs knife-
    skewed,
Rolling and rolling there
Where God seems not to care;   10
Till the fierce Love they bear
   Cramps them in death's extreme decrepitude.

Your voice sings not so soft,—
   Though even as wind murmuring through
    raftered loft,—
Your dear voice is not dear,
Gentle, and evening clear,
As theirs whom none now hear,
   Now earth has stopped their piteous mouths
    that coughed.

Heart, you were never hot,
   Nor large, nor full like hearts made great
    with shot;   20
And though your hand be pale,
Paler are all which trail
Your cross through flame and hail:
   Weep, you may weep, for you may touch
    them not.

                          (1920)

Edgar Lee Masters

Harry Wilmans

I was just turned twenty-one,
And Henry Phipps, the Sunday-school
    superintendent,
Made a speech in Bindle's Opera House.
"The honor of the flag must be upheld," he said,
"Whether it be assailed by a barbarous tribe of
    Tagalogs
Or the greatest power in Europe."
And we cheered and cheered the speech and the
    flag he waved

As he spoke.
And I went to the war in spite of my father,
And followed the flag till I saw it raised   10
By our camp in a rice field near Manila,
And all of us cheered and cheered it.
But there were flies and poisonous things;
And there was the deadly water,
And the cruel heat,
And the sickening, putrid food;
And the smell of the trench just back of the tents
Where the soldiers went to empty themselves;
And there were the whores who followed us,
        full of syphilis;
And beastly acts between ourselves or alone,   20
With bullying, hatred, degradation among us,
And days of loathing and nights of fear
To the hour of the charge through the steaming-
        swamp,
Following the flag,
Till I fell with a scream, shot through the guts.
Now there's a flag over me in Spoon River!
A flag! A flag!

                                        (1914)

Thomas Hardy

The Man He Killed

    'Had he and I but met
      By some old ancient inn,
    We should have sat us down to wet
      Right many a nipperkin!

    'But ranged as infantry,
      And staring face to face,
    I shot at him as he at me,
      And killed him in his place.

    'I shot him dead because—
      Because he was my foe,   10
    Just so: my foe of course he was;
      That's clear enough; although

    'He thought he'd 'list, perhaps,
      Off-hand like—just as I—
    Was out of work—had sold his traps—
      No other reason why.

    'Yes; quaint and curious war is!
      You shoot a fellow down
    You'd treat if met where any bar is,
      Or help to half-a-crown.'   20

                                        (1909)

Stephen Crane

War Is Kind

Do not weep, maiden, for war is kind.
Because your lover threw wild hands toward
      the sky
And the affrighted steed ran on alone,
Do not weep.
War is kind.

    Hoarse, booming drums of the regiment,
    Little souls who thirst for fight,
    These men were born to drill and die.
    The unexplained glory flies above them,
    Great is the Battle-God, great, and his
        Kingdom—   10
    A field where a thousand corpses lie.

Do not weep, babe, for war is kind.
Because your father tumbled in the yellow
      trenches,
Raged at his breast, gulped and died,
Do not weep.
War is kind.

    Swift blazing flag of the regiment,
    Eagle with crest of red and gold,
    These men were born to drill and die.
    Point for them the virtue of slaughter,   20
    Make plain to them the excellence of killing
    And a field where a thousand corpses lie.

Mother whose heart hung humble as a button
On the bright splendid shroud of your son,
Do not weep.
War is kind.

(*1899*)

Walt Whitman

Come Up from the Fields Father

Come up from the fields father, here's a letter
    from our Pete,
And come to the front door mother, here's a
    letter from thy dear son.

Lo, 'tis autumn,
Lo, where the trees, deeper green, yellower and
    redder,
Cool and sweeten Ohio's villages with leaves
    fluttering in the moderate wind,
Where apples ripe in the orchards hang and
    grapes on the trellis'd vines,
(Smell you the smell of the grapes on the vines?
Smell you the buckwheat where the bees were
    lately buzzing?)

Above all, lo, the sky so calm, so transparent
    after the rain, and with wondrous clouds,
Below too, all calm, all vital and beautiful, and
    the farm prospers well.   10

Down in the fields all prospers well,
But now from the fields come father, come at
    the daughter's call,
And come to the entry mother, to the front door
    come right away.

Fast as she can she hurries, something ominous,
    her steps trembling,
She does not tarry to smooth her hair nor adjust
    her cap.

Open the envelope quickly,
O this is not our son's writing, yet his name is
    sign'd,
O a strange hand writes for our dear son, O
    stricken mother's soul!
All swims before her eyes, flashes with black, she
    catches the main words only,
Sentences broken, *gunshot wound in the breast,
    cavalry skirmish, taken to hospital,*   20
At present low, but will soon be better.

Ah now the single figure to me,
Amid all teeming and wealthy Ohio with all its
    cities and farms,
Sickly white in the face and dull in the head,
    very faint,
By the jamb of a door leans.

Grieve not so, dear mother, (the just-grown
    daughter speaks through her sobs,
The little sisters huddle around speechless and
    dismay'd,)
*See, dearest mother, the letter says Pete will soon be
    better.*

Alas poor boy, he will never be better, (nor
    may-be needs to be better, that brave
    and simple soul,)
While they stand at home at the door he is
    dead already,   30
The only son is dead.

But the mother needs to be better,
She with thin form presently drest in black,
By day her meals untouch'd, then at night fitfully
    sleeping, often waking,
In the midnight waking, weeping, longing with
    one deep longing,
O that she might withdraw unnoticed, silent
    from life escape and withdraw,
To follow, to seek, to be with her dear dead son.

(*1865*)

Alfred, Lord Tennyson

Charge of the Light Brigade

Half a league, half a league,
   Half a league onward,
All in the valley of Death
   Rode the six hundred.
"Forward, the Light Brigade!
Charge for the guns!" he said.
Into the valley of Death
   Rode the six hundred.

"Forward, the Light Brigade!"
Was there a man dismayed?   10
Not though the soldier knew
   Someone had blundered.
Theirs not to make reply,
Theirs not to reason why,
Theirs but to do and die.
Into the valley of Death
   Rode the six hundred.

Cannon to right of them,
Cannon to left of them,
Cannon in front of them   20
   Volleyed and thundered;
Stormed at with shot and shell,
Boldly they rode and well,
Into the jaws of Death,
Into the mouth of Hell
   Rode the six hundred.

Flashed all their sabers bare,
Flashed as they turned in air
Sabring the gunners there,
Charging an army, while   30
   All the world wondered.
Plunged in the battery-smoke
Right through the line they broke;
Cossack and Russian
Reeled from the saber-stroke
   Shattered and sundered.
Then they rode back, but not,
   Not the six hundred.

Cannon to right of them,
Cannon to left of them,   40
Cannon behind them
   Volleyed and thundered;
Stormed at with shot and shell,
While horse and hero fell,
They that had fought so well
Came through the jaws of Death,
Back from the mouth of Hell,
All that was left of them,
   Left of six hundred.

When can their glory fade?   50
O the wild charge they made!
   All the world wondered.
Honor the charge they made!
Honor the Light Brigade,
   Noble six hundred!

                                (1854)

EXERCISES

"Audubon, Drafted" [Jones]

1. The draft, or the selection of a qualified person for compulsory military service, has been common to nearly every American generation. Thus, in this poem LeRoi Jones sets up a familiar situation to which human reactions vary widely. Does this poem properly belong in this thematic section, or could it fit others (for example, "Love of Many Kinds" or "Frustration, Outrage, and Violence")? Discuss.

2. LeRoi Jones has been characterized as one of America's angry young men—a black who frankly uses poetry as a form of protest against what he considers to be an inimical white society. Yet, although the subject is admittedly controversial, do you find in this poem any hint of racist propaganda? Discuss.

3. In paraphrasing the poem, do you find it lucid? Are the poet's feeling and tone angry? vehement? destructive? Discuss. How would you describe his feeling and tone?

4. Finally, what is Jones' intention? Is the poem more complex than it at first appears? Does it involve a poetic commentary on such themes as love, separation in love, the brevity of life, grief, a kind of dispassionate anguish, disillusionment, and demoralization? Does the poet communicate his feeling toward his material with a power that you find moving? Discuss.

"A Song about Major Eatherly" [Wain]

5. John Wain, in his provocative work, probes the depth of the hell of war and treats its many tragic facets—especially those often unspoken ones, such as the personal guilt of the killing soldier and the communal guilt of his society. Demanding as it is, this poem requires a variety of critical approaches to enrich our understanding of it. Using New Critical approaches (see pp. 36–45), consider the poem as poetry first. The epigraphic information is obvious enough, but what does the poet tell us about Major Eatherly in Part I? In your discussion treat the persona's sense of guilt—his own war of conscience, so to speak. What are the poet's feeling and tone in Part I? Especially consider his concept of war and manhood in the fourth stanza.

6. Part II introduces the theme of the transcendentality of life, holding that all life is sacred: "To take life is always to die a little . . ." (line 17). Discuss the paradox of the second stanza. What are the reasons for hatred? What is the concept of communal guilt? What is the significance of the fox, the trapper, and the people for whom the trapper works? Is this an analogy of the enemy, Major Eatherly, and the people of America, respectively? What are your observations concerning the final line of Part II?

7. Part III is the most complex portion of the poem. In it Wain reviews in a sweep the Christian tradition of hell and punishment, holding that evil is destroyed by fire in God's great furnace, but the wrongdoer suffers eternally. He brings us ultimately to the age of reason and doubt—especially the eighteenth, nineteenth, and twentieth centuries—during which man began to reduce hell to an impotent myth (note the eighth stanza closely).

Is Wain saying, in so many words, that even if hell is a myth, man's reasons for creating it still exist? Consider the lines, "Only among the thorns can patience weave/A bower where the mind can make its bed" (lines 62–63). Despite our logic and the pleasure principle, do we punish ourselves in more subtle ways for disobedience to our consciences? At any rate, Wain seems to contend that man replaced his belief in orthodox hell with latter-day devils of his own making—the fears with which he makes his own hell. According to the poet, which hell is worse—the old or the new?

8. The last five stanzas of Part III powerfully evoke man's failure as a rational being, and put one in mind of Goya's title of a work, translated, "The Sleep of Reason Brings Forth Monsters." Discuss Wain's reasoning. Is he contending that if man cannot keep his emotional fears, primordial dreads, and destructive urges contained, even in the comforting myths of the past, then when modern man's reason lets down, for whatever cause, tragedy is unleashed—that man may function destructively, perhaps without even knowing it? (The parallel to Yeats' "The Second Coming" should not go unnoticed here.) Within this context, what is the function of Wain's final stanza or line of Part III?

9. Part IV analogically recapitulates Major Eatherly's function of representing modern man. In this connection discuss in detail the symbol of the sea-bird. Do you sense the persona's helplessness and doom, even as he begins his mission (at least, as Wain senses it)? How does Major Eatherly then become the "scapegoat," mentioned in stanza five (line 134)? For whom is he the scapegoat? Has the persona sacrificed himself for the guilt of

mankind? In answering this question, consider the last two stanzas carefully, especially the line "His penitence will not take away our guilt" (line 135). Why does Wain emphasize the technical reason that Major Eatherly is being punished by society? Is this the real reason? Explain the final stanza.

10. Obviously, many other approaches may be taken to the poem. For example, both the historical and socio-cultural critic would want to know more about the "nation, epoch, and milieu," to use Taine's phrase, as they relate to "A Song about Major Eatherly." Much of the dramatic force of the poem relies upon the credibility of the personal and social guilt. The whole problem of the motivation of that guilt, to be specific, would depend, at least in part, upon the related facts of World War II. By August 1945, American casualties were already over 300,000 in the Pacific, the soldiers who had fought through Europe and were arriving in the Pacific were war-weary, and estimates of additional casualties to be inflicted by island-to-island fighting and the mainland invasion of Japan were set at over 1 million. Later it was determined that the militaristic leadership of Japan had anticipated the invasion plans and had mobilized 5,000 Kamikaze (suicide) planes, the fanatical self-immolation of which postwar records proved to be more than 18 percent effective in direct strikes. For weeks leaflets had been dropped over Hiroshima, Nagasaki, and other industrial cities warning the citizens of bombings and urging them to flee. Yet Japanese Premier Suzuki had scorned President Truman's ultimatum in no uncertain terms, calling it "unworthy of notice." Under these circumstances, then, the President made his fateful decision. On August 6, 1945, one atomic bomb was dropped on Hiroshima, obliterating 60 percent of the city and killing more than 78,000 Japanese. Even so, the Japanese refused the President's new surrender ultimatum. At this point, on August 9, the deadly second atomic bomb carried in Major Eatherly's strike ship was dropped on Nagasaki, killing more than 23,000. Only after this second devastation did the Japanese finally agree to surrender and occupation, provided they could keep their emperor.

As early as 1939, Albert Einstein had informed President Roosevelt of the enormously destructive power which could be released through uranium fission. It would seem that these men and all who had participated in this work—Fermi, Szilard, Joliot, and all those who used their talents on the now legendary "Manhattan Project"—would have been even more appropriate "scapegoats" than Major Eatherly. Do such historical and sociocultural approaches dilute the power of Wain's poem? Discuss. What other poetic approaches would enrich the troubling poetic experience of "A Song about Major Eatherly"?

"War" [Langland] and *"Come Up from the Fields Father"* [Whitman]

11. Although Langland's poem deals with World War II and Whitman's with the Civil War, do you still find a common method and substance in the two poems? In framing your answer, consider the following: the use of local color details, images of nature, characterization, and themes. Do the themes of these war poems transcend time?

"Champs d'Honneur" [Hemingway] and *"The Death of the Ball Turret Gunner"* [Jarrell]

12. Compare and contrast these two brief poems. What added impact do the poems gain through their brevity? Does form combine with substance to reveal indirectly a powerful theme—specifically, the short lives of the young men? In your comparison and contrast, treat connotation, irony, feeling, tone, and intention. Finally, compare and contrast the symbols of "red and black" (line 6) in Hemingway's poem and the embryo in Jarrell's. How do they function in the poems? Which poem strikes the stronger chord of response? Why?

"*Short Ode*" [Benét] and "*Dulce et Decorum Est*" [Owen]

13. What similarities do you see in these two poems? What differences? How does each poem delineate the tragic horror of war? Which poet seems closer to his subject? Why? Are the two poets' feelings toward their subjects akin? Are the poets reflective, philosophical, ironic, inimical toward chauvinism—or what?

"*Harry Wilmans*" [Masters] and "*The Man He Killed*" [Hardy]

14. Both poems make heavily ironic commentaries upon war. Yet the two poems differ greatly in form, method, and substance. Masters' persona is speaking from the grave (itself an irony), whereas Hardy's might be talking in a bar. Yet both points of view are first-person. Wilmans is killed, while Hardy's protagonist kills. Yet both are narrators and have a story to tell. What ironic insights into war are illuminated by each? Discuss.

"*War Is Kind*" [Crane] and "*Charge of the Light Brigade*" [Tennyson]

15. Contrast form and meaning in these diverse poems. How does the form of each poem bespeak the feeling and tone of the poet? Do you see relationships between either of these poems and other poems in this section? Discuss.

6. Frustration, Outrage, and Violence

The blood-dimmed tide is loosed, and everywhere
The ceremony of innocence is drowned;
The best lack all conviction, while the worst
Are full of passionate intensity.

[William Butler Yeats, *The Second Coming*]

James Wright

Autumn Begins in Martins Ferry, Ohio

In the Shreve High football stadium,
I think of Polacks nursing long beers in
    Tiltonsville,
And gray faces of Negroes in the blast furnace
    at Benwood,
And the ruptured night watchman of
    Wheeling Steel,
Dreaming of heroes.

All the proud fathers are ashamed to go home.
Their women cluck like starved pullets,
Dying for love.

Therefore,
Their sons grow suicidally beautiful   10
At the beginning of October,
And gallop terribly against each other's bodies.

                (1963)

Laurence Josephs

Passover at Auschwitz

Possibly they thought of it,
Remembering the old days; possibly
They could savor, still, the memory

Of spices, the clean bone, the glass
Of quiet wine left in the cool
Opacity of symbol, for the Guest.

Here were no calendars: perhaps
A knotted cord: more likely
That the stars alone beat time, aware and distant,
Or that clouds, like immaculate grandfathers,   10
Lay against the void of memory.
Here it was Passover all year long! What ghosts

Flamed in their blood; their terrible dreams!
The plague: life! The sea: tears! The serpent:
Hope! For in the dying
Center of history newer than theirs,
The world, like a wingèd horse, flew upside
    down.
They, then, firstborn, were prey of angels,

Where in an endless, idiot night
They waited for a sound of wings or feet.   20
Pass over! or Come down! they must have
    cried.
Or from their myth of sleep, reached out
To the angel death who once, in old bondage,
Did not forget, but held them more than dear.

                (1963)

Derek Walcott

Ruins of a Great House

*though our longest sun sets at right declensions and makes
but winter arches, it cannot be long before we lie down in
darkness, and have our light in ashes . . .*

[Browne, *Urn Burial*]

Stones only, the *disjecta membra* of this Great
    House,
Whose moth-like girls are mixed with candledust,
Remain to file the lizard's dragonish claws;
The mouths of those gate cherubs streaked
    with stain.
Axle and coachwheel silted under the muck
Of cattle droppings.

                Three crows flap for the trees,
And settle, creaking the eucalyptus boughs.
A smell of dead limes quickens in the nose
The leprosy of Empire.   10

             'Farewell, green fields'
             'Farewell, ye happy groves!'

Marble as Greece, like Faulkner's south in stone,
Deciduous beauty prospered and is gone;
But where the lawn breaks in a rash of trees
A spade below dead leaves will ring the bone
Of some dead animal or human thing
Fallen from evil days, from evil times.

It seems that the original crops were limes
Grown in that silt that clogs the river's skirt;   20
The imperious rakes are gone, their bright girls
    gone,
The river flows, obliterating hurt.

I climbed a wall with the grill ironwork
Of exiled craftsmen, protecting that great house
From guilt, perhaps, but not from the worm's
    rent,
Nor from the padded cavalry of the mouse.
And when a wind shook in the limes I heard

What Kipling heard; the death of a great empire,
    the abuse
Of ignorance by Bible and by sword.

A green lawn, broken by low walls of stone   30
Dipped to the rivulet, and pacing, I thought
    next
Of men like Hawkins, Walter Raleigh, Drake,
Ancestral murderers and poets, more perplexed
In memory now by every ulcerous crime.
The world's green age then was a rotting lime
Whose stench became the charnel galleon's text.
The rot remains with us, the men are gone.
But, as dead ash is lifted in a wind,
That fans the blackening ember of the mind,
My eyes burned from the ashen prose of Donne.

Ablaze with rage, I thought   41
Some slave is rotting in this manorial lake,
And still the coal of my compassion fought:
That Albion too, was once
A colony like ours, 'Part of the continent, piece
    of the main'
Nook-shotten, rook o'er blown, deranged
By foaming channels, and the vain expense
Of bitter faction.
                All in compassion ends
So differently from what the heart arranged: 50
'as well as if a manor of thy friend's . . .'
                           (1962)

LeRoi Jones

Preface to a Twenty Volume Suicide Note

Lately, I've become accustomed to the way
The ground opens up and envelops me
Each time I go out to walk the dog.
Or the broad edged silly music the wind
Makes when I run for a bus—

Things have come to that.

And now, each night I count the stars,
And each night I get the same number.
And when they will not come to be counted
I count the holes they leave.   10

Nobody sings anymore.

And then last night, I tiptoed up
To my daughter's room and heard her
Talking to someone, and when I opened
The door, there was no one there . . .
Only she on her knees,
Peeking into her own clasped hands.
                                          (1961)

Louis Simpson

A Dream of Governors

The deepest dream is of mad governors.
                          —Mark Van Doren

The Knight from the world's end
Cut off the dragon's head.
The monster's only friend,
The Witch, insulting, fled.
The Knight was crowned, and took
His Lady. Good and gay,
They lived in a picture-book
Forever and a day.

Or else: When he had sat
So long, the King was old   10
And ludicrous and fat.
At feasts when poets told
How he had shed the blood
Of dragons long ago
He thought, Have I done good
To hear that I did so?

The chorus in a play
Declaimed: "The soul does well
Keeping the middle way."

He thought, That city fell;   20
Man's life is founded on
Folly at the extreme;
When all is said and done
The City is a dream.

At night the King alone
Went to the dragon's cave.
In moonlight on a stone
The Witch sat by the grave.
He grasped her by the hand
And said, "Grant what I ask.   30
Bring evil on the land
That I may have a task!"

The Queen has heard his tread;
She shuts the picture-book.
The King stands by the bed.
In silence as they look
Into each other's eyes
They see a buried thing
That creeps, begins to rise,
And spreads the dragon's wing.   40
                                          (1957)

James Wright

Mutterings Over the Crib of a Deaf Child

"How will he hear the bell at school
Arrange the broken afternoon
And know to run across the cool
Grasses where the starlings cry,
Or understand the day is gone?"

Well, someone lifting cautious brows
Will take the measure of the clock.
And he will see the birchen boughs
Outside sagging dark from the sky, and
The shade crawling upon the rock.   10

"And how will he know to rise at morning?
His mother has other sons to waken,
She has the stove she must build to burning
Before the coals of the night-time die,
And he never stirs when he is shaken."

I take it the air affects the skin,
And you remember, when you were young,
Sometimes you could feel the dawn begin,
And the fire would call you, by and by,
Out of the bed and bring you along.   20

"Well, good enough. To serve his needs
All kinds of arrangements can be made.
But what will you do if his finger bleeds?
Or a bobwhite whistles invisibly
And flutes like an angel off in the shade?"

He will learn pain. And, as for the bird,
It is always darkening when that comes out.
I will putter as though I had not heard,
And lift him into my arms and sing
Whether he hears my song or not.   30

(1957)

Ted Hughes

Secretary

If I should touch her she would shriek and
          weeping
Crawl off to nurse the terrible wound: all
Day like a starling under the bellies of bulls
She hurries among men, ducking, peeping,

Off in a whirl at the first move of a horn.
At dusk she scuttles down the gauntlet of lust
Like a clockwork mouse. Safe home at last
She mends socks with holes, shirts that are torn

For father and brother, and a delicate supper
          cooks:
Goes to bed early, shuts out with the light   10
Her thirty years, and lies with buttocks tight,
Hiding her lovely eyes until day break.

(1956)

Lawrence Ferlinghetti

"The poet's eye obscenely seeing"

The poet's eye obscenely seeing
sees the surface of the round world
          with its drunk rooftops
          and wooden oiseaux on clotheslines
          and its clay males and females
          with hot legs and rosebud breasts
          in rollaway beds
and its trees full of mysteries
and its Sunday parks and speechless statues
and its America   10
          with its ghost towns and empty Ellis Islands

and its surrealist landscape of
> mindless prairies
> supermarket suburbs
> steamheated cemeteries
> cinerama holy days
> and protesting cathedrals

a kissproof world of plastic toiletseats tampax and taxis
> drugged store cowboys and las vegas virgins
> disowned indians and cinemad matrons   20
> unroman senators and conscientious non-objectors

and all the other fatal shorn-up fragments
of the immigrant's dream come too true
> and mislaid
> > among the sunbathers

> > > > *(1955)*

David Ignatow

Sunday at the State Hospital

I am sitting across the table
eating my visit sandwich.
The one I brought him stays suspended
near his mouth; his eyes focus
on the table and seem to think,
his shoulders hunched forward.
I chew methodically,
pretending to take him
as a matter of course.
The sandwich tastes mad   10
and I keep chewing.
My past is sitting in front of me
filled with itself
and trying with almost no success
to bring the present to its mouth.

> > *(1955)*

Scharmel Iris

A Glass Is Splintered

Blue, ever so blue, the glow
Of winter light on snow
Unscuffed of deer or doe
Or tyrant wind. "I've dropped a bird!"
Cried the elated hunter. Heaven scowled. I
> spoke no word.
No other sound was heard
Except the sibilant bleeding of the bird.
Sealed in my throat the word
Endlessly bleeding—the hoarse, fiercely deferred
Unuttered unassailable word.   10

It was my heart, never the ear that heard
The red cry, the last cry of the red-crested fire-
> winged bird.
Because of the bright bird, peony-colored,
> swiftly slain,
And my held-back frozen denial of pain,
Dark went the day and brightened not again.
I remember it well and all too well I know,
The scalding blood of the bird hurriedly ate a
> hole in the snow.

> > *(1953)*

T. S. Eliot

The Hollow Men

MISTAH KURTZ—HE DEAD.
A penny for the Old Guy

I

We are the hollow men
We are the stuffed men
Leaning together
Headpiece filled with straw. Alas!
Our dried voices, when
We whisper together
Are quiet and meaningless
As wind in dry grass
Or rats' feet over broken glass
In our dry cellar   10

Shape without form, shade without color,
Paralysed force, gesture without motion;

Those who have crossed
With direct eyes, to death's other Kingdom
Remember us—if at all—not as lost
Violent souls, but only
As the hollow men
The stuffed men.

II

Eyes I dare not meet in dreams
In death's dream kingdom   20
These do not appear:
There, the eyes are
Sunlight on a broken column
There, is a tree swinging
And voices are
In the wind's singing
More distant and more solemn
Than a fading star.

Let me be no nearer
In death's dream kingdom   30
Let me also wear

Such deliberate disguises
Rat's coat, crowskin, crossed staves
In a field
Behaving as the wind behaves
No nearer—

Not that final meeting
In the twilight kingdom

III

This is the dead land
This is cactus land   40
Here the stone images
Are raised, here they receive
The supplication of a dead man's hand
Under the twinkle of a fading star.

Is it like this
In death's other kingdom
Waking alone
At the hour when we are
Trembling with tenderness
Lips that would kiss   50
Form prayers to broken stone.

IV

The eyes are not here
There are no eyes here
In this valley of dying stars
In this hollow valley
This broken jaw of our lost kingdoms

In this last of meeting places
We grope together
And avoid speech
Gathered on this beach of the tumid river   60

Sightless, unless
The eyes reappear
As the perpetual star
Multifoliate rose
Of death's twilight kingdom
The hope only
Of empty men.

V

Here we go round the prickly pear
Prickly pear prickly pear
Here we go round the prickly pear   70
At five o'clock in the morning.

Between the idea
And the reality
Between the motion
And the act
Falls the Shadow

      For Thine is the Kingdom

Between the conception
And the creation
Between the emotion   80
And the response
Falls the Shadow

       Life is very long

Between the desire
And the spasm
Between the potency
And the existence
Between the essence
And the descent
Falls the Shadow   90

      For Thine is the Kingdom

For Thine is
Life is
For Thine is the

This is the way the world ends
This is the way the world ends
This is the way the world ends
Not with a bang but a whimper.

        (1925)

Robinson Jeffers

Shine, Perishing Republic

While this America settles in the mould of its
  vulgarity, heavily thickening to empire,
And protest, only a bubble in the molten mass,
  pops and sighs out, and the mass hardens,

I sadly smiling remember that the flower fades
  to make fruit, the fruit rots to make earth.
Out of the mother; and through the spring
  exultances, ripeness and decadence; and
  home to the mother.

You making haste haste on decay: not blame-
  worthy; life is good, be it stubbornly
  long or suddenly
A mortal splendor: meteors are not needed less
  than mountains: shine, perishing republic.

But for my children, I would have them keep
  their distance from the thickening center;
  corruption
Never has been compulsory, when the cities
  lie at the monster's feet there are left the
  mountains.

And boys, be in nothing so moderate as in love
  of man, a clever servant, insufferable
  master.
There is the trap that catches noblest spirits,
  that caught—they say—God, when he
  walked on earth.   10

       (1925)

Archibald MacLeish

The End of the World

Quite unexpectedly as Vasserot
The armless ambidextrian was lighting
A match between his great and second toe
And Ralph the lion was engaged in biting
The neck of Madame Sossman while the drum
Pointed, and Teeny was about to cough
In waltz-time swinging Jocko by the thumb—
Quite unexpectedly the top blew off:
And there, there overhead, there, there, hung
  over
Those thousands of white faces, those dazed
  eyes,   10

There in the starless dark, the poise, the hover,
There with vast wings across the canceled skies,
There in the sudden blackness, the black pall
Of nothing, nothing, nothing—nothing at all.

(*1925*)

John Crowe Ransom

Bells for John Whitesides' Daughter

There was such speed in her little body,
And such lightness in her footfall,
It is no wonder that her brown study
Astonishes us all.

Her wars were bruited in our high window.
We looked among orchard trees and beyond,
Where she took arms against her shadow,
Or harried unto the pond

The lazy geese, like a snow cloud
Dripping their snow on the green grass,   10
Tricking and stopping, sleepy and proud,
Who cried in goose, Alas,

For the tireless heart within the little
Lady with rod that made them rise
From their noon apple dreams, and scuttle
Goose-fashion under the skies!

But now go the bells, and we are ready;
In one house we are sternly stopped
To say we are vexed at her brown study,
Lying so primly propped.   20

(*1924*)

John Hall Wheelock

The Black Panther

There is a panther caged within my breast,
    But what his name, there is no breast shall
        know
    Save mine, not what it is that drives him so,
Backward and forward, in relentless quest—
That silent rage, baffled but unsuppressed,
    The soft pad of those stealthy feet that go
    Over my body's prison to and fro,
Trying the walls forever, without rest.

All day I feed him with my living heart,
    But when the night puts forth her dreams and
        stars,   10
    The inexorable frenzy re-wakes:
    His wrath is hurled upon the trembling bars,
The eternal passion stretches me apart,
    And I lie silent—but my body shakes.

(*1923*)

James Stephens

A Glass of Beer

The lanky hank of a she in the inn over there
Nearly killed me for asking the loan of a glass
    of beer;
May the devil grip the whey-faced slut by the
    hair,
And beat bad manners out of her skin for a year.

That parboiled ape, with the toughest jaw you
    will see
On virtue's path, and a voice that would rasp
    the dead,
Came roaring and raging the minute she looked
    at me,
And threw me out of the house on the back of
    my head!

If I asked her master he'd give me a cask a day;
But she, with the beer at hand, not a gill would
    arrange!   10
May she marry a ghost and bear him a kitten,
    and may
The High King of Glory permit her to get the
    mange.

                   (*1918*)

William Butler Yeats

A Deep-Sworn Vow

Others because you did not keep
That deep-sworn vow have been friends of mine;
Yet always when I look death in the face,
When I clamber to the heights of sleep,
Or when I grow excited with wine,
Suddenly I meet your face.

                   (*1917*)

Walter de la Mare

The Listeners

'Is there anybody there?' said the Traveller,
    Knocking on the moonlit door;
And his horse in the silence champed the grasses
    Of the forest's ferny floor:
And a bird flew up out of the turret,
    Above the Traveller's head:
And he smote upon the door again a second
    time;
    'Is there anybody there?' he said.
But no one descended to the Traveller;
    No head from the leaf-fringed sill   10
Leaned over and looked into his grey eyes,
    Where he stood perplexed and still.

But only a host of phantom listeners
    That dwelt in the lone house then
Stood listening in the quiet of the moonlight
    To that voice from the world of men:
Stood thronging the faint moonbeams on the
    dark stair,
    That goes down to the empty hall,
Hearkening in an air stirred and shaken
    By the lonely Traveller's call.   20
And he felt in his heart their strangeness,
    Their stillness answering his cry,
While his horse moved, cropping the dark turf,
    'Neath the starred and leafy sky;
For he suddenly smote on the door, even
    Louder, and lifted his head:—
'Tell them I came, and no one answered,
    That I kept my word,' he said.
Never the least stir made the listeners.
    Though every word he spake   30
Fell echoing through the shadowiness of the
    still house
    From the one man left awake;
Ay, they heard his foot upon the stirrup,
    And the sound of iron on stone,
And how the silence surged softly backward,
    When the plunging hoofs were gone.

                 (*1912*)

William Blake

London

I wander thro' each charter'd street,
Near where the charter'd Thames does flow,
And mark in every face I meet
Marks of weakness, marks of woe.

In every cry of every Man,
In every Infant's cry of fear,
In every voice, in every ban,
The mind-forg'd manacles I hear.

How the Chimney-sweeper's cry
Every black'ning Church appalls;   10
And the hapless Soldier's sigh
Runs in blood down Palace walls.

But most thro' midnight streets I hear
How the youthful Harlot's curse
Blasts the new born Infant's tear,
And blights with plagues the Marriage hearse.

(*1794*)

Anonymous

Western Wind

Western wind, when will thou blow,
The small rain down can rain?
Christ, if my love were in my arms
And I in my bed again!

(*ca. 15th century*)

EXERCISES

"*Autumn Begins in Martins Ferry, Ohio*" and "*Mutterings Over the Crib of a Deaf Child*" [Wright]

1. The form of "Autumn Begins in Martins Ferry, Ohio" is irregular; the poem contains no rhyme (free verse). The first stanza introduces the speaker and three local-color images of different people linked to "All the proud fathers" in line 6. Why are these different kinds of men juxtaposed with "Their women" (line 7) who are likened to "... starved pullets,/Dying for love" (lines 7–8)? Explain. Is Wright's tone satirical? If so, what specific criticism is he making of the relationship between the sexes—especially the married couples in Martins Ferry?

2. The second part of the poem commences with the final stanza. Describe the imagery in correlation with the ritual of football. What is the speaker's attitude toward the popular sport? What is the purpose of associating the football players with horses, and why does

he use the expression "gallop terribly" in the final line? Does the poet look upon football, then, as a substitute for some kind of reality? What is it, and what psychological and sociocultural commentary is he making on the society of Martins Ferry? Or is Wright speaking about all American society? Discuss.

3. Wright's poem "Mutterings Over the Crib of a Deaf Child" is more regular as its form and rhyme scheme indicate. Would you describe the poem as a *dramatic dialogue* or *monologue*? Conversation alternates, as the title informs us, over the little bed of a deaf child. But who is the speaker, or are there two speakers? How does the poet avoid *sentimentality* in withholding easy answers for a tragic human condition? According to the poet, what is the difficult answer to the plight? Explain your observations.

"*Passover at Auschwitz*" [Josephs]

4. Laurence Josephs' poem may be approached historically and socioculturally. Indeed, most readers would need to know that Passover is a Jewish holiday celebrating the escape of the Hebrews, after 430 years of captivity, from Pharaoh's Egypt and that Auschwitz is a city in southwestern Poland, notorious as Nazi

Germany's extermination center. The first stanza of the poem recapitulates the commemoration of Passover, but, in the second stanza, beginning with the word "Here," we are aware that the poet is speaking of Auschwitz. With a knowledge of the organized massacre taking place, especially from 1939–1945, of what added significance does the line "Here it was Passover all year long!" (line 12) assume?

5. How does the poet continue to relate the tradition of Passover to the mad horror of Auschwitz? Discuss.

Relate the poet's tone to the device of *litotes* (understatement). Does violence recounted with such restraint suggest even deeper reaches of frustration and outrage than might otherwise be achieved?

"*Ruins of a Great House*" [Walcott] and "*Preface to a Twenty Volume Suicide Note*" [Jones]

6. These two poems lend themselves well to a comparison and contrast, although each should also be examined separately. First, what does the "Great House" represent in Derek Walcott's poem "Ruins of a Great House"? The poet presents the reader with a tour of the grounds of this home of another era. What details describe not only the house, but also the poet's feeling and tone as well? Although the final stanza expresses the theme of this section, the poet's attitude is tinged with compassion. What lines indicate constructive or affirmative needs even as one may experience frustration and anger? Consider in your answer the expression "the vain expense/Of bitter faction" (lines 47–48).

7. In "Preface to a Twenty Volume Suicide Note," LeRoi Jones paints a verbal picture of disillusionment. How does he make the narrator's sense of frustration concrete through the first four stanzas, concluding, "Nobody sings anymore" (line 11)?

8. The feeling and tone continue into the last stanza, but the reader becomes gradually aware of a shifting emphasis. The persona's daughter is "Talking to someone" (line 14), though "there was no one there . . ." (line 15). The contradiction hovers only a moment, and then the concluding visual image dramatically explains what was only an apparent contradiction. How do the poet's feeling and tone change at this point? Or do they? Explain your answer.

9. Especially compare and contrast the development and conclusion of feeling and tone in Walcott's poem with those of Jones' poem. Do you see other significant similarities? differences?

"*A Dream of Governors*" [Simpson]

10. Achievement, legend, building and dreaming, the desire for challenge (even at the price of evil), and a revelation of the lower and secret depths of evil bespeak, stanza by stanza, Louis Simpson's "A Dream of Governors." In expanding on the theme of how good becomes evil, how youth and achievement come full circle to old age and corruption, point out portions of the poem which support this summarizational commentary.

11. Can you see relationships between Simpson's poem and Tennyson's "Ulysses" (see p. 266)? But what are the differences in ultimate meaning between the two poems?

"*Secretary*" [Hughes], "*Sunday at the State Hospital*" [Ignatow], and "*The Hollow Men*" [Eliot]

12. These three poems indicate various kinds of frustration. How do the phrases "Safe home at last" (line 7) and "lies with buttocks tight" (line 11), when considered with other images in "Secretary," communicate the basic frustration of the persona? Can you amplify her central problems with other images?

13. Ignatow's poem appears to be the briefest kind of comment by a narrator who is visiting a state mental hospital. How do the title and the image of a sandwich in the second line immediately, yet indirectly, succeed in orienting us to the occasion of the poem? Describe the *atmosphere*. What is the significance of the line "My past is sitting in front of me" (line 12)? Or is the line ambiguous? Discuss. Does this poem, too, gain power from understatement?

14. Assuming that Eliot's poem deals with the dilemma of moral consciousness of twentieth-century man, as well as his spiritual frustration, how does the poet

develop the themes throughout the five sections of the poem? In considering your answer, comment upon the wasteland images of part I; the allusive images of "a tree swinging" (line 24) and "a fading star" (line 28) in part II; the linking of the "fading star" (line 44) image and the "twilight kingdom" image to death and aridity in part III; the repetitive emphasis on the star, rose, and "twilight kingdom" images in part IV; the nonsense song of childhood opening part V, and the alternating stanzaic statements with the remotely spaced, yet forcefully interjected single lines *"For Thine is the Kingdom"* and *"Life is very long."*

15. What is the correlation between each stanza in part V and the italicized statement? Are these stanzas especially philosophical? Do they get to biological essences, and if so, why? Discuss.

16. The poem appears to fade into inchoate religious conjecture until it suddenly ends with a kind of repetitive outcry of helplessness. The final stanza in italics is frequently quoted as a commentary upon modern man's concept of the end of the world in a literal sense. If the poem indicates nihilism only, then this interpretation makes sense. However, do you find any hint of spiritual progression in the poem, even for skeptical modern man, which would seem to belie such an interpretation? Here it may be necessary to relate Eliot's epigraph to its source in Joseph Conrad's *Heart of Darkness*, the story of which deals with a Mr. Kurtz who goes to the Congo with the highest of moral intentions but is there corrupted. The name is of *allegorical* significance, for "Kurtz" in German means "short." Could Eliot possibly be contending, then, that modern man, who is morally and spiritually lacking, is also "short of the mark" or "dead" to ultimate meanings in life? If so, Eliot's intention may be vastly different from the usual interpretation of the poem. Discuss.

"The poet's eye obscenely seeing" [Ferlinghetti], *"Shine, Perishing Republic"* [Jeffers], *"London"* [Blake], and *"The End of the World"* [MacLeish]

17. These four poems bear sociocultural similarities that justify grouping them in a single question. Ferlinghetti's "The poet's eye obscenely seeing" exudes frustration in response to certain aspects of the modern world. Point out specific images, metaphorical commentaries upon artifice and hypocrisy. Does the phrase "trees full of mysteries" (line 8) suggest contemporary man's dissociation from nature and preoccupation with material things? As the poet sees them, what are some of our contemporary absurdities? Is "cinerama holy days" (line 16) a deliberate play on words (*pun*)? Does the poet feel that modern man is mad with hygiene—that is, unwholesomely clean? Is he insecure? Is Ferlinghetti's tone basically satirical? Comment.

18. Robinson Jeffers' "Shine, Perishing Republic" is clearly satirical, but the poem is more complex than Ferlinghetti's. Trace the poet's vision of an America growing increasingly corrupt—absorbed with political power, economic hegemony, oblivious of the eternity of nature and arrogantly unaware of the fact that the American's place in it is only a small part. Yet, do you detect that Jeffers' tone is mingled with an appreciation of life, especially in the lines ". . . life is good, be it stubbornly long or suddenly/A mortal splendor . . ." (lines 5–6)? How do you interpret the following statement: "meteors are not needed less than mountains" (line 6)? Assuming such a Republic as Jeffers envisions, what does the persona wish for his own "boys"? His warning may strike you as unexpected, even ambiguous. What is "the trap that catches noblest spirits" (line 10)? Discuss.

19. In "London," William Blake relates in consistently metrical quatrains his persona's response to a London no less tragically plagued than Jeffers' or Ferlinghetti's America. How do you interpret the image "mind-forg'd manacles" (line 8) in context with the preceding lines? Is the "Chimney-sweeper's cry" (line 9) an individual social criticism of child labor in Blake's time, or is it a more universal attack upon the darkness, the hopelessness of the common man's plight? Though the condition of the soldier in this society is "hapless" (line 11) and perhaps even bloody, what is the worst blight on Blake's London?

20. The last moment of Mankind's existence as individual men may experience it is the subject of Archibald MacLeish's "The End of the World." In your opinion,

why does he juxtapose a carnival-like atmosphere with the moment of final destruction? Is the juxtaposition ironic? What images make the catastrophic event believable? Do you find the repetition in the last line, "Of nothing, nothing, nothing—nothing at all," convincing? Explain your answer.

21. Does the fact that MacLeish has chosen a sonnet form for his poem strike you as expected? ironic? How does such a device intensify the poet's rendering of frustration, violence, and outrage?

22. Finally, can you relate the poems treated in this question to other poems either in this section or outside it? Considering MacLeish's "The End of the World," for example, how may the first eight lines be related to Robert Hayden's opening stanza in "Aunt Jemima of the Ocean Waves" (p. 272)? Similarly the poem may in part be compared to and contrasted with Byron's "Darkness" (p. 210), as well as Thomas Campbell's "The Last Man" (p. 251). Discuss such relationships as they illuminate matters of form, content, and theme.

"*A Deep-Sworn Vow*" [Yeats] and "*Western Wind*" [Anonymous]

23. These two poems are superb examples of works that lend themselves to contextualist analysis which, in turn, may enrich our understanding of each poem. Read William Butler Yeats' "A Deep-Sworn Vow" aloud and naturally, trusting your instincts as well as your knowledge of prosody. One discovers that, although the general meter is iambic and anapestic, there are several sequentially accented syllables (spondees), and both the first and last lines begin with accented syllables. Notice that your tendency is to accent "deep sworn vow . . . always when . . . when I grow . . . meet your face." Does Yeats wish to emphasize special meanings by accenting these particular words? If so, how do you interpret the poem, and what are these important ideas deserving of such accentual emphasis? Discuss other meanings of the

poem which may be revealed through their relationship to the devices of sound.

24. Similarly, examine the classic, anonymously written "Western Wind," particularly noting the devices of alliteration in the first line, repetition in the second, the interjection in the third line ("Christ"), caesuras in the first and third lines, and contrast of the exclamation in the fourth line with the question posed in the second. Do you find in the first two lines a use of assonance, especially a subtle play on the *i* and *e* sounds, which actually suggests the sound of blowing wind (onomatopoeia)? Read the poem aloud several times, and listen carefully. Can you discover further correlations between sound and meaning? How do such intensively employed devices tend to give an added impact to the lover's frustration?

"*As Glass Is Splintered*" [Iris] and "*Bells for John Whitesides' Daughter*" [Ransom]

25. These two poems relate profound emotion with a rare kind of artistic purity. Iris' poem tells the story of a hunter who commits an act the ultimate thrust of which is heartless cruelty, although the hunter may himself be ignorant of the fact. How does the poet through his narrator make us realize that the thoughtless act is indeed a cruel one? Describe phrases and images that create sensuous and emotional responses as you experience them.

26. Ransom's poem also tells a story, but it concerns a little girl. Read the poem closely and relate the story in your own words. The abrupt ringing of the bells in the

last stanza captures our attention. Why are the people then "sternly stopped" (line 18)? Why are they "vexed" and what is "her brown study" (line 19)? Why is she "Lying so primly propped" (line 20)? Connotatively, does the use of the word "vexed," rather than—say—"troubled," lend force to the poem's emotional momentum—to the sense of frustration, outrage, and, in this case, despair and helplessness? Does the title of the poem possess an irony which dissolves once you read through the poem and understood its basic level of meaning? Why? Explain your answer.

"The Black Panther" [Wheelock]

27. John Hall Wheelock's poem is an Italian sonnet, a tightly compressed form of poetry. Examine the octave (first eight lines) closely and notice the heavy emphasis on sensuous imagery. How does the sestet (last six lines) build upon the sensuous imagery in the octave? What causes this passion which the poet or his persona describes as "a panther caged within my breast" (line 1)? Are any clues evident to you? Can you relate the passion to some definite kind of frustration, outrage, or violence? In your opinion, does the poem suffer because of the generality of the passion, or do you find it meaningful enough, if not distinctly meaningful? Explain your answer with references to the text of the poem itself.

"A Glass of Beer" [Stephens]

28. James Stephens' poem is also tightly constructed; it is even shorter than a sonnet, bursting with outrage, filled with curses, radiating violence and hatred. The persona is brimming over with anger because of his unfortunate encounter with a barmaid. What are the most vivid terms with which he describes her in the first stanza? Who is the "parboiled ape" (line 5) in the second stanza? Mark Twain once observed that there is a kind of wholesome relief gained from profanity; similarly, others have contended that cursing is a nearly lost art, particularly the colorful, even choric variety. Does "A Glass of Beer" serve as a commentary on either of these statements? Can the poem be related to other themes, such as wit, humor, and folly? Discuss.

"The Listeners" [de la Mare]

29. Walter de la Mare's poem tells the story of a traveler who rides his horse up to a door in the moonlight. Here is a brief paraphrase with questions in parentheses: After asking, "Is there anybody there?" and knocking on the door, he repeats both the question and the action, but no one answers. (Why is the traveler "perplexed and still"?) Inside, we are told, "only a host of phantom listeners" dwell, and they listen quietly to the voice of the traveler, "that voice from the world of men." Sensing their presence inside, the "lonely" traveler also senses "Their strangeness," even as he continues to wait. The only answer to his cry is their stillness. He strikes the door once more and loudly shouts, "Tell them I came, and no one answered,/That I kept my word." But once again his answer is silence, and this time the poet describes the traveler as "the one man left awake." (How do the final four lines assure the reader that the traveler was heard though not answered?)

30. Does the paraphrase help you to understand the poem any more fully than you may otherwise have done? Perhaps you cannot state with certainty, but endeavor to relate the traveler and the listeners to representative ideas, if not to types of people. For example, could the traveler's frustration and anger be caused by personal, or aesthetic, or social efforts to be heard—efforts which are thwarted by a phantom-like silence of society in general?

31. Could the poem have a religious significance, a moral significance, or possibly a prophetic significance? Could you relate the poem to specific historical events or issues of the past, or to your own time? Discuss, keeping as close as possible to the text of the poem.

7. Measure of Man

That's my last Duchess painted on the wall,
Looking as if she were alive. I call
That piece a wonder, now; Fra Pandolf's hands
Worked busily a day, and there she stands.

[Robert Browning, *My Last Duchess*]

Scharmel Iris

The Old Man

I am old now,
I am very old.
The sleep has come upon me
And my words. Today
Have I given all away.
Nor will I join in the talk
Of the old men in the park,
Tapping their canes around the well.
I have forgotten many things
For I am old,   10
Being cloaked in twilight.
I will stuff my pipe with stars
And go to sleep.

(*1953*)

Jesse Stuart

Royster Pennix

The dissipated lines erode my face
Of rough male beauty sprightly springtime bore;
Nothing to show youth went and to what place,
Only the marks to show that pleasure wore
The mortal mansion of my living dust
And through slow process back the way it came
Because the winter of time said it must
Lose strength of living, ecstasy, and flame.
Illicit love to manhood in his prime
Proves waste of mortal flesh and youth in
        flower;   10
But ah, proud ecstasy of passing time
When wine is red and midnight is the hour!
On with the dance, life is still here today,
Tomorrow's silent winter covers all
Where wan cocoons will tame our devilish clay
And lovers we have known will cease to call.

(*1944*)

William Empson

Just a Smack at Auden

Waiting for the end, boys, waiting for the end.
What is there to be or do?
What's become of me or you?
Are we kind or are we true?
Sitting two and two, boys, waiting for the end.

Shall I build a tower, boys, knowing it will rend
Crack upon the hour, boys, waiting for the end?
Shall I pluck a flower, boys, shall I save or spend?
All turns sour, boys, waiting for the end.

Shall I send a wire, boys? Where is there
    to send?   10
All are under fire, boys, waiting for the end.
Shall I turn a sire, boys? Shall I choose a friend?
The fat is in the pyre, boys, waiting for the end.

Shall I make it clear, boys, for all to apprehend,
Those that will not hear, boys, waiting for
    the end,
Knowing it is near, boys, trying to pretend,
Sitting in cold fear, boys, waiting for the end?

Shall we send a cable, boys, accurately penned,
Knowing we are able, boys, waiting for the end,
Via the Tower of Babel, boys? Christ will not
    ascend.   20
He's hiding in his stable, boys, waiting for the
    end.

Shall we blow a bubble, boys, glittering to
    distend,
Hiding from our trouble, boys, waiting for
    the end?
When you build on rubble, boys, Nature will
    append
Double and re-double, boys, waiting for the end.

Shall we make a tale, boys, that things are sure
    to mend,
Playing bluff and hale, boys, waiting for the end?
It will be born stale, boys, stinking to offend,
Dying ere it fail, boys, waiting for the end.

Shall we go all wild, boys, waste and make them
    lend,   30
Playing at the child, boys, waiting for the end?
It has all been filed, boys, history has a trend,
Each of us enisled, boys, waiting for the end.

What was said by Marx, boys, what did he
    perpend?
No good being sparks, boys, waiting for the end.
Treason of the clerks, boys, curtains that descend,
Lights becoming darks, boys, waiting for the
    end.

Waiting for the end, boys, waiting for the end.
Not a chance of blend, boys, things have got to
    tend.
Think of those who vend, boys, think of how we
    wend,   40
Waiting for the end, boys, waiting for the end.
                                 (*1940*)

W. H. Auden

In Memory of W. B. Yeats

I

He disappeared in the dead of winter:
The brooks were frozen, the airports almost
    deserted,
And snow disfigured the public statues;
The mercury sank in the mouth of the dying day.
O all the instruments agree
The day of his death was a dark cold day.

Far from his illness
The wolves ran on through the evergreen forests,
The peasant river was untempted by the
    fashionable quays;
By mourning tongues   10
The death of the poet was kept from his poems.

But for him it was his last afternoon as himself,
An afternoon of nurses and rumors;
The provinces of his body revolted,
The squares of his mind were empty,
Silence invaded the suburbs,
The current of his feeling failed: he became his
    admirers.

Now he is scattered among a hundred cities
And wholly given over to unfamiliar affections;
To find his happiness in another kind of wood 20
And be punished under a foreign code of
    conscience.
The words of a dead man
Are modified in the guts of the living.

But in the importance and noise of tomorrow
When the brokers are roaring like beasts on the
    floor of the Bourse,
And the poor have the sufferings to which they
    are fairly accustomed,
And each in the cell of himself is almost
    convinced of his freedom;
A few thousand will think of this day
As one thinks of a day when one did something
    slightly unusual.

O all the instruments agree   30
The day of his death was a dark cold day.

        2

You were silly like us: your gift survived it all;
The parish of rich women, physical decay,
Yourself; mad Ireland hurt you into poetry.
Now Ireland has her madness and her weather
    still,
For poetry makes nothing happen: it survives
In the valley of its saying where executives
Would never want to tamper; it flows south
From ranches of isolation and the busy griefs,
Raw towns that we believe and die in; it
    survives,   40
A way of happening, a mouth.

        3

Earth, receive an honored guest;
William Yeats is laid to rest;
Let the Irish vessel lie
Emptied of its poetry.

Time that is intolerant
Of the brave and innocent,
And indifferent in a week
To a beautiful physique,

Worships language and forgives   50
Everyone by whom it lives;
Pardons cowardice, conceit,
Lays its honors at their feet.

Time that with this strange excuse
Pardoned Kipling and his views,
And will pardon Paul Claudel,
Pardons him for writing well.

In the nightmare of the dark
All the dogs of Europe bark,
And the living nations wait,   60
Each sequestered in its hate;

Intellectual disgrace
Stares from every human face,
And the seas of pity lie
Locked and frozen in each eye.

Follow, poet, follow right
To the bottom of the night,
With your unconstraining voice
Still persuade us to rejoice;

With the farming of a verse   70
Make a vineyard of the curse,
Sing of human unsuccess
In a rapture of distress;

In the deserts of the heart
Let the healing fountain start,
In the prison of his days
Teach the free man how to praise.

                    (*1939*)

Countee Cullen

Yet Do I Marvel

I doubt not God is good, well-meaning, kind,
And did He stoop to quibble could tell why
The little buried mole continues blind,
Why flesh that mirrors Him must some day die,
Make plain the reason tortured Tantalus
Is baited by the fickle fruit, declare
If merely brute caprice dooms Sisyphus
To struggle up a never-ending stair.

Inscrutable His ways are, and immune
To catechism by a mind too strewn   10
With petty cares to slightly understand
What awful brain compels His awful hand.
Yet do I marvel at this curious thing:
To make a poet black, and bid him sing!

(*1925*)

Edwin Arlington Robinson

Mr. Flood's Party

Old Eben Flood, climbing alone one night
Over the hill between the town below
And the forsaken upland hermitage
That held as much as he should ever know
On earth again of home, paused warily.
The road was his with not a native near;
And Eben, having leisure, said aloud,
For no man else in Tilbury Town to hear:

"Well, Mr. Flood, we have the harvest moon
Again, and we may not have many more;   10
The bird is on the wing, the poet says,
And you and I have said it here before.
Drink to the bird." He raised up to the light
The jug that he had gone so far to fill,
And answered huskily: "Well, Mr. Flood,
Since you propose it, I believe I will."

Alone, as if enduring to the end
A valiant armor of scarred hopes outworn,
He stood there in the middle of the road
Like Roland's ghost winding a silent horn.   20
Below him, in the town among the trees,
Where friends of other days had honored him,
A phantom salutation of the dead
Rang thinly till old Eben's eyes were dim.

Then, as a mother lays her sleeping child
Down tenderly, fearing it may awake,
He set the jug down slowly at his feet
With trembling care, knowing that most things
      break;

And only when assured that on firm earth
It stood, as the uncertain lives of men   30
Assuredly did not, he paced away,
And with his hand extended paused again:

"Well, Mr. Flood, we have not met like this
In a long time; and many a change has come
To both of us, I fear, since last it was
We had a drop together. Welcome home!"
Convivially returning with himself,
Again he raised the jug up to the light;
And with an acquiescent quaver said:
"Well, Mr. Flood, if you insist, I might.   40

"Only a very little, Mr. Flood—
For auld lang syne. No more, sir; that will do."
So, for the time, apparently it did,
And Eben evidently thought so too;
For soon amid the silver loneliness
Of night he lifted up his voice and sang,
Secure, with only two moons listening,
Until the whole harmonious landscape rang—

"For auld lang syne." The weary throat gave
      out,
The last word wavered, and the song was done. 50
He raised again the jug regretfully
And shook his head, and was again alone.
There was not much that was ahead of him,
And there was nothing in the town below—
Where strangers would have shut the many
      doors
That many friends had opened long ago.

(*1920*)

Edgar Lee Masters

Alfonso Churchill

They laughed at me as "Prof. Moon,"
As a boy in Spoon River, born with the thirst
Of knowing about the stars.
They jeered when I spoke of the lunar mountains,

And the thrilling heat and cold,
And the ebon valleys by silver peaks,
And Spica quadrillions of miles away,
And the littleness of man.
But now that my grave is honored, friends,   10
Let it not be because I taught
The lore of the stars in Knox College,
But rather for this: that through the stars
I preached the greatness of man,
Who is none the less a part of the scheme of
    things
For the distance of Spica or the Spiral Nebulæ;
Nor any the less a part of the question
Of what the drama means.

                                        (*1914*)

Edgar Lee Masters

Benjamin Pantier

Together in this grave lie Benjamin Pantier,
    attorney at law,
And Nig, his dog, constant companion, solace
    and friend.
Down the gray road, friends, children, men and
    women,
Passing one by one out of life, left me till I
    was alone
With Nig for partner, bed-fellow, comrade
    in drink.
In the morning of life I knew aspiration and saw
    glory.
Then she, who survives me, snared my soul
With a snare which bled me to death,
Till I, once strong of will, lay broken,
    indifferent,
Living with Nig in a room back of a dingy
    office.   10
Under my jaw-bone is snuggled the bony nose
    of Nig—
Our story is lost in silence. Go by, mad world!

                                        (*1914*)

Edgar Lee Masters

Mrs. Benjamin Pantier

I know that he told that I snared his soul
With a snare which bled him to death.
And all the men loved him,
And most of the women pitied him.
But suppose you are really a lady, and have
    delicate tastes,
And loathe the smell of whiskey and onions.
And the rhythm of Wordsworth's "Ode" runs
    in your ears,
While he goes about from morning till night
Repeating bits of that common thing;
"Oh, why should the spirit of mortal be
    proud?"   10
And then, suppose:
You are a woman well endowed,
And the only man with whom the law and
    morality
Permit you to have the marital relation
Is the very man that fills you with disgust
Every time you think of it—while you think of
    it
Every time you see him?
That's why I drove him away from home
To live with his dog in a dingy room
Back of his office.   20

                                        (*1914*)

Edgar Lee Masters

Editor Whedon

To be able to see every side of every question;
To be on every side, to be everything, to be
    nothing long;
To pervert truth, to ride it for a purpose,
To use great feelings and passions of the human
    family
For base designs, for cunning ends,
To wear a mask like the Greek actors—

Your eight-page paper—behind which you
    huddle,
Bawling through the megaphone of big type:
"This is I, the giant."
Thereby also living the life of a sneak-thief,   10
Poisoned with the anonymous words
Of your clandestine soul.
To scratch dirt over scandal for money,
And exhume it to the winds for revenge,
Or to sell papers,
Crushing reputations, or bodies, if need be,
To win at any cost, save your own life.
To glory in demoniac power, ditching
    civilization,
As a paranoiac boy puts a log on the track
And derails the express train.   20
To be an editor, as I was.
Then to lie here close by the river over the
    place
Where the sewage flows from the village,
And the empty cans and garbage are dumped,
And abortions are hidden.
                           (*1914*)

Marcia Lee Masters

Figure

Night after summer night the drift of pipe-talk
    reached us,
Around the turning of the country stair:
Stories of graves, and ghosts, and vanishings;
The mistried and pathetic lives of men;
The knots of fate—
The things that choked them;—

Grand intent
Shriveled to a quince.

Yet, when the fancy struck you—
You would tell us of the Grinderpuss,   10
The wicked bear who hid out in the woods,
And chewed your toe,
Or crowned your head with honeypots.

But, mostly I remember you
Standing upon a hill alone when sunset
Glowed through the clouds
Like a bright-stepped Acropolis;

Your arms locked beyond all words.
                         (*1963*)

Edward Arlington Robinson

Richard Cory

Whenever Richard Cory went down town,
    We people on the pavement looked at him:
He was a gentleman from sole to crown,
    Clean favored, and imperially slim.

And he was always quietly arrayed,
    And he was always human when he talked;
But still he fluttered pulses when he said,
    "Good-morning," and he glittered when he
        walked.

And he was rich—yes, richer than a king,
    And admirably schooled in every grace: 10
In fine, we thought that he was everything
    To make us wish that we were in his place.

So on we worked, and waited for the light,
    And went without the meat, and cursed the
        bread;
And Richard Cory, one calm summer night,
    Went home and put a bullet through his head.
                         (*1897*)

William Ernest Henley

Invictus

Out of the night that covers me,
    Black as the Pit from pole to pole,
I thank whatever gods may be
    For my unconquerable soul.

In the fell clutch of circumstance
  I have not winced nor cried aloud.
Under the bludgeonings of chance
  My head is bloody, but unbowed.

Beyond this place of wrath and tears
  Looms but the Horror of the shade,   10
And yet the menace of the years
  Finds, and shall find, me unafraid.

It matters not how strait the gate,
  How charged with punishments the scroll,
I am the master of my fate;
  I am the captain of my soul.

                                      (*1888*)

William Johnson Cory

Heraclitus

They told me, Heraclitus, they told me you
      were dead,
They brought me bitter news to hear and
      bitter tears to shed.
I wept, as I remembered, how often you and I
Had tired the sun with talking and sent him
      down the sky.

And now that thou art lying, my dear old
      Carian guest,
A handful of gray ashes, long, long ago at rest,
Still are thy pleasant voices, thy nightingales,
      awake;
For Death, he taketh all away, but them he
      cannot take.

                                      (*1858*)

Robert Browning

The Bishop Orders His Tomb at Saint Praxed's Church

Rome, 15—

Vanity, saith the preacher, vanity!
Draw round my bed: is Anselm keeping back?
Nephews—sons mine . . . ah God, I know not!
      Well—
She, men would have to be your mother once,
Old Gandolf envied me, so fair she was!
What's done is done, and she is dead beside,
Dead long ago, and I am Bishop since,
And as she died so must we die ourselves,
And thence ye may perceive the world's a dream.
Life, how and what is it? As here I lie   10
In this state-chamber, dying by degrees,
Hours and long hours in the dead night, I ask
"Do I live, am I dead?" Peace, peace seems all.
Saint Praxed's ever was the church for peace;
And so, about this tomb of mine. I fought
With tooth and nail to save my niche, ye know:
—Old Gandolf cozened me, despite my care;
Shrewd was that snatch from out the corner
            South
He graced his carrion with, God curse the same!
Yet still my niche is not so cramped but
            thence   20
One sees the pulpit o' the epistle-side,
And somewhat of the choir, those silent seats,
And up into the aery dome where live
The angels, and a sunbeam's sure to lurk:
And I shall fill my slab of basalt there,
And 'neath my tabernacle take my rest,
With those nine columns round me, two and
            two,
The odd one at my feet where Anselm stands:
Peach-blossom marble all, the rare, the ripe
As fresh-poured red wine of a mighty pulse.   30
—Old Gandolf with his paltry onion-stone,
Put me where I may look at him! True peach,
Rosy and flawless: how I earned the prize!

Draw close: that conflagration of my church
—What then? So much was saved if aught were
    missed!
My sons, ye would not be my death! Go dig
The white-grape vineyard where the oil-press
    stood,
Drop water gently till the surface sink,
And if ye find . . . Ah God, I know not, I! . . .
Bedded in store of rotten fig-leaves soft,   40
And corded up in a tight olive-frail,
Some lump, ah God, of *lapis lazuli*,
Big as a Jew's head cut off at the nape,
Blue as a vein o'er the Madonna's breast . . .
Sons, all have I bequeathed you, villas, all,
That brave Frascati villa with its bath,
So, let the blue lump poise between my knees,
Like God the Father's globe on both his hands
Ye worship in the Jesu Church so gay,
For Gandolf shall not choose but see and
    burst!   50
Swift as a weaver's shuttle fleet our years:
Man goeth to the grave, and where is he?
Did I say basalt for my slab, sons? Black—
'T was ever antique-black I meant! How else
Shall ye contrast my frieze to come beneath?
The bas-relief in bronze ye promised me,
Those Pans and Nymphs ye wot of, and
    perchance
Some tripod, thyrsus, with a vase or so,
The Saviour at his sermon on the mount,
Saint Praxed in a glory, and one Pan   60
Ready to twitch the Nymph's last garment off,
And Moses with the tables . . . but I know
Ye mark me not! What do they whisper thee,
Child of my bowels, Anselm? Ah, ye hope
To revel down my villas while I gasp
Bricked o'er with beggar's mouldy travertine
Which Gandolf from his tomb-top chuckles at!
Nay, boys, ye love me—all of jasper, then!
'T is jasper ye stand pledged to, lest I grieve
My bath must needs be left behind, alas!   70
One block, pure green as a pistachio-nut,
There's plenty jasper somewhere in the world—
And have I not Saint Praxed's ear to pray
Horses for ye, and brown Greek manuscripts,

And mistresses with great smooth marbly limbs?
—That's if ye carve my epitaph aright,
Choice Latin, picked phrase, Tully's every word,
No gaudy ware like Gandolf's second line—
Tully, my masters? Ulpian serves his need!
And then how I shall lie through centuries,   80
And hear the blessed mutter of the mass,
And see God made and eaten all day long,
And feel the steady candle-flame, and taste
Good strong thick stupefying incense-smoke!
For as I lie here, hours of the dead night,
Dying in state and by such slow degrees,
I fold my arms as if they clasped a crook,
And stretch my feet forth straight as stone can
    point,
And let the bedclothes, for a mortcloth, drop
Into great laps and folds of sculptor's-work: 90
And as yon tapers dwindle, and strange thoughts
Grow, with a certain humming in my ears,
About the life before I lived this life,
And this life too, popes, cardinals and priests,
Saint Praxed at his sermon on the mount,
Your tall pale mother with her talking eyes,
And new-found agate urns as fresh as day,
And marble's language, Latin pure, discreet,
—Aha, ELUCESCEBAT quoth our friend?
No Tully, said I, Ulpian at the best!   100
Evil and brief hath been my pilgrimage.
All *lapis*, all, sons! Else I give the Pope
My villas! Will ye ever eat my heart?
Ever your eyes were as a lizard's quick,
They glitter like your mother's for my soul,
Or ye would heighten my impoverished frieze,
Piece out its starved design, and fill my vase
With grapes, and add a vizor and a Term,
And to the tripod ye would tie a lynx
That in his struggle throws the thyrsus down,   110
To comfort me on my entablature
Whereon I am to lie till I must ask
"Do I live, am I dead?" There, leave me, there!
For ye have stabbed me with ingratitude
To death—ye wish it—God, ye wish it! Stone—
Gritstone, a-crumble! Clammy squares which
    sweat
As if the corpse they keep were oozing through—

And no more *lapis* to delight the world!
Well, go! I bless ye. Fewer tapers there,
But in a row: and, going, turn your backs 120
—Ay, like departing altar-ministrants,
And leave me in my church, the church for
    peace,
That I may watch at leisure if he leers—
Old Gandolf, at me, from his onion-stone,
As still he envied me, so fair she was!

                    (*1845*)

Robert Browning

My Last Duchess

Ferrara

That's my last Duchess painted on the wall,
Looking as if she were alive. I call
That piece a wonder, now; Fra Pandolf's hands
Worked busily a day, and there she stands.
Will't please you sit and look at her? I said
"Fra Pandolf" by design, for never read
Strangers like you that pictured countenance,
The depth and passion of its earnest glance,
But to myself they turned (since none puts by
The curtain I have drawn for you, but I) 10
And seemed as they would ask me, if they durst,
How such a glance came there; so, not the first
Are you to turn and ask thus. Sir, 'twas not
Her husband's presence only, called that spot
Of joy into the Duchess' cheek; perhaps
Fra Pandolf chanced to say, "Her mantle laps
Over my lady's wrist too much," or, "Paint
Must never hope to reproduce the faint
Half-flush that dies along her throat." Such stuff
Was courtesy, she thought, and cause enough 20
For calling up that spot of joy. She had
A heart—how shall I say?—too soon made
    glad,
Too easily impressed; she liked whate'er
She looked on, and her looks went everywhere.
Sir, 'twas all one! My favor at her breast,
The dropping of the daylight in the West,

The bough of cherries some officious fool
Broke in the orchard for her, the white mule
She rode with round the terrace—all and each
Would draw from her alike the approving
    speech, 30
Or blush, at least. She thanked men—good!
    but thanked
Somehow—I know not how—as if she ranked
My gift of a nine-hundred-years-old name
With anybody's gift. Who'd stoop to blame
This sort of trifling? Even had you skill
In speech—which I have not—to make your will
Quite clear to such an one, and say, "Just this
Or that in you disgusts me; here you miss,
Or there exceed the mark"—and if she let
Herself be lessoned so, nor plainly set 40
Her wits to yours, forsooth, and made
    excuse—
E'en then would be some stooping; and I choose
Never to stoop. Oh, sir, she smiled, no doubt,
Whene'er I passed her; but who passed without
Much the same smile? This grew; I gave
    commands;
Then all smiles stopped together. There she
    stands
As if alive. Will't please you rise? We'll meet
The company below, then. I repeat,
The Count your master's known munificence
Is ample warrant that no just pretense 50
Of mine for dowry will be disallowed;
Though his fair daughter's self, as I avowed
At starting, is my object. Nay, we'll go
Together down, sir. Notice Neptune, though,
Taming a sea-horse, thought a rarity,
Which Claus of Innsbruck cast in bronze for me!

                    (*1842*)

Percy Bysshe Shelley

Ozymandias

I met a traveller from an antique land
Who said: Two vast and trunkless legs of stone
Stand in the desert . . . Near them, on the sand,

Half sunk, a shattered visage lies, whose frown,
And wrinkled lip, and sneer of cold command,
Tell that its sculptor well those passions read
Which yet survive, (stamped on these lifeless
    things,)
The hand that mocked them and the heart that
    fed:

And on the pedestal these words appear:
'My name is Ozymandias, king of kings: 10
Look on my works, ye Mighty, and despair!'
Nothing beside remains. Round the decay
Of that colossal wreck, boundless and bare
The lone and level sands stretch far away.

(1818)

EXERCISES

"The Old Man" [Iris]

1. Scharmel Iris' "The Old Man" may appear to have a self-explanatory title, but when we read the poem we perceive that the persona is not just any old gentleman; he is singular, too. First, consider what may be termed the "poet's voice." An old man declares that he is "old," emphasizes the point, and states that "sleep has come upon me/And my words" (lines 3–4). To what extent is this statement a metaphor—particularly, the word "sleep"? Comment. Continuing, we discern that the persona has "given all away" (line 5), but once again, is he speaking metaphorically? If so, to what may "all" refer (his money, his worldly goods, his talents, his effort to improve the world through giving, or what)? The persona declares that he will not "join in the talk/

Of the old men in the park,/Tapping their canes around the well" (lines 6–8). How does the figure stir richly imaginative associations of what the old man's life—his daily existence—must be like?

2. Note the word "twilight" (line 11) and its transitional relationship to the final two lines. Here the imagery becomes literally, as well as figuratively, celestial. Do you sense an artistic purity evoked by Iris with these concluding lines, "I will stuff my pipe with stars/And go to sleep"?

3. Discuss any distinctive qualities of "The Old Man." For example, does the final figure combine a homely image with a lofty concept in the tradition of great poetry?

"Royster Pennix" [Stuart]

4. How would you describe the personality of Royster Pennix? What was his youth like, and how do we know? How did time affect Pennix's youth? What is his attitude toward earthly pleasures? toward life? toward death? What figures of speech does Stuart develop to make the character of Royster Pennix live for the reader (from the Glossary, consider metaphor, metonymy, consonance)? Do you note a seasonal use of metaphors? Discuss.

Once again, Stuart demonstrates his marked ability to make the abstract concrete. Point out specific examples, including devices by which pleasure is made concrete. Especially discuss the metaphorical treatment of death. How does Stuart make this universal experience concrete, ironically fresh, even for the life-loving Royster Pennix?

"Just a Smack at Auden" [Empson]

5. According to William Empson's satirical poem, what kind of man is the poet W. H. Auden? How does

Empson satirize Auden's pessimism? From Empson we learn much about his attitudes toward Auden, in spite of a bantering tone. What hint do we receive of Auden's views of constructive action in life? toward war? toward Christianity? toward historical trends? toward Marxism? What other subtle aspects of Auden's personality are indicated by Empson through devices of

poetry equally subtle? For example, the rhythm of the poem, its devices of repetition, the use of the term "boys" (especially as repetition) all lend something to the meaning, do they not? Discuss.

"In Memory of W. B. Yeats" [Auden]

6. William Butler Yeats died in a hotel in the south of France, January 29, 1939. Auden indicates the climatic conditions, perhaps of Yeats' native Ireland in the first stanza, rather than those of the Riviera in the second. Commencing with the personification "The mercury sank in the mouth of the dying day" (line 4), a number of lines may seem at first puzzling, but all are explainable within the context of the age and its economic, political, and cultural conditions (a few months before England entered World War II). For example, people articulate themselves through their "mouths"; they also "mouth" sentiments. And Auden links such concepts to "mourning tongues" in line 10—possibly those who eulogized the Nobel laureate upon his death, and by doing so emphasized the living art of a lyric poet who had no superior in his time (relate line 11).

7. Through the remaining lines of the first part, we discern characteristics of Yeats—his strengths and failings—as they emerge. What are they? Then Auden

moves from a personal tone to an increasingly universal one, first relating Yeats to other artists (including Auden himself), to the man's art, habits, country (Ireland)—but ultimately and increasingly he turns his attention to the subject of Yeats as artist.

8. The tone of the third part of the poem elaborates such particularities of the man-artist as his personal faults (What does Auden think of Yeats' political views, for example?) within the larger context of time and even immortality. What is Auden's attitude toward the troubled world in which the aging poet died? What are the different people like? Do they create illusions about "freedom"? How? What are Yeats' redeeming qualities? What does Auden think of Yeats as a poet? Discuss. The form and rhythm of the concluding third section of the poem have stirred some controversy. Do you think such aspects of the section justified? Whatever your opinion, give reasons to support it.

"Mr. Flood's Party" [Robinson] and "My Last Duchess" [Browning]

9. Discuss the differences between and similarities of the two poems. For example, both poems contain dialogue, but Robinson's approach is narrative, whereas Browning's is dramatic. Which poem is the more purely dramatic? Discuss. Both poems reveal individual human characters, too, and both poems deal with lives of men that have changed in some significant way. But the

natures of the two men are vastly different. Discuss. Which poem leaves you with the more vivid impression? To what extent has each poet succeeded in taking the measure of his man (his persona) and imparting his essence to the reader? Discuss, giving specific examples from the text of each poem to support your views.

"The Bishop Orders His Tomb at St. Praxed's Church" [Browning]

10. Examine Browning's poem, widely acknowledged as a work of consummate mastery, richly expressing the poet's psychological insight and historical sense. Comment upon these aspects of the poem as well as upon its

effectiveness as a dramatic monologue, the form in which Browning excelled.

11. Placing the time and atmosphere of the poem into the sixteenth century—the period of the Renaissance in

Rome, specifically the location of St. Praxed's (the Santa Prassede)—what kind of man is the fictive bishop? Point to specific lines to support your viewpoints.

12. In line 17, "Old Gandolf cozened me, despite my care," we perceive that the bishop resents his predecessor. What other lines indicate his resentment toward Gandolf? Does the bishop's preoccupation with Gandolf give you further insights into his character? Discuss.

13. In lines 9 and 10, the bishop appears to be philosophizing even as he is dying. What other lines indicate something of his nonmaterialistic or spiritual attitudes (consider in your answer lines 80–84, 91–93)?

14. Many of the lines may suggest to you that the persona is, basically, a flagrant materialist. Other lines express his sensuality, selfishness, and suspicion. Examine such lines. Also point to those which may allow us some concessions toward him—for example, his learning as a Latin scholar, his appreciation of art, and his humor.

15. Do you see a relationship between Keats' concept of negative capability and Browning's work? Discuss. Again, can you apply to the poem Coleridge's idea of true imaginative creation, "that willing suspension of disbelief for the moment"? In this context, does the poem strike you as a triumph of the imagination? Discuss.

"Alfonso Churchill," "Benjamin Pantier," "Mrs. Benjamin Pantier," and *"Editor Whedon"* [Masters]

A number of poems in this section might be called, to coin a term, "epitaph portraits," especially those of Edgar Lee Masters' *Spoon River Anthology*, for each character speaks, as it were, with the stone tongue of his tomb. Thus, in addition to the inevitable irony, an added premium of validity is placed on the words, for surely the dead speak truly and only what is important—to them, at least.

16. Read first "Alfonso Churchill." Then, in your own words, describe his character. More specifically, how does the poet reveal it? Can you relate this poem not only to the theme of this section, but also to those of other sections? For example, in considering "Wisdom and Beauty," do you see a relationship between this poem and Jack Gilbert's "The Abnormal Is Not Courage" (p. 180)? Discuss these questions and others as they occur to you.

17. What effects of revelation does Masters achieve by juxtaposing the "attorney at law" Benjamin Pantier and his dog "Nig," both in life and death? Do you feel any respect for the lawyer? In considering this question, consider also if honest disillusionment in life may not be better than wishful optimism. What is the purpose of the exclamatory imperative with which the poem concludes, "Go by, mad world!"? Discuss.

18. Now read closely "Mrs. Benjamin Pantier" and relate its persona to "Benjamin Pantier." In that first poem, he states, "Then she . . . snared my soul/With a snare which bled me to death" (lines 7–8). By repeating the essence of the statement in the first line of "Mrs. Benjamin Pantier," what effects of structural unity are achieved, and do the effects go beyond either poem? Discuss, and as you do so determine whether something is added in reading the poems together that would otherwise be missing. What? What kind of person was Mrs. Pantier? Had you the occasion, how would you describe such a couple to your closest friend? How would you phrase their marital conflict (pride versus humility, romanticism versus realism, a sexual mismatch)? Discuss. Are any elements of the poem, especially the conclusion, applicable to themes of other sections of poetry in this collection—for example, "The Shadow World"? Discuss.

19. "Editor Whedon" is a veritable case study in the nature of evil, and yet he is not a simple character. What lines of the poem indicate that he is not "problem-blind"? Still, he is unable to sustain conviction or principle, is he not? How does he use truth to effect his own ends? How does he play upon human passions? How does the poet dramatize the man's falseness? his passions? Are his motivations simple power and selfishness, or what? Discuss. Does Masters suggest that Editor Whedon is irrational? Discuss.

20. Ultimately, in the classic as well as traditional sense, there should be a logical relationship between the life of the hero or "anti-hero" and the action which follows.

Yet, Editor Whedon seems to have moved through life without any particular tragic consequences. Does the poem, then, lack any sense of poetic justice? Or do you find poetic justice in the poem? Discuss.

"Figure" [M. L. Masters]

22. One may well wonder what kind of man could create poems so deeply perceptive of human character as those of Masters. Read Marcia Lee Masters' "Figure," from *Impressions of My Father*. The relationship is that of daughter to father, but she gives us some insights into the creative mystery of a poet that frequently eludes us.

General

23. Each of the following poems creates a striking impact upon the perceptive reader. Choose the ones which shed new light on your ways of thinking and discuss them, relating specific lines and details of each poem to your general remarks. You might commence your discussion with the thematic approach to poetry indicated in parenthesis:

a. Countee Cullen, "Yet Do I Marvel" (suffering, alienation, mystery)
b. Edwin Arlington Robinson, "Richard Cory" (the disparity between appearances and reality, shocked astonishment)
c. William Ernest Henley, "Invictus" (determination, triumph of the human spirit, self-reliance)

21. Finally, to what other single poem in this section do Masters' poems seem most logically to relate? in other sections? Discuss.

What are they? What kind of man was the poet as you perceive him through his daughter's eyes? Discuss. Can you relate this poem to themes of poetry other than "Measure of Man"? to what? Consider "Love of Many Kinds" in answering this question.

d. William Johnson Cory, "Heraclitus" (distinction between nonbeing and memory, or nothingness and grief; consolation)
e. Percy Bysshe Shelley, "Ozymandias" (overweening pride and arrogance, greed and superstition, indifference of nature to man and his vanity)

24. Of the five poems mentioned directly above, you may see certain relationships to other poems in other sections. For example, do you see any lines in Cullen's poem that remind you of William Blake's "The Tyger" (p. 252), and particularly the theme of the awesome mystery of life and the inscrutability of God? As you discern such relationships, discuss them.

8. Wisdom and Beauty

The sea is calm tonight,
The tide is full, the moon lies fair
Upon the straits—on the French coast the light
Gleams and is gone; the cliffs of England stand

[Matthew Arnold, *Dover Beach*]

Gwendolyn Brooks

The Chicago Picasso

August 15, 1967

"Mayor Daley tugged a white ribbon, loosing the blue percale wrap. A hearty cheer went up as the covering slipped off the big steel sculpture that looks at once like a bird and a woman."
—Chicago Sun-Times

(Seiji Ozawa leads the Symphony.
The Mayor smiles.
And 50,000 See.)

Does man love Art? Man visits Art, but squirms.
Art hurts. Art urges voyages—
and it is easier to stay at home,
the nice beer ready.
  In commonrooms
we belch, or sniff, or scratch.
Are raw.

But we must cook ourselves and style ourselves
    for Art,
who is a requiring courtesan.
We squirm.   10
We do not hug the Mona Lisa.
We
may touch or tolerate
an astonishing fountain, or a horse-and-rider.
At most, another Lion.

Observe the tall cold of a Flower
which is as innocent and as guilty,
as meaningful and as meaningless as any
other flower in the western field.

(1968)

Jack Gilbert

The Abnormal Is Not Courage

The Poles rode out from Warsaw against the
    German
Tanks on horses. Rode knowing, in sunlight,
    with sabers.
A magnitude of beauty that allows me no peace.
And yet this poem would lessen that day.
    Question
The bravery. Say it's not courage. Call it a
    passion.
Would say courage isn't that. Not at its best.
It was impossible, and with form. They rode in
    sunlight.
Were mangled. But I say courage is not the
    abnormal.
Not the marvelous act. Not Macbeth with fine
    speeches.
The worthless can manage in public, or for the
    moment.   10
It is too near the whore's heart: the bounty of
    impulse,

And the failure to sustain even small kindness.
Not the marvelous act, but the evident
    conclusion of being.
Not strangeness, but a leap forward of the same
    quality.
Accomplishment. The even loyalty. But fresh.
Not the Prodigal Son, nor Faustus. But Penelope.
The thing steady and clear. Then the crescendo.
The real form. The culmination. And the
    exceeding.
Not the surprise. The amazed understanding.
    The marriage,
Not the month's rapture. Not the exception.
    The beauty   20
That is of many days. Steady and clear.
It is the normal excellence, of long
    accomplishment.

            (*1962*)

Theodore Roethke

The Waking

I wake to sleep, and take my waking slow.
I feel my fate in what I cannot fear.
I learn by going where I have to go.

We think by feeling. What is there to know?
I hear my being dance from ear to ear.
I wake to sleep, and take my waking slow.

Of those so close beside me, which are you?
God bless the Ground! I shall walk softly there,
And learn by going where I have to go.

Light takes the Tree; but who can tell us
    how?   10
The lowly worm climbs up a winding stair;
I wake to sleep, and take my waking slow.

Great Nature has another thing to do
To you and me; so take the lively air,
And, lovely, learn by going where to go.

This shaking keeps me steady. I should know.
What falls away is always. And is near.
I wake to sleep, and take my waking slow.
I learn by going where I have to go.

            (*1953*)

Dylan Thomas

In My Craft or Sullen Art

In my craft or sullen art
Exercised in the still night
When only the moon rages
And the lovers lie abed
With all their griefs in their arms,
I labour by singing light
Not for ambition or bread
Or the strut and trade of charms
On the ivory stages
But for the common wages   10
Of their most secret heart.

Not for the proud man apart
From the raging moon I write
On these spindrift pages
Nor for the towering dead
With their nightingales and psalms
But for the lovers, their arms
Round the griefs of the ages,
Who pay no praise or wages
Nor heed my craft or art.   20

            (*1939*)

William Empson

This Last Pain

This last pain for the damned the Fathers found:
"They knew the bliss with which they were not
    crowned."
    Such, but on earth, let me foretell,
    Is all, of heaven or of hell.

Man, as the prying housemaid of the soul,
May know her happiness by eye to hole:
  He's safe; the key is lost; he knows
  Door will not open, nor hole close.

"What is conceivable can happen too,"
Said Wittgenstein, who had not dreamt of you; 10
  But wisely; if we worked it long
  We should forget where it was wrong.

Those thorns are crowns which, woven into
      knots,
Crackle under and soon boil fool's pots;
  And no man's watching, wise and long,
  Would ever stare them into song.

Thorns burn to a consistent ash, like man;
A splendid cleanser for the frying-pan:
  And those who leap from pan to fire
  Should this brave opposite admire.   20

All those large dreams by which men long live
      well
Are magic-lanterned on the smoke of hell;
  This then is real, I have implied,
  A painted, small, transparent slide.

These the inventive can hand-paint at leisure,
Or most emporia would stock our measure;
  And feasting in their dappled shade
  We should forget how they were made.

Feign then what's by a decent tact believed
And act that state is only so conceived,   30
  And build an edifice of form
  For house where phantoms may keep warm.

Imagine, then, by miracle, with me,
(Ambiguous gifts, as what gods give must be)
  What could not possibly be there,
  And learn a style from a despair.

                  (1935)

Jesse Stuart
"Don Davidson, you walk on earth today"

Don Davidson, you walk on earth today.
The earth is yours and you belong to earth.
Remember Davidson, some things I say,
Since I speak back to you—the actual worth
Of man's not what he takes but all he gives.
I see this now, since I am in the grave.
Happier is he who works and barely lives
And does not get the things he'd like to have.
Power of happiness belongs to him—
Not comfort, now but happiness is bliss.   10
"The dead take to the graves in their clutched
      fingers
That which they gave to the lowly and the
      stranger."
I ask if life at last comes not to this?

                  (1934)

Jesse Stuart
"Oh, Brother, come! Now let us put our hand"

Oh, Brother, come! Now let us put our hand
Upon each other's shoulder and march to cut
The briars and locusts growing in our road;
Oh, let us march and cut and smooth the rut—
For Brother, don't you know that we together
Can march and cut and lift a heavier load!
I hear men crying like the winter weather
Down in the darkness on that thorny road.
Oh, Brother, come! My face and feet are
      bleeding;
The locust thorns have all but pierced my eyes! 10
Come, Brother, we can whip the night and
      darkness;
Oh, we can fight beneath the threatening skies!
We'll take a broad-ax, hew out slabs of night—
Let's go through darkness till we find the light.

                  (1934)

William Butler Yeats

Sailing to Byzantium

I

That is no country for old men. The young
In one another's arms, birds in the trees
—Those dying generations—at their song,
The salmon-falls, the mackerel-crowded seas,
Fish, flesh, or fowl, commend all summer long
Whatever is begotten, born, and dies.
Caught in that sensual music all neglect
Monuments of unageing intellect.

II

An aged man is but a paltry thing,
A tattered coat upon a stick, unless   10
Soul clap its hands and sing, and louder sing
For every tatter in its mortal dress,
Nor is there singing school but studying
Monuments of its own magnificence;
And therefore I have sailed the seas and come
To the holy city of Byzantium.

III

O sages standing in God's holy fire
As in the gold mosaic of a wall,
Come from the holy fire, perne in a gyre,
And be the singing-masters of my soul.   20
Consume my heart away; sick with desire
And fastened to a dying animal
It knows not what it is; and gather me
Into the artifice of eternity.

IV

Once out of nature I shall never take
My bodily form from any natural thing,
But such a form as Grecian goldsmiths make
Of hammered gold and gold enamelling
To keep a drowsy Emperor awake;
Or set upon a golden bough to sing   30
To lords and ladies of Byzantium
Of what is past, or passing, or to come.

(1927)

Amy Lowell

Patterns

I walk down the garden-paths,
And all the daffodils
Are blowing, and the bright blue squills.
I walk down the patterned garden-paths
In my stiff, brocaded gown.
With my powdered hair and jeweled fan,
I too am a rare
Pattern. As I wander down
The garden-paths.

My dress is richly figured,   10
And the train
Makes a pink and silver stain
On the gravel, and the thrift
Of the borders.
Just a plate of current fashion,
Tripping by in high-heeled, ribboned shoes.
Not a softness anywhere about me,
Only whalebone and brocade.
And I sink on a seat in the shade
Of a lime tree. For my passion   20
Wars against the stiff brocade.
The daffodils and squills
Flutter in the breeze
As they please.
And I weep;
For the lime-tree is in blossom
And one small flower has dropped upon my
     bosom.

And the plashing of waterdrops
In the marble fountain
Comes down the garden-paths.   30
The dripping never stops.
Underneath my stiffened gown
Is the softness of a woman bathing in a marble
     basin,
A basin in the midst of hedges grown
So thick, she cannot see her lover hiding,
But she guesses he is near,

And the sliding of the water
Seems the stroking of a dear
Hand upon her.
What is Summer in a fine brocaded gown!　　40
I should like to see it lying in a heap upon the
　　　ground.
All the pink and silver crumpled up on the
　　　ground.

I would be the pink and silver as I ran along the
　　　paths,
And he would stumble after,
Bewildered by my laughter.
I should see the sun flashing from his sword-hilt
　　　and the buckles on his shoes
I would choose
To lead him in a maze along the patterned
　　　paths,
A bright and laughing maze for my heavy-
　　　booted lover.
Till he caught me in the shade,　　50
And the buttons of his waistcoat bruised my
　　　body as he clasped me,
Aching, melting, unafraid.
With the shadows of the leaves and the
　　　sundrops,
And the plopping of the waterdrops,
All about us in the open afternoon—
I am very like to swoon
With the weight of this brocade,
For the sun sifts through the shade.

Underneath the fallen blossom
In my bosom　　60
Is a letter I have hid.
It was brought to me this morning by a rider
　　　from the Duke.
"Madam, we regret to inform you that Lord
　　　Hartwell
Died in action Thursday se'nnight."
As I read it in the white, morning sunlight,
The letters squirmed like snakes.
"Any answer, Madam," said my footman.
"No," I told him.
"See that the messenger takes some refreshment.

No, no answer."　　70
And walked into the garden,
Up and down the patterned paths,
In my stiff, correct brocade.
The blue and yellow flowers stood up proudly
　　　in the sun,
Each one.
I stood upright too,
Held rigid to the pattern
By the stiffness of my gown;
Up and down I walked,
Up and down.　　80

In a month he would have been my husband.
In a month, here, underneath this lime,
We would have broke the pattern;
He for me, and I for him,
He as Colonel, I as Lady,
On this shady seat.
He had a whim
That sunlight carried blessing.
And I answered, "It shall be as you have said."
Now he is dead.　　90

In Summer and in Winter I shall walk
Up and down
The patterned garden-paths
In my stiff, brocaded gown.
The squills and daffodils
Will give place to pillared roses, and to asters,
　　　and to snow.
I shall go
Up and down
In my gown.
Gorgeously arrayed,　　100
Boned and stayed.
And the softness of my body will be guarded
　　　from embrace
By each button, hook, and lace.
For the man who should loose me is dead,
Fighting with the Duke in Flanders,
In a pattern called a war.
Christ! What are patterns for?

(1915)

Walter de la Mare

All But Blind

All but blind
  In his chambered hole
Gropes for worms
  The four-clawed Mole.

All but blind
  In the evening sky,
The hooded Bat
  Twirls softly by.

All but blind
  In the burning day   10
The Barn-Owl blunders
  On her way.

And blind as are
  These three to me,
So, blind to Someone
  I must be.

                  (1913)

Edwin Markham

The Man with the Hoe

God made man in His own image
In the image of God He made him.—Genesis

Bowed by the weight of centuries he leans
Upon his hoe and gazes on the ground,
The emptiness of ages in his face,
And on his back the burden of the world.
Who made him dead to rapture and despair,
A thing that grieves not and that never hopes,
Stolid and stunned, a brother to the ox?
Who loosened and let down this brutal jaw?
Whose was the hand that slanted back this
    brow?
Whose breath blew out the light within this
    brain?   10

Is this the Thing the Lord God made and gave
To have dominion over sea and land;
To trace the stars and search the heavens for
    power;
To feel the passion of Eternity?
Is this the dream He dreamed who shaped the
    suns
And markt their ways upon the ancient deep?
Down all the caverns of Hell to their last gulf
There is no shape more terrible than this—
More tongued with censure of the world's blind
    greed—
More filled with signs and portents for the soul—
More packt with danger to the universe.   21

What gulfs between him and the seraphim!
Slave of the wheel of labor, what to him
Are Plato and the swing of Pleiades?
What the long reaches of the peaks of song,
The rife of dawn, the reddening of the rose?
Through this dread shape the suffering ages
    look;
Time's tragedy is in that aching stoop;
Through this dread shape humanity betrayed,
Plundered, profaned and disinherited,   30
Cries protest to the Powers that made the
    world,
A protest that is also prophecy.

O masters, lords and rulers in all lands,
Is this the handiwork you give to God,
This monstrous thing distorted and soul-
    quencht?
How will you ever straighten up this shape;
Touch it again with immortality;
Give back the upward looking and the light;
Rebuild in it the music and the dream;
Make right the immemorial infamies,   40
Perfidious wrongs, immedicable woes?

O masters, lords and rulers in all lands,
How will the future reckon with this Man?
How answer his brute question in that hour
When whirlwinds of rebellion shake all shores?
How will it be with kingdoms and with kings—

With those who shaped him to the thing
    he is—
When this dumb Terror shall rise to judge the
    world,
After the silence of the centuries?

            (1899)

A. E. Housman

When I Was One and Twenty

When I was one-and-twenty
  I heard a wise man say,
"Give crowns and pounds and guineas
  But not your heart away;
Give pearls away and rubies
  But keep your fancy free."
But I was one-and-twenty,
  No use to talk to me.

When I was one-and-twenty
  I heard him say again,   10
"The heart out of the bosom
  Was never given in vain;
'Tis paid with sighs a-plenty
  And sold for endless rue."
And I am two-and-twenty,
  And oh, 'tis true, 'tis true.

            (1896)

A. E. Housman

Terence, This Is Stupid Stuff

"Terence, this is stupid stuff:
You eat your victuals fast enough;
There can't be much amiss, 'tis clear,
To see the rate you drink your beer.
But oh, good Lord, the verse you make,
It gives a chap the belly-ache.
The cow, the old cow, she is dead;
It sleeps well, the hornèd head:

We poor lads, 'tis our turn now
To hear such tunes as killed the cow.   10
Pretty friendship 'tis to rhyme
Your friends to death before their time
Moping melancholy mad:
Come, pipe a tune to dance to, lad."

Why, if 'tis dancing you would be,
There's brisker pipes than poetry.
Say, for what were hop-yards meant,
Or why was Burton built on Trent?
Oh many a peer of England brews
Livelier liquor than the Muse,   20
And malt does more than Milton can
To justify God's ways to man.
Ale, man, ale's the stuff to drink
For fellows whom it hurts to think:
Look into the pewter pot
To see the world as the world's not.
And faith, 'tis pleasant till 'tis past:
The mischief is that 'twill not last.
Oh, I have been to Ludlow fair
And left my necktie God knows where,   30
And carried half-way home, or near,
Pints and quarts of Ludlow beer:
Then the world seemed none so bad,
And I myself a sterling lad;
And down in lovely muck I've lain,
Happy till I woke again.

Then I saw the morning sky:
Heigho, the tale was all a lie;
The world, it was the old world yet,
I was I, my things were wet,   40
And nothing now remained to do
But begin the game anew.
Therefore, since the world has still
Much good, but much less good than ill,
And while the sun and moon endure
Luck's a chance, but trouble's sure,
I'd face it as a wise man would,
And train for ill and not for good.
'Tis true, the stuff I bring for sale
Is not so brisk a brew as ale: 50

Out of a stem that scored the hand
I wrung it in a weary land.
But take it: if the smack is sour,
The better for the embittered hour;
It should do good to heart and head
When your soul is in my soul's stead;
And I will friend you, if I may,
In the dark and cloudy day.

There was a king reigned in the East:
There, when kings will sit to feast,   60
They get their fill before they think
With poisoned meat and poisoned drink.
He gathered all that springs to birth
From the many-venomed earth;
First a little, thence to more,
He sampled all her killing store;
And easy, smiling, seasoned sound,
Sate the king when healths went round.
They put arsenic in his meat
And stared aghast to watch him eat;   70
They poured strychnine in his cup
And shook to see him drink it up:
They shook, they stared as white's their shirt:
Them it was their poison hurt.
—I tell the tale that I heard told.
Mithridates, he died old.

(*1896*)

Alfred, Lord Tennyson

Dawn

"You are but children."

—*Egyptian Priest to Solon*

Red of the Dawn!
Screams of a babe in the red-hot palms of a
    Moloch of Tyre,
  Man with his brotherless dinner on man in
    the tropical wood,

Priests in the name of the Lord passing souls
    through fire to the fire,
  Head-hunters and boats of Dahomey that
    float upon human blood!

Red of the Dawn!
Godless fury of peoples, and Christless frolic of
    kings,
  And the bolt of war dashing down upon
    cities and blazing farms,
  For Babylon was a child newborn, and Rome
    was a babe in arms,
And London and Paris and all the rest are as yet
    but in leading-strings.   10

Dawn not Day,
While scandal is mouthing a bloodless name at
    her cannibal feast,
  And rake-ruined bodies and souls go down in
    a common wreck,
And the Press of a thousand cities is prized for
    it smells of the beast,
  Or easily violates virgin Truth for a coin or a
    check.

Dawn not Day!
Is it Shame, so few should have climbed from
    the dens in the level below,
  Men, with a heart and a soul, no slaves of a
    four-footed will?
  But if twenty million of summers are stored
    in the sunlight still,
We are far from the noon of man, there is
    time for the race to grow.   20

Red of the Dawn!
Is it turning a fainter red? So be it, but when
    shall we lay
  The Ghost of the Brute that is walking and
    haunting us yet, and be free?
  In a hundred, a thousand winters? Ah, what
    will *our* children be?
The men of a hundred thousand, a million
    summers away?

(*1892*)

Emily Dickinson

I Died for Beauty

I died for Beauty—but was scarce
Adjusted in the Tomb
When One who died for Truth, was lain
In an adjoining Room—

He questioned softly "Why I failed"?
"For Beauty", I replied—
"And I—for Truth—Themself are One—
We Brethren, are", He said—

And so, as Kinsmen, met a Night—
We talked between the Rooms—   10
Until the Moss had reached our lips—
And covered up—our names—

(*1890*)

Emily Dickinson

Much Madness Is Divinest Sense

Much Madness is divinest Sense—
To a discerning Eye—
Much Sense—the starkest Madness—
'Tis the Majority
In this, as All, prevail—
Assent—and you are sane—
Demur—you're straightway dangerous—
And handled with a Chain—

(*1890*)

Matthew Arnold

Dover Beach

The sea is calm tonight,
The tide is full, the moon lies fair
Upon the straits—on the French coast the light
Gleams and is gone; the cliffs of England
    stand,
Glimmering and vast, out in the tranquil bay.
Come to the window, sweet is the night-air!
Only, from the long line of spray
Where the ebb meets the moon-blanched land,
Listen! you hear the grating roar
Of pebbles which the waves draw back, and
    fling,   10
At their return, up the high strand,
Begin, and cease, and then again begin,
With tremulous cadence slow, and bring
The eternal note of sadness in.

Sophocles long ago
Heard it on the Aegean, and it brought
Into his mind the turbid ebb and flow
Of human misery; we
Find also in the sound a thought,
Hearing it by this distant northern sea.   20

The Sea of Faith
Was once, too, at the full, and round earth's
    shore
Lay like the folds of a bright girdle furled.
But now I only hear
Its melancholy, long, withdrawing roar,
Retreating, to the breath
Of the night-wind, down the vast edges drear
And naked shingles of the world.

Ah, love, let us be true
To one another! for the world, which seems   30
To lie before us like a land of dreams,
So various, so beautiful, so new,
Hath really neither joy, nor love, nor light,
Nor certitude, nor peace, nor help for pain;
And we are here as on a darkling plain
Swept with confused alarms of struggle and
    flight,
Where ignorant armies clash by night.

(*1867*)

John Keats

Bright Star

Bright star, would I were stedfast as thou art—
   Not in lone splendour hung aloft the night
And watching, with eternal lids apart,
   Like nature's patient, sleepless Eremite,
The moving waters at their priestlike task
   Of pure ablution round earth's human shores,
Or gazing on the new soft-fallen mask
   Of snow upon the mountains and the
       moors—
No—yet still stedfast, still unchangeable,
   Pillow'd upon my fair love's ripening
       breast,   10
To feel for ever its soft fall and swell,
   Awake for ever in a sweet unrest,
Still, still to hear her tender-taken breath,
And so live ever—or else swoon to death.

                        (1848)

John Keats

To Sleep

O soft embalmer of the still midnight,
   Shutting, with careful fingers and benign,
Our gloom-pleas'd eyes, embower'd from the
       light,
   Enshaded in forgetfulness divine:
O soothest Sleep! if so it please thee, close
   In midst of this thine hymn my willing eyes,
Or wait the 'Amen,' ere thy poppy throws
   Around my bed its lulling charities.
Then save me, or the passed day will shine
Upon my pillow, breeding many woes,—   10
   Save me from curious Conscience, that still
       lords
Its strength for darkness, burrowing like a mole;
   Turn the key deftly in the oiled wards,
And seal the hushed Casket of my Soul.

                        (1848)

Thomas Campbell

The River of Life

The more we live, more brief appear
   Our life's succeeding stages:
A day to childhood seems a year,
   And years like passing ages.

The gladsome current of our youth,
   Ere passion yet disorders,
Steals lingering like a river smooth
   Along its grassy borders.

But as the care-worn cheek grows wan,
   And sorrow's shafts fly thicker,   10
Ye stars, that measure life to man,
   Why seem your courses quicker?

When joys have lost their bloom and breath
   And life itself is vapid,
Why, as we reach the Falls of Death,
   Feel we its tide more rapid?

It may be strange—yet who would change
   Time's course to slower speeding,
When one by one our friends have gone
   And left our bosoms bleeding?   20

Heaven gives our years of fading strength
   Indemnifying fleetness;
And those of youth, a seeming length,
   Proportion'd to their sweetness.

                    (ca. 1823)

John Keats

Ode on a Grecian Urn

I

Thou still unravish'd bride of quietness,
   Thou foster-child of silence and slow time,
Sylvan historian, who canst thus express
   A flower tale more sweetly than our rhyme:

What leaf-fring'd legend haunts about thy shape
  Of deities or mortals, or of both,
    In Tempe or the dales of Arcady?
What men or gods are these? What maidens
    loth?
What mad pursuit? What struggle to escape?
  What pipes and timbrels? What wild
    ecstasy?   10

II

Heard melodies are sweet, but those unheard
  Are sweeter; therefore, ye soft pipes, play on;
Not the sensual ear, but, more endear'd,
  Pipe to the spirit ditties of no tone:
Fair youth, beneath the trees, thou canst not
    leave
  Thy song, nor ever can those trees be bare;
    Bold Lover, never, never canst thou kiss,
Though winning near the goal—yet, do not
    grieve;
  She cannot fade, though thou hast not thy
    bliss,
    For ever wilt thou love, and she be fair!   20

III

Ah, happy, happy boughs! that cannot shed
  Your leaves, nor ever bid the Spring adieu;
And, happy melodist, unwearied,
  For ever piping songs for ever new;
More happy love! more happy, happy love!
  For ever warm and still to be enjoy'd,
    For ever panting, and for ever young;
All breathing human passion far above,
  That leaves a heart high-sorrowful and
    cloy'd,
    A burning forehead, and a parching
    tongue.   30

IV

Who are these coming to the sacrifice?
  To what green altar, O mysterious priest,
Lead'st thou that heifer lowing at the skies,
  And all her silken flanks with garlands drest?

What little town by river or sea shore,
  Or mountain-built with peaceful citadel,
    Is emptied of this folk, this pious morn?
And, little town, thy streets for evermore
  Will silent be; and not a soul to tell
    Why thou art desolate, can e'er return.   40

V

O Attic shape! Fair attitude! with brede
  Of marble men and maidens overwrought,
With forest branches and the trodden weed;
  Thou, silent form, dost tease us out of thought
As doth eternity: Cold Pastoral!
When old age shall this generation waste,
  Thou shalt remain, in midst of other woe
Than ours, a friend to man, to whom thou say'st,
  'Beauty is truth, truth beauty,'—that is all
    Ye know on earth, and all ye need to
    know.   50
                                          (*1820*)

William Wordsworth

The World Is Too Much with Us

The world is too much with us; late and soon,
Getting and spending, we lay waste our powers:
Little we see in Nature that is ours;
We have given our hearts away, a sordid boon!
This Sea that bares her bosom to the moon;
The winds that will be howling at all hours,
And are up-gathered now like sleeping flowers;
For this, for everything, we are out of tune;
It moves us not.—Great God! I'd rather be
A Pagan suckled in a creed outworn;   10
So might I, standing on this pleasant lea,
Have glimpses that would make me less
    forlorn;
Have sight of Proteus rising from the sea;
Or hear old Triton blow his wreathèd horn.
                                          (*1807*)

Robert Burns

To a Mouse

*On Turning Her up in Her Nest, with the Plough,
November 1785*

Wee, sleekit, cowrin, tim'rous beastie,
O, what a panic's in thy breastie!
Thou need na start awa sae hasty,
   Wi bickering brattle!
I wad be laith to rin an' chase thee,
   Wi' murd'ring pattle!

I'm truly sorry Man's dominion
Has broken Nature's social union,
An' justifies that ill opinion,
   Which makes thee startle,   10
At me, thy poor, earth-born companion,
   An' fellow-mortal!

I doubt na, whyles, but thou may thieve;
What then? poor beastie, thou maun live!
A daimen icker in a thrave
   'S a sma' request.
I'll get a blessin wi' the lave,
   An' never miss't!

Thy wee-bit housie, too, in ruin!
Its silly wa's the win's are strewin!   20
An' naething, now, to big a new ane,
   O' foggage green!
An' bleak December's winds ensuin,
   Baith snell an' keen!

Thou saw the fields laid bare an' waste,
An' weary Winter comin fast,
An' cozie here, beneath the blast,
   Thou thought to dwell,
Till crash! the cruel coulter past
   Out through thy cell.   30

That wee-bit heap o' leaves an' stibble
Has cost thee monie a weary nibble!
Now thou's turned out, for a' thy trouble,
   But house or hald,
To thole the Winter's sleety dribble,
   An' cranreuch cauld!

But, Mousie, thou art no thy lane,
In proving foresight may be vain;
The best-laid schemes o' Mice an' Men
   Gang aft a-gley,   40
An' lea'e us nought but grief an' pain,
   For promised joy!

Still thou art blest, compared wi' me!
The present only toucheth thee:
But, Och! I backward cast my e'e
   On prospects drear!
An' forward, though I canna see,
   I guess an' fear!

       (1786)

l. 1. *sleekit:* sleek.
l. 3. *sae:* so.
l. 4. *brattle:* quick scampering.
l. 5. *laith:* loath, reluctant.
l. 6. *pattle:* plough-cleaning paddle.
l. 13. *na:* not.
l. 14. *maun:* must.
l. 15. *thrave:* little grain in a shock.
l. 17. *lave:* what is left.
l. 20. *silly wa's:* weak walls.
l. 21. *big:* build.
l. 22. *foggage:* mosses.
l. 24. *Baith snell:* both bitter.

l. 29. *coulter:* ploughshare.
l. 32. *monie:* many.
l. 34. *But . . . hald:* no house or "holding" (home).
l. 35. *thole:* endure.
l. 36. *cauld:* hoar-frost.
l. 37. *thou . . . lane:* you are not alone.
l. 40. *Gang aft a-gley:* go often astray.

Thomas Gray

Elegy Written in a Country Churchyard

The Curfew tolls the knell of parting day,
The lowing herd wind slowly o'er the lea,
The plowman homeward plods his weary way,
And leaves the world to darkness and to me.

Now fades the glimmering landscape on the
    sight,
And all the air a solemn stillness holds,
Save where the beetle wheels his droning flight,
And drowsy tinklings lull the distant folds;

Save that from yonder ivy-mantled tow'r
The mopeing owl does to the moon complain   10
Of such, as wand'ring near her secret bow'r,
Molest her ancient solitary reign.

Beneath those rugged elms, that yew-tree's
    shade,
Where heaves the turf in many a mould'ring
    heap,
Each in his narrow cell for ever laid,
The rude Forefathers of the hamlet sleep.

The breezy call of incense-breathing Morn,
The swallow twitt'ring from the straw-built
    shed,
The cock's shrill clarion, or the echoing horn,
No more shall rouse them from their lowly
    bed.   20

For them no more the blazing hearth shall burn,
Or busy housewife ply her evening care:
No children run to lisp their sire's return,
Or climb his knees the envied kiss to share.

Oft did the harvest to their sickle yield,
Their furrow oft the stubborn glebe has broke;
How jocund did they drive their team afield!
How bow'd the woods beneath their sturdy
    stroke!

Let not Ambition mock their useful toil,
Their homely joys, and destiny obscure;   30
Nor Grandeur hear with a disdainful smile,
The short and simple annals of the poor.

The boast of heraldry, the pomp of pow'r,
And all that beauty, all that wealth e'er gave,
Awaits alike th' inevitable hour.
The paths of glory lead but to the grave.

Nor you, ye Proud, impute to These the fault,
If Mem'ry o'er their Tomb no Trophies raise,
Where thro' the long-drawn aisle and fretted vault
The pealing anthem swells the note of praise.   40

Can storied urn or animated bust
Back to its mansion call the fleeting breath?
Can Honour's voice provoke the silent dust,
Or Flatt'ry sooth the dull cold ear of Death?

Perhaps in this neglected spot is laid
Some heart once pregnant with celestial fire;
Hands, that the rod of empire might have sway'd,
Or wak'd to extasy the living lyre.

But Knowledge to their eyes her ample page
Rich with the spoils of time did ne'er unroll;   50
Chill Penury repress'd their noble rage,
And froze the genial current of the soul.

Full many a gem of purest ray serene,
The dark unfathom'd caves of ocean bear:
Full many a flower is born to blush unseen,
And waste its sweetness on the desert air.

Some village-Hampden, that with dauntless
    breast
The little Tyrant of his fields withstood;
Some mute inglorious Milton here may rest,
Some Cromwell guiltless of his country's blood.

Th' applause of list'ning senates to command,   61
The threats of pain and ruin to despise,
To scatter plenty o'er a smiling land,
And read their hist'ry in a nation's eyes,

Their lot forbad: nor circumscrib'd alone
Their growing virtues, but their crimes confin'd;
Forbad to wade through slaughter to a throne,
And shut the gates of mercy on mankind,

The struggling pangs of conscious truth to hide,
To quench the blushes of ingenuous shame,   70
Or heap the shrine of Luxury and Pride
With incense kindled at the Muse's flame.

Far from the madding crowd's ignoble strife,
Their sober wishes never learn'd to stray;
Along the cool sequester'd vale of life
They kept the noiseless tenor of their way.

Yet ev'n these bones from insult to protect
Some frail memorial still erected nigh,
With uncouth rhimes and shapeless sculpture
　　deck'd,
Implores the passing tribute of a sigh.　　　　　　80

Their name, their years, spelt by th' unletter'd
　　muse,
The place of fame and elegy supply:
And many a holy text around she strews,
That teach the rustic moralist to die.

For who to dumb Forgetfulness a prey,
This pleasing anxious being e'er resign'd,
Left the warm precincts of the chearful day,
Nor cast one longing ling'ring look behind?

On some fond breast the parting soul relies,
Some pious drops the closing eye requires;　　　90
Ev'n from the tomb the voice of Nature cries,
Ev'n in our Ashes live their wonted Fires.

For thee, who mindful of th' unhonour'd Dead
Dost in these lines their artless tale relate;
If chance, by lonely contemplation led,
Some kindred Spirit shall inquire thy fate,

Haply some hoary-headed Swain may say,
'Oft have we seen him at the peep of dawn
Brushing with hasty steps the dews away
To meet the sun upon the upland lawn.　　　　100

'There at the foot of yonder nodding beech
That wreathes its old fantastic roots so high,
His listless length at noontide would he stretch,
And pore upon the brook that babbles by.

'Hard by yon wood, now smiling as in scorn,
Mutt'ring his wayward fancies he would rove,
Now drooping, woeful wan, like one forlorn,
Or craz'd with care, or cross'd in hopeless love.

'One morn I miss'd him on the custom'd hill,
Along the heath and near his fav'rite tree;　　　110
Another came; nor yet beside the rill,
Nor up the lawn, nor at the wood was he;

'The next with dirges due in sad array
Slow thro' the church-way path we saw him
　　borne.
Approach and read (for thou can'st read) the
　　lay,
Grav'd on the stone beneath yon aged thorn.'

　　The Epitaph
Here rests his head upon the lap of Earth
A Youth to Fortune and to Fame unknown.
Fair Science frown'd not on his humble birth,
And Melancholy mark'd him for her own.　　　120

Large was his bounty, and his soul sincere,
Heav'n did a recompence as largely send:
He gave to Mis'ry all he had, a tear,
He gain'd from Heav'n ('twas all he wish'd) a
　　friend.

No farther seek his merits to disclose,
Or draw his frailties from their dread abode,
(There they alike in trembling hope repose,)
The bosom of his Father and his God.

　　　　　　　　　　　　　　　　(1751)

Thomas Gray

Ode on the Death of a Favourite Cat

'Twas on a lofty vase's side,
Where China's gayest art had dyed
　　The azure flowers that blow;
Demurest of the tabby kind,
The pensive Selima reclined,
　　Gazed on the lake below.

Her conscious tail her joy declared;
The fair round face, the snowy beard,
  The velvet of her paws,
Her coat, that with the tortoise vies,   10
Her ears of jet, and emerald eyes,
  She saw; and purred applause.

Still had she gazed; but 'midst the tide
Two angel forms were seen to glide.
  The genii of the stream:
Their scaly armor's Tyrian hue
Through richest purple to the view
  Betrayed a golden gleam.

The hapless nymph with wonder saw;
A whisker first and then a claw,   20
  With many an ardent wish,
She stretched in vain to reach the prize.
What female heart can gold despise?
  What cat's averse to fish?

Presumptuous maid! with looks intent
Again she stretched, again she bent,
  Nor knew the gulf between.
(Malignant Fate sat by, and smiled)
The slippery verge her feet beguiled,
  She tumbled headlong in.   30

Eight times emerging from the flood
She mewed to every watry god,
  Some speedy aid to send.
No dolphin came, no nereid stirred,
Nor cruel Tom nor Susan heard.
  A favorite has no friend!

From hence, ye beauties, undeceived,
Know, one false step is ne'er retrieved,
  And be with caution bold.
Not all that tempts your wandering eyes   40
And heedless hearts is lawful prize;
  Nor all that glisters, gold.

                                            (*1748*)

EXERCISES

"The Chicago Picasso" [Brooks] and *"The Abnormal Is Not Courage"* [Gilbert]

1. There are many views of wisdom and beauty and many of them are contradictory and often ambiguous. The first two poems of this section illustrate this point; both evince unconventional attitudes toward wisdom and beauty. There is a certain wisdom in the very honesty, however, paradoxically revealed in both poems. *Paraphrase* Gwendolyn Brooks' poem. What questions does she raise about man in relationship to art, possibly man's closest approach to beauty? Why may art make man uneasy? Or does it? Similarly, if art hurts man, why and how does it do so? Why does art make man uncomfortable with his lot in life? What effect does the poet gain by likening art to a "requiring courtesan" (line 9)? How do you interpret Brooks' statement, "We/may touch or tolerate" (lines 12–13) *objets d'art*, but "We do not hug the Mona Lisa" (line 11)? Comment.

2. After absorbing Jack Gilbert's "The Abnormal Is Not Courage," what is the poet's *feeling* toward the Polish cavalrymen who rode out on horses to face the German tanks? To what war is he referring? For many many people such a response would be considered a courageous action in the face of impossible odds. As Gilbert notes, "They rode in sunlight./Were mangled" (lines 7–8). Yet, the poet contends that such action, though "marvelous," is not courage. Is Gilbert attempting to distinguish between what might be considered abnormal human action or foolishness on the one hand, and his concept of a greater human courage on the other— much as Mark Twain demonstrated with his example of a small flea attacking a man, an act which takes no courage for the flea because he lacks a commensurate fear which most human beings feel in final moments of

truth? Or are the two examples different? How? Would you agree with Gilbert's argument?

3. Toward what other examples of so-called courage, even classic examples, does the poet take pejorative attitudes? Notice that he praises Penelope. Who was Penelope in Greek mythology? Why is she known as a symbol of loyalty? According to Gilbert, of what does courage really exist? Do you agree with him? If not, do you think his point of view is worth considering? Can you think of examples of what he terms, "the normal excellence, of long accomplishment" (line 22)? Discuss.

"The Waking" [Roethke]

4. After reading Theodore Roethke's poem and considering its substance, examine closely his method—particularly his metrical technique and the relationships between rhythm, rhyme, and meaning. The poem is an example of the complex verse form the *villanelle*, having nineteen lines which break down into five three-line stanzas known as *tercets* and a concluding stanza of four lines. There are only two basic rhymes used in the villanelle, and traditionally they follow the form *aba, aba, aba, aba, aba, abaa*, with two sets of lines repeated as a *refrain* according to a certain pattern: the first line is repeated in the sixth, twelfth, and eighteenth lines; and the third line is repeated in the ninth, fifteenth, and nineteenth lines—making a total of four refrains of each of two lines.

For what reasons do you think Roethke chose *iambic pentameter* as his basic metrical form or rhythm? Discuss. Even within the traditional form of the villanelle, notice that several of Roethke's rhymes are approximate or *slant rhymes*, those in lines 7, 8, 10, 11, 13, and 14, while all the others are regular rhymes. Do you sense in any of these lines, especially from the standpoint of content, that Roethke intended to give them an added emphasis? If so, which lines and why? For example, in line 7, "Of those so close beside me, which are you?" one can perceive that the question is given added emphasis by slant rhyme—the subtle distinction between the assonance of "you" in line 7 and the previous "slow" in line 6. Does Roethke desire the reader to shift his attention from "I" to "you" in "The Waking," and, if so, does the "you" become increasingly important? Why would the poet wish to suspend the reader's thought processes in other lines containing *slant rhymes*? Discuss.

5. From standpoints of content as well as sound, what effects does the poet achieve by making refrains out of lines 1 (repeated in lines 6, 12, 18) and line 3 (repeated in lines 9, 15, 19)? The refrains are all nearly consistent ("I" is changed to "And" in line 9) except for line 15. Why does Roethke vary the wording in this line? By bringing the two lines together in the concluding *couplet*, does Roethke render an added force of *unity* to the poem? Discuss.

6. Consider the seemingly odd juxtapositions of words, phrases, or clauses in line 1 ("I wake to sleep"), line 4 ("We think by feeling"), line 6 ("I wake to sleep"), and line 16 ("This shaking keeps me steady."). Such a figurative expression is known as *antithesis*, unless it is extremely condensed, as in "hot ice," and then it is called *oxymoron*. Why does the poet employ the device, and do you think the reasons justify the usage? For example, does he wish merely to oppose ideas and deliberately to startle the reader, or are his purposes more functional? Discuss.

7. Finally, in your own opinion what is Roethke's intention in "The Waking," and could you compose a statement indicating how form and substance combine to clarify, intensify, and give a powerful poetic impulse to his utterance? Discuss.

"In My Craft or Sullen Art" [Thomas]

8. The contextualist would notice in detail the form of Dylan Thomas' famous poem. Some of the contextualist's observations would possibly include the following: there are 20 lines in the entire poem, 11 in the first stanza, 9 in the second. Each line has 7 syllables with the exception of the final line of the first stanza, "Of their most secret heart," which has 6; the third line of the second stanza, "On these spindrift pages," which likewise has 6;

and the final line, "Nor heed my craft or art," which also contains 6 syllables. He would notice, too, that although the basic metrical form is iambic, there are numerous trochaic feet in the poem; and he would see an unusual number of sequential accents, lines which could be scanned as *spondees* or hovering accents—for example, "only" in line 3, "I la . . ." in line 6, "But for" in line 10, "Not for" in line 11, "On these" in line 13. Especially he would observe that the first line of the second stanza possibly could be scanned with 6 accented syllables out of the 7: "Not for the proud man apart."

Most New Critics, however, would want to know the relationships between these devices of sound—including the rhyme scheme (*abcdebdecca abcdeecca*), rhythm or patterns of accents (meter), line lengths, and all other such technical devices—and the poet's inten-

tion and artistic vision. In other words, how does Dylan Thomas' technique function to make the poem meaningful and its impact strong? You might commence your consideration of this broad question by examining the three six-syllable lines mentioned. How may all three be linked in relationship to meaning? Discuss other relationships between Thomas' technical devices and meaning.

9. What is the basic *irony* of this poem, and how does it relate to the theme of this section, "Wisdom and Beauty"? Read the poem aloud before making your final observations. Would you say, despite the irregularity of the meter, that the verbal impression is natural? If so, would you also contend that Dylan Thomas' naturalness is achieved because the devices of sound tend to support the poet's intention or meaning?

"This Last Pain" [Empson]

10. The poem "This Last Pain" virtually cries out for a *paraphrase*, for the wisdom one finds in the poem is so complex that one must begin simply. What is the relationship between the first stanza and the traditional concepts of heaven and hell? Is Empson's general contention in the second stanza achieved through the comparison of man to a "prying housemaid of the soul" (line 5), that modern man is somehow shut off from a functioning soul, a *living* soul—that he is, so to speak, only a perverse voyeur of his soul?

11. Note, in line 9, Empson's reference to Wittgenstein. Ludwig Wittgenstein (1889–1951) was one of the Vienna Circle of philosophers driven out of Austria in 1938 by Hitler. With his stringent efforts to clarify language, his linguistics become ever more complicated and sophisticated. In his efforts to implement logic, for example, he found that there were nearly as many "logics" as there were words—that each word, in a sense, required its own system of logic. Does this brief summary of Wittgenstein's ideas shed any light on Empson's contention that aestheticism tends to kill language by dissipating its sense "under a multiplicity of associations"? Who is the "you," by the way, of whom Wittgenstein "had not dreamt" in the third stanza? Is Empson's allusive implication here that the Austrian philosopher became lost in theory, and therefore ineffectual?

12. What is the significance of the thorn figure in the fourth and fifth stanzas? Is the ". . . leap from pan to fire" (line 19) some kind of philosophical leap? What do you think? The magic-lantern was an optical instrument similar to our slide projector. Does modern man in any sense create "large dreams" (line 21) which he projects upon a kind of "smoke of hell" (line 22)? Explain.

13. Is there a diluted satirical tone in the eighth stanza, and is Empson here contending that modern man, in a sense, conducts a kind of philosophical commerce in modern-day marketplaces ("emporia") of ideas? If so, what is Empson's argument concerning the hollowness of modern man's beliefs and convictions? Can you relate your responses in any way to William Butler Yeats' "The Second Coming," treated in Chapter 9 (see pp. 57–75)? Does this stanza, with others, suggest any *mythopoeic* approaches?

14. The last two stanzas appear to sum up the poem and are characterized by an imperative tone. How would you interpret Empson's statement in these stanzas—more specifically, "an edifice of form" (line 31)? Is this phrase central to his concluding statement? How does the final line relate to the theme of this section, "Wisdom and Beauty"? Do you see any connections between "style" and "art," as well as "style" and a way of life (a philosophy or religion)? Is Empson contending, then,

that religion or philosophy may in some way be equated with his own poetic art? Assuming the possibility, can you establish relationships between the idea of art as religion, and Matthew Arnold's concept of poetry? Comment.

15. Finally, does the title, "This Last Pain," refer to man's awareness of his own limitations? his awareness of his struggle and doubt? Is man the only creature who realizes that his life on this earth is limited and who must bear the burden of that knowledge all his mature life—and from life into ultimate nonbeing without illusions, easy answers, and sugar-coated happiness pills? Or how do you interpret the title?

"*Don Davidson, you walk on earth today*" and "*Oh, Brother, come!*" [Stuart]

16. Both of these poems are sonnet variations, and both poems speak clearly. Discuss the themes of wisdom and beauty as they are revealed in the first poem, including the lines, ". . . the actual worth/Of man's not what he takes but all he gives" (lines 4-5).

17. The second sonnet variation is as lucid as the first. His theme appears to be brotherhood (*agape*). Although Stuart's poems often seem simple, the impression is frequently deceptive. In this poem what lines strike you as especially fresh and meaningful? Stuart is given to placing abstract concepts within concrete terms of nature. For example, consider line 13. "We'll take a broad-ax, hew out slabs of night—." Can you point out other examples of this technique? What other effective devices do you find in Stuart's poetry?

18. Despite the surface differences, do you see any similarities between Stuart's poems and Empson's work? Consider in your answer the tone of exhortation and concern with man's moral consciousness (humanistic approaches). To what other approaches does Stuart's poetry lend itself? For example, do you find in the socio-cultural approach especially timely possibilities? Discuss.

"*Sailing to Byzantium*" [Yeats]

19. Read William Butler Yeats' "Sailing to Byzantium." The Byzantium referred to is the eastern portion of the original Roman Empire, centered in Istanbul (then Constantinople). Even as Rome was falling in the west, the eastern empire reached its highest civilization under the reign of Justinian (A.D. 527-565). This civilization lasted over a thousand years and served to influence much of subsequent eastern European art, especially Russia's.

How does such information illuminate the poem? With this background, endeavor to answer the following questions:

a. What is the age of the narrator-persona of the poem?
b. Do you see *archetypal* and *mythopoeic* symbols of birth and procreative power in the first stanza? Specify.

c. What is the motivation for the persona's having "sailed the seas and come/To the holy city of Byzantium" (lines 15-16)?

d. Are the first three lines of the second stanza memorable enough in your judgment to qualify as "touch-stones" in Matthew Arnold's concept of what they should be—that is, do they possess the "very highest poetical quality" and are we "thoroughly penetrated by their power"? Do any lines of the third stanza fall into this category?

e. How does the final stanza sum up Yeats' concept of the immortality of art in contrast to the transient existence of each human being?

"*Ode on a Grecian Urn*" [Keats]

20. Do you see any similarity of images between John Keats' poem and Yeats' "Sailing to Byzantium"? Discuss them.

21. Keats has been called the most sensuous of the Romantic poets. Choose several images in the poem which appeal to your five senses. Discuss the lines in

the poem through which you are most "thoroughly penetrated by their power." Again, do you find thematic parallels with any lines from Yeats' poem? Discuss.

22. Note in the final stanza that interpretation of the famous lines, "'Beauty is truth, truth beauty,'" is dependent upon the poet's feeling and tone. First, in an apostrophe he addresses the Grecian urn, "O Attic shape!" Consider in determining feeling and tone in this final stanza that the poet states the "silent form" of the urn "dost tease us out of thought/As doth eternity" (lines 44–45). The theme which follows then is clearly expressed: all men and women grow old, but art remains eternally young. How does this context affect the meaning of the well-known statement on beauty and truth, and how do you interpret this statement?

"Dover Beach" [Arnold]

23. Generally conceded to be one of the great poems in English, Matthew Arnold's "Dover Beach" lends itself to numerous poetic approaches. First, note the date of the publication of the poem (1867). The French Revolution had swept Europe half a century before; social upheavals were still erupting—yet most revolutions had failed; Karl Marx and Friedrich Engels published their *Communist Manifesto* in 1848; traditional concepts of religious faith were being undermined by scientific explorations—for example, the work of Jean Lamarck, Robert Chambers, and Charles Darwin; psychological research was already under way, culminating in the age of Freud (1856–1939).

Does such a background suggest historical, humanistic, and sociocultural approaches one may take to the poem? May the poem be approached variously as a view of civilization, a treatment of shifting moral and ethical concepts, or a statement of protest at one's human plight? Evidence indicates that the date of the work's composition could be as early as 1851. Does this dating alter your views of the poem?

24. Note the second stanza closely. Could the water imagery indicate the *archetype* of birth, as night (darkness) dimly asserts the imperative of nonbeing or death?

25. Generally, then, the poem commences with an emotional assertion of inspiration, beauty, and peace, but concludes with a powerful image of disillusionment, turmoil, ignorance, and ugliness. Does the structural inversion strengthen the tone of the poem and its emotional impact—the disparity between the beauty of nature (what could be) and the ugliness of reality (human conditions as they are)? Discuss. In this connection, do you detect an increasing use of abstract terms or a decreasing concreteness of word choice as the poem progresses? Give examples and explain.

26. After treatment of these points, how would you phrase the major theme of the poem? Are the lovers searching for a merely physical relationship (the seduction motif)? a spiritual fulfillment, or a kind of metaphorical rebirth? On a more universal level, is the persona questing for order out of chaos? Discuss. Do you see relationships between this poem and other poems in this section, or other sections? Why, do you suppose, was this poem placed in this section rather than—say—"Love of Many Kinds"? Discuss.

27. Finally, how does a synthesis of approaches help one to do more justice to interpreting the poem than any single approach could? Discuss. Does the poem still exceed our critical grasp? In considering your answer, does one take from the poem a sensibility that transcends critical approaches? Do you find the poem singularly applicable to human suffering with which you are familiar? Is it personally meaningful, and even if it is, do you feel its power in a way that is difficult to express? Do you feel with the poet (let us say metaphorically) any identification with the "ebb and flow/ Of human misery" (lines 17–18) and any remaining contradictions between "The Sea of Faith" (line 21) and the stark realities which one must confront in his daily life? Discuss these and other aspects of the poem as you find them significant.

General

There are several well-known poems in this section which powerfully stir our awareness and lend themselves to detailed questions. Select three poems from the following and make a commentary on each, beginning with the approaches suggested.

28. Amy Lowell's "Patterns" reads aloud so well probably because it is such a seemingly natural dramatic monologue. Amy Lowell was an imagist in poetry. Speaking for her and other imagists, Ezra Pound noted three qualities of such poetry: (a) "direct treatment of the 'thing,' whether subjective or objective"; (b) "to use absolutely no word that does not contribute to the presentation"; and (c) as regarding rhythm, "to compose in sequence of the musical phrase, not in sequence of the metronome." Apply these tenets of imagism to Amy Lowell's poem. How closely do they approximate her technique and purposes?

29. Comment upon the dramatic impact of A. E. Housman's "Terence, This Is Stupid Stuff"—relating the pertinent aspects of the poem to the theme of wisdom and including responses to these questions in your commentary:

a. How many people are talking in this poem?

b. Who is Terence? Why is he being criticized by his friend?

c. What is it that his friend wants Terence to do?

d. In the second stanza, center your remarks on Terence's reply to his friend.

e. Examine in detail the tone of the speaker in the second and third stanzas, especially his attitudes toward poetry and reality.

f. How does Terence justify writing poetry which, as he puts it, "Is not so brisk a brew as ale"?

g. As a matter of fact, he states his poetry may taste "sour," but what is his rationale for writing it?

h. What is the significance of the anecdote of King Mithridates, who lived in the East, to the nature of serious poetry and reality? In summary, is the tone of the poem pessimistic, offensive, sorrowful, unpleasant, apologetic, rational, wise—or what?

30. Discuss the irony of Emily Dickinson's "Much Madness Is Divinest Sense," and relate it to the issues of the day. Establish relationships between her poem "I Died for Beauty" and John Keats' "Ode on a Grecian Urn." Discuss similarities and differences.

31. Discuss humanistic values—especially aspects of philosophy and morality—in Thomas Gray's masterpiece "Elegy Written in a Country Churchyard." In your judgment, why has this poem endeared itself to generations of English-speaking peoples everywhere? Relate selected lines to the themes of wisdom and beauty. Would you consider any of these lines "touchstones" of great poetry? Discuss.

9. The Shadow World

Weave a circle round him thrice,
And close your eyes with holy dread,
For he on honey-dew hath fed,
And drunk the milk of Paradise.

[Samuel Taylor Coleridge, *Kubla Khan*]

James Dickey

Falling

A 29-year-old stewardess fell . . . to her death tonight when
she was swept through an emergency door that suddenly
sprang open . . . The body . . . was found . . . three hours after
the accident.

—*New York Times*

The states when they black out and lie there
    rolling when they turn
To something transcontinental move by
    drawing moonlight out of the great
One-sided stone hung off the starboard wingtip
    some sleeper next to
An engine is groaning for coffee and there is
    faintly coming in
Somewhere the vast beast-whistle of space. In
    the galley with its racks
Of trays she rummages for a blanket and
    moves in her slim tailored
Uniform to pin it over the cry at the top of the
    door. As though she blew

The door down with a silent blast from her lungs
    frozen she is black
Out finding herself with the plane nowhere
    and her body taking by the throat
The undying cry of the void falling living
    beginning to be something   10
That no one has ever been and lived through

    screaming without enough air
Still neat lipsticked stockinged girdled by
    regulation her hat
Still on her arms and legs in no world and
    yet spaced also strangely
With utter placid rightness on thin air taking
    her time she holds it
In many places and now, still thousands of
    feet from her death she seems
To slow she develops interest she turns in her
    maneuverable body

To watch it. She is hung high up in the
    overwhelming middle of things in her
Self in low body-whistling wrapped intensely
    in all her dark dance-weight
Coming down from a marvellous leap with
    the delaying, dumfounding ease
Of a dream of being drawn like endless
    moonlight to the harvest soil   20
Of a central state of one's country with a great
    gradual warmth coming
Over her floating finding more and more
    breath in what she has been using
For breath as the levels become more human
    seeing clouds placed honestly
Below her left and right riding slowly toward
    them she clasps it all
To her and can hang her hands and feet in it in
    peculiar ways and
Her eyes opened wide by wind, can open her
    mouth as wide wider and suck

All the heat from the cornfields   can go down
    on her back with a feeling
Of stupendous pillows stacked under her   and
    can turn   turn as to someone
In bed   smile, understood in darkness   can go
    away   slant   slide
Off tumbling   into the emblem of a bird with
    its wings half-spread   30
Or whirl madly on herself   in endless gymnastics
    in the growing warmth
Of wheatfields rising toward the harvest moon.
    There is time to live
In superhuman health   seeing mortal
    unreachable lights far down seeing
An ultimate highway with one late priceless
    car probing it   arriving
In a square town   and off her starboard arm the
    glitter of water catches
The moon by its one shaken side   scaled,
    roaming silver   My God it is good
And evil   lying in one after another of all the
    positions for love
Making   dancing   sleeping   and now cloud
    wisps at her no
Raincoat   no matter   all small towns brokenly
    brighter from inside
Cloud   she walks over them like rain   bursts   40
    out to behold a Greyhound
Bus shooting light through its sides   it is the
    signal to go straight
Down like a glorious diver   then feet first
    her skirt stripped beautifully
Up   her face in fear-scented cloths   her legs
    deliriously bare   then
Arms out   she slow-rolls over   steadies out
    waits for something great
To take control of her   trembles near feathers
    planes head-down
The quick movements of bird-necks turning
    her head   gold eyes   the insight-
eyesight of owls blazing into the hencoops   a
    taste for chicken overwhelming
Her   the long-range vision of hawks enlarging
    all human lights of cars
Freight trains   looped ridges   enlarging the

moon racing slowly
Through all the curves of a river   all the darks
    of the midwest blazing   50
From above. A rabbit in a bush turns white
    the smothering chickens
Huddle   for over them there is still time for
    something to live
With the streaming half-idea of a long stoop
    a hurtling   a fall
That is controlled   that plummets as it wills
    turns gravity
Into a new condition, showing its other side
    like a moon   shining
New Powers   there is still time to live on a
    breath made of nothing
But the whole night   time for her to remember
    to arrange her skirt
Like a diagram of a bat   tightly it guides her
    she has this flying-skin
Made of garments   and there are also those sky-
    divers on TV   sailing
In sunlight   smiling under their goggles
    swapping batons back and forth   60
And He who jumped without a chute and was
    handed one by a diving
Buddy. She looks for her grinning companion
    white teeth   nowhere
She is screaming   singing hymns   her thin
    human wings spread out
From her neat shoulders   the air beast-crooning
    to her   warbling
And she can no longer behold the huge partial
    form of the world   now
She is watching her country lose its evoked
    master shape   watching it lose
And gain   get back its houses and peoples
    watching it bring up
Its local lights   single homes   lamps on barn
    roofs   if she fell
Into water she might live   like a diver
    cleaving   perfect   plunge

Into another   heavy silver   unbreathable
    slowing   saving   70

Element: there is water   there is time to perfect
    all the fine
Points of diving   feet together   toes pointed
    hands shaped right
To insert her into water like a needle   to come
    out healthily dripping
And be handed a Coca-Cola   there they are
    there are the waters
Of life   the moon packed and coiled in a
    reservoir   so let me begin
To plane across the night air of Kansas   opening
    my eyes superhumanly
Bright   to the dammed moon   opening the natural
    wings of my jacket
By Don Loper   moving like a hunting owl toward
    the glitter of water
One cannot just fall   just tumble screaming all
    that time   one must use
It   she is now through with all   through all
    clouds   damp   hair   80
Straightened   the last wisp of fog pulled apart
    on her face like wool   revealing
New darks   new progressions of headlights
    along dirt roads   from chaos

And night   a gradual warming   a new-made,
    inevitable world of one's own
Country   a great stone of light in its waiting
    waters   hold   hold out
For water: who knows when what correct young
    woman must take up her body
And fly   and head for the moon-crazed inner
    eye of midwest imprisoned
Water   stored up for her for years   the arms
    of her jacket slipping
Air up her sleeves to go   all over her? What
    final things can be said
Of one who starts out sheerly in her body in
    the high middle of night
Air   to track down water like a rabbit where it
    lies like life itself   90
Off to the right in Kansas? She goes toward
    the blazing-bare lake
Her skirts neat   her hands and face warmed

more and more by the air
Rising from pastures of beans   and under her
    under chenille bedspreads
The farm girls are feeling the goddess in them
    struggle and rise brooding
On the scratch-shining posts of the bed
    dreaming of female signs
Of the moon   male blood like iron   of what is
    really said by the moan
Of airliners passing over them at dead of midwest
    midnight   passing
Over brush fires   burning out in silence on little
    hills   and will wake
To see the woman they should be   struggling
    on the rooftree to become
Stars: for her the ground is closer   water is
    nearer   she passes   100
It   then banks   turns   her sleeves fluttering
    differently as she rolls
Out to face the east, where the sun shall come
    up from wheatfields she must
Do something with water   fly to it   fall in it
    drink it   rise
From it   but there is none left upon earth   the
    clouds have drunk it back
The plants have sucked it down   there are
    standing toward her only
The common fields of death   she comes back
    from flying to falling
Returns to a powerful cry   the silent scream
    with which she blew down
The coupled door of the airliner   nearly
    nearly losing hold
Of what she has done   remembers   remembers
    the shape at the heart
Of cloud   fashionably swirling   remembers
    she still has time to die   110
Beyond explanation. Let her now take off her
    hat in summer air the contour
Of cornfields   and have enough time to kick
    off her one remaining
Shoe with the toes   of the other foot   to
    unhook her stockings
With calm fingers, noting how fatally easy it
    is to undress in midair

Near death   when the body will assume without
    effort any position
Except the one that will sustain it   enable it to
    rise   live
Not die   nine farms hover close   widen
    eight of them separate, leaving
One in the middle   then the fields of that farm
    do the same   there is no
Way to back off   from her chosen ground
    but she sheds the jacket
With its silver sad impotent wings   sheds the
    bat's guiding tailpiece   120
Of her skirt   the lightning-charged clinging of
    her blouse   the intimate
Inner flying-garment of her slip in which she
    rides like the holy ghost
Of a virgin   sheds the long windsocks of her
    stockings   absurd
Brassiere   then feels the girdle required by
    regulations squirming
Off her: no longer monobuttocked   she feels
    the girdle flutter   shake
In her hand   and float upward   her clothes
    rising off her ascending
Into cloud   and fights away from her head the
    last sharp dangerous shoe
Like a dumb bird   and now will drop in
    SOON   now will drop

In like this   the greatest thing that ever came
    to Kansas   down from all
Heights   all levels of American breath
    layered in the lungs   130
Chill of space to the loam where extinction
    slumbers in corn tassels thickly
And breathes like rich farmers counting: will
    come among them after
Her last superhuman act   the last slow careful
    passing of her hands
All over her unharmed body   desired by every
    sleeper in his dream:
Boys finding for the first time their loins filled
    with heart's blood
Widowed farmers whose hands float under light
    covers to find themselves

Arisen at sunrise   the splendid position of
    blood unearthly drawn
Toward clouds   all feel something   pass over
    them as she passes
Her palms over *her* long legs   *her* small breasts
    and deeply between
Her thighs   her hair shot loose from all pins
    streaming in the wind   140
Of her body   let her come openly   trying at
    the last second to land
On her back   This is it   THIS
              And those who find her impressed
In the soft loam   gone down   driven well into
    the image of her body
The furrows for miles flowing in upon her
    where she lies very deep
In her mortal outline   in the earth as it is in
    cloud   can tell nothing
But that she is there   inexplicable
    unquestionable   and remember
That something broke in them as well   and
    began to live and die more
When they walked for no reason into their
    fields to where the whole earth
Caught her   interrupted her maiden flight   told
    her how to lie   she cannot   150
Turn   go away   cannot move   cannot slide
    off it and assume another
Position   no sky-diver with any grin could
    save her   hold her in his arms
Plummet with her   unfold above her his
    wedding silks   she can no longer
Mark the rain with whirling women that take
    the place of a dead wife
Or the goddess in Norwegian farm girls   or
    all the back-breaking whores
Of Wichita. All the known air above her is not
    giving up quite one
Breath   it is all gone   and yet not dead   not
    anywhere else
Quite   lying still in the field on her back
    sensing the smells
Of incessant growth try to lift her   a little
    sight left in the corner
Of one eye   fading   seeing something wave

lies believing   160
That she could have made it   at the best part
      of her brief goddess
State   to water   gone in headfirst   come out
      smiling   invulnerable
Girl in a bathing-suit ad   but she is lying like a
      sunbather at the last
Of moonlight   half-buried in her impact on
      the earth   not far
From a railroad trestle   a water tank   she
      could see if she could
Raise her head from her modest hole   with her
      clothes beginning
To come down all over Kansas   into bushes   on
      the dewy sixth green
Of a golf course   one shoe   her girdle coming
      down fantastically
On a clothesline, where it belongs   her blouse
      on a lightning rod:

Lies in the fields   in *this* field   on her broken
      back as though on   170
A cloud she cannot drop through   while
      farmers sleepwalk without
Their women from houses   a walk like falling
      toward the far waters
Of life   in moonlight   toward the dreamed
      eternal meaning of their farms
Toward the flowering of the harvest in their
      hands   that tragic cost
Feels herself go   go toward   go outward
      breathes at last fully
Not   and tries   less   once   tries   tries
      AH, GOD—

                                             (*1967*)

Melvin B. Tolson

The Sea Turtle and the Shark

            Strange but true is the story
            of the sea-turtle and the shark—
      the instinctive drive of the weak to survive
            in the oceanic ark.

Driven,
      riven
   by hunger
from abyss to shoal,
sometimes the shark swallows
   the sea-turtle whole.   10
"The sly reptilian marine
      withdraws,
      into the shell
   of his undersea craft,
his leathery head and the rapacious claws
         that can rip
      a rhinoceros' hide
         or strip
   a crocodile to fare-thee-well;
         now,   20
      inside the shark,
the sea-turtle begins the churning seesaws
   of his descent into pelagic hell;
      then . . . *then,*
   with ravenous jaws
   that can cut sheet steel scrap,
   the sea-turtle gnaws
. . . and gnaws . . . and gnaws . . .
his way in a way that appalls—
   his way to freedom,   30
   beyond the vomiting dark,
   beyond the stomach walls
      of the shark."

                                             (*1965*)

Anne Sexton

Her Kind

I have gone out, a possessed witch,
haunting the black air, braver at night;
dreaming evil, I have done my hitch
over the plain houses, light by light:
lonely thing, twelve-fingered, out of mind.
A woman like that is not a woman, quite.
I have been her kind.

I have found the warm caves in the woods,
filled them with skillets, carvings, shelves,
closets, silks, innumerable goods;   10
fixed the suppers for the worms and the elves:
whining, rearranging the disaligned.
A woman like that is misunderstood.
I have been her kind.

I have ridden in your cart, driver,
waved my nude arms at villages going by,
learning the last bright routes, survivor
where your flames still bite my thigh
and my ribs crack where your wheels wind.
A woman like that is not ashamed to die.   20
I have been her kind.

(*1959*)

Lawrence Ferlinghetti

"This life is not a circus where"

This life is not a circus where
the shy performing dogs of love
                    look on
as time flicks out
          its tricky whip
                  to race us thru our paces
Yet gay parading floats drift by
          decorated with gorgeous gussies in silk tights
        and attended by moithering monkeys
              make-believe monks   10
              horny hiawathas
        and baboons astride tame tigers
          with ladies inside
      while googly horns make merrygoround music
    and pantomimic pierrots castrate disaster
      with strange sad laughter
and gory gorillas toss tender maidens heavenward
    while cakewalkers and carnie hustlers
      all gassed to the gills
        strike playbill poses   20
     and stagger after every
                wheeling thing
While still around the ring
            lope the misshapen camels of lust
and all us Emmett Kelly clowns
      always making up imaginary scenes

with all our masks for faces
      even eat fake Last Suppers
          at collapsible tables
   and mocking cross ourselves   30
          in sawdust crosses
And yet gobble up at last
      to shrive our circus souls
  the also imaginary
        wafers of grace

                  (1955)

Stephen Vincent Benét

Ghosts of a Lunatic Asylum

Here, where men's eyes were empty and as
    bright
As the blank windows set in glaring brick,
When the wind strengthens from the sea—and
    night
Drops like a fog and makes the breath come thick;

By the deserted paths, the vacant halls,
One may see figures, twisted shades and lean,
Like the mad shapes that crawl an Indian screen,
Or paunchy smears you find on prison walls.

Turn the knob gently! There's the Thumbless
    Man,
Still weaving glass and silk into a dream,   10
Although the wall shows through him—and
    the Khan
Journeys Cathay beside a paper stream.

A Rabbit Woman chitters by the door—
—Chilly the grave-smell comes from the
    turned sod—
Come—lift the curtain—and the cold before
The silence of the eight men who were God!

              (1918)

James Joyce

I Hear an Army

I hear an army charging upon the land,
    And the thunder of horses plunging, foam
      about their knees:
Arrogant, in black armor, behind them stand,
    Disdaining the reins, with fluttering whips,
      the charioteers.

They cry unto the night their battle-name:
    I moan in sleep when I hear afar their whirling
      laughter.
They cleave the gloom of dreams, a blinding
    flame,
    Clanging, clanging upon the heart as upon an
      anvil.

They come shaking in triumph their long, green
    hair:
    They come out of the sea and run shouting
      by the shore.   10
My heart, have you no wisdom thus to despair?
    My love, my love, my love, why have you
      left me alone?

              (1914)

Edgar Lee Masters
Fletcher McGee

She took my strength by minutes,
She took my life by hours,
She drained me like a fevered moon
That saps the spinning world.
The days went by like shadows,
The minutes wheeled like stars.
She took the pity from my heart,
And made it into smiles.
She was a hunk of sculptor's clay,
My secret thoughts were fingers: 10
They flew behind her pensive brow
And lined it deep with pain.
They set the lips, and sagged the cheeks,
And drooped the eyes with sorrow.
My soul had entered in the clay,
Fighting like seven devils.
It was not mine, it was not hers;
She held it, but its struggles
Modeled a face she hated,
And a face I feared to see.   20
I beat the windows, shook the bolts.
I hid me in a corner—
And then she died and haunted me,
And hunted me for life.

(*1914*)

Oscar Wilde
The Harlot's House

We caught the tread of dancing feet,
We loitered down the moonlit street,
And stopped beneath the harlot's house.

Inside, above the din and fray,
We heard the loud musicians play
The "Treues Liebes Herz" of Strauss.

Like strange mechanical grotesques,
Making fantastic arabesques,
The shadows raced across the blind.

We watched the ghostly dancers spin   10
To sound of horn and violin,
Like black leaves wheeling in the wind.

Like wire-pulled automatons,
Slim silhouetted skeletons
Went sidling through the slow quadrille.

They took each other by the hand,
And danced a stately saraband;
Their laughter echoed thin and shrill.

Sometimes a clockwork puppet pressed
A phantom lover to her breast,   20
Sometimes they seemed to try to sing.

Sometimes a horrible marionette
Came out, and smoked its cigarette
Upon the steps like a live thing.

Then, turning to my love, I said,
"The dead are dancing with the dead,
The dust is whirling with the dust."

But she—she heard the violin,
And left my side and entered in:
Love passed into the house of lust.   30

Then suddenly the tune went false,
The dancers wearied of the waltz,
The shadows ceased to wheel and whirl.

And down the long and silent street,
The dawn, with silver-sandaled feet,
Crept like a frightened girl.

(*1885*)

Edgar Allan Poe
Sonnet—Silence

There are some qualities—some incorporate
          things,
    That have a double life, which thus is made

A type of that twin entity which springs
  From matter and light, evinced in solid and
    shade.
There is a two-fold *Silence*—sea and shore—
  Body and soul. One dwells in lonely places,
  Newly with grass o'ergrown; some solemn
    graces,
Some human memories and tearful lore,
Render him terrorless; his name's "No More."
He is the corporate Silence; dread him not!   10
  No power hath he of evil in himself;
But should some urgent fate (untimely lot!)
  Bring thee to meet this shadow (nameless
    elf,
That haunteth the lone regions where hath trod
No foot of man), commend thyself to God!
                             (*1845*)

George Gordon, Lord Byron

Darkness

I had a dream, which was not all a dream.
The bright sun was extinguish'd, and the stars
Did wander darkling in the eternal space,
Rayless, and pathless, and the icy earth
Swung blind and blackening in the moonless air;
Morn came and went—and came, and brought
  no day,
And men forgot their passions in the dread
Of this their desolation; and all hearts
Were chill'd into a selfish prayer for light:
And they did live by watchfires—and the
  thrones,   10
The palaces of crowned kings—the huts,
The habitations of all things which dwell,
Were burnt for beacons; cities were consumed,
And men were gather'd round their blazing
  homes
To look once more into each other's face;
Happy were those who dwelt within the eye
Of the volcanos, and their mountain-torch:
A fearful hope was all the world contain'd;
Forests were set on fire—but hour by hour

They fell and faded—and the crackling trunks 20
Extinguish'd with a crash—and all was black.
The brows of men by the despairing light
Wore an unearthly aspect, as by fits
The flashes fell upon them; some lay down
And hid their eyes and wept; and some did rest
Their chins upon their clenched hands, and
  smiled;
And others hurried to and fro, and fed
Their funeral piles with fuel, and look'd up
With mad disquietude on the dull sky,
The pall of a past world; and then again   30
With curses cast them down upon the dust,
And gnash'd their teeth and howl'd: the wild
  birds shriek'd
And, terrified, did flutter on the ground,
And flap their useless wings; the wildest brutes
Came tame and tremulous; and vipers crawl'd
And twined themselves among the multitude,
Hissing, but stingless—they were slain for food.
And War, which for a moment was no more,
Did glut himself again:—a meal was bought
With blood, and each sate sullenly apart   40
Gorging himself in gloom: no love was left;
All earth was but one thought—and that was
  death
Immediate and inglorious; and the pang
Of famine fed upon all entrails—men
Died, and their bones were tombless as their
  flesh;
The meagre by the meagre were devour'd,
Even dogs assail'd their masters, all save one,
And he was faithful to a corse, and kept
The birds and beasts and famish'd men at bay,
Till hunger clung them, or the dropping dead 50
Lured their lank jaws; himself sought out no
  food,
But with a piteous and perpetual moan,
And a quick desolate cry, licking the hand
Which answer'd not with a caress—he died.
The crowd was famish'd by degrees; but two
Of an enormous city did survive,
And they were enemies: they met beside
The dying embers of an altar-place
Where had been heap'd a mass of holy things

For an unholy usage; they raked up,   60
And shivering scraped with their cold skeleton
      hands
The feeble ashes, and their feeble breath
Blew for a little life, and made a flame
Which was a mockery; then they lifted up
Their eyes as it grew lighter, and beheld
Each other's aspects—saw, and shriek'd, and
      died—
Even of their mutual hideousness they died,
Unknowing who he was upon whose brow
Famine had written Fiend. The world was void.
The populous and the powerful was a lump.   70
Seasonless, herbless, treeless, manless, lifeless.
A lump of death—a chaos of hard clay.
The rivers, lakes, and ocean all stood still,
And nothing stirr'd within their silent depths:
Ships sailorless lay rotting on the sea,
And their masts fell down piecemeal: as they
      dropp'd
They slept on the abyss without a surge—
The waves were dead; the tides were in their
      grave,
The moon, their mistress, had expired before;
The winds were wither'd in the stagnant air,   80
And the clouds perish'd: Darkness had no need
Of aid from them—She was the Universe.

                                      (*1816*)

Samuel Taylor Coleridge

Kubla Khan

In Xanadu did Kubla Khan
A stately pleasure-dome decree:
Where Alph, the sacred river, ran
Through caverns measureless to man
    Down to a sunless sea.
So twice five miles of fertile ground
With walls and towers were girdled round:
And there were gardens bright with sinuous rills,
Where blossomed many an incense-bearing tree;
And here were forests ancient as the hills,   10
Enfolding sunny spots of greenery.

But oh! that deep romantic chasm which slanted
Down the green hill athwart a cedarn cover!
A savage place! as holy and enchanted
As e'er beneath a waning moon was haunted
By woman wailing for her demon-lover!
And from this chasm, with ceaseless turmoil
      seething,
As if this earth in fast thick pants were breathing,
A mighty fountain momently was forced:
Amid whose swift half-intermitted burst   20
Huge fragments vaulted like rebounding hail,
Or chaffy grain beneath the thresher's flail:
And 'mid these dancing rocks at once and ever
It flung up momently the sacred river.
Five miles meandering with a mazy motion
Through wood and dale the sacred river ran,
Then reached the caverns measureless to man,
And sank in tumult to a lifeless ocean:
And 'mid this tumult Kubla heard from far
Ancestral voices prophesying war!   30
    The shadow of the dome of pleasure
    Floated midway on the waves;
    Where was heard the mingled measure
    From the fountain and the caves.
It was a miracle of rare device,
A sunny pleasure-dome with caves of ice!

    A damsel with a dulcimer
    In a vision once I saw:
    It was an Abyssinian maid,
    And on her dulcimer she played,   40
    Singing of Mount Abora.
    Could I revive within me
    Her symphony and song,
    To such a deep delight 'twould win me,
That with music loud and long,
I would build that dome in air,
That sunny dome! those caves of ice!
And all who heard should see them there,
And all should cry, Beware! Beware!
His flashing eyes, his floating hair!   50
Weave a circle round him thrice,
And close your eyes with holy dread,
For he on honey-dew hath fed,
And drunk the milk of Paradise.

                                      (*1816*)

EXERCISES

"*Kubla Khan*" [Coleridge]

1. Read this poem. According to the poet, one of the cardinal points to be implemented in poetry was the "power of giving the interest of novelty by modifying colors of imagination," including the creation of poems with a "supernatural" quality. Within the poem, do you feel that Coleridge gives novelty to his work? In so doing, does he place startlingly new images within familiar contexts? Give examples.

2. Coleridge stated that he wrote his poem after an opium-induced dream was interrupted, and could never finish the poem. Do you believe him? Discuss. Do you find the poem entrancing, terrifying, suggestive of sexual aspects (Freudian approaches), wondrous, haunting, hauntingly beautiful? Discuss.

"*Sonnet—Silence*" [Poe]

3. In spite of Poe's declaration that poetry is the rhythmic creation of beauty, he was fond of achieving otherworldly effects and titillating with the occult. The tone is often strange, melancholy, harrowing, neurasthenic, fantastic, and shocking. But like Coleridge, he often achieved thrilling heights of imaginative experience. Read his "Sonnet—Silence." This poem requires a careful paraphrase. How do the first four lines introduce Poe's concept of a "twin entity," and how can "matter and light" and "solid and shade" be related to his thesis? Is it important to note he is writing of "*incorporate things*" (italics added)? Extending his comparison, then, he speaks of a "two-fold *Silence*." How does he make the abstraction of silence concrete? Discuss. How do you conceive of the "corporate Silence"? What is the poet's feeling toward it? By contrast, what are his *feeling* and *tone* toward the incorporate silence? Discuss. Can you develop a rationale which lends credence to Poe's horrific attitudes toward what might be termed incorporeal silence? In your discussion, consider the power of the imagination, which even the rational Dr. Johnson feared, and the comparatively modern term "hallucination." Finally, do you see any relationships between Poe's poem and Coleridge's "Kubla Khan"? Discuss.

"*Her Kind*" [Sexton] and "*Fletcher McGee*" [Masters]

4. Certain relationships may be observed between these two poems. With a comparison of the two in mind, read both poems. According to Sexton, what are the habits of a "possessed witch" (line 1)? Peruse the final stanza. How were witches treated in public? Does the "your" indicate a specific person? society in general? or what? How does the answer affect the meaning of "Her Kind"? Discuss.

5. How is the "She" in "Fletcher McGee" similar to the "I" in Sexton's poem? different? For example, does line 3 suggest that the "She" may be more than a witch—for example, a succubus? What lines and phrases indicate an unearthly or strange tone? What is the function of the metaphor, Fletcher McGee as sculptor and She as statue? How do you interpret the lines, "My soul had entered in the clay,/Fighting like seven devils" (lines 15–16)? What effects does the poet create by extending the basic metaphor? How may both poems be related to the haunting misery of love? Discuss.

"*This life is not a circus*" [Ferlinghetti]

6. Read Lawrence Ferlinghetti's "This life is not a circus." What uncanny elements do you find in the poem? Consider in your answer the phrases "dogs of love," "gorgeous gussies in silktights," "make-believe monks" juxtaposed with "horny hiawathas," "panto-mimic pierrots" who "castrate disaster," "misshapen camels of lust," "all us Emmett Kelly clowns," "all our masks for faces," and the *verbal irony* of the religious imagery at the conclusion, beginning with "fake Last Suppers" and continuing through "circus souls" and "imaginary wafers of grace." How does Ferlinghetti turn beauty into a phantasm or illusion with the line "and gory gorillas toss tender maidens heavenward"?

7. Beyond the immediate devices of Ferlinghetti's shadow world, does the poem take on sociocultural aspects? For example, could it be considered a poem of protest against the artifice of the "civilized world," or man's tendency to exaggerate and distort human relationships into grotesqueries? Discuss. In this sense, do you see any relationship between this poem and T. S. Eliot's "The Love Song of J. Alfred Prufrock" (see pp. 284–286)? Discuss.

"*Ghosts of a Lunatic Asylum*" [Benét]

8. An unusual number of parallels may be suggested by reading Stephen Vincent Benét's poem along with Ferlinghetti's "This life is not a circus." Both immediately partake of weird and unearthly aspects, although within the shadow world they deal primarily with humanity. Do you find the simile in the first stanza of Benét's poem ironic? How? Benét's inmates are likened to "twisted shades" (line 6) that "lean" (line 6), and ". . . mad shapes that crawl on Indian screen" (line 7) or "paunchy smears you find on prison walls" (line 8). What uncanny elements do you find in this stanza? Does the first line of the third stanza, "Turn the knob gently!" produce a dramatic effect? What are the fantastic and bizarre aspects of the last two stanzas? How does Benét manage to juxtapose the familiar with the strange, especially through the use of names and abstractions? What is the dramatic function of the line, "Come—lift the curtain . . ." (line 15)?

9. Notice that both Benét's and Ferlinghetti's poems conclude with religious allusions. Does this aspect of their poetic organization tend to lead the reader progressively toward ever greater heights of supersensuous experience, allowing the reader to transcend external reality and to glimpse what Coleridge termed "the shadows of imagination"? Discuss.

"*I Hear an Army*" [Joyce]

10. Why is James Joyce's poem in this section rather than in "War"?

11. Is the mood of the narrator-persona dreamlike? unearthly? Point out lines and images which support your view. What nightmarish dimensions of the poem are evident to you? Note especially the image of the soldiers coming "shaking in triumph their long, green hair" (line 9), emerging "out of the sea" (line 10). The color green may at first seem mystifying, but compare the use of the same color in Wilfred Owen's poem "Dulcet et Decorum Est" (see p. 144). As grotesque as it is, how may the color imagery as well as the sea imagery be explained in terms of war (especially World War I)? Discuss. Does war also produce the curse of loneliness and the distortions of life which people tend to associate with a shadow world? Discuss.

"*The Harlot's House*" [Wilde]

12. Is Oscar Wilde's poem thematically related to the other poems in this section? How? What is the basic irony of line 6? The last two stanzas, in particular, exude an unearthly and weird tone. How do the images tend to effectuate this result? Relate specific images to your ideas.

"*The Sea Turtle and the Shark*" [Tolson]

13. Melvin Tolson verbally paints his story in quick, bold, lucid strokes. The hungry shark swallows the sea turtle. But the "sly reptilian" (line 11) withdraws into his carapace and, though swallowed, with powerful, "rapacious claws" (line 15) gnaws his way from "*inside the shark*" (line 21) out, "to freedom" (line 30). It is, one must admit with the poet, a "Strange but true . . . story" (line 1). Would you describe Tolson's subject as eerie, uncanny, even unearthly? Why? Discuss.

14. Examining the poet's feeling and tone more closely, do you see any sociocultural meanings in the poem? In your discussion, note the excerpts, "the instinctive drive of the weak to survive" (line 3), the turtle's "descent into pelagic [relating to ocean rather than coastal waters] hell" (line 23), and "gnaws . . . and gnaws . . ./ his way in a way that appalls—/his way to freedom" (lines 28–30)? Can you relate these meanings to any issues of the present? Discuss. In the broadest sense, do you see any social parallels with Wilde's "The Harlot's House"?

"*Falling*" [Dickey]

15. One of the most recent of strange and eerie poems in English is James Dickey's "Falling." Even though the poem is based on an actual event—a horrifying accident—do you find in it a tendency to suspend your disbelief and to accept the poet's vision of the stewardess' death plunge from a jet at night? What sensuous images tend to move you toward the supersensuous dimension of the imagination as you read? How does the poet produce his slow-motion effects? Are they convincing? Do you have any difficulty relating the removal of the stewardess' clothing under such extraordinary circumstances to reality? Or are you concerned so much with reality as you read? Discuss.

16. Although Freud denied any personal experience with dreams of flying and falling, he was familiar with such phenomena in others, relating them to "'exciting' games of childhood" and "voluptuous feelings . . . transformed into anxiety." What aspects of Dickey's poem tend to support such psychological approaches? Discuss.

"*Darkness*" [Byron]

17. Lord Byron's poem commences with a dream but moves quickly to a paradox: with morning no day comes. In this nightmare world, there is no light. In fear, men pray for light. Everywhere people "burnt for beacons" (line 13) all combustible items "To look once more into each other's face" (line 15). What is the irony of their unified action? Discuss.

18. Byron proceeds mercilessly, describing the unearthly darkness. What further changes occur in "civilized" man? Discuss his ghoulish and horrific actions, including cannibalism. What is the significance of the one faithful dog? Is his purpose in the poem symbolical? What of the fate of the last two living human beings and their relationship to each other? Of course, they are physically weak, but do they die from this cause so much as from their fear of each other?

Does the source of their fear lie in mutual hostility? Discuss. Finally, all is still and lifeless in "Darkness."

19. After carefully reviewing the poem, what do you think is the poet's intention? Is he making an ironic commentary upon man? If so, how do the devices of Byron's shadow world give strength to his argument? Discuss.

10. Myth and Archetype

The stars will shine forever over you,
But they will never reach down to your face;
    •   •   •
Out of the womb of woman at your birth.
At death you go back to the womb of earth.

[Jesse Stuart, "The stars will shine forever over you"]

Bink Noll

The Picador Bit

Inside that figure rides opaque malice
who by drilling makes the great heart lift
its fountain and waste the lake of blood.
His lance strikes, holds. Longer, the don's full
    weight.

Men for this circumstance of sport have made
laws that order place, gear, conduct and four tries
but the bull learns rage instead. He erupts
through headlong pain and strikes wrath back
    again.

Today's malice, part horse saved by blindfold
and morphine from panic at horns, stands,   10
its legal right side out, and standing so
tempts this, the next enlargement of the hole

—and part brawny don, mechanic who finds
and fits his point to drain the immense will.
Again the spot. The centaur shocks sideward
till the hole is important, like a whale's spout.

The crowd feels the lance in its own ripe hole,
in its hump knows the monster with two
    heads,
the blackness of its law, this letting of force
and the pump emptying the tongue of red.   20

Blood foams down. The head is dropped forever
    now.
Justice is satisfied. Its constable trots
darkly off. Left to his killers, the bull—
danger's substance, lure, huge hate itself—

thrills every male groin while he swings there
and, helpless, spills the fire of his urine.

                    (1962)

Kathleen Raine

The Pythoness

I am that serpent-haunted cave
Whose navel breeds the fates of men.
All wisdom issues from a hole in the earth:
The gods form in my darkness, and dissolve
    again.

From my blind womb all kingdoms come,
And from my grave seven sleepers prophesy.
No babe unborn but wakens to my dream,
No lover but at last entombed in me shall lie.

I am that feared and longed-for burning place
Where man and phoenix are consumed away,   10
And from my low polluted bed arise
New sons, new suns, new skies.

                    (1948)

Robert Hayden

O Daedalus, Fly Away Home

Drifting night in the Georgia pines,
coonskin drum and jubilee banjo.
    Pretty Malinda, dance with me.

Night is juba, night is conjo.
    Pretty Malinda, dance with me.

Night is an African juju man
weaving a wish and a weariness together
    to make two wings.

    O fly away home fly away

Do you remember Africa?   10

    O cleave the air fly away home

My gran, he flew back to Africa,
just spread his arms and
    flew away home.

Drifting night in the windy pines;
night is a laughing, night is a longing.
    Pretty Malinda, come to me.

Night is a mourning juju man
weaving a wish and a weariness together
    to make two wings.   20

    O fly away home fly away

                    (1943)

Jesse Stuart

"The stars will shine forever over you"

The stars will shine forever over you,
But they will never reach down to your face;
And the dead leaves will hover over you
To leave a blanket on your resting place.
In summer, burdock leaves will flap and wave
And sumac sprouts will grow and spit red leaves
That will lodge on a net, brown love-vine
    weaves
And webs that spiders weave above your grave.
You will not care for rhymes and gold leaves
    when
You lie in this place I am speaking of.   10

I don't think you will know about them then,
And I don't think that you will dream of love
When you lie blind to drifting skies above.
Out of the womb of woman at your birth.
At death you go back to the womb of earth.

(*1934*)

Stephen Vincent Benét

Daniel Boone

(*1735–1820*)

When Daniel Boone goes by, at night,
The phantom deer arise
And all lost, wild America
Is burning in their eyes.

(*1933*)

Hart Crane

To Brooklyn Bridge

How many dawns, chill from his rippling rest
The seagull's wings shall dip and pivot him,
Shedding white rings of tumult, building high
Over the chained bay waters Liberty—

Then, with inviolate curve, forsake our eyes
As apparitional as sails that cross
Some page of figures to be filed away;
—Till elevators drop us from our day . . .

I think of cinemas, panoramic sleights
With multitudes bent toward some flashing
       scene   10
Never disclosed, but hastened to again,
Foretold to other eyes on the same screen;

And Thee, across the harbor, silver-paced
As though the sun took step of thee, yet left
Some motion ever unspent in thy stride,—
Implicitly thy freedom staying thee!

Out of some subway scuttle, cell or loft
A bedlamite speeds to thy parapets,
Tilting there momently, shrill shirt ballooning,
A jest falls from the speechless caravan.   20

Down Wall, from girder into street noon leaks,
A rip-tooth of the sky's acetylene;
All afternoon the cloud-flown derricks turn . . .
Thy cables breathe the North Atlantic still.

And obscure as that heaven of the Jews,
Thy guerdon . . . Accolade thou dost bestow
Of anonymity time cannot raise:
Vibrant reprieve and pardon thou dost show.

O harp and altar, of the fury fused,
(How could mere toil align thy choiring
            strings!)   30
Terrific threshold of the prophet's pledge,
Prayer of pariah, and the lover's cry,—

Again the traffic lights that skim thy swift
Unfractioned idiom, immaculate sigh of stars,
Beading thy path—condense eternity:
And we have seen night lifted in thine arms.

Under thy shadow by the piers I waited;
Only in darkness is thy shadow clear.
The City's fiery parcels all undone,
Already snow submerges an iron year . . .   40

O Sleepless as the river under thee,
Vaulting the sea, the prairies' dreaming sod,
Unto us lowliest sometime sweep, descend
And of the curveship lend a myth to God.

(*1930*)

Robert Frost

West-Running Brook

"Fred, where is north?"

"North? North is there, my love.

The brook runs west."

"West-Running Brook then call it."
(West-Running Brook men call it to this day.)
"What does it think it's doing running west
When all the other country brooks flow east
To reach the ocean? It must be the brook
Can trust itself to go by contraries
The way I can with you—and you with me—
Because we're—we're—I don't know what we are.
What are we?"

"Young or new?"

"We must be something.   10
We've said we two. Let's change that to we three.
As you and I are married to each other,
We'll both be married to the brook. We'll build
Our bridge across it, and the bridge shall be
Our arm thrown over it asleep beside it.
Look, look, it's waving to us with a wave
To let us know it hears me."

"Why, my dear,
That wave's been standing off this jut of shore—"
(The black stream, catching on a sunken rock,
Flung backward on itself in one white wave,   20
And the white water rode the black forever,
Not gaining but not losing, like a bird
White feathers from the struggle of whose breast
Flecked the dark stream and flecked the darker pool
Below the point, and were at last driven wrinkled
In a white scarf against the far-shore alders.)
"That wave's been standing off this jut of shore

Ever since rivers, I was going to say,
Were made in heaven. It wasn't waved to us."

"It wasn't, yet it was. If not to you,   30
It was to me—in an annunciation."

"Oh, if you take it off to lady-land,
As't were the country of the Amazons
We men must see you to the confines of
And leave you there, ourselves forbid to enter—
It is your brook! I have no more to say."

"Yes, you have, too. Go on. You thought of something."

"Speaking of contraries, see how the brook
In that white wave runs counter to itself.
It is from that in water we were from   40
Long, long before we were from any creature.
Here we, in our impatience of the steps,
Get back to the beginning of beginnings,
The stream of everything that runs away.
Some say existence like a Pirouot
And Pirouette, forever in one place,
Stands still and dances, but it runs away;
It seriously, sadly, runs away
To fill the abyss's void with emptiness.
It flows beside us in this water brook,   50
But it flows over us. It flows between us
To separate us for a panic moment.
It flows between us, over us, and *with* us.
And it is time, strength, tone, light, life, and love—
And even substance lapsing unsubstantial;
The universal cataract of death
That spends to nothingness—and unresisted,
Save by some strange resistance in itself,
Not just a swerving, but a throwing back,
As if regret were in it and were sacred.   60
It has this throwing backward on itself
So that the fall of most of it is always
Raising a little, sending up a little.
Our life runs down in sending up the clock.
The brook runs down in sending up our life.
The sun runs down in sending up the brook.
And there is something sending up the sun.
It is this backward motion toward the source,

Against the stream, that most we see ourselves in,
The tribute of the current to the source.   70
It is from this in nature we are from.
It is most us."

       "Today will be the day

You said so."

       "No, today will be the day
You said the brook was called West-Running Brook."

"Today will be the day of what we both said."
                 (*1928*)

Langston Hughes

Our Land

We should have a land of sun,
  Of gorgeous sun,
And a land of fragrant water
Where the twilight is a soft bandanna
    handkerchief
Of rose and gold,
And not this land
Where life is cold.

           (*1926*)

William Butler Yeats

Leda and the Swan

A sudden blow: the great wings beating still
Above the staggering girl, her thighs caressed
By the dark webs, her nape caught in his bill,
He holds her helpless breast upon his breast.

How can those terrified vague fingers push
The feathered glory from her loosening thighs?

And how can body, laid in that white rush,
But feel the strange heart beating where it lies?

A shudder in the loins engenders there
The broken wall, the burning roof and tower   10
And Agamemnon dead.
                  Being so caught up,
So mastered by the brute blood of the air,
Did she put on his knowledge with his power
Before the indifferent beak could let her drop?
                (*1924*)

Stephen Vincent Benét

The Ballad of William Sycamore

My father, he was a mountaineer,
  His fist was a knotty hammer;
He was quick on his feet as a running deer,
  And he spoke with a Yankee stammer.

My mother, she was merry and brave,
  And so she came to her labor,
With a tall green fir for her doctor grave
  And a stream for her comforting neighbor.

And some are wrapped in the linen fine,
And some like a godling's scion; 10
But I was cradled on twigs of pine
In the skin of a mountain lion.

And some remember a white, starched lap
And a ewer with silver handles;
But I remember a coonskin cap
And the smell of bayberry candles.

The cabin logs, with the bark still rough,
And my mother who laughed at trifles,
And the tall, lank visitors, brown as snuff,
With their long, straight squirrel-rifles. 20

I can hear them dance, like a foggy song,
Through the deepest one of my slumbers,
The fiddle squeaking the boots along
And my father calling the numbers.

The quick feet shaking the puncheon-floor,
The fiddle squeaking and squealing,
Till the dried herbs rattled above the door
And the dust went up to the ceiling.

There are children lucky from dawn till dusk,
But never a child so lucky! 30
For I cut my teeth on "Money Musk"
In the Bloody Ground of Kentucky!

When I grew tall as the Indian corn,
My father had little to lend me,
But he gave me his great, old powder-horn
And his woodsman's skill to befriend me.

With a leather shirt to cover my back,
And a redskin nose to unravel
Each forest sign, I carried my pack
As far as a scout could travel. 40

Till I lost my boyhood and found my wife,
A girl like a Salem clipper!
A woman straight as a hunting-knife
With eyes as bright as the Dipper!

We cleared our camp where the buffalo feed,
Unheard-of streams were our flagons;
And I sowed my sons like apple-seed
On the trail of the Western wagons.

They were right, tight boys, never sulky or
slow,
A fruitful, a goodly muster. 50
The eldest died at the Alamo.
The youngest fell with Custer.

The letter that told it burned my hand.
Yet we smiled and said, "So be it!"
But I could not live when they fenced the
land,
For it broke my heart to see it.

I saddled a red, unbroken colt
And rode him into the day there;
And he threw me down like a thunderbolt
And rolled on me as I lay there. 60

The hunter's whistle hummed in my ear
As the city-men tried to move me,
And I died in my boots like a pioneer
With the whole wide sky above me.

Now I lie in the heart of the fat, black soil,
Like the seed of a prairie-thistle;
It has washed my bones with honey and oil
And picked them clean as a whistle.

And my youth returns, like the rains of
Spring,
And my sons, like the wild-geese flying; 70
And I lie and hear the meadow-lark sing
And have much content in my dying.

Go play with the towns you have built of
blocks
The towns where you would have bound me!
I sleep in my earth like a tired fox,
And my buffalo have found me.

(1922)

John Masefield

Sea Fever

I must down to the seas again, to the lonely sea
    and the sky,
And all I ask is a tall ship and a star to steer her
    by,
And the wheel's kick and the wind's song and
    the white sail's shaking
And a gray mist on the sea's face and a gray
    dawn breaking.

I must down to the seas again, for the call of
    the running tide
Is a wild call and a clear call that may not be
    denied;
And all I ask is a windy day with the white
    clouds flying,
And the flung spray and the blown spume, and
    the sea-gulls crying.

I must down to the seas again to the vagrant
    gypsy life,
To the gull's way and the whale's way where
    the wind's like a whetted knife;   10
And all I ask is a merry yarn from a laughing
    fellow-rover,
And quiet sleep and a sweet dream when the
    long trick's over.

                         (*1902*)

Dante Gabriel Rossetti

The Ballad of Dead Ladies

[*From François Villon*]

Tell me now in what hidden way is
    Lady Flora the lovely Roman?
Where's Hipparchia, and where is Thaïs,
    Neither of them the fairer woman?
    Where is Echo, beheld of no man,
Only heard on river and mere—
    She whose beauty was more than human?—
But where are the snows of yester-year?

Where's Héloïse, the learned nun,
    For whose sake Abeillard, I ween,   10
Lost manhood and put priesthood on?
    (From Love he won such dule and teen!)
    And where, I pray you, is the Queen
Who willed that Buridan should steer
    Sewed in a sack's mouth down the Seine?—
But where are the snows of yester-year?

White Queen Blanche, like a queen of lilies,
    With a voice like any mermaiden—
Bertha Broadfoot, Beatrice, Alice,
    And Ermengarde the lady of Maine—   20
    And that good Joan whom Englishmen
At Rouen doomed and burned her there—
    Mother of God, where are they then?—
But where are the snows of yester-year?

Nay, never ask this week, fair lord,
    Where they are gone, nor yet this year,
Except with this for an overword—
    But where are the snows of yester-year?

                         (*1869*)

Algernon Charles Swinburne

When the Hounds of Spring

Chorus from Atalanta in Calydon

When the hounds of spring are on winter's
    traces,
    The mother of months in meadow or plain
Fills the shadows and windy places
    With lisp of leaves and ripple of rain;

Atalanta in Calydon: after Artemis had sent a wild boar to ravage the Grecian city of Calydon, Meleager slew it and gave the remains to the lovely, swift-footed Arcadian huntress, Atalanta, whom he loved. Although this chorus does not treat the rest of the myth, Atalanta offered to marry any man who could defeat her in a race. By dropping three golden apples along the course, which Atalanta could not resist stopping to pick up, Hippomenes contrived to defeat her and succeeded.
l. 2. *mother of months:* mythic allusion to Artemis, goddess of the moon.

And the brown bright nightingale amorous
Is half assuaged for Itylus,
For the Thracian ships and the foreign faces,
   The tongueless vigil, and all the pain.

Come with bows bent and with emptying of
     quivers,
   Maiden most perfect, lady of light,   10
With a noise of winds and many rivers,
   With a clamour of waters, and with might;
Bind on thy sandals, O thou most fleet,
Over the splendour and speed of thy feet;
For the faint east quickens, the wan west shivers,
   Round the feet of the day and the feet of the
     night.

Where shall we find her, how shall we sing to
     her,
   Fold our hands round her knees, and cling?
O that man's heart were as fire and could spring
     to her,
   Fire, or the strength of the streams that spring!
For the stars and the winds are unto her   21
As raiment, as songs of the harp-player;
For the risen stars and the fallen cling to her,
   And the southwest-wind and the west-wind
     sing.

For winter's rains and ruins are over,
   And all the season of snows and sins;
The day dividing lover and lover,
   The light that loses, the night that wins;
And time remembered is grief forgotten,
And frosts are slain and flowers begotten,   30
And in green underwood and cover
   Blossom by blossom the spring begins.

The full streams feed on flower of rushes,
   Ripe grasses trammel a travelling foot,
The faint fresh flame of the young year flushes
   From leaf to flower and flower to fruit;

l. 6. *Itylus:* son of Tereus and Procne, slain by his mother
Procne as vengeance for the rape of her sister Philomela
by Tereus, who afterward cut out Philomela's tongue to
keep her from talking. Philomela was later changed into
the nightingale.

And fruit and leaf are as gold and fire,
And the oat is heard above the lyre,
And the hoofèd heel of a satyr crushes
   The chestnut-husk at the chestnut-root.   40

And Pan by noon and Bacchus by night,
   Fleeter of foot than the fleet-foot kid,
Follows with dancing and fills with delight
   The Mænad and the Bassarid;
And soft as lips that laugh and hide
The laughing leaves of the trees divide,
And screen from seeing and leave in sight
   The god pursuing, the maiden hid.

The ivy falls with the Bacchanal's hair
   Over her eyebrows hiding her eyes;   50
The wild vine slipping down leaves bare
   Her bright breast shortening into sighs;
The wild vine slips with the weight of its
     leaves,
But the berried ivy catches and cleaves
To the limbs that glitter, the feet that scare
   The wolf that follows, the fawn that flies.

                    (1865)

l. 39. *satyr:* half-man, half-goat, given to licentiousness.
l. 41. *Bacchus:* god of wine and festivity.
l. 44. *Mænad . . . Bassarid:* female and male worshipers of
Bacchus, given to frenzied sexual play.

Elizabeth Barrett Browning

A Musical Instrument

What was he doing, the great god Pan,
   Down in the reeds by the river?
Spreading ruin and scattering ban,
Splashing and paddling with hoofs of a goat,
And breaking the golden lilies afloat
   With the dragon-fly on the river?

He tore out a reed, the great god Pan,
   From the deep cool bed of the river;
The limpid water turbidly ran,
And the broken lilies a-dying lay,   10
And the dragon-fly had fled away,
   Ere he brought it out of the river.

High on the shore sat the great god Pan
   While turbidly flowed the river;
And hacked and hewed as a great god can,
With his hard bleak steel at the patient reed,
Till there was not a sign of the leaf indeed
   To prove it fresh from the river.

He cut it short, did the great god Pan
   (How tall it stood in the river!)   20
Then drew the pith, like the heart of a man,
Steadily from the outside ring,
And notched the poor dry empty thing
   In holes, as he sat by the river.

"This is the way," laughed the great god Pan
   (Laughed while he sat by the river),
"The only way, since gods began
To make sweet music, they could succeed."
Then, dropping his mouth to a hole in the reed,
   He blew in power by the river.   30

Sweet, sweet, sweet, O Pan!
   Piercing sweet by the river!
Blinding sweet, O great god Pan!
The sun on the hill forgot to die,
And the lilies revived, and the dragon-fly
   Came back to dream on the river.

Yet half a beast is the great god Pan,
   To laugh as he sits by the river,
Making a poet out of a man.
The true gods sigh for the cost and pain—   40
For the reed which grows nevermore again
   As a reed with the reeds in the river.
                           (1860)

John Keats

La Belle Dame Sans Merci

O what can ail thee, Knight at arms
   Alone and palely loitering?
The sedge has withered from the Lake,
   And no birds sing!

O what can ail thee, Knight at arms,
   So haggard and so woe-begone?
The Squirrel's granary is full,
   And the harvest's done.

I see a lily on thy brow,
   With anguish moist and fever dew;   10
And on thy cheeks a fading rose
   Fast withereth too.

I met a Lady in the Meads,
   Full beautiful, a faery's child;
Her hair was long, her foot was light,
   And her eyes were wild.

I made a Garland for her head,
   And bracelets, too, and fragrant Zone;
She look'd at me as she did love,
   And made sweet moan.   20

I set her on my pacing steed,
   And nothing else saw, all day long;
For sidelong would she bend, and sing
   A faery's song.

She found me roots of relish sweet,
   And honey wild, and manna dew;
And sure in language strange she said,
   'I love thee true.'

She took me to her elfin grot,
   And there she wept and sigh'd full sore;   30
And there I shut her wild, wild eyes
   With kisses four.

And there she lulled me asleep,
  And there I dreamed, ah woe betide!
The latest dream I ever dreamt,
  On the cold hill side.

I saw pale Kings, and Princes too,
  Pale warriors, death pale were they all;
They cried, 'La belle dame sans merci
  Hath thee in thrall!'   40

I saw their starv'd lips in the gloam
  With horrid warning gaped wide—
And I awoke, and found me here,
  On the cold hill's side.

And this is why I sojourn here,
  Alone and palely loitering;
Though the sedge is withered from the Lake,
  And no birds sing.

                            (*1820*)

Thomas Campion

My Sweetest Lesbia

My sweetest Lesbia, let us live and love,
And though the sager sort our deeds reprove,
Let us not weigh them. Heaven's great lamps do
    dive
Into their west, and straight again revive;
But soon as once set is our little light,
Then must we sleep one ever-during night.

If all would lead their lives in love like me,
Then bloody swords and armor should not be;
No drum nor trumpet peaceful sleeps should
    move,
Unless alarm came from the camp of love.   10
But fools do live and waste their little light,
And seek with pain their ever-during night.

When timely death my life and fortune ends,
Let not my hearse be vexed with mourning
    friends;
But let all lovers rich in triumph come,
And with sweet pastimes grace my happy tomb.
And, Lesbia, close up thou my little light,
And crown with love my ever-during night.

                            (*1601*)

Anonymous

Sir Patrick Spence

The king sits in Dumferling toune,
  Drinking the blude-reid wine:
'O quhar will I get guid sailor,
  To sail this schip of mine?'

Up and spak an eldern knicht,
  Sat at the kings richt kne:
'Sir Patrick Spence is the best sailor,
  That sails upon the se.'

The king has written a braid letter
  And signd it wi' his hand;   10
And sent it to Sir Patrick Spence,
  Was walking on the sand.

The first line that Sir Patrick red,
  A loud lauch lauched he:
The next line that Sir Patrick red,
  The teir blinded his ee.

'O quha is this has don this deid,
  This ill deid don to me;
To send me out this time o' the zeir,
  To sail upon the se?   20

l. 1. *toune:* town.
l. 2. *blude-reid:* blood-red.
l. 3. *quhar:* where; *guid:* good.
l. 6. *richt:* right.
l. 9. *braid:* broad.
l. 14. *lauch:* laugh.
l. 16. *ee:* eye.
l. 19. *zeir:* year.

'Mak hast, mak haste, my mirry men all,
    Our guid schip sails the morne';
'O say na sae, my master deir,
    For I feir a deadlie storme.

'Late, late yestreen I saw the new moone,
    Wi' the auld moone in hir arme;
And I feir, I feir, my deir master,
    That we will com to harme.'

O our Scots nobles wer richt laith
    To weet their cork-heild schoone;   30
Bot lang owre a' the play wer playd,
    Thair hats they swam aboone.

O lang, lang, may thair ladies sit
    Wi' thair fans in their hand,
Or eir they se Sir Patrick Spence
    Cum sailing to the land.

O lang, lang, may the ladies stand
    Wi' thair gold kems in their hair,
Waiting for thair ain deir lords,
    For they'll se thame na mair.   40

Have owre, have owre to Aberdour,
    It's fiftie fadom deip:
And thair lies guid Sir Patrick Spence,
    Wi' the Scots lords at his feit.

(ca. 13th century)

l. 23. *sae:* so.
l. 29. *wer richt laith:* were right loath.
l. 30. *weet . . . schoone:* wet their cork-heeled shoes.
l. 31. *owre:* before.
l. 32. *aboone:* above them.

l. 35. *Or eir:* ere.
l. 38. *kems:* combs.
l. 41. *Have owre:* half way over.
l. 42. *fadom:* fathom—a fathom is six feet of water depth.

EXERCISES

"The Picador Bit" [Noll]

1. The picador is the horseman in the *corrida de toros* (inaccurately translated, "bullfight") who pricks the bull with a lance to irritate him into savage ferocity for the climax of the performance, when the bull and matador face each other. The first three stanzas indicate something of the poet's attitude toward the picador. What is it? If "don" (lines 4 and 13) is a Spanish title of respect, denoting a distinguished man, then how do you explain the picador's description as both a don and a figure of "opaque malice" (line 1)?

2. Could "don" possibly apply to any of those gentlemen who watch the *corrida*? How? Does such an application clarify the meaning of lines 23–24? Discuss.

3. In the fourth stanza, note the various connotations of the picador—a "brawny don," a "mechanic" (line 13), and a "centaur" (line 15). How does the poet achieve new effects with such broadened concepts of the picador? For example, in mythology the centaur was a man down to the waist, a horse in body and legs. How does the use of centaur affect your view of the picador?

4. Finally, we should remember that the poet in treating archetypal themes enriches old legends and mythologies. One ancient meaning of the complete *corrida* (ceremonial performance) requires that the majestic black bull be genuinely fierce—thus a totemic force of evil, just as the matador symbolizes the power of goodness. The *aficionado* (expert in bullfighting) knows this and, in a mythic dimension, perceives of the whole *corrida* as possessing spiritual significance. Thus, the picador is a "bit" of the battle between evil and good that goes on inside mankind always, even as it is symbolized before him in the *corrida*. How do stanzas five and six render the deeper archetypal and mythic levels of the *corrida*?

Consider especially such phrases as "the monster with two heads" (line 18), "the blackness of its law" (line 19), "Justice is satisfied" (line 22), and "huge hate itself" (line 24).

"*O Daedalus, Fly Away Home*" [Hayden] and "*To Brooklyn Bridge*" [Crane]

5. Pointing to lines that support your answer, what is the locale of Hayden's poem? How do such words as "juba" (line 4, a rhythmic Southern Negro dance with clapping of hands), "conjo" (line 4, a localism for "magic" or "incantatory"), and "juju man" (line 6, a conjurer using "jujus," or charms and fetishes) lend a valid imperative to the single-line stanza, "*O fly away home fly away*" (line 9)?

6. What is the purpose of the interrogative, "Do you remember Africa?" (line 10) and why did the poet place the line near the center of the poem rather than—say—at the beginning? How is the image "to make two wings" (line 20) related to the myth of Icarus and Daedalus (see a brief summary of the myth in the question on Vassar Miller's "The New Icarus," p. 122)? In what other ways is the myth of Daedalus related to Hayden's poem?

7. In spite of obvious differences, Crane's poem, "To Brooklyn Bridge," may be correlated with Hayden's poem in several ways. For example, both poems have a definite physical location, both are musical, both deal with transcendent subjects, both reveal abstract concepts through concrete imagery, and both are mythopoeic. Read Crane's poem closely, noting especially the concluding line, "And of the curveship lend a myth to God." What do you think is Crane's meaning of Brooklyn Bridge as a spanning object—spanning from what to what? Is it symbolical, and if so, how? Similarly, does Hayden's poem suggest that he also may be creating a kind of symbolical bridge, as it were? Discuss. After treating the correlations between the two poems, observe the differences.

"*The stars will shine forever over you*" [Stuart], "*The Pythoness*" [Raine], and "*La Belle Dame Sans Merci*" [Keats]

8. On the surface, these poems appear to be quite different. Stuart's poem is a sonnet, which relates in detail the death and an ironic posthumous memory of a human life bespeaking itself, presented within a cyclical context of ever-changing nature. A twelve-line work of slant rhyme, Raine's poem would appear to be about a large snake; yet, in Greek mythology, the pythoness was a woman soothsayer, the priestess of Apollo at Delphi (Apollo being the god of sun, music, poetry, healing, and prophecy). Keats' poem, generally a ballad measure with mixed quatrains, introduces a Knight at arms who is "palely loitering" both at the outset and conclusion of the poem. The knight relates a most amazing love story: he takes a beautiful woman with him upon his steed. She sings to him all day and finds him "roots of relish sweet,/And honey wild, and manna dew" (lines 25–26). She takes him to her mysterious cave, where she weeps and sighs, and there he shuts her eyes with kisses. But *she*, ultimately, lulls *him* to sleep. His dream convinces him that he, like many others before him, is under the spell of a lovely woman without mercy. And he awakens to find himself on a cold hillside where "no birds sing." Despite these surface differences, what images do you find which all three poems share in common? Among others in your answer, also consider these: caves, holes in the earth, or entombment; darkness; love and life; and death.

9. Both Jung and Eliot have remarked in substance that archetypes (themes) are preexisting configurations that often are revealed powerfully through poetry. Among many archetypes emerging through symbols and allegories are these: cyclical motifs (including life-death); woman as temptress and destroyer; various procreation and sexual themes; womb of woman and birth motif; earth as mother; and the womb of woman and earth as natural "death mother." Point to lines in two or more of the poems which share these images and, through them, render these deeper archetypal motifs.

"Daniel Boone" and "The Ballad of William Sycamore" [Benét]

10. Both poems deal with heroes of mythic proportions. The very brevity of "Daniel Boone" rivets the attention of the reader like a flash on a screen. He may read the poem quickly, only to discover its meaning catching up with him, urging him to read it again and to reflect upon it. Do certain images and words produce a quiet, perhaps eerie, mysterious, yet vitally living quality in the poet's feeling and tone? What is the dominant emotion of the poem? What images make it emotionally effective, and in doing so produce its mythic dimension? Discuss.

11. Mention a few lines from "The Ballad of William Sycamore" that describe the hero's personality. Beginning with the second stanza, point out any images suggestive of the "tall tale" in America (hyperbole), all of which accumulate to produce a mythic stature of William Sycamore.

12. Does the longer poem generate a stronger emotional response than the shorter? Noting the dominant tones of both poems, how do you think Benét conceived of his country and its pioneering people? Discuss. Do you see any relationships between the "westering" spirit—the sense of discovery and wild surmise—of these poems and the world of today? Discuss.

"Leda and the Swan" [Yeats]

13. It is important to understand allusions in any poem, but especially in this one. The woman Leda was impregnated by Zeus in the form of a swan. From this union came Clytemnestra, who murdered Agamemnon, and Helen, whose beauty led to the Trojan War. How does a knowledge of these myths give an insight into Yeats' concept of fate?

14. Do you see any relationships between the Pagan myth as treated by Yeats, and other religions? Discuss.

15. The imagery of the first eleven and one-half lines is rapidly presented; its tone is sudden, forceful, vivid, even overpowering. But then the tone changes in the final three and one-half lines. The break in line 11 (caesura), and the dropping of the second half of the line commencing "Being so caught up" helps the reader to adjust to the shift of tone and the profound question the poet poses. What is this question, and why is it an important one in understanding the experience of the poem?

"West-Running Brook" [Frost]

16. This poem is a dialogue between two people. Who are they? What is their relationship? What are they like?

17. Beneath the informality of the atmosphere, there are various symbols which help to develop the poet's tone, basically a philosophical one. Consider lines, then, which support these symbolical observations: water as a symbol of life; the bridge as connection, love, and a movement from point to point toward fulfillment of human aspirations (lines 13–15); and the "white wave" which "runs counter to itself" (lines 38–72). Of these three dominant symbols, this last is the most complex. Pointing to specific lines, interpret different levels of the symbol. Do you see any other symbols in the poem? Discuss them.

"Sea Fever" [Masefield] and "Sir Patrick Spence" [Anonymous]

18. These two poems may be compared and contrasted in form, content, and emotional impact. Paraphrase them both.

19. In contrasting the two poems, consider distinctions in meter, rhyme, and stanzaic form. Note differences in respective attitudes of the poets (feeling) toward the sea, the desire to leave land and to sail, and expectations of the forthcoming voyage. Point out lines to support your views.

20. The similarities between the two poems consist mainly in content and imagery. But an unusual parallel is contained in the conclusions of the two poems—in

meaning. That of "Sir Patrick Spence" is stated directly, but Masefield's conclusion is more subtle. What is this similarity?

21. Finally, do you see a symbolical relationship between Masefield's last line, "And quiet sleep and a sweet dream when the long trick's over," and the conclusions of Robert Frost's "Stopping by Woods on a Snowy Evening" (p. 98) or "After Apple-Picking" (p. 286)? Discuss.

"*When the Hounds of Spring*" [Swinburne]

22. The musicality of Swinburne's poetry is so luxuriant that it often dominates the meaning. Such is the case here. Read the poem aloud and examine first the many examples of alliteration in the first stanza. What is the rhyme scheme of the eight-line stanzas, and are they consistent throughout the poem?

23. How do such musical devices contribute to the poet's feeling, tone, and ultimate meaning? In considering Swinburne's meaning, of course, it is important to discern the mythological allusions throughout the poem. The footnotes will help you to understand his references. What bearing do the allusions have on the poet's intention, and how is that intention ultimately revealed in this famous chorus of *Atalanta in Calydon*? Discuss.

24. Do you find that feeling tends to dominate reason in this poem, that emotion dominates logic? How may this question possibly be related to Swinburne's intention?

General

25. Each of the seventeen poems of this section may be correlated with the theme of myth and archetype. Keeping in mind your understanding of myth and archetype, select any of the poems not yet directly treated through questions and relate it or them to mythopoeic or archetypal motifs.

26. If we are to appreciate poetry fully, we should be able to establish as many ways as possible of understanding the genre—especially through perceiving relationships between poems. Implementing your own poetic judgments, can you discern any relationships in form, or content, or theme between poems within this section, or between a selected poem in this section and any other poem in another section? Discuss.

11. Humor, Wit, and Folly

Miss J. Hunter Dunn, Miss J. Hunter Dunn,
Furnish'd and burnish'd by Aldershot sun,
What strenuous singles we played after tea,
We in the tournament—you against me!

[John Betjeman, *A Subaltern's Love-Song*]

Donald Hall

Dr. Fatt, Instructor

And why does *Fatt* teach English? Why, because
A law school felt he could not learn the laws.
He waddles brilliantly from class to class,
Smiling at everyone, and at the grass.
"*Hamlet*," he tells his students, "you will find,
Concerns a man who can't make up his mind.
The Tempest? . . . It's the one with Ariel.
Are there more questions now?" But one can tell
That all his will, brains, and imagination
Are concentrated on a higher station: 10
He wants to be in the Administration.
Sometimes at parties he observes the Dean;
He giggles, coughs, and turns aquamarine.
Yet some day we will hear of "Dr. *Fatt*,
Vice-President in Charge of This or That."
I heard the Dean observe, at tea and cakes,
Face stuffed and sneering, "*Fatt* has what it takes."

(*1960*)

Louis Simpson

The Custom of the World

O, we loved long and happily, God knows!
The ocean danced, the green leaves tossed, the air
Was filled with petals, and pale Venus rose
When we began to kiss. Kisses brought care,
And closeness caused the taking off of clothes.
O, we loved long and happily, God knows!

"The watchdogs are asleep, the doormen
        doze. . . ."
We huddled in the corners of the stair,
And then we climbed it. What had we to lose?
What would we gain? The best way to
        compare   10
And quickest, was by taking off our clothes.
O, we loved long and happily, God knows!

Between us two a silent treason grows,
Our pleasures have been changed into despair.
Wild is the wind, from a cold country blows,
In which these tender blossoms disappear.
And did this come of taking off our clothes?
O, we loved long and happily, God knows!

Mistress, my song is drawing to a close.
Put on your rumpled skirt and comb your
        hair,   20
And when we meet again let us suppose
We never loved or ever naked were.
For though this nakedness was good, God
        knows,
The custom of the world is wearing clothes.

(*1959*)

John Betjeman

A Subaltern's Love-Song

Miss J. Hunter Dunn, Miss J. Hunter Dunn,
Furnish'd and burnish'd by Aldershot sun,
What strenuous singles we played after tea,
We in the tournament—you against me!

Love-thirty, love-forty, oh! weakness of joy,
The speed of a swallow, the grace of a boy,
With carefullest carelessness, gaily you won,
I am weak from your loveliness, Joan Hunter
    Dunn.

Miss Joan Hunter Dunn, Miss Joan Hunter Dunn,
How mad I am, sad I am, glad that you won.   10
The arm-handled racket is back in its press,
But my shock-headed victor, she loves me no
    less.

Her father's euonymus shines as we walk,
And swing past the summer-house, buried in
    talk,
And cool the verandah that welcomes us in
To the six-o'clock news and a lime-juice and
    gin.

The scent of the conifers, sound of the bath,
The view from my bedroom of moss-dappled
    path,
As I struggle with double-end evening tie,
For we dance at the Golf Club, my victor
    and I.   20

On the floor of her bedroom lie blazer and shorts
And the cream-colored walls are be-trophied
    with sports,
And westering, questioning settles the sun
On your low-leaded window, Miss Joan
    Hunter Dunn.

The Hillman is waiting, the light's in the hall,
The pictures of Egypt are bright on the wall,
My sweet, I am standing beside the oak stair
And there on the landing's the light on your
    hair.

By roads "not adopted", by woodlanded ways,
She drove to the club in the late summer haze,   30
Into nine-o'clock Camberley, heavy with bells
And mushroomy, pine-woody, evergreen smells.

Miss Joan Hunter Dunn, Miss Joan Hunter
    Dunn,
I can hear from the car-park the dance has begun.
Oh! full Surrey twilight! importunate band!
Oh! strongly adorable tennis-girl's hand!

Around us are Rovers and Austins afar,
Above us, the intimate roof of the car,
And here on my right is the girl of my choice,
With the tilt of her nose and the chime of her
    voice,   40

And the scent of her wrap, and the words never
    said,
And the ominous, ominous dancing ahead,
We sat in the car-park till twenty to one
And now I'm engaged to Miss Joan Hunter
    Dunn.

                              (1958)

Philip H. Rhinelander

Hangover

My head is like lead, and my temples they bulge,
And my tongue feels like something I wouldn't
    divulge,
But it's always the way when I overindulge,
                              Overindulge . . .

The wages of sin they tell me is death,
Like the grim retribution that fell on Macbeth,
And the wages of gin is a terrible breath,
    Terrible breath . . .

My eyes are on fire, my forehead I clutch,
And it's hard to stand up, my condition is such, 10
But it's always this way when I've taken too
  much,
    Taken too much . . .

I feel like a fish that has recently died,
Like the rind of a melon that's left at low tide,
And I can't eat my breakfast, I know 'cause I've
  tried,
    My, how I tried . . .

I'm feeling unhappy, I needn't relate.
I wish I could blame it on something I ate,
But it's always this way when I stay up too late,
    Stay up too late . . .

My feet are unsteady, the carpet revolves   21
With a sinister eddy. My courage dissolves,
And I wish I had followed my better resolves,
    My better resolves . . .
      (1945)

Ogden Nash

The Turtle

The turtle lives 'twixt plated decks
Which practically conceal its sex.
I think it clever of the turtle
In such a fix to be so fertile.
      (1940)

F. Scott Fitzgerald

Obit on Parnassus

Death before forty's no bar. Lo!
 These had accomplished their feats:
Chatterton, Burns, and Kit Marlowe,
 Byron and Shelley and Keats.

Death, the eventual censor,
 Lays for the forties, and so
Took off Jane Austen and Spenser,
 Stevenson, Hood, and poor Poe.

You'll leave a better-lined wallet
 By reaching the end of your rope   10
After fifty, like Shakespeare and Smollett,
 Thackeray, Dickens, and Pope.

Try for the sixties—but say, boy,
 That's when the tombstones were built on
Butler and Sheridan, the play boy,
 Arnold and Coleridge and Milton.

Three score and ten—the tides rippling
 Over the bar; slip the hawser.
Godspeed to Clemens and Kipling,
 Swinburne and Browning and Chaucer.   20

Some staved the debt off but paid it
 At eighty—that's after the law.
Wordsworth and Tennyson made it,
 And Meredith, Hardy, and Shaw.

But Death, while you make up your quota,
 Please note this confession of candor—
That I wouldn't give an iota
 To linger till ninety, like Landor.
      (1937)

Arthur Guiterman

On the Vanity of Earthly Greatness

The tusks that clashed in mighty brawls
Of mastodons, are billiard balls.

The sword of Charlemagne the Just
Is ferric oxide, known as rust.

The grizzly bear whose potent hug
Was feared by all, is now a rug.

Great Caesar's bust is on the shelf,
And I don't feel so well myself!

(1930)

Franklin P. Adams

Us Potes

Swift was sweet on Stella;
   Poe had his Lenore;
Burns's fancy turned to Nancy
   And a dozen more.

Pope was quite a trifler;
   Goldsmith was a case;
Byron'd flirt with any skirt
   From Liverpool to Thrace.

Sheridan philandered;
   Shelley, Keats, and Moore   10
All were there with some affair
   Far from lit'rachoor.

Fickle is the heart of
   Each immortal bard.
Mine alone is made of stone—
   Gotta work too hard.

(1928)

E. E. Cummings

nobody loses all the time

nobody loses all the time

i had an uncle named
Sol who was a born failure and
nearly everybody said he should have gone
into vaudeville perhaps because my Uncle Sol
   could

sing McCann He Was A Diver on Xmas Eve
   like Hell Itself which
may or may not account for the fact that my
   Uncle

Sol indulged in that possibly most inexcusable
of all to use a highfalootin phrase
luxuries that is or to   10
wit farming and be
it needlessly
added

my Uncle Sol's farm
failed because the chickens
ate the vegetables so
my Uncle Sol had a
chicken farm till the
skunks ate the chickens when

my Uncle Sol   20
had a skunk farm but
the skunks caught cold and
died and so
my Uncle Sol imitated the
skunks in a subtle manner

or by drowning himself in the watertank
but somebody who'd given my Uncle Sol a
   Victor
Victrola and records while he lived presented to
him upon the auspicious occasion of his decease a
scrumptious not to mention splendiferous funeral
   with   30
tall boys in black gloves and flowers and
   everything and

i remember we all cried like the Missouri
when my Uncle Sol's coffin lurched because
somebody pressed a button
(and down went
my Uncle
Sol

and started a worm farm)

(1926)

Dorothy Parker

Résumé

Razors pain you;
Rivers are damp;
Acids stain you;
And drugs cause cramp.
Guns aren't lawful;
Nooses give;
Gas smells awful;
You might as well live.

(*1926*)

Countee Cullen

For a Lady I Know

She even thinks that up in heaven
    Her class lies late and snores,
While poor black cherubs rise at seven
    To do celestial chores.

(*1925*)

Robert Frost

Brown's Descent

Brown lived at such a lofty farm
    That everyone for miles could see
His lantern when he did his chores
    In winter after half-past three.

And many must have seen him make
    His wild descent from there one night,
'Cross lots, 'cross walls, 'cross everything,
    Describing rings of lantern-light.

Between the house and barn the gale
    Got him by something he had on   10
And blew him out on the icy crust
    That cased the world, and he was gone!

Walls were all buried, trees were few:
    He saw no stay unless he stove
A hole in somewhere with his heel.
    But though repeatedly he strove

And stamped and said things to himself,
    And sometimes something seemed to yield,
He gained no foothold, but pursued
    His journey down from field to field.   20

Sometimes he came with arms outspread
    Like wings, revolving in the scene
Upon his longer axis, and
    With no small dignity of mien.

Faster or slower as he chanced,
    Sitting or standing as he chose,
According as he feared to risk
    His neck, or thought to spare his clothes.

He never let the lantern drop.
    And some exclaimed who saw afar   30
The figures he described with it,
    "I wonder what those signals are

"Brown makes at such an hour of night!
    He's celebrating something strange.
I wonder if he's sold his farm,
    Or been made Master of the Grange."

He reeled, he lurched, he bobbed, he checked;
    He fell and made the lantern rattle
(But saved the light from going out).
    So half way down he fought the battle,   40

Incredulous of his own bad luck.
    And then becoming reconciled
To everything, he gave it up
    And came down like a coasting child.

"Well—I—be—" that was all he said,
    As standing in the river road
He looked back up the slippery slope
    (Two miles it was) to his abode.

Sometimes as an authority
  On motorcars, I'm asked if I   50
Should say our stock was petered out,
  And this is my sincere reply:

Yankees are what they always were.
  Don't think Brown ever gave up hope
Of getting home again because
  He couldn't climb that slippery slope;

Or even thought of standing there
  Until the January thaw
Should take the polish off the crust.
  He bowed with grace to natural law,   60

And then went round it on his feet,
  After the manner of our stock;
Not much concerned for those to whom,
  At that particular time o'clock,

It must have looked as if the course
  He steered was really straight away
From that which he was headed for—
  Not much concerned for them, I say;

No more so than became a man—
  And politician at odd seasons.   70
I've kept Brown standing in the cold
  While I invested him with reasons;

But now he snapped his eyes three times;
  Then shook his lantern, saying, "Ile's
'Bout out!" and took the long way home
  By road, a matter of several miles.

                                        (1916)

Richard Porson

Epigram on an Academic Visit to the Continent

I went to Frankfort, and got drunk
With that most learn'd professor—Brunck:
I went to Worts, and got more drunken
With that more learn'd professor—Ruhncken.

Sir W. S. Gilbert

There Lived a King

There lived a King, as I've been told,
In the wonder-working days of old,
When hearts were twice as good as gold,
  And twenty times as mellow.
Good-temper triumphed in his face,
And in his heart he found a place
For all the erring human race
  And every wretched fellow.
When he had Rhenish wine to drink
It made him very sad to think   10
That some, at junket or at jink,
  Must be content with toddy.
He wished all men as rich as he
(And he was rich as rich could be),
So to the top of every tree
  Promoted everybody.

Lord Chancellors were cheap as sprats,
And Bishops in their shovel hats
Were plentiful as tabby cats—
  In point of fact, too many.   20
Ambassadors cropped up like hay,
Prime Ministers and such as they
Grew like asparagus in May,
  And Dukes were three a penny.
On every side Field Marshals gleamed,
Small beer were Lords Lieutenant deemed,
With Admirals the ocean teemed
  All round his wide dominions.
And Party Leaders you might meet
In twos and threes in every street,   30
Maintaining, with no little heat,
  Their various opinions.

That King, although no one denies
His heart was of abnormal size,
Yet he'd have acted otherwise
  If he had been acuter.
The end is easily foretold,
When every blessed thing you hold

Is made of silver, or of gold,
    You long for simple pewter.   40
When you have nothing else to wear
But cloth of gold and satins rare,
For cloth of gold you cease to care—
    Up goes the price of shoddy.
In short, whoever you may be,
To this conclusion you'll agree,
When every one is somebodee,
    Then no one's anybody!

A. E. Housman

Is My Team Ploughing?

"Is my team ploughing,
    That I used to drive
And hear the harness jingle
    When I was man alive?"

Aye, the horses trample,
    The harness jingles now;
No change though you lie under
    The land you used to plough.

"Is football playing
    Along the river shore,   10
With lads to chase the leather,
    Now I stand up no more?"

Aye, the ball is flying,
    The lads play heart and soul;
The goal stands up, the keeper
    Stands up to keep the goal.

"Is my girl happy,
    That I thought hard to leave,
And has she tired of weeping
    As she lies down at eve?"   20

Aye, she lies down lightly,
    She lies not down to weep:
Your girl is well contented.
    Be still, my lad, and sleep.

"Is my friend hearty,
    Now I am thin and pine;
And has he found to sleep in
    A better bed than mine?"

Aye, lad, I lie easy,
    I lie as lads would choose;   30
I cheer a dead man's sweetheart.
    Never ask me whose.

                   (1896)

Lewis Carroll

Jabberwocky

'Twas brillig, and the slithy toves
    Did gyre and gimble in the wabe;
All mimsy were the borogoves,
    And the mome raths outgrabe.

"Beware the Jabberwock, my son!
    The jaws that bite, the claws that catch!
Beware the Jubjub bird, and shun
    The frumious Bandersnatch!"

He took his vorpal sword in hand;
    Long time the manxome foe he sought—   10
So rested he by the Tumtum tree,
    And stood awhile in thought.

And, as in uffish thought he stood,
    The Jabberwock, with eyes of flame,
Came whiffling through the tulgey wood,
    And burbled as it came!

Lewis Carroll: the pseudonym of Charles Lutwidge Dodgson, the creator of *Alice in Wonderland.*
l. 3. *mimsy:* a portmanteau word for "miserable" and "flimsy."

One, two! One, two! And through and
    through
  The vorpal blade went snicker-snack!
He left it dead, and with its head
  He went galumphing back.   20

"And hast thou slain the Jabberwock?
  Come to my arms, my beamish boy!
O frabjous day! Callooh! Callay!"
  He chortled in his joy.

'Twas brillig, and the slithy toves
  Did gyre and gimble in the wabe;
All mimsy were the borogoves,
  And the mome raths outgrabe.

                (1872)

Firth

Britannia Rules of Orthography

From British novels a thrill I get
That I sadly miss in the American tale—
The thrill of a heroine suffragette
In gaol.

They touch on Life in the Quivering Raw,
With the frankest noun and the straightest verb,
And all of them—Hewlett, Bennett, and Shaw—
Say kerb.

Domestic voices are flabby and weak
In the Search for Truth that the age requires.   10
Would Ade or Tarkington dare to speak
Of tyres?

Hail to Conrad, Galsworthy, Wells,
To the crunching might of their books and
      dramas,
And the Lure of the East when Kipling spells
Pyjamas.

Benjamin Franklin

The Difference

When man and woman die, as poets sung,
His heart's the last part moves,—her last, the
    tongue.

Alexander Pope

Engraved on the Collar of His Highness' Dog

I am his Highness' dog at Kew.
Pray tell me, sir, whose dog are you?

                (1739)

John Wilmot, Earl of Rochester

Epitaph on Charles II

Here lies our Sovereign Lord the King,
  Whose word no man relies on,
Who never said a foolish thing,
  Nor ever did a wise one.

Anonymous

"There was a young fellow named Hall"

There was a young fellow named Hall,
Who fell in the spring in the fall;
  'Twould have been a sad thing
  If he'd died in the spring,
But he didn't—he died in the fall.

Anonymous

"There was a young fellow of Perth"

There was a young fellow of Perth,
Who was born on the day of his birth;
　He was married, they say,
　On his wife's wedding day,
And he died when he quitted the earth.

Anonymous

"Miss Minnie McFinney, of Butte"

Miss Minnie McFinney, of Butte,
Fed always, and only, on frutte.
　Said she: "Let the coarse
　Eat of beef and of horse,
I'm a peach, and that's all there is tutte."

EXERCISES

"Humor" originally was a physiological term, related by early "natural philosophers" or physicians to fluids of living creatures and to their health. For example, one of the "four humors" was black bile, indicative of a melancholy temperament. This basic meaning broadened over the centuries to refer to a person's attitude, state of mind, or disposition. Today the meaning has broadened further, extending beyond one's mood, and has come to refer to what is amusing, comical, or ludicrous. Indeed, there is some indication that the meaning of the word is restricting itself again to denote, primarily, the comical.

Humor is now closely related to "wit." Originally, wit was concerned with knowledge, having been derived from the concept of wisdom. The term was increasingly linked with the idea of pleasure, however, and ultimately became associated with that which makes one amused or amusing. Thus, both humor and wit are often closely associated—so closely, in fact, that one is inclined to agree with the wag who observed that anyone attempting to distinguish between humor and wit possessed neither the comic spirit of the one nor the delighting intellect of the other.

Still we tend today to discriminate between the two. Humor denotes perception and expression of the comic and laughable (not that the comic is always ludicrous, for it may consist of pathos, too, as Emmett Kelly's sad clown reminds us), but humor suggests a kindness and geniality evocative of sympathetic amusement. Wit still denotes perception, too, but the emphasis is on intelligence, a sense of proportion, sparkling verbal thrusts, piquancy, imaginative fancy, the ready pleasantry and pleasurable repartee. One associates it with the flashing intellect and scintillant smile. The emphasis is on brightness and alertness, as when we say, "A ready wit." English writer and critic George Saintsbury (1845–1933) wittily observed, "Humor always laughs, however earnestly it feels, and sometimes chuckles; but it never sniggers." Wit, though, is involved more obviously with such comic devices as pithy epigrams, sharp irony of various kinds, the ridicule of satire, and the verbal knifings of sarcasm, the sharp retort, or the perfect squelch.

Folly denotes foolishness, a lack of understanding or rational behavior. The types of folly vary from the idiotic and asinine to the giddy and fatuous. They range from mere imprudence or a lack of judgment, on the one hand, to stupid rashness and laughable madness, on the other. The connotations may be those of extravagant senselessness—even nonsense.

Whatever the particular kind of humor, wit, or folly, each involves in its ideal form a desirable release of pleasure on part of the recipient of the human foible revealed, the sudden incongruity, the swift play upon the mind, the startling vapidity—the art and nature of the laughable. Below are listed some aspects of the comic along with selected poets and their poems. Read the poems and consider them in light of the specific aspect of the comic to which they are related or to other aspects as you perceive them. Finally, discuss the broadest aspects of the comic inherent in each poem. As the terms are generally described above, does the individual poem seem to partake most of humor, wit, or folly—or does it blend more than one or all of the three? Read and respond—guffaw, laugh, smile (outwardly or inwardly), weep, or gaze with a vacant stare—as you like it. Here are the groupings:

1. *Comedy through change of context:*
   Donald Hall, "Dr. Fatt, Instructor"
   Alexander Pope, "Engraved on the Collar of His Highness' Dog"
   Dorothy Parker, "Résumé"

2. *Comedy of expectation:*
   Donald Hall, "Dr. Fatt, Instructor"
   Countee Cullen, "For a Lady I Know"
   Louis Simpson, "The Custom of the World"
   Arthur Guiterman, "On the Vanity of Earthly Greatness"
   Sir W. S. Gilbert, "There Lived a King"
   A. E. Housman, "Is My Team Ploughing?"
   Benjamin Franklin, "The Difference"
   John Wilmot, Earl of Rochester, "Epitaph on Charles II"

3. *Comedy of the naïve:*
   John Betjeman, "A Subaltern's Love-Song"

4. *Comedy through making the situation difficult:*
   Philip H. Rhinelander, "Hangover"
   Robert Frost, "Brown's Descent"
   Ogden Nash, "The Turtle"
   Dorothy Parker, "Résumé"

5. *Comedy through making the situation easy:*
   Donald Hall, "Dr. Fatt, Instructor"
   Sir W. S. Gilbert, "There Lived a King"

6. *Comedy through caricature* (exaggeration of ordinary parts):
   Donald Hall, "Dr. Fatt, Instructor"
   Franklin P. Adams, "Us Potes"
   Louis Simpson, "The Custom of the World"
   Countee Cullen, "For a Lady I Know"
   Philip H. Rhinelander, "Hangover"

7. *Comedy of "unmasking"* (parody, travesty):
   Countee Cullen, "For a Lady I Know"
   Sir W. S. Gilbert, "There Lived a King"
   Lewis Carroll, "Jabberwocky"
   John Wilmot, Earl of Rochester, "Epitaph on Charles II"

8. *Comedy of motion:*
   E. E. Cummings, "nobody loses all the time"
   Robert Frost, "Brown's Descent"

9. *Comedy of mimicry:*
   Richard Porson, "Epigram on an Academic Visit to the Continent"
   Firth, "Britannia Rules of Orthography"
   A. E. Housman, "Is My Team Ploughing?"
   Anonymous, "Miss Minnie McFinney, of Butte"

10. *Comedy through condensation* (economy of expression, i.e., compression):
    Donald Hall, "Dr. Fatt, Instructor"
    Arthur Guiterman, "On the Vanity of Earthly Greatness"
    Countee Cullen, "For a Lady I Know"
    Benjamin Franklin, "The Difference"

11. *Comedy of ambiguity:*
    Lewis Carroll, "Jabberwocky"
    John Betjeman, "A Subaltern's Love-Song"

12. *Comedy through puns, displacement of meaning, word play:*
    Sir W. S. Gilbert, "There Lived a King"
    Lewis Carroll, "Jabberwocky"
    Anonymous, "Miss Minnie McFinney, of Butte"

Firth, "Britannia Rules of Orthography"
Benjamin Franklin, "The Difference"
Anonymous, "There was a young fellow named Hall"

13. *Comedy through comparison:*

Richard Porson, "Epigram on an Academic Visit to the Continent"
Firth, "Britannia Rules of Orthography"
John Wilmot, Earl of Rochester, "Epitaph on Charles II"

14. *Comedy of nonsense:*

Arthur Guiterman, "On the Vanity of Earthly Greatness"
Alexander Pope, "Engraved on the Collar of His Highness' Dog"
Sir W. S. Gilbert, "There Lived a King"
Lewis Carroll, "Jabberwocky"
Firth, "Britannia Rules of Orthography"
Anonymous, "There was a young fellow of Perth"
Anonymous, "There was a young fellow named Hall"

15. *Comedy of burlesque* (especially the disparity between subject and style):

Donald Hall, "Dr. Fatt, Instructor"
John Betjeman, "A Subaltern's Love-Song"
F. Scott Fitzgerald, "Obit on Parnassus"
Lewis Carroll, "Jabberwocky"
Benjamin Franklin, "The Difference"

16. *Comedy of retort* (the *bon mot*):

A. E. Housman, "Is My Team Ploughing?"
Alexander Pope, "Engraved on the Collar of His Highness' Dog"

17. *Comedy of revealed cynicism* (as in the *carpe diem* motif):
Donald Hall, "Dr. Fatt, Instructor"
Louis Simpson, "The Custom of the World"

18. *Humor through conflict of individual and society* (the small and the large):

Louis Simpson, "The Custom of the World"
E. E. Cummings, "nobody loses all the time"

19. *Comedy through degradation* (imposed by conditions outside the individual's control and with whom we feel sympathy):

Louis Simpson, "The Custom of the World"
John Betjeman, "A Subaltern's Love-Song"
Philip H. Rhinelander, "Hangover"
F. Scott Fitzgerald, "Obit on Parnassus"
Arthur Guiterman, "On the Vanity of Earthly Greatness"
E. E. Cummings, "nobody loses all the time"
Dorothy Parker, "Résumé"
Countee Cullen, "For a Lady I Know"
Robert Frost, "Brown's Descent"
A. E. Housman, "Is My Team Ploughing?"

20. *Tragicomedy:*

E. E. Cummings, "nobody loses all the time"
A. E. Housman, "Is My Team Ploughing?"

12. God and Man

I caught this morning morning's minion, kingdom
of daylight's dauphin, dapple-dawn-drawn
Falcon, in his riding
Of the rolling level underneath him steady air . . .
[Gerard Manley Hopkins, *The Windhover*]

Louis Simpson

The Cradle Trap

A bell and rattle,
a smell of roses,
a leather Bible,
and angry voices . . .

They say, I love you.
They shout, You must!
The light is telling
terrible stories.

But night at the window
whispers, Never mind.   10
Be true, be true
to your own strange kind.

(1963)

Howard Nemerov

Boom!

Sees Boom in Religion, Too
Atlantic City, June 23, 1957 (AP).—President Eisenhower's
pastor said tonight that Americans are living in a period of
"unprecedented religious activity" caused partially by paid
vacations, the eight-hour day and modern conveniences.
  "These fruits of material progress," said the Rev. Edward
L. R. Elson of the National Presbyterian Church, Washington,
"have provided the leisure, the energy, and the means for a
level of human and spiritual values never before reached."

Here at the Vespasian-Carlton, it's just one
religious activity after another; the sky
is constantly being crossed by cruciform
airplanes, in which nobody disbelieves
for a second, and the tide, the tide
of spiritual progress and prosperity
miraculously keeps rising, to a level
never before attained. The churches are full,
the beaches are full, and the filling-stations
are full, God's great ocean is full   10
of paid vacationers praying an eight-hour day
to the human and spiritual values, the fruits,
the leisure, the energy, and the means, Lord,
the means for the level, the unprecedented level,
and the modern conveniences, which also are full.
Never before, O Lord, have the prayers and
          praises
from belfry and phonebooth, from ballpark and
          barbecue
the sacrifices, so endlessly ascended.

It was not thus when Job in Palestine
sat in the dust and cried, cried bitterly;   20
when Damien kissed the lepers on their wounds
it was not thus; it was not thus
when Francis worked a fourteen-hour day
strictly for the birds; when Dante took
a week's vacation without pay and it rained
part of the time, O Lord, it was not thus.

242

But now the gears mesh and the tires burn
and the ice chatters in the shaker and the priest
in the pulpit, and Thy Name, O Lord,
is kept before the public, while the fruits   30
ripen and religion booms and the level rises
and every modern convenience runneth over,
that it may never be with us as it hath been
with Athens and Karnak and Nagasaki,
nor Thy sun for one instant refrain from shining
on the rainbow Buick by the breezeway
or the Chris Craft with the uplift life raft;
that we may continue to be the just folks we are,
plain people with ordinary superliners and
disposable diaperliners, people of the
      stop'n'shop   40
'n'pray as you go, of hotel, motel, boatel,
the humble pilgrims of no deposit no return
and please adjust thy clothing, who will give
      to Thee,
if Thee will keep us going, our annual
Miss Universe, for Thy Name's Sake, Amen.

                    (*1958*)

Lawrence Ferlinghetti

Christ Climbed Down

Christ climbed down
from His bare Tree
this year
and ran away to where
there were no rootless Christmas trees
hung with candycanes and breakable stars

Christ climbed down
from His bare Tree
this year
and ran away to where   10
there were no gilded Christmas trees
and no tinsel Christmas trees

Christ Climbed Down: this poem, along with several others, was composed especially for jazz accompaniment; therefore, spontaneity and oral significance of the work should be emphasized in reading the poem.

and no tinfoil Christmas trees
and no pink plastic Christmas trees
and no gold Christmas trees
and no black Christmas trees
and no powderblue Christmas trees
hung with electric candles
and encircled by tin electric trains
and clever cornball relatives   20

Christ climbed down
from His bare Tree
this year
and ran away to where
no intrepid Bible salesmen
covered the territory
in two-tone cadillacs
and where no Sears Roebuck creches
complete with plastic babe in manger
arrived by parcel post   30
the babe by special delivery
and where no televised Wise Men
praised the Lord Calvert Whiskey

Christ climbed down
from His bare Tree
this year
and ran away to where
no fat handshaking stranger
in a red flannel suit
and a fake white beard   40
went around passing himself off
as some sort of North Pole saint
crossing the desert to Bethlehem
Pennsylvania
in a Volkswagon sled
drawn by rollicking Adirondack reindeer
with German names
and bearing sacks of Humble Gifts
from Saks Fifth Avenue
for everybody's imagined Christ child   50

Christ climbed down
from His bare Tree
this year
and ran away to where

no Bing Crosby carollers
groaned of a tight Christmas
and where no Radio City angels
iceskated wingless
thru a winter wonderland
into a jinglebell heaven   60
daily at 8:30
with Midnight Mass matinees

Christ climbed down
from His bare Tree
this year
and softly stole away into
some anonymous Mary's womb again
where in the darkest night
of everybody's anonymous soul
He awaits again   70
an unimaginable
and impossibly
Immaculate Reconception
the very craziest
of Second Comings   (1955)

Robert Lowell

Winter in Dunbarton

Time smiling on this sundial of a world
Sweltered about the snowman and the worm,
Sacker of painted idols and the peers
Of Europe, but my cat is cold, is curled
Tight as a boulder: she no longer smears
Her catnip mouse from Christmas, for the
              germ—
Mindless and ice, a world against our world—
Has tamped her round of brains into her ears.

This winter all the snowmen turn to stone,
Or, sick of the long hurly-burly, rise   10
Like butterflies into Jehovah's eyes
And shift until their crystals must atone

In water. Belle, the cat that used to rat
About my father's books, is dead. All day

Dunbarton: Lowell's ancestral town in New Hampshire.

The wastes of snow about my house stare in
Through idle windows at the brainless cat;
The coke-barrel in the corner whimpers. May
The snow recede and red clay furrows set
In the grim grin of their erosion, in
The caterpillar tents and roadslides, fat   20

With muck and winter dropsy, where the tall
Snow-monster wipes the coke-fumes from his
              eyes
And scatters his corruption and it lies
Gaping until the fungus-eyeballs fall

Into this eldest of the seasons. Cold
Snaps the bronze toes and fingers of the Christ
My father fetched from Florence, and the dead
Chatters to nothing in the thankless ground
His father screwed from Charlie Stark and sold
To the selectmen. Cold has cramped his head   30
Against his heart: my father's stone is crowned
With snowflakes and the bronze-age shards of
              Christ.
                                              (1944)

Jesse Stuart

Robert Diesel

You ask me if there is a living God.
I say it does not matter when I see
God in the fresh turned slopes of loamy sod,
God in the white blooms on the apple tree.
I feel God in the lilac lips of night
And see Him in the sky and sun and star;
To be with Him is laughter and delight,
To feel and touch these parts of Him that are.
I know spring-scented wind that bites my cheeks
Is God caressing me in showers of spring;   10
I know in April winds it's God who speaks;
His language is such quiet and simple thing.
God walks with me around the slopes I plow
And soothes me with the fern and wild jonquils;
He often sees the sweat run from my brow....
God is eternal here among these hills.
                                              (1944)

Dylan Thomas

Incarnate Devil

Incarnate devil in a talking snake,
The central plains of Asia in his garden,
In shaping-time the circle stung awake,
In shapes of sin forked out the bearded apple,
And God walked there who was a fiddling
    warden
And played down pardon from the heavens'
    hill.

When we were strangers to the guided seas,
A handmade moon half holy in a cloud,
The wisemen tell me that the garden gods   10
Twined good and evil on an eastern tree;
And when the moon rose windily it was
Black as the beast and paler than the cross.

We in our Eden knew the secret guardian
In sacred waters that no frost could harden,
And in the mighty mornings of the earth;
Hell in a horn of sulphur and the cloven myth,
All heaven in a midnight of the sun,
A serpent fiddled in the shaping-time.

                        (1936)

Louis MacNeice

Sunday Morning

Down the road someone is practising scales,
The notes like little fishes vanish with a wink
    of tails,
Man's heart expands to tinker with his car
For this is Sunday morning, Fate's great bazaar;
Regard these means as ends, concentrate on this
    Now,
And you may grow to music or drive beyond
    Hindhead anyhow,
Take corners on two wheels until you go so fast

That you can clutch a fringe or two of the windy
    past,
That you can abstract this day and make it to
    the week of time
A small eternity, a sonnet self-contained in
    rhyme.   10

But listen, up the road, something gulps, the
    church spire
Opens its eight bells out, skulls' mouths which
    will not tire
To tell how there is no music or movement
    which secures
Escape from the weekday time. Which deadens
    and endures.

                        (1935)

Robinson Jeffers

Hurt Hawks

I

The broken pillar of the wing jags from the
    clotted shoulder,
The wing trails like a banner in defeat,
No more to use the sky forever but live with
    famine
And pain a few days: cat nor coyote
Will shorten the week of waiting for death,
    there is game without talons.
He stands under the oak-bush and waits
The lame feet of salvation; at night he
    remembers freedom
And flies in a dream, the dawns ruin it.
He is strong and pain is worse to the strong,
    incapacity is worse.
The curs of the day come and torment him   10
At distance, no one but death the redeemer will
    humble that head,
The intrepid readiness, the terrible eyes.
The wild God of the world is sometimes
    merciful to those
That ask mercy, not often to the arrogant.

You do not know him, you communal
     people, or you have forgotten him;
Intemperate and savage, the hawk remembers
     him;
Beautiful and wild, the hawks, and men that
     are dying, remember him.

II

I'd sooner, except the penalties, kill a man than
     a hawk; but the great redtail
Had nothing left but unable misery
From the bone too shattered for mending, the
     wing that trailed under his talons when
     he moved.   20
We had fed him six weeks, I gave him
     freedom,
He wandered over the foreland hill and returned
     in the evening, asking for death,
Not like a beggar, still eyed with the old
Implacable arrogance. I gave him the lead
     gift in the twilight.
     What fell was relaxed,
Owl-downy, soft feminine feathers; but what
Soared: the fierce rush: the night-herons by the
     flooded river cried fear at its rising
Before it was quite unsheathed from reality.

(1928)

Gerard Manley Hopkins

Pied Beauty

Glory be to God for dappled things—
     For skies of couple-color as a brindle cow;
        For rose-moles all in stipple upon trout that
        swim;
Fresh-firecoal chestnut-falls; finches' wings;
     Landscape plotted and pieced—fold, fallow,
        and plow;
        And all trades, their gear and tackle and
        trim.

All things counter, original, spare, strange;
     Whatever is fickle, freckled (who knows
        how?)
        With swift, slow; sweet, sour; adazzle,
        dim;
He fathers-forth whose beauty is past change— 10
     Praise Him.

(1918)

Gerard Manley Hopkins

The Windhover

To Christ Our Lord

I caught this morning morning's minion,
     kingdom of daylight's dauphin, dapple-
     dawn-drawn Falcon, in his riding
     Of the rolling level underneath him steady
     air, and striding
High there, how he rung upon the rein of a
     wimpling wing
In his ecstasy! then off, off forth on swing,
     As a skate's heel sweeps smooth on a
     bowbend; the hurl and gliding
     Rebuffed the big wind. My heart in hiding
Stirred for a bird—the achieve of, the mastery
     of the thing!

Brute beauty and valor and act, oh, air, pride,
     plume, here
     Buckle! and the fire that breaks from thee
     then, a billion
Times told lovelier, more dangerous, O my
     chevalier!   10

     No wonder of it; sheer plod makes plow
     down sillion
Shine, and blue-bleak embers, ah my dear,
     Fall, gall themselves, and gash gold-vermilion.

(1918)

Rupert Brooke

Heaven

Fish (fly-replete, in depth of June,
Dawdling away their wat'ry noon)
Ponder deep wisdom, dark or clear,
Each secret fishy hope or fear.
Fish say, they have their Stream and Pond;
But is there anything Beyond?
This life cannot be All, they swear,
For how unpleasant, if it were!
One may not doubt that, somehow, Good
Shall come of Water and of Mud;   10
And, sure, the reverent eye must see
A purpose in Liquidity.
We darkly know, by Faith we cry,
The future is not Wholly Dry.
Mud unto mud!—Death eddies near—
Not here the appointed End, not here!
But somewhere, beyond Space and Time,
Is wetter water, slimier slime!
And there (they trust) there swimmeth One
Who swam ere rivers were begun,   20
Immense, of fishy form and mind,
Squamous, omnipotent, and kind;
And under that Almighty Fin,
The littlest fish may enter in.
Oh! never fly conceals a hook,
Fish say, in the Eternal Brook,
But more than mundane weeds are there,
And mud, celestially fair;
Fat caterpillars drift around,
And Paradisal grubs are found;   30
Unfading moths, immortal flies,
And the worm that never dies.
And in that Heaven of all their wish,
There shall be no more land, say fish.

                                    (1914)

Paul Laurence Dunbar

We Wear the Mask

We wear the mask that grins and lies,
It hides our cheeks and shades our eyes,—
This debt we pay to human guile;
With torn and bleeding hearts we smile,
And mouth with myriad subtleties.
Why should the world be overwise,
In counting all our tears and sighs?
Nay, let them only see us, while
    We wear the mask.

We smile, but, O great Christ, our cries   10
To Thee from tortured souls arise.
We sing, but oh, the clay is vile
Beneath our feet, and long the mile;
But let the world dream otherwise,
    We wear the mask.

                                    (1895)

Rudyard Kipling

Recessional

God of our fathers, known of old,
    Lord of our far-flung battle-line,
Beneath whose awful Hand we hold
    Dominion over palm and pine—
Lord God of Hosts, be with us yet,
Lest we forget—lest we forget!

The tumult and the shouting dies;
    The Captains and the Kings depart;
Still stands Thine ancient sacrifice,
    An humble and a contrite heart.   10
Lord God of Hosts, be with us yet,
Lest we forget—lest we forget!

Far-called, our navies melt away;
    On dune and headland sinks the fire;
Lo, all our pomp of yesterday
    Is one with Nineveh and Tyre!
Judge of the Nations, spare us yet,
Lest we forget—lest we forget!

If, drunk with sight of power, we loose
    Wild tongues that have not Thee in awe,   20
Such boastings as the Gentiles use,
    Or lesser breeds without the Law—
Lord God of Hosts, be with us yet,
Lest we forget—lest we forget!

For heathen heart that puts her trust
    In reeking tube and iron shard,
All valiant dust that builds on dust,
    And guarding, calls not Thee to guard,
For frantic boast and foolish word—
Thy Mercy on Thy People, Lord!   30

        (1897)

Stephen Crane

The Blades of Grass

In Heaven,
Some little blades of grass
Stood before God.
"What did you do?"
Then all save one of the little blades
Began eagerly to relate
The merits of their lives.
This one stayed a small way behind,
Ashamed.

Presently, God said,   10
"And what did you do?"
The little blade answered, "Oh, my Lord,
Memory is bitter to me,
For, if I did good deeds,
I know not of them."
Then God, in all his splendor,
Arose from his throne.
"Oh, best little blade of grass!" he said.

        (1895)

William Butler Yeats

The Indian Upon God

I passed along the water's edge below the
    humid trees,
My spirit rocked in evening light, the rushes
    round my knees,
My spirit rocked in sleep and sighs; and saw the
    moorfowl pace
All dripping on a grassy slope, and saw them
    cease to chase
Each other round in circles, and heard the eldest
    speak:
Who holds the world between His bill and made
    us strong or weak
Is an undying moorfowl, and He lives beyond the
    sky.
The rains are from His dripping wing, the moon-
    beams from His eye.
I passed a little further on and heard a lotus
    talk:
Who made the world and ruleth it, He hangeth
    on a stalk,   10
For I am in His image made, and all this tinkling
    tide
Is but a sliding drop of rain between His petals wide.
A little way within the gloom a roebuck raised
    his eyes
Brimful of starlight, and he said: *The Stamper of*
    the Skies,
He is a gentle roebuck; for how else, I pray, could
    He
Conceive a thing so sad and soft, a gentle thing
    like me?
I passed a little further on and heard a peacock
    say:
Who made this grass and made the worms and
    made my feathers gay,
He is a monstrous peacock, and He waveth all the
    night
His languid tail above us, lit with myriad spots
    of light.   20

        (1889)

Rudyard Kipling

"When Earth's last picture is painted"

When Earth's last picture is painted and the
    tubes are twisted and dried,
When the oldest colors have faded, and the
    youngest critic has died,
We shall rest, and, faith, we shall need it—lie
    down for an aeon or two,
Till the Master of All Good Workmen shall put
    us to work anew.

And those that were good shall be happy: they
    shall sit in a golden chair;
They shall splash at a ten-league canvas with
    brushes of comets' hair.
They shall find real saints to draw from—
    Magdalene, Peter, and Paul;
They shall work for an age at a sitting and
    never be tired at all!

And only the Master shall praise us, and only
    the Master shall blame;
And no one shall work for money, and no one
    shall work for fame,   10
But each for the joy of the working, and each,
    in his separate star,
Shall draw the Thing as he sees It for the God
    of Things as They are!

               (1892)

George Meredith

Lucifer in Starlight

On a starred night Prince Lucifer uprose.
Tired of his dark dominion, swung the fiend
Above the rolling ball in cloud part screened,
Where sinners hugged their specter of repose.
Poor prey to his hot fit of pride were those.
And now upon his western wing he leaned,
Now his huge bulk o'er Afric's sands careened,
Now the black planet shadowed Arctic snows.
Soaring through wider zones that pricked his scars
With memory of the old revolt from Awe,   10
He reached a middle height, and at the stars,
Which are the brain of heaven, he looked, and
    sank.
Around the ancient track marched, rank on rank,
The army of unalterable law.

               (1883)

Alfred, Lord Tennyson

Flower in the Crannied Wall

Flower in the crannied wall,
I pluck you out of the crannies,
I hold you here, root and all, in my hand,
Little flower—but if I could understand
What you are, root and all, and all in all,
I should know what God and man is.

               (1869)

Walt Whitman

When I Heard the Learn'd Astronomer

When I heard the learn'd astronomer,
When the proofs, the figures, were ranged in
    columns before me,
When I was shown the charts and diagrams, to
    add, divide, and measure them,
When I sitting heard the astronomer where he
    lectured with much applause in the
    lecture-room,
How soon unaccountable I became tired and sick,
Till rising and gliding out I wander'd off by
    myself,
In the mystical moist night-air, and from time
    to time,
Look'd up in perfect silence at the stars.

               (1865)

Ralph Waldo Emerson

Brahma

If the red slayer think he slays,
  Or if the slain think he is slain,
They know not well the subtle ways
  I keep, and pass, and turn again.

Far or forgot to me is near;
  Shadow and sunlight are the same;
The vanished gods to me appear;
  And one to me are shame and fame.

They reckon ill who leave me out;
  When me they fly, I am the wings;   10
I am the doubter and the doubt,
  And I the hymn the Brahmin sings.

The strong gods pine for my abode,
  And pine in vain the sacred Seven;
But thou, meek lover of the good!
  Find me, and turn thy back on heaven.

                                    (1857)

Thomas Campbell

The Last Man

All worldly shapes shall melt in gloom,
  The Sun himself must die,
Before this mortal shall assume
  Its Immortality!
I saw a vision in my sleep
That gave my spirit strength to sweep
  Adown the gulf of Time!
I saw the last of human mould
That shall Creation's death behold,
  As Adam saw her prime!   10

The Sun's eye had a sickly glare,
  The Earth with age was wan,
The skeletons of nations were
  Around that lonely man!

Some had expired in fight—the brands
Still rusted in their bony hands;
  In plague and famine some!
Earth's cities had no sound nor tread;
And ships were drifting with the dead
  To shores where all was dumb!   20

Yet, prophet-like, that lone one stood
  With dauntless words and high,
That shook the sere leaves from the wood
  As if a storm passed by,
Saying, 'We are twins in death, proud Sun!
Thy face is cold, thy race is run,
  'Tis Mercy bids thee go;
For thou ten thousand thousand years
Hast seen the tide of human tears,
  That shall no longer flow.   30

'What though beneath thee man put forth
  His pomp, his pride, his skill,
And arts that made fire, flood, and earth,
  The vassals of his will?
Yet mourn I not thy parted sway,
Thou dim discrowned king of day.
  For all those trophied arts
And triumphs that beneath thee sprang
Healed not a passion or a pang
  Entailed on human hearts.   40

'Go, let oblivion's curtain fall
  Upon the stage of men,
Nor with thy rising beams recall
  Life's tragedy again,
Its piteous pageants bring not back,
Nor waken flesh upon the rack
  Of pain anew to writhe—
Stretched in disease's shapes abhorred,
  Or mown in battle by the sword
Like grass beneath the scythe.   50

'Even I am weary in yon skies
  To watch thy fading fire;
Test of all sumless agonies,
  Behold not me expire!

My lips that speak thy dirge of death—
Their rounded gasp and gurgling breath
  To see thou shalt not boast;
The eclipse of Nature spreads my pall,—
The majesty of Darkness shall
  Receive my parting ghost!   60

'This spirit shall return to Him
  Who gave its heavenly spark:
Yet think not, Sun, it shall be dim
  When thou thyself art dark!
No! it shall live again, and shine
In bliss unknown to beams of thine,
  By him recalled to breath
Who captive led captivity,
Who robbed the grave of Victory,
  And took the sting from Death!   70

'Go, Sun, while Mercy holds me up
  On Nature's awful waste
To drink this last and bitter cup
  Of grief that man shall taste—
Go, tell the night that hides thy face
Thou saw'st the last of Adam's race
  On Earth's sepulchral clod
The darkening universe defy
To quench his immortality
  Or shake his trust in God!'   80
                    (*1823*)

William Cullen Bryant

To a Waterfowl

  Whither, 'midst falling dew,
While glow the heavens with the last steps of day,
Far, through their rosy depths, dost thou pursue
  Thy solitary way!

  Vainly the fowler's eye
Might mark thy distant flight to do thee wrong,
As, darkly painted on the crimson sky,
  Thy figure floats along.

  Seek'st thou the plashy brink
Of weedy lake, or marge of river wide,   10
Or where the rocking billows rise and sink
  On the chafed ocean side?

  There is a power whose care
Teaches thy way along that pathless coast,—
The desert and illimitable air,—
  Lone wandering, but not lost.

  All day thy wings have fanned,
At that far height, the cold, thin atmosphere,
Yet stoop not, weary, to the welcome land,
  Though the dark night is near.   20

  And soon that toil shall end;
Soon shalt thou find a summer home, and rest,
And scream among thy fellows; reeds shall
    bend,
  Soon, o'er thy sheltered nest.

  Thou'rt gone, the abyss of heaven
Hath swallowed up thy form; yet, on my heart
Deeply hath sunk the lesson thou hast given,
  And shall not soon depart.

  He who, from zone to zone,
Guides through the boundless sky thy certain
    flight,   30
In the long way that I must tread alone,
  Will lead my steps aright.
                    (*1821*)

William Blake

The Tyger

Tyger! Tyger! burning bright
In the forests of the night,
What immortal hand or eye
Could frame thy fearful symmetry?

In what distant deeps or skies
Burnt the fire of thine eyes?
On what wings dare he aspire?
What the hand dare seize the fire?

And what shoulder, & what art,
Could twist the sinews of thy heart?   10
And when thy heart began to beat,
What dread hand? & what dread feet?

What the hammer? what the chain?
In what furnace was thy brain?
What the anvil? what dread grasp
Dare its deadly terrors clasp?

When the stars threw down their spears,
And water'd heaven with their tears,
Did he smile his work to see?
Did he who made the Lamb make thee?   20

Tyger! Tyger! burning bright
In the forests of the night,
What immortal hand or eye,
Dare frame thy fearful symmetry?

(*1794*)

John Milton

On His Blindness

When I consider how my light is spent
Ere half my days in this dark world and wide,
And that one talent which is death to hide
Lodged with me useless, though my soul more
        bent
To serve therewith my Maker, and present
My true account, lest he returning chide,
"Doth God exact day-labor, light denied?"
I fondly ask. But Patience, to prevent
That murmur, soon replies, "God doth not
        need
Either man's work or his own gifts. Who best   10
Bear his mild yoke, they serve him best. His
        state
Is kingly: thousands at his bidding speed,
And post o'er land and ocean without rest;
They also serve who only stand and wait."

(*1655*)

EXERCISES

The poems in this section have been placed into sixteen groupings below. Those in each group contain certain relationships which, to some extent, make them especially comparable. You should read the poems by groups. As you do so be aware of similarities in *form* (prosody, figures of speech, sense imagery, and various technical matters); *content* (prevailing themes, symbolism, allegory); and *effect* or *impact* (intellectual and emotional response). Discuss similarities and differences as you perceive them.

Do the poems provide new insights into the age-old motif of "God and Man"? As you consider each poem, also be aware of possible relationships to other poems in other sections. For example, Thomas Campbell's "The Last Man" (in Group 13 below) is in many ways reminiscent of Lord Byron's "Darkness" (p. 210), being closely associated even in chronology. Despite the similarities, however, there is a major distinction between the two: Campbell's poem is demonstrative of man's faith in something larger than even the last man, something beyond man—in God—whereas Byron's poem is stark in its nihilism as humankind vanishes into a chaos of eternal darkness. Can you establish relationships in a similar way between the poems in this section and other sections? or between poems in different groups?

Group 1:
Louis Simpson, "The Cradle Trap"
Ralph Waldo Emerson, "Brahma"

Group 2:
Howard Nemerov, "Boom!"
Lawrence Ferlinghetti, "Christ Climbed Down"

Group 3:
Jesse Stuart, "Robert Diesel"
Robinson Jeffers, "Hurt Hawks"

Group 4:
Gerard Manley Hopkins, "Pied Beauty" and "The
Windhover"

Group 5:
Robinson Jeffers, "Hurt Hawks"
Gerard Manley Hopkins, "The Windhover"

Group 6:
Jesse Stuart, "Robert Diesel"
Louis MacNeice, "Sunday Morning"
George Meredith, "Lucifer in Starlight"
John Milton, "On His Blindness"

Group 7:
Rupert Brooke, "Heaven"
William Butler Yeats, "The Indian Upon God"

Group 8:
Alfred, Lord Tennyson, "Flower in the Crannied
Wall"
Walt Whitman, "When I Heard the Learned As-
tronomer"

Group 9:
Louis MacNeice, "Sunday Morning"
Paul Laurence Dunbar, "We Wear the Mask"

Group 10:
Dylan Thomas, "Incarnate Devil"
George Meredith, "Lucifer in Starlight"

Group 11:
Alfred, Lord Tennyson, "Flower in the Crannied
Wall"
William Blake, "The Tyger"

Group 12:
Robert Lowell, "Winter in Dunbarton"
Louis MacNeice, "Sunday Morning"

Group 13:
Rudyard Kipling, "Recessional"
Ralph Waldo Emerson, "Brahma"
Thomas Campbell, "The Last Man"
William Cullen Bryant, "To a Waterfowl"
John Milton, "On His Blindness"

Group 14:
Dylan Thomas, "Incarnate Devil"
Rupert Brooke, "Heaven"
Rudyard Kipling, "When Earth's last picture is
painted"

Group 15:
Howard Nemerov, "Boom!"
Louis MacNeice, "Sunday Morning"

Group 16:
Jesse Stuart, "Robert Diesel"
Gerard Manley Hopkins, "Pied Beauty"

13. Death and Affirmation

And you, my father, there on the sad height,
Curse, bless, me now with your fierce tears, I pray.
Do not go gentle into that good night.
Rage, rage against the dying of the light.

[Dylan Thomas, *Do Not Go Gentle into That Good Night*]

Sylvia Plath

Tulips

The tulips are too excitable, it is winter here.
Look how white everything is, how quiet,
     how snowed-in.
I am learning peacefulness, lying by myself
     quietly
As the light lies on these white walls, this bed,
     these hands.
I am nobody; I have nothing to do with
     explosions.
I have given my name and my day-clothes up
     to the nurses
And my history to the anaesthetist and my body
     to surgeons.

They have propped my head between the pillow
     and the sheet-cuff
Like an eye between two white lids that will
     not shut.
Stupid pupil, it has to take everything in.   10
The nurses pass and pass, they are no trouble,
They pass the way gulls pass inland in their white
     caps,
Doing things with their hands, one just the
     same as another,
So it is impossible to tell how many there are.

My body is a pebble to them, they tend it as
     water
Tends to the pebbles it must run over, smoothing
     them gently.
They bring me numbness in their bright needles,
     they bring me sleep.
Now I have lost myself I am sick of baggage—
My patent leather overnight case like a black
     pillbox,
My husband and child smiling out of the family
     photo;   20
Their smiles catch onto my skin, little smiling
     hooks.

I have let things slip, a thirty-year-old cargo boat
Stubbornly hanging on to my name and address.
They have swabbed me clear of my loving
     associations.
Scared and bare on the green plastic-pillowed
     trolley
I watched my tea-set, my bureaus of linen, my
     books
Sink out of sight, and the water went over my
     head.
I am a nun now, I have never been so pure.

I didn't want any flowers, I only wanted
To lie with my hands turned up and be utterly
     empty.   30
How free it is, you have no idea how free—

The peacefulness is so big it dazes you,
And it asks nothing, a name tag, a few trinkets.
It is what the dead close on, finally; I imagine
    them
Shutting their mouths on it, like a Communion
    tablet.

The tulips are too red in the first place, they
    hurt me.
Even through the gift paper I could hear them
    breathe
Lightly, through their white swaddlings, like
    an awful baby.
Their redness talks to my wound, it corresponds.
They are subtle: they seem to float, though they
    weigh me down,   40
Upsetting me with their sudden tongues and
    their colour,
A dozen red lead sinkers round my neck.

Nobody watched me before, now I am watched.
The tulips turn to me, and the window behind
    me
Where once a day the light slowly widens and
    slowly thins,
And I see myself, flat, ridiculous, a cut-paper
    shadow
Between the eye of the sun and the eyes of the
    tulips,
And I have no face, I have wanted to efface
    myself.
The vivid tulips eat my oxygen.

Before they came the air was calm enough,   50
Coming and going, breath by breath, without
    any fuss.
Then the tulips filled it up like a loud noise.
Now the air snags and eddies round them the
    way a river
Snags and eddies round a sunken rust-red engine.
They concentrate my attention, that was happy
Playing and resting without commiting itself.

The walls, also, seem to be warming themselves.
The tulips should be behind bars like dangerous
    animals;
They are opening like the mouth of some great
    African cat,
And I am aware of my heart: it opens and closes
Its bowl of red blooms out of sheer love of me. 61
The water I taste is warm and salt, like the sea,
And comes from a country far away as health.

                           (1962)

Anne Sexton

The Starry Night

That does not keep me from having a terrible need of—
shall I say the word—religion. Then I go out at night to
paint the stars.
              Vincent Van Gogh in a letter to his brother

The town does not exist
except where one black-haired tree slips
up like a drowned woman into the hot sky.
The town is silent. The night boils with eleven
    stars.
Oh starry starry night! This is how
I want to die.

It moves. They are all alive.
Even the moon bulges in its orange irons
to push children, like a god, from its eye.
The old unseen serpent swallows up the stars.   10
Oh starry starry night! This is how
I want to die:

into that rushing beast of the night,
sucked up by that great dragon, to split
from my life with no flag,
no belly,
no cry.

                           (1961)

Thomas Merton

Elegy for the Monastery Barn

As though an aged person were to wear
Too gay a dress
And walk about the neighborhood
Announcing the hour of her death,

So now, one summer day's end,
At suppertime, when wheels are still,
The long barn suddenly puts on the traitor,
        beauty,
And hails us with a dangerous cry,
For: "Look!" she calls to the country,
"Look how fast I dress myself in fire!"   10

Had we half guessed how long her spacious
        shadows
Harbored a woman's vanity
We would be less surprised to see her now
So loved, and so attended, and so feared.

She, in whose airless heart
We burst our veins to fill her full of hay,
Now stands apart.
She will not have us near her. Terribly,
Sweet Christ, how terribly her beauty burns us
        now!

And yet she has another legacy,   20
More delicate, to leave us, and more rare.

Who knew her solitude?
Who heard the peace downstairs
While flames ran whispering among the rafters?
Who felt the silence, there,
The long, hushed gallery
Clean and resigned and waiting for the fire?

Look! They have all come back to speak their
        summary:
Fifty invisible cattle, the past years
Assume their solemn places one by one.   30
This is the little minute of their destiny.
Here is their meaning found. Here is their end.

Laved in the flame as in a Sacrament
The brilliant walls are holy
In their first-last hour of joy.

Fly from within the barn! Fly from the silence
Of this creature sanctified by fire!
Let no man stay inside to look upon the Lord!
Let no man wait within and see the Holy
One sitting in the presence of disaster   40
Thinking upon this barn His gentle doom!

                              (1952)

Dylan Thomas

Do Not Go Gentle into That Good Night

Do not go gentle into that good night,
Old age should burn and rave at close of day;
Rage, rage against the dying of the light.

Though wise men at their end know dark is
        right,
Because their words had forked no lightning
        they
Do not go gentle into that good night.

Good men, the last wave by, crying how bright
Their frail deeds might have danced in a green
        bay,
Rage, rage against the dying of the light.

Wild men who caught and sang the sun in
        flight,   10
And learn, too late, they grieved it on its way,
Do not go gentle into that good night.

Grave men, near death, who see with blinding
        sight
Blind eyes could blaze like meteors and be gay,
Rage, rage against the dying of the light.

And you, my father, there on the sad height,
Curse, bless, me now with your fierce tears, I
    pray.
Do not go gentle into that good night.
Rage, rage against the dying of the light.

(1939)

Jesse Stuart

"Maybe there is the sound of windless rain"

Maybe there is the sound of windless rain,
The steady thump of rain on my grave rock;
I have no way to tell with this dead brain
The sound of rain that's ticking like a clock.
Though flesh is close related to the time;
My ears are deaf to any ticking sound
Though life is close related to the rhyme;
What chance has one now lying under ground?
And then to think each comes and takes his turn.
Each man's a god and each is crucified—   10
Each goes back to the dirt and grass and fern
After the temple of his flesh has died.
Each comes and goes and each must go alone;
Each life is dirt and time and rhyme and stone.

(1934)

William Faulkner

My Epitaph

If there be grief, then let it be but rain,
And this but silver grief for grieving's sake,
If these green woods be dreaming here to wake
Within my heart, if I should rouse again.

But I shall sleep, for where is any death
While in these blue hills slumbrous overhead
I'm rooted like a tree? Though I be dead,
This earth that holds me fast will find me breath.

(1932)

James Weldon Johnson

Go Down Death

(A Funeral Sermon)

Weep not, weep not,
She is not dead;
She's resting in the bosom of Jesus.
Heart-broken husband—weep no more;
Grief-stricken son—weep no more;
She's only just gone home.
Day before yesterday morning,
God was looking down from his great, high
    heaven,
Looking down on all his children,
And his eye fell on Sister Caroline,   10
Tossing on her bed of pain.
And God's big heart was touched with pity,
With the everlasting pity.

And God sat back on his throne,
And he commanded that tall, bright angel
    standing at his right hand:
Call me Death!
And that tall, bright angel cried in a voice
That broke like a clap of thunder:
Call Death!—Call Death!
And the echo sounded down the streets of
    heaven   20
Till it reached away back to that shadowy place,
Where Death waits with his pale, white horses.

And Death heard the summons,
And he leaped on his fastest horse,
Pale as a sheet in the moonlight.
Up the golden street Death galloped,
And the hoof of his horse struck fire from the
    gold,
But they didn't make no sound.
Up Death rode to the Great White Throne,
And waited for God's command.   30

And God said: Go down, Death, go down,
Go down to Savannah, Georgia,
Down in Yamacraw,

And find Sister Caroline.
She's borne the burden and heat of the day,
She's labored long in my vineyard,
And she's tired—
She's weary—
Go down, Death, and bring her to me.

And Death didn't say a word,   40
But he loosed the reins on his pale, white horse,
And he clamped the spurs to his bloodless sides,
And out and down he rode,
Through heaven's pearly gates,
Past suns and moons and stars;
On Death rode,
And the foam from his horse was like a comet
    in the sky;
On Death rode,
Leaving the lightning's flash behind;
Straight on down he came.   50

While we were watching round her bed,
She turned her eyes and looked away,
She saw what we couldn't see;
She saw Old Death. She saw Old Death.
Coming like a falling star.
But Death didn't frighten Sister Caroline;

He looked to her like a welcome friend.
And she whispered to us: I'm going home,
And she smiled and closed her eyes.

And Death took her up like a baby,   60
And she lay in his icy arms,
But she didn't feel no chill.
And Death began to ride again—
Up beyond the evening star,
Out beyond the morning star,
Into the glittering light of glory,
On to the Great White Throne.
And there he laid Sister Caroline
On the loving breast of Jesus.

And Jesus took his own hand and wiped away
    her tears,   70
And he smoothed the furrows from her face,
And the angels sang a little song,
And Jesus rocked her in his arms,
And kept a-saying: Take your rest,
Take your rest, take your rest.
Weep not—weep not,
She is not dead;
She's resting in the bosom of Jesus.

                                            (*1927*)

E. E. Cummings

Buffalo Bill's Defunct

Buffalo Bill's
defunct
      who used to
      ride a watersmooth-silver
                    stallion
and break onetwothreefourfive pigeonsjustlikethat
                            Jesus
he was a handsome man
               and what i want to know is
how do you like your blueeyed boy   10
Mister Death

                    (*1923*)

Conrad Aiken

The Morning Song of Senlin

It is morning, Senlin says, and in the morning
When the light drips through the shutters like
    the dew,
I arise, I face the sunrise,
And do the things my fathers learned to do.
Stars in the purple dusk above the rooftops
Pale in a saffron mist and seem to die,
And I myself on a swiftly tilting planet
Stand before a glass and tie my tie.

Vine leaves tap my window,
Dew-drops sing to the garden stones,   10
The robin chirps in the chinaberry tree
Repeating three clear tones.

It is morning. I stand by the mirror
And tie my tie once more.
While waves far off in a pale rose twilight
Crash on a coral shore.
I stand by a mirror and comb my hair:
How small and white my face!—
The green earth tilts through a sphere of air
And bathes in a flame of space.   20

There are houses hanging above the stars
And stars hung under a sea.
And a sun far off in a shell of silence
Dapples my walls for me.

It is morning, Senlin says, and in the morning
Should I not pause in the light to remember
    god?
Upright and firm I stand on a star unstable,
He is immense and lonely as a cloud.
I will dedicate this moment before my mirror
To him alone, for him I will comb my hair.   30
Accept these humble offerings, cloud of silence!
I will think of you as I descend the stair.

Vine leaves tap my window,
The snail-track shines on the stones,
Dew-drops flash from the chinaberry tree
Repeating two clear tones.

It is morning, I awake from a bed of silence,
Shining I rise from the starless waters of sleep.
The walls are about me still as in the evening,
I am the same, and the same name still I keep.   40
The earth revolves with me, yet makes no
        motion,
The stars pale silently in a coral sky.
In a whistling void I stand before my mirror,
Unconcerned, and tie my tie.

There are horses neighing on far-off hills
Tossing their long white manes,
And mountains flash in the rose-white dusk,
Their shoulders black with rains.
It is morning. I stand by the mirror
And surprise my soul once more;   50
The blue air rushes above my ceiling,
There are suns beneath my floor.

. . . It is morning, Senlin says, I ascend from
    darkness
And depart on the winds of space for I know
    not where,
My watch is wound, a key is in my pocket,
And the sky is darkened as I descend the stair.
There are shadows across the windows, clouds
    in heaven,
And a god among the stars; and I will go
Thinking of him as I might think of daybreak
And humming a tune I know.   60

Vine leaves tap at the window,
Dew-drops sing to the garden stones,
The robin chirps in the chinaberry tree
Repeating three clear tones.

(*1918*)

Rupert Brooke

The Great Lover

I have been so great a lover: filled my days
So proudly with the splendor of Love's praise,
The pain, the calm, and the astonishment,
Desire illimitable, and still content,
And all dear names men use, to cheat despair,
For the perplexed and viewless streams that
    bear
Our hearts at random down the dark of life.
Now, ere the unthinking silence on that strife
Steals down, I would cheat drowsy Death so far,
My night shall be remembered for a star   10
That outshone all the suns of all men's days.
Shall I not crown them with immortal praise
Whom I have loved, who have given me, dared
    with me
High secrets, and in darkness knelt to see
The inenarrable godhead of delight?
Love is a flame:—we have beaconed the
    world's night.
A city:—and we have built it, these and I.
An emperor:—we have taught the world to die.
So, for their sakes I loved, ere I go hence,
And the high cause of Love's magnificence,   20
And to keep loyalties young, I'll write those
    names
Golden for ever, eagles, crying flames,
And set them as a banner, that men may know,
To dare the generations, burn, and blow
Out on the wind of Time, shining and
    streaming. . . .

These I have loved:
      White plates and cups, clean-gleaming,
Ringed with blue lines; and feathery, faëry dust;
Wet roofs, beneath the lamp-light; the strong
    crust
Of friendly bread; and many-tasting food;   30
Rainbows; and the blue bitter smoke of wood;
And radiant raindrops couching in cool flowers;

And flowers themselves, that sway through
    sunny hours;
Dreaming of moths that drink them under the
    moon;
Then, the cool kindliness of sheets, that soon
Smooth away trouble; and the rough male kiss
Of blankets; grainy wood; live hair that is
Shining and free; blue-massing clouds; the keen
Unpassioned beauty of a great machine;
The benison of hot water; furs to touch;   40
The good smell of old clothes; and other such—
The comfortable smell of friendly fingers,
Hair's fragrance, and the musty reek that
    lingers
About dead leaves and last year's ferns. . . .
                            Dear names,
And thousand others throng to me! Royal
    flames;
Sweet water's dimpling laugh from tap or
    spring;
Holes in the ground; and voices that do sing:
Voices in laughter, too; and body's pain,
Soon turned to peace; and the deep-panting
    train;   50
Firm sands; the little dulling edge of foam
That browns and dwindles as the wave goes
    home;
And washen stones, gay for an hour; the cold
Graveness of iron; moist black earthen mold;
Sleep; and high places; footprints in the dew;
And oaks; and brown horse-chestnuts,
    glossy-new;
And new-peeled sticks; and shining pools on
    grass;—
All these have been my loves. And these shall
    pass,
Whatever passes not, in the great hour,
Nor all my passion, all my prayers, have power 60
To hold them with me through the gates of
    Death.
They'll play deserter, turn with the traitor
    breath,
Break the high bond we made, and sell Love's
    trust
And sacramental covenant to the dust.

—Oh, never a doubt but, somewhere, I shall
     wake,
And give what's left of love again, and make
New friends now strangers. . . .
                  But the best I've known
Stays here, and changes, breaks, grows old, is
     blown
About the winds of the world, and fades from
     brains   70
Of living men, and dies.
                  Nothing remains.
O dear my loves, O faithless, once again
This one last gift I give: that after men
Shall know, and later lovers, far-removed
Praise you, "All these were lovely"; say, "He
     loved."

                           (*1916*)

Carl Sandburg

Cool Tombs

When Abraham Lincoln was shoveled into the
     tombs, he forgot the copperheads and the
     assassin . . . in the dust, in the cool
     tombs.
And Ulysses Grant lost all thought of con men
     and Wall Street, cash and collateral
     turned ashes . . . in the dust, in the cool
     tombs.
Pocahontas' body, lovely as a poplar, sweet as
     a red haw in November or a pawpaw
     in May, did she wonder? does she
     remember? . . . in the dust, in the cool
     tombs?

Take any streetful of people buying clothes and
     groceries, cheering a hero or throwing
     confetti and blowing tin horns . . . tell
     me if the lovers are losers . . . tell me if
     any get more than the lovers . . . in the
     dust . . . in the cool tombs.

                           (*1916*)

Edgar Lee Masters

Lucinda Matlock

I went to the dances at Chandlerville,
And played snap-out at Winchester.
One time we changed partners,
Driving home in the moonlight of middle June,
And then I found Davis.
We were married and lived together for seventy
     years,
Enjoying, working, raising the twelve children,
Eight of whom we lost
Ere I had reached the age of sixty.
I spun, I wove, I kept the house, I nursed the
     sick,   10
I made the garden, and for holiday
Rambled over the fields where sang the larks,
And by Spoon River gathering many a shell,
And many a flower and medicinal weed—
Shouting to the wooded hills, singing to the
     green valleys.
At ninety-six I had lived enough, that is all,
And passed to a sweet repose.
What is this I hear of sorrow and weariness,
Anger, discontent and drooping hopes?
Degenerate sons and daughters,   20
Life is too strong for you—
It takes life to love life.

                           (*1914*)

Thomas Hardy

The Darkling Thrush

I leant upon a coppice gate
     When Frost was spectre-gray,
And Winter's dregs made desolate
     The weakening eye of day.
The tangled bine-stems scored the sky
     Like strings of broken lyres,
And all mankind that haunted nigh
     Had sought their household fires.

The land's sharp features seemed to be
   The Century's corpse outleant,   10
His crypt the cloudy canopy,
   The wind his death-lament.
The ancient pulse of germ and birth
   Was shrunken hard and dry,
And every spirit upon earth
   Seemed fervourless as I.

At once a voice arose among
   The bleak twigs overhead
In a full-hearted evensong
   Of joy illimited;   20
An aged thrush, frail, gaunt, and small,
   In blast-beruffled plume,
Had chosen thus to fling his soul
   Upon the growing gloom.

So little cause for carolings
   Of such ecstatic sound
Was written on terrestrial things
   Afar or nigh around,
That I could think there trembled through
   His happy good-night air   30
Some blessed Hope, whereof he knew
   And I was unaware.

                    (*1900*)

A. E. Housman

To an Athlete Dying Young

The time you won your town the race
We chaired you through the market-place;
Man and boy stood cheering by,
And home we brought you shoulder-high.

To-day, the road all runners come,
Shoulder-high we bring you home,
And set you at your threshold down,
Townsman of a stiller town.

Smart lad, to slip betimes away
From fields where glory does not stay   10
And early though the laurel grows
It withers quicker than the rose.

Eyes the shady night has shut
Cannot see the record cut,
And silence sounds no worse than cheers
After earth has stopped the ears:

Now you will not swell the rout
Of lads that wore their honours out,
Runners whom renown outran
And the name died before the man.   20

So set, before its echoes fade,
The fleet foot on the sill of shade,
And hold to the low lintel up
The still-defended challenge-cup.

And round that early-laurelled head
Will flock to gaze the strengthless dead,
And find unwithered on its curls
The garland briefer than a girl's.

                    (*1896*)

Walt Whitman

Good-bye My Fancy!

Good-bye my Fancy!
Farewell dear mate, dear love!
I'm going away, I know not where,
Or to what fortune, or whether I may ever see
     you again,
So Good-bye my Fancy.

Now for my last—let me look back a moment;
The slower fainter ticking of the clock is in me.
Exit, nightfall, and soon the heart-thud stopping.

Long have we lived, joyed, caressed together;
Delightful!—now separation—Good-bye my
     Fancy.   10

Yet let me not be too hasty,
Long indeed have we lived, slept, filtered,
    become really blended into one;
Then if we die together, (yes, we'll
    remain one,)
If we go anywhere we'll go together to meet
    what happens,
Maybe we'll be better off and blither, and learn
    something,
Maybe it is yourself now really ushering me to
    the true songs, (who knows?)
Maybe it is you the mortal knob really undoing,
    turning—so now finally,
Good-bye—and hail! my Fancy.

(1891)

Emily Dickinson

Because I Could Not Stop for Death

Because I could not stop for Death—
He kindly stopped for me—
The Carriage held but just Ourselves—
And Immortality.

We slowly drove—He knew no haste
And I had put away
My labor and my leisure too,
For His Civility—

We passed the School, where Children strove
At Recess—in the Ring—   10
We passed the Fields of Gazing Grain—
We passed the Setting Sun—

Or rather—He passed Us—
The Dews drew quivering and chill—
For only Gossamer, my Gown—
My Tippet—only Tulle—

We paused before a House that seemed
A Swelling of the Ground—
The Roof was scarcely visible—
The Cornice—in the Ground—   20

Since then—'tis Centuries—and yet
Feels shorter than the Day
I first surmised the Horses Heads
Were toward Eternity—

(1890)

Emily Dickinson

If I Shouldn't Be Alive

If I shouldn't be alive
When the Robins come,
Give the one in Red Cravat,
A Memorial crumb.

If I couldn't thank you,
Being fast asleep,
You will know I'm trying
With my Granite lip!

(1890)

Alfred, Lord Tennyson

Crossing the Bar

Sunset and evening star,
    And one clear call for me!
And may there be no moaning of the bar,
    When I put out to sea,

But such a tide as moving seems asleep,
    Too full for sound and foam,
When that which drew from out the boundless
    deep
    Turns again home.

Twilight and evening bell,
    And after that the dark!   10
And may there be no sadness of farewell,
    When I embark;

For though from out our bourne of Time and
    Place
  The flood may bear me far,
I hope to see my Pilot face to face
  When I have crossed the bar.

                (*1889*)

Robert Louis Stevenson

Requiem

Under the wide and starry sky,
Dig the grave and let me lie.
Glad did I live and gladly die,
  And I laid me down with a will.

This be the verse you grave for me:
Here he lies where he longed to be,
Home is the sailor, home from sea,
  And the hunter home from the hill.

                (*1887*)

Walter Savage Landor

I Strove with None

I strove with none, for none was worth my
    strife:
  Nature I loved, and, next to Nature, Art:
I warm'd both hands before the fire of Life;
  It sinks; and I am ready to depart.

                (*1849*)

Alfred, Lord Tennyson

Ulysses

It little profits that an idle king,
By this still hearth, among these barren crags,
Matched with an aged wife, I mete and dole
Unequal laws unto a savage race,

That hoard, and sleep, and feed, and know not
  me.
I cannot rest from travel; I will drink
Life to the lees. All times I have enjoyed
Greatly, have suffered greatly, both with those
That loved me, and alone; on shore, and when
Through scudding drifts the rainy Hyades   10
Vexed the dim sea. I am become a name;
For always roaming with a hungry heart
Much have I seen and known—cities of men,
And manners, climates, councils, governments,
Myself not least, but honored of them all—
And drunk delight of battle with my peers,
Far on the ringing plains of windy Troy.
I am a part of all that I have met;
Yet all experience is an arch wherethrough
Gleams that untraveled world whose margin
  fades   20
Forever and forever when I move.
How dull it is to pause, to make an end,
To rust unburnished, not to shine in use!
As though to breathe were life! Life piled on life
Were all too little, and of one to me
Little remains; but every hour is saved
From that eternal silence, something more,
A bringer of new things; and vile it were
For some three suns to store and hoard myself,
And this gray spirit yearning in desire   30
To follow knowledge like a sinking star,
Beyond the utmost bound of human thought.
    This is my son, mine own Telemachus,
To whom I leave the scepter and the isle—
Well-loved of me, discerning to fulfill
This labor, by slow prudence to make mild
A rugged people, and through soft degrees
Subdue them to the useful and the good.
Most blameless is he, centered in the sphere
Of common duties, decent not to fail   40
In offices of tenderness, and pay
Meet adoration to my household gods,
When I am gone. He works his work, I mine.
    There lies the port; the vessel puffs her sail;
There gloom the dark, broad seas. My mariners,
Souls that have toiled, and wrought, and
    thought with me—

That ever with a frolic welcome took
The thunder and the sunshine, and opposed
Free hearts, free foreheads—you and I are old;
Old age hath yet his honor and his toil; 50
Death closes all. But something ere the end,
Some work of noble note, may yet be done,
Not unbecoming men that strove with Gods.
The lights begin to twinkle from the rocks;
The long day wanes; the slow moon climbs; the
     deep
Moans round with many voices. Come, my
     friends.
'Tis not too late to seek a newer world.
Push off, and sitting well in order smite
The sounding furrows; for my purpose holds
To sail beyond the sunset, and the baths 60
Of all the western stars, until I die.
It may be that the gulfs will wash us down;
It may be we shall touch the Happy Isles,
And see the great Achilles, whom we knew.
Though much is taken, much abides; and though
We are not now that strength which in old days
Moved earth and heaven, that which we are,
     we are—
One equal temper of heroic hearts,
Made weak by time and fate, but strong in will
To strive, to seek, to find, and not to yield. 70

(1842)

John Keats

Ode to a Nightingale

I

My heart aches, and a drowsy numbness pains
     My sense, as though of hemlock I had
          drunk,
Or emptied some dull opiate to the drains
     One minute past, and Lethe-wards had
          sunk:

'Tis not through envy of thy happy lot,
     But being too happy in thine happiness,—
          That thou, light-wingèd Dryad of the
               trees,
               In some melodious plot
Of beechen green, and shadows numberless,
     Singest of summer in full-throated ease. 10

II

O, for a draught of vintage! that hath been
     Cool'd a long age in the deep-delvèd earth,
Tasting of Flora and the country green,
     Dance, and Provençal song, and sunburnt
          mirth!
O for a beaker full of the warm South,
     Full of the true, the blushful Hippocrene,
          With beaded bubbles winking at the brim,
               And purple-stainèd mouth;
That I might drink, and leave the world
     unseen,
          And with thee fade away into the
               forest dim: 20

III

Fade far away, dissolve, and quite forget
     What thou among the leaves hast never
          known,
The weariness, the fever, and the fret
     Here, where men sit and hear each other
          groan;
Where palsy shakes a few, sad, last grey hairs,
     Where youth grows pale, and spectre-thin,
          and dies;
          Where but to think is to be full of sorrow
               And leaden-eyed despairs,
Where Beauty cannot keep her lustrous eyes,
     Or new Love pine at them beyond
          tomorrow. 30

IV

Away! away! for I will fly to thee,
     Not charioted by Bacchus and his pards,
But on the viewless wings of Poesy,
     Though the dull brain perplexes and
          retards:

Already with thee! tender is the night,
  And haply the Queen-Moon is on her
      throne,
    Cluster'd around by all her starry Fays;
      But here there is no light,
  Save what from heaven is with the breezes
      blown
    Through verdurous glooms and winding
    mossy ways.   40

V

I cannot see what flowers are at my feet,
  Nor what soft incense hangs upon the
      boughs,
But, in embalmèd darkness, guess each sweet
  Wherewith the seasonable month endows
The grass, the thicket, and the fruit-tree wild;
  White hawthorn, and the pastoral eglantine;
    Fast fading violets cover'd up in leaves;
      And mid-May's eldest child,
  The coming musk-rose, full of dewy wine,
    The murmurous haunt of flies on summer
    eves.   50

VI

Darkling I listen; and, for many a time
  I have been half in love with easeful Death,
Call'd him soft names in many a musèd rhyme,
  To take into the air my quiet breath;
Now more than ever seems it rich to die,
  To cease upon the midnight with no pain,
    While thou art pouring forth thy soul
      abroad
      In such an ecstasy!
  Still wouldst thou sing, and I have ears in
    vain—
    To thy high requiem become a sod.   60

VII

Thou wast not born for death, immortal
    Bird!
  No hungry generations tread thee down;

The voice I hear this passing night was heard
  In ancient days by emperor and clown:
Perhaps the self-same song that found a path
Through the sad heart of Ruth, when, sick for
    home,
  She stood in tears amid the alien corn;
    The same that oft-times hath
Charm'd magic casements, opening on the
    foam
  Of perilous seas, in faery lands forlorn.   70

VIII

Forlorn! the very word is like a bell
  To toll me back from thee to my sole self!
Adieu! the fancy cannot cheat so well
  As she is fam'd to do, deceiving elf.
Adieu! adieu! thy plaintive anthem fades
  Past the near meadows, over the still stream,
    Up the hill-side; and now 'tis buried deep
      In the next valley-glades:
  Was it a vision, or a waking dream?
    Fled is that music:—Do I wake or sleep?   80
                      (*1820*)

John Donne

Death, Be Not Proud

Death, be not proud, though some have callèd
    thee
Mighty and dreadful, for thou art not so;
For those whom thou think'st thou dost
    overthrow
Die not, poor Death; nor yet canst thou kill me.
From rest and sleep, which but thy pictures be,
Much pleasure; then from thee much more
    must flow;
And soonest our best men with thee do go—
Rest of their bones and souls' delivery!
Thou'rt slave to fate, chance, kings, and desperate
    men,

And dost with poison, war, and sickness dwell; 10
And poppy or charms can make us sleep as well
And better than thy stroke. Why swell'st thou
    then ?

One short sleep past, we wake eternally,
And Death shall be no more : Death, thou shalt
    die.

(1633)

EXERCISES

"Tulips" [Plath] and *"The Great Lover"* [Brooke]

1. Sylvia Plath's "Tulips" can be read along with Rupert Brooke's "The Great Lover" for purposes of comparison and contrast. Both poems deal with things loved, the essences of life, and even with pain. Both are profuse with images, and both are extremely detailed. However, which poem seems to you to be the more specific? the more general? Discuss. Notice the frequent use of similes and metaphors, especially in Plath's poem. Do you see any similarities to those of Brooke? Discuss. Do both poems deal with the yearning for life? Which does so more directly? more indirectly? Discuss.

2. What is the major irony of "Tulips"? Discuss. Do you conceive of Plath's use of the tulips as a device—as a means to other ends? Is the poem really about tulips? What is the function of the tulips? Discuss the effect of contrast in her poem—the juxtaposition of sickness and health, restraint and freedom, death and life. In spite of the frequent seriousness of feeling and tone in "Tulips," do you discern associations with humor? Finally, is the poem basically affirmative? Discuss.

"The Starry Night" [Sexton] and *"Ode to a Nightingale"* [Keats]

3. Do you see any correlations between these two poems? Discuss them, including the pervading night-death motif in both works. Though similarities exist, there are sharp contrasts in feeling and tone. Distinctions merge into disparate interpretations also. How does the persona of "The Starry Night" prefer to meet death as opposed to Keats' persona?

4. Finally, can you relate the device of synecdoche (or metonymy) to the last three lines of "The Starry Night"? If so, how? If you are familiar with Vincent Van Gogh's painting *The Starry Night*, can you perceive a relevance between the poetic art and the spacial art? Discuss.

"Elegy for the Monastery Barn" [Merton] and *"Crossing the Bar"* [Tennyson]

5. Read Thomas Merton's "Elegy for the Monastery Barn." Both this poem and Alfred, Lord Tennyson's "Crossing the Bar" are excellent examples of extended metaphors. Draw out both protracted comparisons in detail, and then contrast the poets' respective feelings, tones, and intentions.

6. What are Merton's attitudes toward the monastery barn? How does he relate its burning to woman, to capriciousness, to the past, to a "legacy," to beauty and death, and to religious concepts of life and death? Discuss. For what reasons does the poet—a Trappist monk at Gethsemani in Nelson County, Kentucky, for most of his adult life—shift to an imperative tone (apostrophe) in the final stanza? Is the shift justified through meanings inherent in the expressions? Discuss.

"*My Epitaph*" [Faulkner] and "*Requiem*" [Stevenson]

7. The Nobel laureate William Faulkner wrote poetry before he wrote fiction. He once called himself a "failed poet." Read his poem and compare it to Robert Louis Stevenson's "Requiem," which it resembles in some ways. How may the two be compared? Discuss. How do both poets reveal a basically affirmative attitude toward the life process, including death? Do you think Faulkner was, in all respects, a "failed poet"? Why or why not?

"*Do Not Go Gentle into That Good Night*" [Thomas]

8. Dylan Thomas' poem is a skillfully wrought villa-nelle, and its form may be consistently compared with the analysis of that form in the question on Theodore Roethke's "The Waking" (see p. 181). In your own opinion, which poet generates the greater compression and power of expression within this form? Discuss.
9. Examine Thomas' poem closely. In each stanza, he introduces different kinds of men; sequentially they are old men, wise men, good men, wild men, grave men, and, directly, his own father. Describe the thoughts of each of these kinds of men at the crisis of death, and the relationships between their thoughts and the ways in which they respond to death.

"*Maybe there is the sound of windless rain*" [Stuart] and "*The Morning Song of Senlin*" [Aiken]

10. Read Jesse Stuart's poem along with Conrad Aiken's poem. Both poems contain notable devices of unity, especially as repetition is subtly interwoven through both works. Particularly notice Stuart's use of the images of stone, time, rhyme, and earth (dirt, grass, fern). The form and substance of the poem are tightly organized within the framework of a Shakes-pearean sonnet, as they should be. Observe how each of the four images progresses through the first three quatrains, and how all four images are unified in the concluding couplet. In the considerably longer poem by Aiken, the devices of unity center about images of morning, waking, time, earth and color, earth as a planet in space, God, and song. Especially observe how the next-to-last stanza draws the images together, and how the final stanza serves as a repetition emphasizing a pattern of musicality in the poem.

"*Go Down Death*" [Johnson]

11. "Go Down Death (A Funeral Sermon)" is a narrative poem reflecting southern Negro folklore, an aspect of the rich tradition of local color in American literature. In addition, the subject of the poem is a blend of Christian subjects and attitudes: death, myths, and a wide range of richly imaginative associations among them. How does Johnson achieve the effect of a sermon through the form of the poem (free verse)? through the various figures of speech (euphemisms, metaphors, similes, mythic allusions)? Give several examples of each device. How do you account for the inherent power of this poem? Considering in your answer Emily Dickinson's "Because I Could Not Stop for Death," do you see relationships between Johnson's poem and others in this section? in other sections? Discuss.

"*Buffalo Bill's Defunct*" [Cummings]

12. "Buffalo Bill's Defunct," by E. E. Cummings, blends approaches of irony and the feeling and tone of innocence. The poem is ironic in that the view of the death of the folk hero of the American West, Buffalo

Bill, is anything but the expected one of serious, solemn, and reverent response. What are some of the unusual effects Cummings produces by spacing, running some words together, and virtually isolating others? In considering your answer, note the correspondence between sound and meaning.

13. Describe the "voice" of the poem (not Buffalo Bill) as you perceive him. Does the action, as it is remembered, take place in a Wild West Show? What are the clues that makes one think so? What kind of person attended such shows and felt such enthusiasm in watching them? Why does the poet use "Boy" rather than "man"

before referring to "Mister Death" at the end of the poem, and why is Death designated so flippantly? In your description of Cummings' "voice," what would you guess his age to be, and what is the pertinence of his age to his attitudes? Discuss.

14. Considering the heavy emphasis on irony in this poem, can you relate a similar emphasis to James Weldon Johnson's poem, "Go Down Death"? to A. E. Housman's "To an Athlete Dying Young"? to Carl Sandburg's "Cool Tombs"? to John Donne's "Death, Be Not Proud"? Discuss the central irony of each and the function of irony as a whole.

"Ode to a Nightingale" [Keats]

15. This is one of the great poems in the English language. Read it carefully. In form, notice that the poem contains eight stanzas of ten lines each, with a rhyme scheme of *ababcdecde*; yet the poem moves so naturally, so leisurely that one is conscious of the meter only as a kind of musical theme supporting meaning. Keats' "Ode" requires a close *paraphrase* if we are to understand not only the surface level of the poem, but also its deeper soundings of meaning—especially Keats' view of death as the ultimate experience of all living things. In tracing the persona's "drowsy" mood from the opening of the poem to its dreamlike conclusion and the abrupt awakening, examine the rich sensuous images of the poem and how they evoke meanings. The appeal to the senses of taste and touch is obvious enough, but notice how Keats links image to image, and the reader moves from thirst and coolness to pleasant warmth, and then back into the imagination of the persona. What images do you find, then, of death and how Keats viewed it through his persona? Observe that the view is not static, but changing—the concept of distance, the fading away, the dissolution.

16. In the third stanza especially, notice the images of pain in the actual world. What is the function of such

images, and how is the function related to the beginning line of the fourth stanza, "Away! away! for I will fly to thee." Does "to thee" mean "to death"? If so, how will he "fly" or go? What is the night of death like? Is there suffering as on earth, or is all gentleness? How does the world of death correspond to the world of nature?

17. In the sixth stanza, the persona states clearly his attitude toward death, or appears to for the moment. Here, too, observe that the reader becomes increasingly conscious of the nightingale. How does the seventh stanza serve to link the present to the past, and how does the nightingale itself become a kind of medium of association? In the famous concluding lines of this stanza, and in the final stanza, the persona's attitude toward death changes, does it not? Discuss. Considering the whole poem, what is the poet's concept of death? What is the function of the dream ending?

18. Can you relate the dreaming ending of Keats' poem to Alfred, Lord Tennyson's "Ulysses"? How? In what ways can you establish a correspondence between Keats' poem and Dylan Thomas' "Do Not Go Gentle into That Good Night"? with Thomas Hardy's "The Darkling Thrush"? Discuss.

General

19. Consider the following poems as they reveal the archetypal motif of death as a journey: James Weldon Johnson's "Go Down Death"; Walt Whitman's "Goodbye My Fancy!"; Emily Dickinson's "Because I Could Not Stop for Death"; and Alfred, Lord Tennyson's "Crossing the Bar" and "Ulysses."

20. As you have probably observed, a number of the poems in this section may echo or anticipate poems in other sections. Among the ones already mentioned and those you may have noted yourself, consider these possibilities:

William Faulkner's "My Epitaph" and Walter de la Mare's "Silver" (2. Nature and the Human Spirit)

Conrad Aiken's "The Morning Song of Senlin" and Dylan Thomas' "Fern Hill" (1. Childhood and Loss of Innocence); T. S. Eliot's "The Love Song of J. Alfred Prufrock" (14. The Complexity of Poetry)

John Keats' "Ode to a Nightingale" and William Butler Yeats' "Sailing to Byzantium" (8. Wisdom and Beauty); Walt Whitman's "Out of the Cradle Endlessly Rocking" (3. The Struggle for Identity)

Carl Sandburg's "Cool Tombs" and Dylan Thomas' "In My Craft or Sullen Art" (8. Wisdom and Beauty)

Edgar Lee Masters' "Lucinda Matlock" and William Ernest Henley's "Invictus" (7. Measure of Man)

Thomas Hardy's "The Darkling Thrush" and Matthew Arnold's "Dover Beach" (8. Wisdom and Beauty)

Walt Whitman's "Good-bye My Fancy!" and Ralph Waldo Emerson's "Brahma" (12. God and Man)

Walter Savage Landor's "I Strove with None" and Scharmel Iris' "The Old Man" (7. Measure of Man)

John Donne's "Death, Be Not Proud" and Thomas Campbell's "The Last Man" (12. God and Man)

14. The Complexity of Poetry

Let us go then, you and I,
When the evening is spread out against the sky
Like a patient etherised upon a table;

. . .

In the room the women come and go
Talking of Michelangelo.

[T. S. Eliot, The Love Song of J. Alfred Prufrock]

Robert Hayden

Aunt Jemima of the Ocean Waves

I

Enacting someone's notion of themselves
(and me), The One And Only Aunt Jemima
and Kokimo The Dixie Dancing Fool
do a bally for the freak show.

I watch a moment, then move on,
pondering the logic that makes of them
(and me) confederates
of The Spider Girl, The Snake-skinned Man . . .

Poor devils have to live somehow.
I cross the boardwalk to the beach,
lie in the sand and gaze beyond
the clutter at the sea.

10

II

Trouble you for a light?
I turn as Aunt Jemima settles down
beside me, her blue-rinsed hair
without the red bandanna now.

I hold the lighter to her cigarette.
Much obliged. Unmindful (perhaps)
of my embarrassment, she looks
at me and smiles: You sure   20

do favor a friend I used to have.
Guess that's why I bothered you
for a light. So much like him that I—
She pauses, watching white horses rush

to the shore. Way them big old waves
come slamming whopping in,
sometimes it's like they mean to smash
this no-good world to hell.

Well, it could happen. A book I read—
Crossed that very ocean years ago.   30
London, Paris, Rome,
Constantinople too—I've seen them all.

Back when they billed me everywhere
as the Sepia High Stepper.
Crowned heads applauded me.
Years before your time. Years and years.

I wore me plenty diamonds then,
and counts or dukes or whatever they were
would fill my dressing room
with the costliest flowers. But of course   40

there was this one you resemble so.
Get me? The sweetest gentleman.
Dead before his time. Killed in the war
to save the world for another war.

High-stepping days for me
were over after that. Still I'm not one
to let grief idle me for long.
I went out with a mental act—

mind-reading—Mysteria From
The Mystic East—veils and beads   50
and telling suckers how to get
stolen rings and sweethearts back.

One night he was standing by my bed,
seen him plain as I see you,
and warned me without a single word:
Baby, quit playing with spiritual stuff.

So here I am, so here I am,
fake mammy to God's mistakes.
And that's the beauty part,
I mean, ain't that the beauty part.   60

She laughs, but I do not, knowing what
her laughter shields. And mocks.
I light another cigarette for her.
She smokes, not saying any more.

Scream of children in the surf,
adagios of sun and flashing foam,
the sexual glitter and oppressive fun. . . .
An antique etching comes to mind:

"The Sable Venus" naked on
a baroque Cellini shell—voluptuous   70
imago floating in the wake
of slave-ships on fantastic seas.

Jemima sighs, Reckon I'd best
be getting back. I help her up.
Don't you take no wooden nickels, hear?
Tin dimes neither. So long, pal.

(1970)

Peter Wild

Death of a Cat on Rt. 84

Wounded in the middle of the road
she clung to the warm pavement,
biting her tongue,
          the icy stars

eating into the back of her head.
at 4 A. M.
      the cold and black vacuum
of the desert
          moving alongside me,
windshield smeared with the guts   10
    of mayflies and spots of rain,
the black road standing still;
I clobbered her
      at sixty-five miles an hour
seeing her, too quick,
  a wind-blown rag
         near the center line,
she struggling up into the light
      to heal her broken flesh
and didn't jar the wheel.   20
the desert, cold and black,
    moved along with me,
beyond the Galiuros
    the night enflamed with lightning.

                (*1968*)

Laurence Lieberman

The Unblinding

(For my student, upon the anniversary of the operation that restored his sight)

When I think of my fear
of moving through my dreamed
life into the tough, unknown, real
images that burn my senses and mind
more fiercely than human
events that stick

in the craw of biographies,
when I shy away
from the incandescent moments that fall
into my hands unsought, un-   10
deservedly given or lent
to me, visions,

so to say, that can—and do
on occasion—sweep me off into their own
orbits, shattering my known self
into ill-fitting puzzle
pieces, and grinding
each fragment to smithereens,

leaving me numb to objects,
to the feel of a thing, to all identities   20
clogged, hopelessly blocked, I find
I try again, taught
by my student, Robert Beegle,
who was here today

leaning sail on a puff
of wind five thousand miles out from Cal-
ifornia to say hello   here
I am   fully bearded   one hundred years
younger than the eighteen-year-old
death-of-me you met   30

two years ago   Mr. Lieberman.
And it is true.
He has grown younger more quickly
than anyone old I have
known. When I first
fastened my twenty-twenty two eyes on two

totally blinded at age
four in a traffic
mishap, two stillborn egg yolks
immobile in vacant   40
sockets, I saw a being sunk
within and drilling

deeper, as the innermost rings
in the trunk of a withered
sycamore, dying inward.
In the front row
next to the door (at his feet, the seeing-
eye German shepherd, head

on his paws, licking
and snuffling toward bell-time,   50
often mistaking a distant horn or whistle

for the hour-gong), the handicapped
listener shivered his lips
to decipher braille

that flew past shortwave
of fingertips,
the lips racing to overtake the fingers,
casting about within for broken
tape-ends of emotions
straggling from reels of earliest   60

childhood. I felt my eyes
clamber into hollowness, opening
in him like a bottomless
pit. Once exposed, it overflowed his face
and spread around the class,
like a skin

tightening. We could not breathe.
He shut his eyes.
Words failed—our voices
drawn into declivities of his nose   70
and mouth—
the room becoming an abyss

over which we teetered
dizzily. I looked and looked. Where
I had seen clearly
before grew blind spots
now. I saw too near,
too far, sight

locked. I had
to try not to see him,   80
to lay violent hands upon the light,
to make it bend
around his chair and twist
over his clenched,

sight-slaying face.
My skull bones grew
in weight,
converging on the delicate
flesh of eyeballs. Then, for days,
I walked shakily,   90

one foot stretched
before me, hunting anchorage (safe
lodging) like the tip of a white
cane, tapping. . . . One morning, I glanced
about, dazedly—he stood
beside me, no one

I had ever seen before
outside his dog's
life, extending the pink absence slip
for my O.K. I saw (powerless   100
to believe) he saw my face,
smiling his first

look of me, the words
loosening from his tongue
as sparrows from a shaken clothesline.
One flick of a surgeon's knife
struck long-idle retinas
into perfect sight.

(1967)

Thom Gunn

Black Jackets

In the silence that prolongs the span
Rawly of music when the record ends,
  The red-haired boy who drove a van
In weekday overalls but, like his friends,

  Wore cycle boots and jacket here
To suit the Sunday hangout he was in,
  Heard, as he stretched back from his beer,
Leather creak softly round his neck and chin.

  Before him, on a coal-black sleeve
Remote exertion had lined, scratched, and
      burned   10
  Insignia that could not revive
The heroic fall or climb where they were earned.

On the other drinkers bent together,
Concocting selves for their impervious kit,
   He saw it as no more than leather
Which, taut across the shoulders grown to it,

   Sent through the dimness of a bar
As sudden and anonymous hints of light
   As those that shipping give, that are
Now flickers in the Bay, now lost in night.   20

   He stretched out like a cat, and rolled
The bitterish taste of beer upon his tongue,
   And listened to a joke being told:
The present was the things he stayed among.

   If it was only loss he wore,
He wore it to assert, with fierce devotion,
   Complicity and nothing more.
He recollected his initiation,

   And one especially of the rites.
For on his shoulders they had put tattoos: 30
   The group's name on the left, The Knights,
And on the right the slogan Born To Lose.
                               (1958)

Kingsley Amis

A Dream of Fair Women

The door still swinging to, and girls revive,
Aeronauts in the utmost altitudes
   Of boredom fainting, dive
In the bright oxygen of my nod;
Angels as well, a squadron of draped nudes,
   They roar towards their god.

Militant all, they fight to take my hat,
No more as yet; the other men retire
   Insulted, gestured at;
Each girl presses on me her share of what   10
Makes up the barn-door target of desire:
   And I am a crack shot.

Speech fails them, amorous, but each one's
   look,
Endorsed in other ways, begs me to sign
   Her body's autograph-book;
"Me first, Kingsley; I'm cleverest" each declares,
But no gourmet races downstairs to dine,
   Nor will I race upstairs.

Feigning aplomb, perhaps for half an hour,
I hover, and am shown by each princess   20
   The entrance to her tower;
Open, in that its tenant throws the key
At once to anyone, but not unless
   The anyone is me.

Now from the corridor their fathers cheer,
Their brothers, their young men; the cheers
   increase
   As soon as I appear;
From each I win a handshake and sincere
Congratulations; from the chief of police
   A nod, a wink, a leer.   30

This over, all delay is over too;
The first eight girls (the roster now agreed)
   Leap on me, and undo . . .
But honesty impels me to confess
That this is 'all a dream', which was, indeed,
   Not difficult to guess.

But wait; not 'just a dream', because, though
   good
And beautiful, it is also true, and hence
   Is rarely understood;
Who would choose any feasible ideal   40
In here and now's giant circumference,
   If that small room were real?

Only the best; the others find, have found
Love's ordinary distances too great,
   And eager, stand their ground;
Map-drunk explorers, dry-land sailors, they
See no arrival that can compensate
   For boredom on the way;

And, seeming doctrinaire, but really weak,
Limelighted dolls guttering in their brain,   50
  They come with me, to seek
The halls of theoretical delight,
The women of that ever-fresh terrain,
  The night after to-night.

(*1956*)

David Ignatow

The News Photo

This idiot had suffered his own faults,
but since it was this country
and he had done a thing beyond himself,
by the axe, and since it was an act
that could be called public,
in the interest of the public to be known,
he was to be shown in this act,
in its way instructive: they had been his parents
and he had tried not to,
shouting at them to beware, as they slept;   10
he had wept, and since in this manner
he had cleansed himself,
he could grin for his picture.

(*1955*)

Howard Moss

The Gift to Be Simple

Breathing something German at the end,
Which no one understood, he died, a friend,
  Or so he meant to be, to all of us.
  Only the stars defined his radius;
His life, restricted to a wooden house,

Was in his head. He saw a fledgling fall.
  Two times he tried to nest it, but it fell
  Once more, and died; he wandered home
    again—
  We save so plain a story for great men.
    An angel in ill-fitting sweaters,   10
    Writing children naive letters,
  A violin player lacking vanities,
  A giant wit among the homilies—
We have no parallel to that immense
    Intelligence.

But if he were remembered for the Bomb,
As some may well remember him, such a tomb,
  For one who hated violence and ceremony
  Equally, would be a wasted irony.
He flew to formal heavens from his perch,   20
A scientist become his own research,
  And even if the flames were never gold
  That lapped his body to an ash gone cold,
  Even if his death no trumpets tolled,
    There is enough of myth inside the truth
    To make a monument to fit him with;
  And since the universe is in a jar,
  There is no weeping where his heavens are,
And I would remember, now the world is less,
    His gentleness.   30

(*1955*)

Scharmel Iris

A Poem

A poem is a magic thing—
It must be lucid, it should sing.
A cry that cuts the heart in two
Needs be true.
If it has a golden ring,
A poem is a magic thing—
It will sing.

(*1953*)

Robinson Jeffers

The Inquisitors

Coming around a corner of the dark trail . . .
    what was wrong with the valley?
Azevedo checked his horse and sat staring: it
    was all changed. It was occupied. There
    were three hills
Where none had been: and firelight flickered
    red on their knees between them: if
    they were hills:
They were more like Red Indians around a
    camp-fire grave and dark, mountain-high,
    hams on heels
Squating around a little fire of hundred-foot
    logs. Azevedo remembers he felt an
    ice-brook
Glide on his spine; he slipped down from the
    saddle and hid
In the brush by the trail, above the black
    redwood forest. There was the Little
    Sur South Fork,
Its forest valley; the man had come in at nightfall
    over Bowcher's Gap, and a high moon
    hunted
Through running clouds. He heard the rumble
    of a voice, heavy not loud, saying,
    "I gathered some,
You can inspect them." One of the hills moved
    a huge hand   10
And poured its contents on a table-topped rock
    that stood in the firelight; men and
    women fell out;
Some crawled and some lay quiet; the hills
    leaned to eye them. One said: "It seems
    hardly possible
Such fragile creatures could be so noxious."
    Another answered,
"True, but we've seen. But it is only recently
    they have the power." The third
    answered, "That bomb?"
"Oh," he said, "—and the rest." He reached
    across and picked up one of the mites
    from the rock, and held it

Close to his eyes, and very carefully with finger
    and thumbnail peeled it: by chance a
    young female
With long black hair: it was too helpless even
    to scream. He held it by one white leg
    and stared at it:
"I can see nothing strange: only so fragile."
    The third hill answered, "We suppose it
    is something
Inside the head." Then the other split the skull
    with his thumbnail, squinting his eyes
    and peering, and said,
"A drop of marrow. How could that spoil the
    earth?" "Nevertheless," he answered,   20
"They have that bomb. The blasts and the fires
    are nothing: freckles on the earth: the
    emanations
Might set the whole planet into a tricky fever
And destroy much." "Themselves," he answered.
    "Let them. Why not?" "No," he
    answered, "life."

                        (1948)

E. E. Cummings

anyone lived in a pretty how town

anyone lived in a pretty how town
(with up so floating many bells down)
spring summer autumn winter
he sang his didn't he danced his did.

Women and men (both little and small)
cared for anyone not at all
they sowed their isn't they reaped their same
sun moon stars rain

children guessed (but only a few
and down they forgot as up they grew   10
autumn winter spring summer)
that noone loved him more by more

when by now and tree by leaf
she laughed his joy she cried his grief
bird by snow and stir by still
anyone's any was all to her

someones married their everyones
laughed their cryings and did their dance
(sleep wake hope and then) they
said their nevers they slept their dream   20

stars rain sun moon
(and only the snow can begin to explain
how children are apt to forget to remember
with up so floating many bells down)

one day anyone died i guess
(and noone stooped to kiss his face)
busy folk buried them side by side
little by little and was by was

all by all and deep by deep
and more by more they dream their sleep   30
noone and anyone earth by april
wish by spirit and if by yes.

Woman and men (both dong and ding)
summer autumn winter spring
reaped their sowing and went their came
sun moon stars rain

                              (*1940*)

Henry Reed

Naming of Parts

Today we have naming of parts. Yesterday,
We had daily cleaning. And tomorrow morning,
We shall have what to do after firing. But
          today,
Today we have naming of parts. Japonica
Glistens like coral in all of the neighboring
          gardens,
          And today we have naming of parts.

This is the lower sling swivel. And this
Is the upper sling swivel, whose use you will
          see,
When you are given your slings. And this is
          the piling swivel,
Which in your case you have not got. The
          branches   10
Hold in the gardens their silent, eloquent
          gestures,
          Which in our case we have not got.

This is the safety-catch, which is always released
With an easy flick of the thumb. And please do
          not let me
See anyone using his finger. You can do it
          quite easy
If you have any strength in your thumb. The
          blossoms
Are fragile and motionless, never letting anyone
          see
          Any of them using their finger.

And this you can see is the bolt. The purpose of
          this
Is to open the breech, as you see. We can slide it
Rapidly backwards and forwards: we call this   21
Easing the spring. And rapidly backwards and
          forwards
The early bees are assaulting and fumbling the
          flowers:
          They call it easing the Spring.

They call it easing the Spring: it is perfectly
          easy
If you have any strength in your thumb: like
          the bolt,
And the breech, and the cocking-piece, and the
          point of balance,
Which in our case we have not got; and the
          almond-blossom
Silent in all of the gardens and the bees going
          backwards and forwards,
          For today we have naming of parts.   30
                              (*1942*)

Karl Shapiro

Auto Wreck

Its quick soft silver bell beating, beating
And down the dark one ruby flare
Pulsing out red light like an artery,
The ambulance at top speed floating down
Past beacons and illuminated clocks
Wings in a heavy curve, dips down,
And brakes speed, entering the crowd.
The doors leap open, emptying light;
Stretchers are laid out, the mangled lifted
And stowed into the little hospital.   10
Then the bell, breaking the hush, tolls once,
And the ambulance with its terrible cargo
Rocking, slightly rocking, moves away,
As the doors, an afterthought, are closed.

We are deranged, walking among the cops
Who sweep glass and are large and composed.
One is still making notes under the light.
One with a bucket douches ponds of blood
Into the street and gutter.
One hangs lanterns on the wrecks that cling,   20
Empty husks of locusts, to iron poles.

Our throats were tight as tourniquets,
Our feet were bound with splints, but now
Like convalescents intimate and gauche,
We speak through sickly smiles and warn
With the stubborn saw of common sense,
The grim joke and the banal resolution.
The traffic moves around with care,
But we remain, touching a wound
That opens to our richest horror.   30

Already old, the question Who shall die?
Becomes unspoken Who is innocent?
For death in war is done by hands;
Suicide has cause and stillbirth, logic.
But this invites the occult mind,

Cancels our physics with a sneer,
And spatters all we knew of dénouement
Across the expedient and wicked stones.

(1942)

Karl Shapiro

The Dirty Word

The dirty word hops in the cage of the mind like the Pondicherry vulture, stomping with its heavy left claw on the sweet meat of the brain and tearing it with its vicious beak, ripping and chopping the flesh. Terrified, the small boy bears the big bird of the dirty word into the house, and grunting, puffing, carries it up the stairs to his own room in the skull. Bits of black feather cling to his clothes and his hair as he locks the staring creature in the dark closet.   10

All day the small boy returns to the closet to examine and feed the bird, to caress and kick the bird, that now snaps and flaps its wings savagely whenever the door is opened. How the boy trembles and delights at the sight of the white excrement of the bird! How the bird leaps and rushes against the walls of the skull, trying to escape from the zoo of the vocabulary! How wildly snaps the sweet meat of the brain in its rage.   20

And the bird outlives the man, being freed at the man's death-funeral by a word from the rabbi.

(But I one morning went upstairs and opened the door and entered the closet and found in the cage of my mind the great bird dead. Softly I wept it and softly removed it and softly buried the body of the bird in the hollyhock garden of the house I lived in twenty years before. And out of the worn black feathers of the wing have I made these pens to write these elegies, for I have outlived 30
the bird, and I have murdered it in my early manhood.)

(1942)

W. H. Auden

Paysage Moralisé

Hearing of harvests rotting in the valleys,
Seeing at end of street the barren mountains,
Round corners coming suddenly on water,
Knowing them shipwrecked who were launched
    for islands,
We honour founders of these starving cities
Whose honour is the image of our sorrow,

Which cannot see its likeness in their sorrow
That brought them desperate to the brink of
    valleys;
Dreaming of evening walks through learned
    cities
They reined their violent horses on the
    mountains,   10
Those fields like ships to castaways on islands,
Visions of green to them who craved for water.

They built by rivers and at night the water
Running past windows comforted their sorrow;
Each in his little bed conceived of islands
Where every day was dancing in the valleys
And all the green trees blossomed on the
    mountains,
Where love was innocent, being far from cities.

But dawn came back and they were still in
    cities;
No marvellous creature rose up from the water; 20
There was still gold and silver in the mountains
But hunger was a more immediate sorrow,
Although to moping villages in valleys
Some waving pilgrims were describing islands . . .

'The gods,' they promised, 'visit us from islands,
Are stalking, head-up, lovely, through our
    cities;
Now is the time to leave your wretched valleys

And sail with them across the lime-green water,
Sitting at their white sides, forget your sorrow,
The shadow cast across your lives by
    mountains.'   30

So many, doubtful, perished in the mountains,
Climbing up crags to get a view of islands,
So many, fearful, took with them their sorrow
Which stayed them when they reached unhappy
    cities,
So many, careless, dived and drowned in water,
So many, wretched, would not leave their
    valleys.

It is our sorrow. Shall it melt? Then water
Would gush, flush, green these mountains and
    these valleys,
And we rebuild our cities, not dream of
    islands.

                         (*1933*)

Roy Campbell

The Zebras

From the dark woods that breathe of fallen
    showers,
Harnessed with level rays in golden reins,
The zebras draw the dawn across the plains
Wading knee-deep among the scarlet flowers.
The sunlight, zithering their flanks with fire,
Flashes between the shadows as they pass
Barred with electric tremors through the grass
Like wind along the gold strings of a lyre.
Into the flushed air snorting rosy plumes
That smoulder round their feet in drifting
    fumes,   10
With dove-like voices call the distant fillies,
While round the herds the stallion wheels his
    flight,
Engine of beauty volted with delight,
To roll his mare among the trampled lilies.

                         (*1928*)

Wallace Stevens

Peter Quince at the Clavier

I

Just as my fingers on these keys
Make music, so the selfsame sounds
On my spirit make a music, too.

Music is feeling, then, not sound;
And thus it is that what I feel,
Here in this room, desiring you,

Thinking of your blue-shadowed silk,
Is music. It is like the strain
Waked in the elders by Susanna.

Of a green evening, clear and warm,   10
She bathed in her still garden, while
The red-eyed elders watching, felt

The basses of their beings throb
In witching chords, and their thin blood
Pulse pizzicati of Hosanna.

II

In the green water, clear and warm,
Susanna lay.
She searched
The touch of springs,
And found   20
Concealed imaginings.
She sighed,
For so much melody.

Upon the bank, she stood
In the cool
Of spent emotions.
She felt, among the leaves,
The dew
Of old devotions.

She walked upon the grass,   30
Still quavering.
The winds were like her maids,

On timid feet,
Fetching her woven scarves,
Yet wavering.

A breath upon her hand
Muted the night.
She turned—
A cymbal crashed,
And roaring horns.   40

III

Soon, with a noise like tambourines,
Came her attendant Byzantines.

They wondered why Susanna cried
Against the elders by her side;

And as they whispered, the refrain
Was like a willow swept by rain.

Anon, their lamps' uplifted flame
Revealed Susanna and her shame.

And then, the simpering Byzantines
Fled, with a noise like tambourines.   50

IV

Beauty is momentary in the mind—
The fitful tracing of a portal;
But in the flesh it is immortal.
The body dies; the body's beauty lives.
So evenings die, in their green going,
A wave, interminably flowing.
So gardens die, their meek breath scenting
The cowl of winter, done repenting.
So maidens die, to the auroral
Celebration of a maiden's choral.   60
Susanna's music touched the bawdy strings
Of those white elders; but, escaping,
Left only Death's ironic scraping.
Now, in its immortality, it plays
On the clear viol of her memory,
And makes a constant sacrament of praise.

(1915)

T. S. Eliot

The Love Song of J. Alfred Prufrock

S'io credesse che mia risposta fosse
A persona che mai tornasse al mondo,
Questa fiamma staria senza piu scosse.
Ma perciocche giammai di questo fondo
Non torno vivo alcun, s'i'odo il vero
Senza tema d'infamia ti rispondo.

Let us go then, you and I,
When the evening is spread out against the sky
Like a patient etherised upon a table;
Let us go, through certain half-deserted streets,
The muttering retreats
Of restless nights in one-night cheap hotels
And sawdust restaurants with oyster-shells:
Streets that follow like a tedious argument
Of insidious intent
To lead you to an overwhelming question . . .   10
Oh, do not ask, "What is it?"
Let us go and make our visit.

In the room the women come and go
Talking of Michelangelo.

The yellow fog that rubs its back upon the
    window-panes,
The yellow smoke that rubs its muzzle on the
    window-panes
Licked its tongue into the corners of the evening,
Lingered upon the pools that stand in drains,
Let fall upon its back the soot that falls from
    chimneys,
Slipped by the terrace, made a sudden leap,   20
And seeing that it was a soft October night,
Curled once about the house, and fell asleep.

S'io . . . rispondo: a damned soul in Dante's *Inferno*, Guido
da Montefeltro, replies to a questioning of his name in
these words—"If I thought my reply were being addressed
to one who might return to the living earth, this flame
would quiver no more [*i.e.*, the spirit would not talk].
But since no one alive goes back from this depth, if what
I hear be true, then without fear of infamy I answer you."

And indeed there will be time
For the yellow smoke that slides along the
    street,
Rubbing its back upon the window-panes;
There will be time, there will be time
To prepare a face to meet the faces that you
    meet;
There will be time to murder and create,
And time for all the works and days of hands
That lift and drop a question on your plate;   30
Time for you and time for me,
And time yet for a hundred indecisions,
And for a hundred visions and revisions,
Before the taking of a toast and tea.

In the room the women come and go
Talking of Michelangelo.

And indeed there will be time
To wonder, "Do I dare?" and, "Do I dare?"
Time to turn back and descend the stair,
With a bald spot in the middle of my hair—   40
(They will say: "How his hair is growing thin!")
My morning coat, my collar mounting firmly
    to the chin,
My necktie rich and modest, but asserted by a
    simple pin—
(They will say: "But how his arms and legs are
    thin!")
Do I dare
Disturb the universe?
In a minute there is time
For decisions and revisions which a minute will
    reverse.

For I have known them all already, known them
    all:
Have known the evenings, mornings,
    afternoons,   50
I have measured out my life with coffee spoons;
I know the voices dying with a dying fall
Beneath the music from a farther room.
   So how should I presume?

And I have known the eyes already, known
     them all—
The eyes that fix you in a formulated phrase,
And when I am formulated, sprawling on a pin,
When I am pinned and wriggling on the wall,
Then how should I begin
To spit out all the butt-ends of my days and
     ways?   60
     And how should I presume?

And I have known the arms already, known
     them all—
Arms that are braceleted and white and bare
(But in the lamplight, downed with light brown
     hair!)
Is it perfume from a dress
That makes me so digress?
Arms that lie along a table, or wrap about a shawl.
     And should I then presume?
     And how should I begin?

. . . .

Shall I say, I have gone at dusk through narrow
     streets   70
And watched the smoke that rises from the pipes
Of lonely men in shirt-sleeves, leaning out of
     windows? . . .

I should have been a pair of ragged claws
Scuttling across the floors of silent seas.

. . . .

And the afternoon, the evening, sleeps so
     peacefully!
Smoothed by long fingers,
Asleep . . . tired . . . or it malingers,
Stretched on the floor, here beside you and me.
Should I, after tea and cakes and ices,
Have the strength to force the moment to its
     crisis?   80
But though I have wept and fasted, wept and
     prayed,
Though I have seen my head (grown slightly
     bald) brought in upon a platter,

I am no prophet—and here's no great matter;
I have seen the moment of my greatness flicker,
And I have seen the eternal Footman hold my
     coat, and snicker,
And in short, I was afraid.

And would it have been worth it, after all,
After the cups, the marmalade, the tea,
Among the porcelain, among some talk of you
     and me,
Would it have been worth while,   90
To have bitten off the matter with a smile,
To have squeezed the universe into a ball
To roll it toward some overwhelming question,
To say: "I am Lazarus, come from the dead,
Come back to tell you all, I shall tell you all"—
If one, settling a pillow by her head,
     Should say: "That is not what I meant at all;
     That is not it, at all."

And would it have been worth it, after all,
Would it have been worth while,   100
After the sunsets and the dooryards and the
     sprinkled streets,
After the novels, after the teacups, after the
     skirts that trail along the floor—
And this, and so much more?—
It is impossible to say just what I mean!
But as if a magic lantern threw the nerves in
     patterns on a screen:
Would it have been worth while
If one, settling a pillow or throwing off a
     shawl,
And turning toward the window, should say:
     "That is not it at all,
     That is not what I meant, at all."   110

No! I am not Prince Hamlet, nor was meant to
     be;
Am an attendant lord, one that will do
To swell a progress, start a scene or two,
Advise the prince; no doubt, an easy tool,
Deferential, glad to be of use,
Politic, cautious, and meticulous;

Full of high sentence, but a bit obtuse;
At times, indeed, almost ridiculous—
Almost, at times, the Fool.

I grow old . . . I grow old . . . 120
I shall wear the bottoms of my trousers rolled.
Shall I part my hair behind? Do I dare to eat
    a peach?
I shall wear white flannel trousers, and walk
    upon the beach.
I have heard the mermaids singing, each to each.

I do not think that they will sing to me.

I have seen them riding seaward on the waves
Combing the white hair of the waves blown
    back
When the wind blows the water white and
    black.

We have lingered in the chambers of the sea
By sea-girls wreathed with seaweed red and
    brown 130
Till human voices wake us, and we drown.
                   (*1915*)

Robert Frost

After Apple-Picking

My long two-pointed ladder's sticking through
    a tree
Toward heaven still,
And there's a barrel that I didn't fill
Beside it, and there may be two or three
Apples I didn't pick upon some bough.
But I am done with apple-picking now.
Essence of winter sleep is on the night,
The scent of apples: I am drowsing off.
I cannot rub the strangeness from my sight
I got from looking through a pane of glass 10
I skimmed this morning from the drinking
    trough

And held against the world of hoary grass.
It melted, and I let it fall and break.
But I was well
Upon my way to sleep before it fell,
And I could tell
What form my dreaming was about to take.
Magnified apples appear and disappear,
Stem end and blossom end,
And every fleck of russet showing clear. 20
My instep arch not only keeps the ache,
It keeps the pressure of a ladder-round.
I feel the ladder sway as the boughs bend.
And I keep hearing from the cellar bin
The rumbling sound
Of load on load of apples coming in.
For I have had too much
Of apple-picking: I am overtired
Of the great harvest I myself desired.
There were ten thousand thousand fruit to
    touch, 30
Cherish in hand, lift down, and not let fall.
For all
That struck the earth,
No matter if not bruised or spiked with stubble,
Went surely to the cider-apple heap
As of no worth.
One can see what will trouble
This sleep of mine, whatever sleep it is.
Were he not gone,
The woodchuck could say whether it's like his 40
Long sleep, as I describe its coming on,
Or just some human sleep.
                   (*1914*)

Thomas Hardy

The Convergence of the Twain

(*Lines on the loss of the "Titanic"*)

    In a solitude of the sea
      Deep from human vanity,
And the Pride of Life that planned her, stilly
    couches she.

Steel chambers, late the pyres
  Of her salamandrine fires,
Cold currents thrid, and turn to rhythmic tidal
    lyres.

   Over the mirrors meant
    To glass the opulent
The sea-worm crawls—grotesque, slimed,
    dumb, indifferent.

   Jewels in joy designed   10
    To ravish the sensuous mind
Lie lightless, all their sparkles bleared and black
    and blind.

   Dim moon-eyed fishes near
    Gaze at the gilded gear
And query: 'What does this vaingloriousness
    down here?'

   Well: while was fashioning
    This creature of cleaving wing,
The Immanent Will that stirs and urges
    everything

   Prepared a sinister mate
    For her—so gaily great—   20
A Shape of Ice, for the time far and dissociate.

   And as the smart ship grew
    In stature, grace, and hue,
In shadowy silent distance grew the Iceberg too.

   Alien they seemed to be:
    No mortal eye could see
The intimate welding of their later history.

   Or sign that they were bent
    By paths coincident
On being anon twin halves of one august
    event,   30

   Till the Spinner of the Years
    Said 'Now!' And each one hears,
And consummation comes, and jars two
    hemispheres.

                  (1912)

John Donne

The Flea

Mark but this flea, and mark in this,
How little that which thou deny'st me is;
It sucked me first, and now sucks thee,
And in this flea our two bloods mingled be;
Thou know'st that this cannot be said
A sin, nor shame, nor loss of maidenhead;
    Yet this enjoys before it woo,
      And pampered swells with one blood made
        of two,
    And this, alas, is more than we would do.

Oh stay, three lives in one flea spare,   10
Where we almost, yea, more than married are.
This flea is you and I, and this
Our marriage bed, and marriage temple is;
Though parents grudge, and you, w' are met,
And cloistered in these living walls of jet.
    Though use make you apt to kill me,
    Let not to that, self-murder added be,
    And sacrilege, three sins in killing three.

Cruel and sudden, hast thou since
Purpled thy nail in blood of innocence?   20
Wherein could this flea guilty be,
Except in that drop which it sucked from thee?
Yet thou triumph'st and say'st that thou
Find'st not thyself, nor me the weaker now;
    'Tis true, then learn how false fears be:
    Just so much honor, when thou yield'st to
      me,
    Will waste, as this flea's death took life from
      thee.

                  (1633)

William Shakespeare

When That I Was and a Little Tiny Boy

When that I was and a little tiny boy,
   With hey, ho, the wind and the rain,
A foolish thing was but a toy,
   For the rain it raineth every day.

But when I came to man's estate
   With hey, ho, the wind and the rain,
'Gainst knaves and thieves men shut the gate,
   For the rain it raineth every day.

But when I came, alas! to wive,
   With hey, ho, the wind and the rain,   10
By swaggering could I never thrive,
   For the rain it raineth every day.

But when I came unto my beds,
   With hey, ho, the wind and the rain,
With toss-pots still had drunken heads,
   For the rain it raineth every day.

A great while ago the world begun,
   With hey, ho, the wind and the rain,
But that's all one, our play is done,
   And we'll strive to please you every day.   20

                 (1623)

EXERCISES

"Aunt Jemima of the Ocean Waves" [Hayden]

1. Notice that the first two stanzas of this poem commence with images of a freak show. Considering the oddities of each freak, why does the "I" or persona of the poem feel a kinship with them, "pondering the logic that makes of them/(and me) confederates" (lines 6–7)?

2. Where is the persona as the second part of the poem commences? Why is the setting important for the dramatic dialogue which follows between him and the woman who has played the role of "Aunt Jemima" in the freak show? What details of her experience emerge from their conversation, and how do they let the reader know what kind of person Aunt Jemima is? Is her tone flirtatious? disillusioned? angry? vivid with happy memories? meditative and philosophical? or a combination of all these? How do you interpret the lines, "So here I am, so here I am,/fake mammy to God's mistakes" (lines 57–58)?

3. Do you discern a kind of mystic presence of a third person in the poem? If so, who is he and what was his relationship to Aunt Jemima?

4. Notice that Aunt Jemima laughs after relating her story, but the persona does not, "knowing what/her laughter shields" and "mocks" (lines 61–62). How do you interpret his reaction to Aunt Jemima's story? Do you find any hint of his attitude in the last three stanzas? Discuss.

5. Finally, what is the purpose of the conversational banter in the final stanza? How does its tone affect the meaning of the poem? Is the overall effect of the last stanza to lend a familiar balance to more subtle, introspective ironies revealed elsewhere in the poem?

"Black Jackets" [Gunn]

6. What Thom Gunn terms a "Sunday hangout" is the setting for his poem "Black Jackets." The poet virtually bombards the reader with sense images in describing the atmosphere and the character of "The red-haired boy

who drove a van/In weekday overalls" (lines 3–4). What sense responses are stirred by "silence" and "music" in the first two lines; "stretched back from his beer" and "Leather creak softly" in the second stanza; "lined, scratched, and burned" in the third stanza? Similarly what visual images do you find in the fifth stanza? What images of taste and sound in the seventh stanza? How do setting and atmosphere, combined with sensuous images, help to explain meaning in the final stanzas—especially meaning inherent in "fierce devotion," "Complicity," and the red-haired boy's "initiation"? What ironies do you see in the tattoos of "The Knights" and "Born To Lose"?

7. Do you see obvious similarities between this poem and Thom Gunn's "On the Move" (see p. 109)? What are the differences? Discuss.

"The Unblinding" [Lieberman]

8. Laurence Lieberman's poem is unusual in that the poet himself is the frankly admitted persona. Read the first four stanzas closely. When, or upon what kind of occasions, does Mr. Lieberman remember his student who taught him something? Describe this student, Robert Beegle, as he appeared to Mr. Lieberman when for the first time he "fastened" his "twenty-twenty two eyes" on him (line 36). What moods of inner conflict are produced by this image? By stating, "I had/to try not to see him,/to lay violent hands upon the light" (lines 79–81), does Mr. Lieberman give vent to his own sense of frustration in helping his blind student to perceive as others do? What other images add to this tone of frustration?

9. What effect is achieved by stating that one morning he saw his student "outside his dog's/life, extending the pink absence slip/for my O.K." (lines 98–100)? Why is this kind of indirection more effective than simply stating, "He saw"? In the same way, why are Robert Beegle's words perceived of by his teacher as "loosening from his tongue/as sparrows from a shaken clothesline" (lines 104–105)?

10. Can you describe in your own words how this poem helps one to understand the plight of those caught in circumstances less fortunate than our own? Can you go a step farther and express how the poem affects your own attitudes, if it does? Discuss.

"A Dream of Fair Women" [Amis]

11. How do you explain the first six stanzas of this poem, for surely the reader's response must be, "All this cannot be happening!" Notice that the poet uses such terms as "Aeronauts" in the first stanza as well as "Angels." From the dreamlike state, what is the position of the "I" or persona in the first stanza (relate to the lines, "a squadron of draped nudes,/They roar towards their god"—lines 5–6)?

12. The images in this poem are not only graphic, but also sexually suggestive. Explore such images as they suggest meanings. Consider the feminine body as an "autograph-book" to be signed (third stanza); the male lover as a "gourmet"; the feminine image of "entrance to her tower" and "key" (fourth stanza); the significance of congratulations given the lover from the most unlikely of sources—the families of the girls and "A nod, a wink, a leer" from the chief of police (fifth stanza); then, at the height of fantasy the admission of a dream rather than reality (stanzas six and seven).

13. Considering the last three stanzas, what has been the purpose of the graphic dream, and the poet's voice, as it were, insisting that the dream is "good," "beautiful," and "also true" (how can the dream be "true"?) though "rarely understood"? Why does the poet contend that "Only the best" would choose instead a reasonable hope ("any feasible ideal") or ambition if such a room with such girls were "real"? Then how can it be that such dreams are indeed good, beautiful, and true? Consider in your answer how the "Lime-lighted dolls guttering in their brain" and the "halls of theoretical delight" bespeak the reality of most men's hopes for love that remain unfulfilled? How are such

men "really weak" although "seeming doctrinaire"? Does the poet, then, probe for our hidden secrets and help us to acknowledge them? Discuss.

14. In what ways do you discern correspondences between Kingsley Amis' "A Dream of Fair Women" and Henry Reed's "Naming of Parts"? Is Reed's poem also symbolical and suggestive of a level of reality that lies beneath the literal surface? The literal surfaces of the two poems obviously differ, and you might note them; but how are the portions that ladder down into our secret wishes and fantasies similar? Discuss.

"*The News Photo*" [Ignatow], "*Auto Wreck*" [Shapiro], "*The Dirty Word*" [Shapiro], and "*The Zebras*" [Campbell]

15. Several of the poems in this section are short and create a powerful impact through a variety of poetic devices. Consider first David Ignatow's "The News Photo," particularly its reportorial tone. In the idiot's having "done a thing beyond himself" (line 3) with an axe we are prepared for the shock, but the conclusion of the poem, with its emphasis on public interest and "The News Photo" itself nearly forces the reader into a prolonged, yet strangely neutral, horror. How do you react to this poem? What effects has the poet produced by the indirection of his statement (irony)? Has he stirred you, for example, to imagine what the photo would be like? Discuss.

16. Compare the tone of Ignatow's poem to that of Karl Shapiro's in "Auto Wreck," noting similarities. For example, what images produce shock and horror? How is the tone prolonged beyond the first stanzas? What indirections add to the tone, and what are the ironies? Discuss differences between the two poems— for example, Shapiro's conclusion is clearly more direct and philosophical than Ignatow's. How is it that the poet can find a kind of logic even in war, suicide, and stillbirth, and yet can find no such rationalizations in an automobile wreck? Discuss.

17. Emotive response to Karl Shapiro's "The Dirty Word" may include shock also. How does the poet relate profanity to childhood, adolescence, man in rage, and man at death? The final stanza is summarizational, is it not? How do you interpret the death of the "Pondicherry vulture" of the "dirty word" as treated by the poet in the final stanza, his response to the death of the bird, his use of its black wing feathers for "pens to write these elegies," and his contention that he has "outlived the bird," having "murdered it in my early manhood"? Explain your answer.

18. "The Zebras," an Italian sonnet by Roy Campbell, may also be termed a poem of shock, but the response of the reader varies widely from that of other poems treated in this question. How do the profuse images, rich in color and sensuosity, create a distinctly different kind of emotional impact? How does the form of the poem with its patterned rhyme and such lines as that describing the zebra stallion, "Engine of beauty volted with delight" (line 13), summarize the poet's attitude toward his subject and reader?

"*The Gift to Be Simple*" [Moss], "*Peter Quince at the Clavier*" [Stevens], and "*Convergence of the Twain*" [Hardy]

19. These three poems are based upon historical events or real people. What each poet has to say about his reaction to the situation is complex and will require more than a single observation. First, consider Howard Moss' "The Gift to Be Simple." What lines suggest the different ways he feels toward the death of Albert Einstein? his influence upon people all over the world from the most innocent to the most renowned? the contrasts between his great achievement and his humble personal life? How do the last few lines summarize the poet's ultimate feeling? What is the connection between the title and the body of the poem? Can you relate this poem in any way (perhaps by contrast) to aspects of John Wain's "A Song about Major Eatherly" (p. 140)?

20. Wallace Stevens' "Peter Quince at the Clavier" takes its incentive from the clownish director of low comedy in Shakespeare's play *A Midsummer Night's Dream*, in which remarkable mixups and confused passions occur between some of the major characters. The story of Susanna and the elders, from the Apocrypha, reveals the sudden passions of two churchmen. Having seen Susanna bathing nude, they attempt to make her submit to them under threat of bogus incrimination; but she resists. Her servants rush to her when the elders cry out their charges, but Daniel saves her by proving the elders themselves guilty. How and for what reasons does the poet allude to these sources in the first stanza?

21. If he desires to relate music and passion, then how does the comic effect of the title, bordering on absurdity, add to the meaning of the poem?

22. For what possible reasons does the persona relate his own passion ("desiring you") to that of the "red-eyed elders watching" Susanna bathe? Do the allusions help the reader indirectly to define or to imagine more clearly the love affair? For example, may not the relationship of the man and woman ("I" and "you") be in some ways comparable to that of an elder and Susanna? Consider the possibilities. In contrast to the lust of the elders for Susanna's body, how does the final stanza render an impression of beauty which transcends physical passion?

23. Thomas Hardy's "Convergence of the Twain" depicts the sinking of the famous ship *Titanic*. Yet, the opening of the poem is ironic, for the ship is at the bottom of the sea. What ironies are achieved by Hardy in placing the opulent mirrors next to "grotesque, slimed, dumb, indifferent" (line 9) seaworms, or in juxtaposing "Jewels in joy designed" (line 10) with a lightless depth of the sea, "all their sparkles bleared and black and blind" (line 12)? This is, of course, human expectation unfulfilled, pride thwarted, joy reduced to grief, hope to tragedy. Yet, the second half of Hardy's poem (stanzas 6–11) explain the unexpected in terms of what the poet calls "The Immanent Will" (stanza six) and "the Spinner of the Years" (last stanza). Although the intervening stanzas treat the ship ("her") and iceberg ("sinister mate") metaphorically as destined lovers and their disastrous coming together as "The intimate welding of their later history," does the basic irony satisfy you? Explain your answer.

24. Taking all three poems together, do you feel that the poets manage to produce a different perspective or to give a new view of the historical event upon which they base their poems? If so, what is the value of such new perspectives and views? Do they enrich human experience, and if so, how? Discuss.

"*The Love Song of J. Alfred Prufrock*" [Eliot] and "*anyone lived in a pretty how town*"[Cummings]

25. These two poems may be compared thematically. To illustrate, both poems deal with the nature of human experience and relationships of the individual to society. In another sense, they deal with conformity, especially as twentieth-century man knows it. In "Prufrock" by combining the epigraph with the first stanza, how can we discern the poet's tone as despairing, half-alive, half-dead, problematic, even hellish in a Dante-esque sense? The poem then assumes a philosophical tone without losing its other intonations. Prufrock is uncertain, hesitant, indecisive, too self-conscious, but he is familiar with society, has thought a great deal, listened to music, made love to women. Point to lines which assure us of these aspects of his experience.

26. What does Prufrock mean when he says, "There will be time . . ./To prepare a face to meet the faces that you meet" (lines 26–27)? Or, "I have measured out my life with coffee spoons" (line 51)? What other lines present complex associations? Point out these lines and attempt to relate them to logical interpretations.

27. In what way does the final stanza of the poem, in which we see Prufrock turn away from the sea and his fantasies of mermaids there and return to his society, recapitulate the opening tone of the poem? How can Prufrock, or all of us for that matter, "drown" in the midst of society? How does the concluding stanza bear a direct relationship to the title of the poem? Give reasons for your answers.

28. Cummings' poem may at first appear to be rough treatment on the reader, for the words and lines do not

fit familiar, expected patterns, Gradually, though, we perceive the reiteration of "anyone" and "noone," suggesting people, especially lovers. Similarly, other patterns also make sense, such as "stars rain sun moon," with which we may associate the cycle of life or the passing of time. What expressions in the second stanza can you relate to conformity? in the third stanza to the loss of innocence and what might be called the adjustment of idealism within the framework of practicality? How is love emphasized in the fourth stanza?

29. As the cycle of life continues, and we read, "some-ones married their everyones" in the fifth stanza, the meaning is obvious enough, but how do you interpret the more specific "said their nevers they slept their dream"? Trace the remainder of the life cycle.

30. How does Cummings suggest that he is speaking about the lives and loves of people on a universal level? Does the image of man and woman as sounds of bells (metonymy) strike you as fitting? If so, explain. Does the association give clarity to the other examples of bell imagery in the poem?

31. In what ways are Eliot's and Cummings' poems different? For example, discuss the tone of the conclusion of "anyone lived in a pretty how town," and contrast it with that of Eliot's final tone previously treated.

"*Paysage Moralisé*" [Auden]

32. W. H. Auden's unrhymed poem "*Paysage Moralisé*" (the Moral Country) is written in the complex French form called *sestina*. Note that each of the end words of the six lines of the first stanza recurs in a varied form throughout all six stanzas, and the last *envoy* has compressed within it all six end words, two of them in each of the three lines. The form may appear at first to be highly artificial, the meaning either nonexistent or forced. Consider the six end words, however, in association with the following ideas:

a. "valleys"—farmlands
b. "mountains"—human effort

c. "water"—spiritual or renewed life
d. "islands"—individual isolation, private pursuits
e. "cities"—modern industrialized society
f. "sorrow"—human grief and failure

Assuming you do find an emergent meaning in the first stanza, can you trace a progression of meaning throughout the remainder of the poem? If so, can you correlate Auden's description of civilization with history? with a sociocultural approach to problems facing society today? Do you see any political implications in Auden's "Moral Country"? Give reasons for your answer.

"*After Apple-Picking*" [Frost]

33. Some critics have commented that this poem deals with nature and man's workaday world—such life processes as human responsibility, fatigue, and sleep. Others have observed that it is an attempt to depict earthbound man in relation to his heavenly aspirations. They ask, for example, why Frost employs "heaven" as a directional word in the second line rather than the more natural "sky"? They also contend that the emphasis on "sleep" in three of the last five lines is suggestive of more than sleep—death, in fact. Examine this poem from these two points of view and interpret the poem as you see it. Giving reasons for your observations, which of the two views do you tend to support? Or do you have other interpretations that you can support?

"*A Poem*" [Iris]

34. Perhaps it is fitting that our last series of questions in this section should deal with a first-rate poet's concept of what a poem, in its highest sense, should be. William Butler Yeats noted in Iris' work simplicity, order, an

intense beauty, and a passion for perfection. What lines in this poem express these four qualities?

35. If you do, indeed, find "A Poem" to be a work of artistic purity, then describe your feeling toward poetry as a whole after reading it.

36. Can you relate Iris' concepts of poetry, as he deals with them here, to any other poem in this section—for example, to Shakespeare's song, "When That I Was and a Little Tiny Boy" or to John Donne's more complex "The Flea"? Discuss.

37. Does Iris in any way increase your understanding of what great poetry encompasses, of what it may consist, and of how it creates an imaginative experience all its own?

38. Finally, of all the approaches to poetry treated in the first part of this book, which ones may be applied to Iris' "A Poem"? some of them? all of them, including a unity of approaches? As briefly as possible, demonstrate how such applications may be made. Does such an exercise increase your enjoyment of poetry, even though it also increases your understanding of it? Discuss.

PART THREE / *The Basics of Poetry and Glossary*

The Basics of Poetry

The Structure of Poetry

Poetry has a structure which is different from that of prose, although the prose poem may appear to be an exception. Sometimes a poet may superimpose a structure or form on his idea, but usually, the shape which the poem takes on the page is a natural outgrowth of what the poet wants to say—his intention. In this way, then, content may influence poetic form. Form, in turn, may determine content, in that the poet's method often dictates the subjects which he considers for poems; he may tend to choose subjects which fit the forms he prefers to use.

The structure of poetry is both temporal and spatial. The story, argument, or sense of the poem is read over a period of time, thereby allowing for a progressive development of ideas. The lines of the poem take up a certain amount of space on the page, and in the best poetry, this spatial arrangement coordinates itself with the temporal one. Not unlike human experience itself, then, genuine poetry is a time-space event. A poet may reinforce a logical flow of ideas with a regular line structure, as Andrew Marvell did in "To His Coy Mistress," or he may break up the line structure in order to avoid a regular pattern of reading or to create new patterns for other purposes. William Carlos Williams sometimes arranged regular patterns of meter and then deliberately broke them, thus frustrating the reader's expectation and achieving ironic effects. Though the poet may choose to give his poem almost any overall form, certain established forms should be recognized by the student.

Forms of Poetry

In ancient Greek poetry a LYRIC was a poem sung by one person who accompanied the song by playing a lyre. The lyric may be defined as a brief poem expressing an emotion. It has a musical quality and is a more or less direct personal expression of the speaker's emotion. We apply the word "lyric" to poems which achieve a melodic quality through the rhythm of the words. "Lyric" is a broad term, then, applied to poetry which is imaginative, unified, and melodic. Other forms, such as ballads, sonnets, and odes, may be considered varieties of lyrics. John Donne's poem "Song" ("Go and catch a falling star") is a lyric of disillusionment, whereas this work of E. E. Cummings is a lyric of joy:

I thank You God for most this amazing

i thank You God for most this amazing
day: for the leaping greenly spirits of trees
and a blue true dream of sky; and for everything
which is natural which is infinite which is yes

(i who have died am alive again today,
and this is the sun's birthday; this is the birth
day of life and of love and wings: and of the gay
great happening illimitably earth)

how should tasting touching hearing seeing
breathing any—lifted from the no
of all nothing—human merely being
doubt unimaginable You?

(now the ears of my ears awake and
now the eyes of my eyes are opened)

(1950)

The EPIC is a long narrative poem that tells of the adventures of a heroic character who is important in the history of a race or nation. The epic is characterized by a vast setting and a formal, elevated style. FOLK EPICS, such as *Beowulf*, are by unknown authors. Dante's *Divine Comedy* is a literary epic of the fourteenth century. LITERARY

EPICS are by known authors. The MOCK EPIC, like Pope's *Rape of the Lock*, parodies epic style for ironic or satiric effects.

The SONNET is a fourteen-line poem following one of two traditional models. The PETRARCHAN OR ITALIAN SONNET is divided into two parts. The first eight lines, or octave, have the rhyme scheme *abbaabba*. In this section a question is raised or a proposition is stated. The sestet, or last six lines, answers the question or applies the proposition. These lines most frequently have a rhyme scheme of *cdecde*, but this may vary, as in John Milton's "On His Having Arrived at the Age of Twenty-Three":

How soon hath Time, the subtle thief of youth,	*a*
Stol'n on his wing my three-and-twentieth year!	*b*
My hasting days fly on with full career,	*b*
But my late spring no bud or blossom shew'th.	*a*
Perhaps my semblence might deceive the truth,	*a*
That I to manhood am arriv'd so near,	*b*
And inward ripeness doth much less appear,	*b*
That some more timely-happy spirits indu'th.	*a*
Yet it be less or more, or soon or slow,	*c*
It shall be still in strictest measure ev'n,	*d*
To that same lot, however mean or high,	*e*
Toward which Time leads me, and the will of Heav'n;	*d*
All is, if I have grace to use it so,	*c*
As ever in my great Taskmaster's eye.	*e*

(1645)

The SHAKESPEAREAN or ENGLISH SONNET has four divisions—three quatrains and a rhymed couplet at the end. The rhyme scheme is typically *abab cdcd efef gg*. The epigrammatic couplet, *gg*, is usually a clever commentary on the preceding twelve lines. Consider this sonnet by Shakespeare:

Sonnet 30

When to the sessions of sweet silent thought	*a*
I summon up remembrance of things past,	*b*
I sigh the lack of many a thing I sought,	*a*
And with old woes new wail my dear time's waste:	*b*
Then can I drown an eye, unus'd to flow,	*c*
For precious friends hid in death's dateless night,	*d*
And weep afresh love's long-since cancell'd woe,	*c*
And moan the expense of many a vanish'd sight.	*d*
Then can I grieve at grievances foregone,	*e*

And heavily from woe to woe tell o'er	*f*
The sad account of fore-bemoanèd moan,	*e*
Which I new pay as if not paid before:	*f*
But if the while I think on thee, dear friend,	*g*
All losses are restor'd, and sorrows end.	*g*

(1609)

The ELEGY is a formal poem on a serious theme—most often, the death of a friend. Moving from the death, the poet goes on to make general observations on man and society. Tennyson's "In Memoriam" and Whitman's "When Lilacs Last in the Dooryard Bloom'd" are both elegies, the former on the death of Tennyson's friend Arthur Henry Hallam, and the latter on the assassination of Abraham Lincoln. Traditionally, the elegy begins with the occasion that stirred the poet into song, expresses sorrow, then moves through a complex rationalization to the acceptance of death, even joyous acceptance as in Whitman's elegy on Lincoln.

The PASTORAL ELEGY employs the pastoral imagery of country life and shepherds. Its theme is the death of a friend or admired person, and the poem is an expression of grief for the departed "shepherd." Milton's "Lycidas" is a pastoral elegy in which both Milton and his departed college friend, Edward King, appear as shepherds.

The ODE is an elaborate poem of heightened emotion and lyrical verse written for a special purpose. Originally a Greek form used in drama, the ode in English poetry may be classified in three types: Pindaric, Horatian, and irregular. The PINDARIC ODE consists of strophes (stanzas) and antistrophes (stanzas) similar in metrical form followed by contrasting epodes (stanzas). The HORATIAN ODE has one stanzaic form, the strophe, repeated with variations. The IRREGULAR ODE, lacking a strict complex form, is written in a series of irregular strophes. Gray's "The Bard" is a Pindaric ode; Coleridge's "Ode to France" is a Horatian ode; Keats' "Ode to a Nightingale" is an irregular ode.

A DRAMATIC MONOLOGUE is a poem told in first-person narration at a dramatic moment in the speaker's life. The speaker is narrating his situation either to a silent listener or to others, and he reveals a great deal about himself in the process. T. S. Eliot's "The Love Song of J. Alfred Prufrock" is a modern dramatic monologue, but the greatest craftsman of this form was Robert Browning, as exemplified by the first stanza of his "Soliloquy of the Spanish Cloister":

Gr-r-r—there go, my heart's abhorrence!
  Water your damned flower-pots, do!
If hate killed men, Brother Lawrence,
  God's blood, would not mine kill you!
What? your myrtle-bush wants trimming?
  Oh, that rose has prior claims—
Needs its leaden vase filled brimming?
  Hell dry you up with its flames!

                              (1842)

The BALLAD is a story in verse intended for singing and employing simple language. Most FOLK BALLADS, such as "The Twa Corbies," are anonymous:

The Twa Corbies

As I was walking all alane,
I heard twa corbies making a mane;
The tane unto the t'other say,
"Where sall we gang and dine to-day?"

"In behint yon auld fail dyke,
I wot there lies a new slain knight;
And naebody kens that he lies there,
But his hawk, his hound, and lady fair.

"His hound is to the hunting gane,
His hawk to fetch the wild-fowl hame,
His lady's ta'en another mate,
So we may mak our dinner sweet.

"Ye'll sit on his white hause-bane,
And I'll pike out his bonny blue een;
Wi' ae lock o' his gowden hair
We'll theek our nest when it grows bare.

"Mony a one for him makes mane,
But nane sall ken where he is gane;
O'er his white banes, when they are bare,
The wind sall blaw for evermair."

The rhyme scheme of "The Twa Corbies" is an exception to the usual ballad stanza, which rhymes *abcb*, as in "Sir Patrick Spens." Repetition is also characteristic of the ballad.

LITERARY BALLADS, or ART BALLADS, are known poets' more sophisticated adaptations of the ballad form. There are a great many famous literary ballads. Among them are Samuel Taylor Coleridge's "The Rime of the Ancient Mariner," John Keats' "La Belle Dame Sans Merci," and A. E. Housman's "The True Lover":

The True Lover

The lad came to the door at night,
  When lovers crown their vows.
And whistled soft and out of sight
  In shadow of the boughs.

"I shall not vex you with my face
  Henceforth, my love, for aye;
So take me in your arms a space
  Before the east is grey.

"When I from hence away am past
  I shall not find a bride,
And you shall be the first and last
  I ever lay beside."

She heard and went and knew not why;
  Her heart to his she laid;
Light was the air beneath the sky
  But dark under the shade.

"Oh do you breathe, lad, that your breast
  Seems not to rise and fall,
And here upon my bosom prest
  There beats no heart at all?"

"Oh loud, my girl, it once would knock,
  You should have felt it then;
But since for you I stopped the clock
  It never goes again."

"Oh lad, what is it, lad, that drips
  Wet from your neck on mine?
What is it falling on my lips,
  My lad, that tastes of brine?"

"Oh like enough 'tis blood, my dear,
  For when the knife has slit
The throat across from ear to ear
  'Twill bleed because of it."

Under the stars the air was light
  But dark below the boughs,
The still air of the speechless night,
  When lovers crown their vows.

                       (*1896*)

The self-contradictory term PROSE POEM is used to describe a poem which has no particular meter or rhyme and is structured like a prose paragraph. It relies on imagery and original diction to give it impact. Karl Shapiro is a contemporary poet who has used this method successfully in this work:

August Saturday Night on the Negro Street

August Saturday night on the Negro street the trolleys clang and break sweet dusty smoke. Cars hoot meaningless signals. The air is in a sweat of Jim Crow gaiety, shopping, milling, rubbing of flesh, five miles of laughter in white Baltimore. The second floor dance hall has a famous trumpet. You can't move on the floor, which rolls like waves and is in actual danger of giving way. The temperature adds to the frenzy. There is a no pause in the jump and scream of the jazz, heatwaves of laughter, untranslatable slang. The dancing is demotic, terpsichorean. It's like a war of pleasure. It's the joy of work. The fatigue is its own reward.

                       (*1962*)

An EPIGRAM is a concise, pointed saying. Originally an inscription, in the seventeenth century it was a short two-line poem. Today it has no set form. "I can resist everything except temptation" is an epigram by Oscar Wilde.

An EPITAPH is an inscription on a burial marker. It may be either humorous or serious, but is most often the latter. The epitaph marking Shakespeare's burial place reads more like a threat:

Good frend, for Jesus sake forbeare
To digg the dust encloased here;
Bleste be ye man y^t spares thes stones,
And curst be he y^t moves my bones.

An EPITHET is a brief phrase or adjective which describes the main feature or trait of a person or object. "Richard the Lion-Hearted" and "swift-footed" Achilles are examples.

The HAIKU is a Japanese poetic form consisting of seventeen syllables originally distributed over three lines, but in English, possibly spaced over either two or three lines. With haiku, poets attempt to present a distinct picture and give sudden insight as Onitsura does here:

The World Upside Down

A trout leaps high—
  below him, in the river bottom
    clouds flow by.

Stanza Forms

Within the poem itself various stanza forms may be used. A STANZA is a group of two or more lines composing a division within the poem. It may exhibit a particular rhyme scheme or it may lack rhyme altogether. Stanzas may differ in the number of lines they contain, and they are sometimes divided according to thought as well as form.

The QUATRAIN, or four-line stanza, is the most familiar, as in William Blake's "The Tyger":

Tyger! Tyger! burning bright
In the forests of the night,
What immortal hand or eye
Could frame thy fearful symmetry?

The BALLAD STANZA is a quatrain rhyming *abcb*. The TERCET is a three-line stanza.

A SPENSERIAN STANZA consists of nine lines— eight iambic pentameter lines, and an iambic hexameter line, known as an ALEXANDRINE, at the end. The rhyme scheme is *ababbcbcc*. This stanza was made famous by and named for Edmund Spenser. A sample stanza from his *The Faerie Queene* is given below:

Upon a great adventure he was bond,
  That greatest *Gloriana* to him gave,
  That greatest Glorious Queene of *Faerie* lond,

To winne him worship and her grace to have,
Which of all earthly things he most did crave;
And ever as he rode, his hart did earne
To prove his puissance in battell brave
Upon his foe, and his new force to learne;
Upon his foe, a Dragon horrible and stearne.

A COUPLET consists of two successive lines of poetry with an end rhyme, as in Marvell's "To His Coy Mistress":

Had we but world enough, and time,
This coyness, lady, were no crime.

A CLOSED COUPLET is a couplet in which an idea begun in the first line is completed in the second. Alexander Pope is the master of the closed couplet:

True wit is nature to advantage dressed,
What oft was thought, but ne'er so well express'd.

A HEROIC COUPLET is a closed couplet in iambic pentameter. Pope's closed couplet above is also a heroic couplet.

An ALEXANDRINE is the last line of a Spenserian stanza, or an iambic hexameter line.

Prosody: The Rhythm and Meter of Poetry

Poetry is characterized by rhythm. This rhythm, or meter, consists of a regular pattern of accented and unaccented syllables. The smallest unit of accented and unaccented syllables is called a FOOT.

An unaccented syllable followed by an accented syllable (for example, today) is called an IAMBIC FOOT, or IAMB:

The plowman homeward plods his weary way.

If the accented syllable comes first, followed by an unaccented syllable (for example, brother), it is a TROCHAIC FOOT, or TROCHEE:

There they are, my fifty men and women.

In a SPONDEE, both syllables are stressed (for example, breakfast). Rarely is the spondaic foot the prevailing pattern of a line.

One metric foot with three syllables, the first accented, the latter two unaccented, is a DACTYL (for example, passenger) which is also infrequently used.

Another is the ANAPEST (for example, introduce), a meter which is more frequently used:

And the sound of a voice that is still

The number of these feet in a line of poetry is prefaced to the word "meter" when describing the meter of the poem. Thus one foot is MONOMETER, two feet is DIMETER, three feet is TRIMETER, four feet is TETRAMETER, five feet is PENTAMETER, six feet is HEXAMETER, seven feet is HEPTAMETER, and eight feet is OCTAMETER. After eight feet the line tends to break in two. Using these terms, we can describe the accent structure and number of feet per line in a poem, as, for example, "iambic pentameter," meaning that the poem has five feet in the line and that each foot has an unaccented syllable followed by an accented syllable. The most common meter in English poetry is, in fact, iambic pentameter. The majority of Shakespeare's plays are written in this line form:

Make dust our paper, and with rainy eyes
Write sorrow on the bosom of the earth

This particular type of nonrhyming iambic pentameter is called BLANK VERSE. Poets, however, do not rigidly maintain the same metrical structure throughout blank verse poems, so that each line may vary somewhat.

FREE VERSE is just as the name implies—free. That is, it is liberated from any particular metric structure. This is the form used by Walt Whitman in *Song of Myself*:

I celebrate myself, and sing myself,
And what I assume you shall assume,
For every atom belonging to me as good belongs to you.

Free verse employs repetition of words and ideas as well as parallel grammatical structures to create its rhythm. The lack of rigidity of this form may make it appear to be an easier form to write in than more regularly structured forms. Yet to be successful, free verse must follow the rhythm of the ideas of the poem and flow as the mind moves along with the idea. That is, the meter is often carefully chosen to enhance the meaning which the poet wishes to impart.

Another less rigid metric form is SYLLABIC VERSE. This form employs a certain number of syllables for each line without regard to accent. The modern poet Marianne Moore, in her poem "Nevertheless," used syllabic verse:

Nevertheless

you've seen a strawberry
   that's had a struggle; yet
   was, where the fragments met,

a hedgehog or a star-
   fish for the multitude
   of seeds. What better food

than apple seeds—the fruit
   within the fruit—locked in
   like counter-curved twin

hazelnuts? Frost that kills
   the little rubber-plant-
   leaves of *kok-saghyz*-stalks, can't

harm the roots; they still grow
   in frozen ground. Once where
   there was a prickly-pear-

leaf clinging to barbed wire,
   a root shot down to grow
   in earth two feet below;

as carrots from mandrakes
   or a ram's-horn some-
   times. Victory won't come

to me unless I go
   to it; a grape tendril
   ties a knot in knots till

knotted thirty times—so
   the bound twig that's under-
   gone and over-gone, can't stir.

The weak overcomes its
   menace, the strong over-
   comes itself. What is there

like fortitude! What sap
   went through that little thread
   to make the cherry red!

                (*1944*)

ACCENTUAL VERSE, on the other hand, is based on the number of accents per line without regard to the number of syllables. *Beowulf* is an example of accentual verse.

Many an earl of Beowulf brandished

His ancient iron to guard his lord,

To shelter safely the peerless prince.

The Sounds of Poetry

Poetry may have several different rhyme arrangements. Certain types of rhyme have been popular during certain literary periods. The END RHYME, as in Pope's couplet quoted earlier (p. 301), is the most conventional kind of rhyme.

The pause in the middle of the second line of the couplet between the words "thought" and "but," indicated by the comma in this case, is an example of a CAESURA.

When we pause at the end of the line, as we do in the same couplet after the word "dressed," we call it an END-STOPPED LINE.

In Milton's sonnet "When I Consider How My Light Is Spent" (p. 253), however, the thought often moves from one line into the next without pause:

Lodged with me useless, though my soul more bent
To serve therewith my Maker, and present
My true account, lest he returning chide.

This RUN-ON LINE (an example of ENJAMBEMENT) presents a contrast to the end-stopped line and allows for a more natural flow of words and thought through successive lines of poetry.

An INTERNAL RHYME is a rhyme within the line, usually a word within the line rhyming with the end word, as in the following lines from Coleridge's "The Rime of the Ancient Mariner":

We were the *first* that ever *burst*
Into that silent sea.

SLANT RHYMES have the same final consonant, but the preceding vowel sound is different. The result is a near-rhyme, as in soul/oil, or vain/man. Slant rhymes avoid becoming singsong as occasionally occurs with end rhymes. In addition, they may create such effects as suspended thought, the frozen moment, thus enhancing the poet's impact upon the reader. For these and other reasons, slant rhymes became popular with modern poets, especially Emily Dickinson.

Words which look as if they would rhyme, from the way they are spelled, but which have different sounds, are called EYE RHYMES. Examples are h*a*ve/r*a*ve and g*one*/l*one*.

Lines using MASCULINE RHYMES end with an accented syllable—bríght, and líght—whereas lines using FEMININE RHYMES end with an unaccented syllable—wíther and híther.

Another pattern of word sounds is called ALLITERATION. Alliteration is the repetition of initial consonants in a word sequence, as in Donne's line, "*b*reak, *b*low, *b*urn, and make me new."

ASSONANCE is the repetition of vowel sounds. It is less obvious than alliteration. In the following quote there is a repetition of the "a" vowel sound:

There open f*a*nes and g*a*ping gr*a*ves.

Words in which the sound evokes the sense are called ONOMATOPOEIC words. The words "buzz," "crash," "moo," "sigh," and "splash" have approximately the same sound as the thing which they describe. Onomatopoeic words create a sense of the scene which the poem describes. Consider the effect of the ONOMATOPOEIA and alliteration in the following line from Coleridge's "The Rime of the Ancient Mariner":

And the sails did sigh like sedge.

The Language of Poetry

The DICTION of poetry—the poet's choice of language—is the most important part of poetry. Each word must be selected not only for its dictionary definition, but for the feelings and ideas with which the word is associated. The meaning of a word as defined by the dictionary is called its DENOTATIVE MEANING. The denotation of a word is thus impersonal, verifiable, and direct. What the word suggests in addition to the above is known as its CONNOTATION. The connotation of a word is emotional and indirect; it involves our personal response to it. "Communist," "Eden," and "sex" are highly connotative words. Calling someone a "Communist" is completely different from calling him a "Socialist," because the word "Communism" in the United States in the 1970s has connotations or suggestions beyond the meaning of a form of government. In choosing the right word, the poet must be very sensitive to connotations:

William Stafford

Adults Only

Animals own a fur world;
people own worlds that are variously, pleasingly, bare.
And the way these worlds *are* once arrived for us kids
   with a jolt,
that night when the wild woman danced
in the giant cage we found we were all in
at the state fair.

Better women exist, no doubt, than that one,
and occasions more edifying, too, I suppose.
But we have to witness for ourselves what comes for
   us,

nor be distracted by barkers of irrelevant ware;
and a pretty good world, I say, arrived that night
when that woman came farming right out of her
  clothes,
by God,

At the state fair.

                           (1960)

The language in William Stafford's poem above is, for the most part, not unusual. The poem contains no archaic, eloquent, or lofty words. The expressions "pretty good" (line 11) and "by God" (line 13) are, in fact, colloquial. To this simple diction he adds an exotic dimension, however, with the words "wild woman" (line 4) and "giant cage" (line 5). In the second stanza he goes on to interpret the meaning of his experience, using such words as "edifying" (line 8) and "irrelevant" (line 10), which hint at the poet's sophistication. He concludes affirmatively that ". . . a pretty good world, I say, arrived that night/when that woman came farming right out of her clothes,/by God,/At the state fair" (lines 11–14). If he had said "dancing" or "stripping" out of her clothes, the impact would have been lost. "Farming" not only suits the plain rural-like diction of the poem but is unexpected and unusual and somehow so connotatively correct that we cannot help but conclude the poem with a smiling sense of satisfaction. Stafford skillfully blends ordinary, unusual, and sophisticated language into a delightful poem about growing up. The poet, in short, must be able to select the right words connotatively to achieve the desired outcome.

Images

An IMAGE is a concrete representation of a sensory experience. Images appeal to our senses. Visual images are used most often, but aural, gustatory, tactile, and olfactory images, as well as those that elicit any combination of sensory Impressions (SYNESTHESIA) may be employed. images may be either LITERAL or FIGURATIVE.

LITERAL IMAGES call up a sensory experience by using the conventional meanings of the words:

Nine bean-rows will I have there, a hive for the
  honeybee,
And live alone in the bee-loud glade.

These lines by William Butler Yeats create a literal image of a grassy plain buzzing with bees. "Bee-loud glade" is both a visual and an auditory image.

A FIGURATIVE IMAGE, on the other hand, is an extension of the normal description, using words together which do not ordinarily go together:

Silent as the sleeve-worn stone.

This is a figurative image by Archibald MacLeish. It calls for an extension of our usual association. Stones are ordinarily just hard or perhaps smooth. But "silent" stone suggests new sensory and imaginative associations.

Figures of Speech

A METAPHOR is an implied comparison between two seemingly dissimilar things. When Macbeth says,

Life's but a walking shadow, a poor player
That struts and frets his hour upon the stage
And then is heard no more . . .

he is using acting as a metaphor for human life. Shakespeare compares the brief time we spend on earth to the brief time an actor performs on stage.

A SIMILE is a direct comparison which uses a word such as "like" or "as." Wordsworth compares himself directly to a cloud in "I wandered Lonely *as* a Cloud." In "Amoretti," Spenser uses the simile: "My love is like to ice." If he had said "My love is ice," it would have been a metaphor.

A CONCEIT is a figure of speech which ingeniously compares two dissimilar things. The ELIZABETHAN CONCEIT, usually found in love poems, makes an extended and elaborate comparison of the subject to some object. Thomas Campion compares his love to a garden in "There Is a Garden in Her Face":

There is a garden in her face,
    Where roses and white lilies grow,
A heavenly paradise is that place,
    Wherein all pleasant fruits do flow.

The METAPHYSICAL CONCEIT makes a witty, complex, and striking analogy such as the one Donne made between the attachment of two lovers and a draftsman's compass in "A Valediction Forbidding Mourning":

If they be two, they are two so
    As stiff twin *compasses* are two:
Thy soul, the fixed foot, makes no show
    To move, but doth, if the other do.

ANTITHESIS places one idea in opposition to another. Pope often used antithesis in his verse essays. The following is from his *Essay on Man*:

The learned is happy nature to explore,
The fool is happy that he knows no more.

HYPERBOLE is overstatement or gross exaggeration. Pope's "Rape of the Lock" is an example of a hyperbolic statement. The clipping of a single lock of hair, to which the title refers, would hardly be called "rape."

METONYMY involves the substitution of a word or idea closely associated with the object or of an attribute of an object for the object itself, such as "city" for inhabitants, or "crown" for king. Metonymy is closely related to synecdoche.

An OXYMORON is a linking together of two contradictory terms such as "bitter-sweet," "joyful pain," "falsely true," and "quest for failure." "Parting is such sweet sorrow" is a common oxymoron.

PARADOX is a statement which is seemingly self-contradictory but is true in a deeper sense. "This love feel I, that feel no love in this!" is a paradoxical statement from *Romeo and Juliet*.

PERSONIFICATION is the attribution of life or personality to an inanimate object or idea, as in "The angry wind shouted harsh words of defiance." "Death has reared himself a throne" is a personification by Edgar Allan Poe.

SYNECDOCHE uses the part for the whole, as in "All *hands* on deck." It may use the whole to represent a part, as "The *world* is too much with us." Synecdoche is closely related to metonymy.

An UNDERSTATEMENT is a figure of speech which, as the name implies, understates the situation. Iago gives Othello the idea that Desdemona is unfaithful to him, and then understates Othello's despair when he comments: "I see this hath a little dashed your spirits." Othello's reply is also an understatement: "Not a jot, not a jot."

Poets often use words or figures of speech for their symbolic value. A SYMBOL is something which is not only itself, but also stands for something else. A short time ago, Congress and the public were enraged over the burning of the American flag by war protesters. Obviously no one was alarmed over the burning of a piece of red, white, and blue cloth. The uproar occurred because the American flag is considered a symbol, or representation, of America itself. In poetry the winged horse Pegasus is a symbol of poetic inspiration, just as the cross is a symbol of Christianity.

Feeling and Tone in Poetry

An aspect of all the parts of a poem previously mentioned, and yet one that overlays all of them, is the TONE of the poem. By "feeling" and "tone" are meant the attitude of the author toward his subject and audience. "Ode to a Nightingale," like many of Keats' poems, has a melancholy tone. E. E. Cummings' poetry, on the other hand, often has a lively, good-humored tone, as in his poem "i thank You God for most this amazing" on page 297. Just as one's tone of voice reveals one's mood, the tone of a poem reveals whether the poet is light-hearted, sympathetic, sad, ironic, philosophical, or whatever, in his feeling toward his subject and reader.

An IRONIC statement is one in which the feeling is expressed in words which have the opposite meaning. To say "My, you look neat" to someone who looks particularly messy is to speak ironically. Hyperbole is an ironic device which Pope uses in "The Rape of the Lock" when he says:

This nymph, to the destruction of mankind,
Nourished two locks, which graceful hung behind.

To say that the loss of Belinda's locks will destroy mankind is an overstatement. What Pope really means is just the opposite—that the loss of her locks is insignificant to mankind. Oftentimes we cannot accept the statements of the speaker in the poem because he speaks ironically. In ascertaining the poet's tone, the reader must be careful not to accept an ironic voice as a sincere one.

Glossary

The page number following the defined word indicates where a more complete discussion can be found.

Acatalectic: A line of poetry that is metrically complete. For example, an iambic pentameter line is acatalectic provided each of its five metrical feet has an initial unaccented syllable followed by an accented syllable. If a syllable were dropped in any foot, it would be a catalectic, or incomplete, line.

Accent (p. 301): The vocal stress given to a syllable in pronunciation. "Accent" refers to the *emphasis* of a sound rather than its duration. Three types of accent are: word accent, which is stress upon a word or syllable of a word; rhetorical accent, which is accent placed in order to bring out the meaning of a sentence; and metrical accent, which is accent placed according to the metrical structure of the line.

Accentual Verse (p. 302): Verse based on the number of accents per line without regard to the number of syllables.

Acrostic: A form in which letters form words both horizontally and vertically. The form may be either prose or verse. It presents names, phrases, or sentences in a regular pattern. In the simple acrostic below, the first letter of each word spells a word vertically.

> Poetry
> Often
> Endures
> Time

Alexandrine (pp. 300, 301): A line of verse that has six iambic feet—in other words, an iambic hexameter line. Spenser is noted for using an Alexandrine as the last line of his Spenserian stanza.

Allegory: A lengthy metaphor in prose or verse in which objects and people are personifications of abstract qualities. Thus, it depicts one thing in the guise of another. Allegory may employ a one-to-one ratio between object and representation, as in Bunyan's *Pilgrim's Progress,* in which the character "Christian" stands for every Christian. It may use a character to represent many things. For example, the Red Cross Knight in Spenser's *The Faerie Queene* is not only England, but also Protestantism, the Anglican Church, Everyman, and so forth. Thus, in allegory, meanings are presented which are independent of the surface story.

Alliteration (p. 303): Repetition of identical initial consonant sounds in a succession of words.

> And the smooth stream in smoother numbers flows
>
> *(Pope)*

Some critics also speak of vowel alliteration, but these sounds are more accurately defined as assonance.

Allusion: A reference to a historical or literary event or figure, as in "He exhibited the patience of a Job."

Ambiguity: The condition of being open to several interpretations, of having more than one possible meaning.

Amphibrach: A metrical foot containing three syllables in the following order: unstressed, stressed, and unstressed, as in "together."

Anacoluthon: Purposeful or accidental failure to complete a sentence according to its original plan, as in "If you don't watch out . . . Oh, never mind."

Anagoge (Anagogy): Traditionally, the mystical or spiritual meaning of literature; more broadly, the total or universal meaning of literature.

Anapest (p. 301): A metrical foot consisting of three syllables—two unaccented syllables followed by an accented one, such as intercede.

Anaphora: The repetition of the same word or words at the beginning of two or more successive lines, clauses, or sentences. This device is found often in Whitman's poetry.

Animism: In a literary sense, the convention that assumes that natural phenomena and natural objects possess feelings and consciousness. "As the storm approached, the leaves trembled in fear" is an example of its use. Closely akin to pathetic fallacy.

Anticlimax: A situation that works against the climax. In other words, the trivial or ludicrous confronts us where we expect a serious climactic event. Anticlimax may occur unintentionally due to poor plotting, or it may be employed intentionally to undercut the importance of previous events, as Pope employs it in "The Rape of the Lock":

To fifty chosen sylphs, of special note,
We trust the important charge, the petticoat.

Antithesis (p. 305): A figure of speech that contrasts words, sentences, or ideas, thus balancing one against the other. An example is Pope's famous "Man Proposes, God disposes."

Aposiopesis: A sudden deliberate breaking off of a sentence, as in "Touch me again and I'll . . ." In aposiopesis the sentence remains incomplete; in anacoluthon the sentence is completed in a grammatically irregular way.

Apostrophe: A figure of speech in which someone or something is addressed as though present—whether it is actually present or not.

Archetype: A recurrent image or symbol that has become a recognizable part of our literary experience. The term is borrowed from the psychological studies of Carl Jung, who believed archetypes to be a part of our primordial (preconscious) experience and thus able to evoke profound emotional responses. An example is the sea, which may be interpreted as an archetypal symbol for the origin of life.

Argument: A prose summarization or explication of meaning accompanying a long poem or play. George Bernard Shaw's prefaces to his plays and Milton's prefaces to the books of *Paradise Lost* are examples. The term is also used to describe a prose paraphrase of the meaning of a poem.

Art Ballad (p. 299): A ballad of known authorship, also called a "literary ballad." "La Belle Dame Sans Merci" by Keats and "The Rime of the Ancient Mariner" by Coleridge are both art ballads.

Art Epic (p. 297): An epic of known authorship, also called a "literary epic." Dante's "Divine Comedy" and Milton's *Paradise Lost* are both art epics.

Assonance (p. 303): Repetition of vowel sounds in a group of two or more words.

Than t*i*red *eye*lids upon t*i*red *eye*s.

(*Tennyson*)

Atmosphere: The predominant mood or feeling of a poem, especially as produced by setting or background.

Aubade: A lyrical poem about the coming of morning. Often it is concerned with lovers who must part now that day approaches. Depending upon the circumstances, it can be either happy or sad.

Autotelic: A poem that does not seek to comment upon the external world or—in an objective sense—to teach or preach. Keats' "Ode to Autumn" is a good example of an autotelic poem. Using autumn as the object of his poem, Keats creates a sensuous, nondidactic poetic "experience."

Ballad (p. 299): A form of verse that narrates a story or an exciting episode. Common subjects for ballads are love and the supernatural. Distinction is made between folk ballads (those of anonymous authorship) and art ballads (those by known authors).

Ballad Stanza (p. 300): The stanza form of the ballad, usually consisting of four lines rhyming *abcb*. The first and third lines have four accents; the second and fourth have three. A refrain, or recurring line, is common to the ballad stanza.

Bathos: Unsuccessful pathos. Bathos results from the failure of an attempt to achieve dignity, and it results in a drop from the lofty to the ridiculous. The outcome is an unintentional anticlimax.

Belles-Lettres: Literature that depends upon imaginative and artistic foundations rather than upon intellectual and factual ones. In a pejorative sense, the term suggests writing that is bubbly with beauty but is without substantial content.

Blank Verse (p. 301): Nonrhyming iambic pentameter verse. Blank verse is the most suitable form for long poems and poetic dramas because of its flexibility. Christopher Marlowe was the first to explore the possibilities of blank verse. Shakespeare and Milton are its masters.

Bon Mot: A witty, just-right statement or saying. Often found in sophisticated drama, as well as in life. When Oscar Wilde remarked, "I wish I had said that," Whistler replied, "You will, Oscar, you will." That is a bon mot!

Burlesque: An approach that creates comedy by exaggeration and by incongruity of style and subject. Donald Hall's poem "Dr. Fatt, Instructor" is an example.

Cacophany: The use of sounds that seem harsh and discordant when read aloud. The opposite of Euphony.

Cadence: The rhythmical beat, or movement, of poetry or prose. When one speaks, one does so in a varying, accentual pattern that forms a rhythm; in poetry this pattern, built in by the poet, is the cadence.

Caesura (pp. 57, 302): A pause within a line of poetry (usually in the middle), which breaks the line's metrical pattern.

Canto: A division of a long poem. Dante's "Divine Comedy," for example, is divided into cantos.

Carpe Diem: Literally, "Seize the day." Carpe diem poetry suggests that since we all must die, we had better take what pleasures we can while we are alive. In effect, this kind of poem says, "Eat, drink and be merry, for tomorrow you die."

Catalectic: Lacking part of the last foot in a line of poetry.

Chanson de Geste: A medieval poetic tale of valorous deeds of kings and lords on the field of battle. The twelfth-century French epic *Chanson de Roland* is probably the first, and certainly the best, example.

Chantey: A heavily rhythmic sailor's song, usually sung by men doing a difficult task together. Its pragmatic function was to insure that everyone pulled together. Traditionally, the "chantey man" was the leader of the group who alone sang several lines, after which the entire crew joined in a refrain. "Blow the man down" is an example.

Cliché: An expression that may once have been quite effective but is now stale, dull, and hackneyed. Examples are "fit as a fiddle," "there's something rotten in Denmark," and "the more the merrier."

Closed Couplet (p. 301): A couplet that contains its complete meaning within itself and can therefore exist independently of other lines within the poem. Many of Pope's couplets are closed and therefore not dependent on the lines that precede or follow them:

The general order, since the whole began
Is kept in nature, and is kept in man.

Common Meter: A four-line stanza characterized by metrical regularity. The first and third lines have eight syllables (iambic tetrameter), and the second and fourth lines have six (iambic trimeter). Sometimes called "common measure."

Conceit (p. 304): A figure of speech or metaphor expressing an elaborate and extravagant analogy between two seemingly dissimilar things. Conceits tend to be clever and intellectual rather than emotional. Eliot refers to "The evening is spread out against the sky/ Like a patient etherised upon a table."

Connotation (p. 303): The implied meaning of a word— the meaning the word suggests. Connotation involves the feelings and biases that a word brings to mind. These feelings may be strictly personal, but they are more often national or universal.

Consonantal Rhyme: A form of slant rhyme in which the final consonants in the stressed syllables of words agree but the preceding vowels do not, as in the case of "seen" rhymed with "own."

Context: The total work. Sometimes in poetry a word's nuances of meaning may be determined only by the total work in which it appears. Note the different meaning of the word "bitch" in the following sentences. "Baying twice, the bitch loped in pursuit of the fleeing fox." "She's beautiful," he agreed, "but she's a bitch."

Convention: A style, device, or approach that is acceptable even though logically it is indefensible. For example, at a performance of Shakespeare the playgoer willingly suspends his disbelief and accepts the convention of months passing in a few hours and the convention of people speaking in verse. Similarly, the reader accepts rhyming dialogue and the other conventions of poetry.

Couplet (p. 301): Two successive lines of verse with similar end rhymes. Couplets customarily have the same number of syllables per line, but they may violate this custom and still qualify as couplets.

Crisis: In drama, fiction, and narrative poetry, the point at which all of the forces involved come together and determine the final turn of the plot.

Dactyl (p. 301): A metrical foot of three syllables, consisting of an accented syllable followed by two unaccented syllables, as in "réndèzvoùs."

Dadaism: A movement in art and literature during and shortly after World War I which attacked all conventional standards of aesthetics.

Decorum: The appropriateness of style to subject matter. Decorum calls for kings to speak in an elevated style, farmers in a rustic style, clowns in prose, and so on. Awareness of decorum helps to maintain character consistency and credibility, although rigid adherence to these rules can lead to stereotyping of characters.

Denotation (p. 303): The dictionary, or exact, meaning of a word. Denotation is the meaning of a word devoid of its emotional implications and associations.

Deus ex Machina: Literally, the "god from the machine." In Greek drama when a "god" came on stage to decide matters among men, he was lowered from above by "machine." Today the phrase means simply an improbable way of resolving an issue in literature. The writer who gets rid of a villain by having him struck by lightning is resorting to this device.

Diction (p. 303): The choice of words in spoken or written language.

Didactic Verse: Poetry written to teach lessons, instruct, or serve as a pulpit for preachments. Longfellow's "A Psalm of Life" is a good example.

Distich: Two lines of poetry that rhyme. Often such lines are epigrammatic and thus, though they may be a couplet in a larger poem, are complete in themselves. The following from Pope's "An Essay on Man" is an example:

Know then thyself, presume not God to scan,
The proper study of mankind is man.

Doggerel: Bad poetry, usually maudlin, with obvious or forced rhymes and pogo-stick rhythm.

Double Rhyme: See Feminine Rhyme.

Dramatic Irony: When a character in a play, fiction, or poetry doesn't know something that we know and he says something that unknown to him describes his real situation, we have dramatic irony. If a character approaches his bed and says, "I'm so tired, I don't think I'll ever wake up," and we know that a murderer is in a closet waiting to kill him, the victim's observation becomes dramatically ironic.

Dramatic Monologue (p. 298): A poem told in first-person narration at a dramatic moment in the speaker's life.

Duple Meter: Meter that uses two syllable feet, such as iambic and trochaic meter.

Eclogue: A formal pastoral poem. Characters include— not always in the same poem—shepherds, shepherd-esses, and swains. The setting is some remote, idyllic wood. When such a poem is written to lament the death of a friend, it is called a pastoral elegy. Milton's "Lycidas" and Shelley's "Adonais" are major examples of the pastoral elegy.

Effect: What a work does to its reader emotionally. If a poet wants to create a haunting impression such as Keats creates in "La Belle Dame Sans Merci," he utilizes every device in his poem to achieve that effect.

Elizabethan Conceit (p. 304): A figure of speech that makes an extended and elaborate comparison of the subject with some object such as a garden or ship.

End Rhyme (p. 302): Rhyme that occurs at the end of a line of verse. The two lines by Coleridge below utilize end rhymes:

Where Alph, the sacred river, ran
Through caverns measureless to man

(*Kubla Khan*)

End-Stopped Line (p. 302): A line that stops or pauses at the end instead of carrying over to the next line.

Enjambement (pp. 57, 303): The continuation of sense and grammatic structure from one line to the next.

Envoy (Envoi): A terminal stanza, usually addressed to some person of great importance, that in effect repeats what the entire poem has been saying. See D. G. Rossetti's translation of François Villon's "Ballad of Dead Ladies."

Epic (p. 297): A long poem narrating the adventures of a larger-than-life hero. The style of an epic is elevated and serious, as befits a historical hero. *Beowulf* and *Paradise Lost* are two English epics.

Epic Simile: A simile that is extended, involved, and ornate, in imitation of the similes of Homer's *Iliad* and *Odyssey.*

Epigram (p. 300): A concise pointed saying.

Epistle: A letter; in literature, a formal literary composition. See Pope's "Epistle to Dr. Arbuthnot."

Epitaph (p. 300): A burial inscription. Epitaphs can be either serious or humorous. They generally contain the name of the dead person and some motto.

Epithet (p. 300): A phrase that points out a particular and outstanding characteristic of a person. For example, the English King Ethelred was called "Ethelred the Unready."

Eulogy: A formal speech praising someone or something.

Euphemism: A way of stating indirectly something that directly stated might be considered offensive. Thus, instead of saying of a couple that they are having sexual relations, one might observe that they are "sleeping together." An older example of a euphemism is the Victorian substitution of "white meat" for "breast" when asking for a piece of chicken.

Euphony: In literature, a style of writing that when read sounds pleasant to the reader's ear.

Exemplum: A story told for the purpose of making a doctrinal or moral point. Medieval preachers found this form most effective when sermonizing. For example, Chaucer's "Pardoner's Tale" shows how the love of money is the root of all evil.

Explication de Texte: A critical approach, French in origin, used especially by the New Critics. The method is to probe minutely each element in a literary work—words, images, and so forth—to determine all possible meanings contained by these elements, their relationships, and their ambiguities.

Extended Metaphor: A single metaphor developed at length, sometimes throughout a whole work.

Eye Rhyme (p. 303): Rhyme by sight rather than by sound, based on word endings spelled alike but pronounced differently, as in "rain" and "again" and "done" and "alone."

Fabliau: A medieval humorous tale in verse, characterized by a satiric, often bawdy approach to human life. Chaucer's "The Miller's Tale" is an excellent example of the form.

Falling Meter: Meter beginning with stressed and ending with unstressed syllables, such as trochaic and dactylic meter.

Feminine Ending (p. 303): An unstressed syllable at the end of a line of verse.

Feminine Rhyme (p. 303): A rhyme of two syllables, the first stressed and the second unstressed, as in these lines by Swinburne:

In fierce March weather
White waves break tether.

     (Four Songs of Four Seasons)

Figurative Image (p. 304): An image based on an extension of the literal meaning of the words, which adds extra dimensions of meaning.

Fin de siècle: Although it can refer to the last years of any century, the term is usually used in connection with those of the nineteenth, especially in the England of Wilde and Shaw, to imply the presence of a "decadent" literary culture.

Fixed Form: Poetic form as established by convention and adhered to without variation. For example, the sonnet is a fixed form consisting of fourteen lines in iambic pentameter with a strict rhyme scheme.

Flexible Form: The opposite of Fixed Form. Poetry that is not bound by fixed patterns of form.

Folk Ballad (p. 299): A story in verse, intended for singing, employing simple language. Usually anonymous.

Folk Epic (p. 297): An epic of vague origin, such as *Beowulf*.

Foot (p. 301): A unit consisting of two or more stressed or unstressed syllables. It is a unit of rhythm.

Form (p. 297): The pattern or structure of a poem—that is, the meter, rhyme scheme, and so forth. The sonnet is a particular form, different from the ballad form.

Formal English: Written English as opposed to spoken, characterized by serious tone and elevated diction.

Fourteener: A verse form consisting of fourteen syllables arranged in iambic feet, found mainly in medieval and renaissance poetry.

Free Verse (p. 301): Verse free from any set metrical pattern. Whitman's "Out of the Cradle Endlessly Rocking" is in free verse.

Genre: A type or category of literature, classified by form or technique. The lyric is a genre.

Gnomic: Pithy, aphoristic. Describing a maxim, often in poetic form, that states a general truth and is usually moralistic or magic in content.

Grammatical Pause: A pause dictated by the grammatical structure or sense unit of the sentence.

Haiku (p. 300): A Japanese poetic form using only seventeen syllables. Originally, there were three lines of five, seven, and five syllables each, but now a haiku may consist of only two lines.

Hemistich: Half of a stich or poetic line, especially as divided by a caesura.

Heroic Couplet (p. 301): Two iambic pentameter lines with end rhymes.

Heroic Simile: See Epic Simile.

Hyperbole (p. 305): An overstatement or exaggeration.

Iamb (p. 301): A metrical foot containing an unaccented syllable followed by an accented syllable, such as "embrace."

Ictus: The metrical stress that falls on a given syllable (not the syllable itself).

Image (p. 304): The communication by words of a particular sense impression. An image may be of any kind: visual, tactile, auditory, and so forth. Most often, images are visual; that is, they create a picture of something, as Keats does in the following lines from "The Eve of St. Agnes."

He followed through a lowly archéd way,
Brushing the cobwebs with his lofty plume.

Incremental Repetition: The use of repetition with variations. Usually associated with ballads. The following lines from Charles Algernon Swinburne's art ballad "The King's Daughter" show the nature of incremental repetition:

We were ten maidens in the green corn,
 Small red leaves in the mill-water:
Fairer maidens never were born,
 Apples of gold for the king's daughter.

We were ten maidens by a well-head,
  Small white birds in the mill-water:
Sweeter maidens never were wed,
  Rings of red for the king's daughter.

Initial Rhyme: Rhyme occurring in the initial syllable or syllables.

The moon rises quickly
When June follows May.

Internal Rhyme (p. 303): A rhyme within a line of verse—usually the end word rhyming with a word in the middle of the line. Hopkins' line below is a less common internal rhyme:

The ear, it strikes like lightning to hear him sing.

Inverted Word Order: Reversal of normal word order for poetic effect, as in "When spring arrives, I will journey to thee."

Invocation: A request to a god for help in writing. Epic poets customarily begin their epics with an invocation to the gods.

Irony (p. 306): A technique contrasting appearance with actuality. An ironic situation is one in which events fall short of, or are the reverse of, our expectation. An ironic statement is one expressing an idea in words that carry the opposite meaning.

Italian Sonnet or Petrarchan Sonnet (p. 298): A fourteen-line poem with a rhyme scheme of *abbaabba cdecde*. The poem is divided into two sections—the first section of eight lines called the octave, and the last section of six lines called the sestet.

Kenning: Usually a metaphor substituted for a noun; a poetic stereotype, characteristic of Old English poetry. There are many kennings to be found in *Beowulf*, such as "the whale road" for the ocean.

Lay (Lai): A short narrative poem, especially one to be sung. The term is applied to various French and English poetic forms written from the twelfth century on.

Light Verse: Humorous, witty poetry, jesting in tone, usually short. It can be quite biting or satiric. The limerick is a form of light verse, as is the parody. Lewis Carroll's "Jabberwocky" and "Father William" are examples of light-verse parodies.

Limerick: A five-line humorous poem in anapestic meter, rhyming *aabba*. The first, second, and fifth lines have three feet; the third and fourth lines have two feet.

Literal Image (p. 304): An image that evokes a sensory experience through the normal—denotative—meanings of the words used.

Literary Ballad: See Art Ballad.

Literary Epic (p. 297): An epic of known authorship, such as Milton's *Paradise Lost*.

Litotes: A figure of speech in which the affirmative is expressed by the negation of its opposite, as in "not bad at all."

Lyric (p. 297): A short musical poem expressing a strong emotional feeling. Originally, the lyric was a song accompanied by a musical instrument—the lyre. The word "lyric" has now become a very general term used to describe a great many varieties of poems. Long poems such as epics may have lyric qualities at times, and the sonnet is a kind of lyric too.

Madrigal: A brief lyric designed as a musical piece and dealing with the theme of love or rustic life.

Magnum Opus: A poet's greatest work, or one of the great works of its kind. Originally the term meant masterpiece, but today it may be used sarcastically to suggest that the work under consideration is not very good.

Malapropism: The ridiculous misuse of a word by substituting it for a word similar in sound but unrelated in meaning. "I'm ravished" for "I'm famished" is an example. Named after Mrs. Malaprop, a character who committed such blunders in Sheridan's play *The Rivals.*

Masculine Rhyme (p. 303): A rhyme involving only the final stressed syllable, as in these lines by Robert Herrick:

Come, let us go while we are in our prime;
And take the harmless folly of the time.
              (*"Corinna's Going A-Maying"*)

Metaphor (p. 304): A figure of speech implying a comparison between two essentially unlike objects or ideas. An example is the comparison of passing time to a bird in Sir Philip Sidney's line, "Time shall moult away his wings."

Metaphysical Conceit (p. 305): The type of conceit used by the metaphysical poets, characterized by startling and unusual analogies.

Meter (p. 301): The rhythmical pattern of poetry. Meter is determined by the kind of feet used and the number of feet per line.

Metonymy (p. 305): The use of one name or object to represent another, such as "the White House" to represent the President.

Mock Epic (p. 298): A literary form that parodies the epic by using elevated style and other epic devices to treat a trivial subject for comic or satiric purposes.

Montage: A series of brief scenes presented impressionistically in rapid succession.

Myth: An ancient story presented in supernatural episodes and concerned with important events in the lives of men and in nature, such as birth, death, initiation, and trial. Examples of mythical subjects are Prometheus, and Leda and the Swan. Myth is the plot pattern that embodies archetypal themes and images.

Neologism: A new word consciously introduced into the language, especially to enhance literary style.

Objective Correlative (p. 44): An objective means of communicating an emotion. The term was popularized by T. S. Eliot, who considered it to be "the only way of expressing emotion in the form of art." An objective correlative is an image, event, or situation that evokes a particular emotion rather than expressing the emotion directly.

Octave (p. 298): The first eight lines of an Italian sonnet.

Ode (p. 298): A solemn, elaborate poem divided into strophes (stanzas). Pinderic odes have a strict metrical form; Horatian and irregular odes are freer. Wordsworth's "Ode on Intimations of Immortality," an irregular ode, is irregular in both the length of its lines and the number of lines per stanza. Usually, the subject of the ode is that which the poet addresses.

Old Native Meter: Based on Old English versification, it has four stressed syllables and a varying number of unstressed syllables, often with alliteration.

Onomatopoeia (p. 303): A technique in which the sound of a word simulates the sense. "Whiz," "crash," "bang," and "moo" are a few examples.

Otiose: Wordy and redundant. In literary criticism, a term used to describe a style.

Ottava Rima: An eight-line stanza rhyming *abababcc*. The end couplet, *cc*, has a witty turn to it.

Oxymoron (p. 305): A combination of words with apparently contradictory meanings, such as "serious vanity" and "cold fire."

Paean: A song of praise, joy, or triumph.

Palindrome: A word or line reading the same backward as forward, such as the maxim, jokingly attributed to Napoleon, "Able was I ere I saw Elba."

Panegyric: A formal composition written or spoken in praise of a person, living or dead. The term is often used in a derogatory sense now.

Paradox (p. 305): A seemingly self-contradictory phrase that reveals an underlying truth, such as "Nothing is won without a loss."

Paraphrase: The rendering of a poem in the words of the reader on the level of the language of information.

Parody: A humorous distortion or exaggeration of a serious work, seeking to mimic or ridicule that work.

Pastoral (p. 298): A form of poetry involving shepherds and shepherdesses who live in a rural setting.

Pastoral Elegy (p. 298): An elegy situated in a pastoral setting. The shepherds mourn the death of their friend.

Pathetic Fallacy: A term coined by John Ruskin to denote the attribution of human emotions to nature. Inappropriate emotion of this kind can make a poem absurd.

Pegasus (p. 305): The winged horse that inspires poets.

Periphrasis: A roundabout way of expression. A rhetorical device that may be successful or merely verbose, depending on the skill of the poet.

Persona: The speaker of a poem from whose point of view the poem is written. The man who speaks from prison to his lover is the persona of Lovelace's poem "To Althea, From Prison."

Personification (p. 305): The attribution of human qualities to an abstraction or an inanimate object. "Mother Earth" and "Father Time" are personifications.

Petrarchan Sonnet: See Italian Sonnet.

Philippic: A discourse or speech of bitter denunciation. The term is derived from the orations of Demosthenes denouncing Philip, King of Macedon, in the fourth century B.C.

Preciosity: A literary style with fastidious or affected refinement in diction and manner.

Primary Stress: The heaviest accent within a metrical foot.

Prose Poem (p. 300): A poem structured like a prose paragraph without regard to meter or rhyme scheme.

Prosody (p. 301): The metric pattern, stanza, and rhyme scheme of poetry.

Pun: A play upon words revolving around words that sound alike but have different meanings. Puns may also be based on two different meanings of the same word. In *Romeo and Juliet*, the dying Mercutio puns when he says, "Look for me tomorrow and you shall find me a grave man" ("grave" meaning not just serious, but in the grave).

Pyrrhic: A metrical foot characterized by two unaccented

syllables, such as ŏf thĕ. Seldom encountered in English poetry.

Quantitative Verse: Verse whose rhythm is based on the duration of sound rather than the stress or number of syllables per line.

Quatrain (p. 300): A four-line stanza.

Refrain: A recurring line or phrase.

Requiem: A hymn or dirge dedicated to the repose of the dead.

Rhyme: Two or more words that sound alike.

Rhyme Royal: Seven iambic pentameter lines rhyming *ababbcc*.

Rhyme Scheme (p. 301): The arrangement of the rhyming words at the end of the lines in a poem. The first rhyming words are customarily labeled a, the second b, and so on.

Rhythm (p. 301): The regular or fairly regular recurrence of a beat or accent, which forms a pattern pleasing to the ear.

Rising Meter: Meter that begins with unstressed and ends with stressed syllables such as iambic and anapestic meter.

Roundel: An eleven-line verse form with a refrain in the fourth and eleventh lines that repeats part of the first line.

Run-on Line (p. 303): A line carrying over into the next line of a poem without pause.

Sapphic: A complex stanzaic pattern, named after the Greek poetess Sappho. It has four lines, the first three with eleven syllables and the fourth with five syllables, in the following metrical form:

ll. 1–3 — ∪ | — — | — ∪ ∪ | — ∪ | — ∪ |

l. 4   — ∪ ∪ | — ∪ |

Sarcasm: An expression of bitter or harsh emotion. Often a cutting taunt in personal derision of someone.

Satire: Humor that employs irony and sarcasm to expose human vice or folly.

Scansion: The metrical analysis of a poem.

Scop: An entertainer who brightened the Anglo-Saxon courts by composing and reciting heroic poetry. Much in demand, he was an honored member of such courts.

Secondary Stress: In metrical analysis this term has two meanings: (1) in any foot the unaccented syllable(s) as opposed to the accented syllable; (2) variation in levels of accent from not quite as light as an unaccented syllable to not as heavy as an accented syllable. The

mark " is used to indicate this kind of secondary stress.

Sentimentality: A direct appeal by the poet to the emotions of the reader, unjustified by the substance of the poem. Emotive words like God, mother, and honor are often used in place of substantive poetry to produce a sentimental effect. Such subjects are the most difficult of all to write about, because the poet must cut through the heavily laden emotional connotations that have accumulated. Notice how E. E. Cummings avoids sentimentality by giving a fresh treatment of death in "Buffalo Bill's defunct."

Sestet (p. 298): The second division of a Petrarchan or Italian sonnet; that is, the last six lines. It follows the octave, or eight-line, division.

Sestina: A poem of six six-line stanzas and a three-line envoy, usually unrhymed. Each stanza repeats the final words of the lines of the first stanza in a varied but fixed sequence. The six end words are used again in the envoy, two in each of the three lines.

Shakespearean or Elizabethan Sonnet (p. 298): A sonnet that has three quatrains rhyming *abab cdcd efef* and a couplet rhyming *gg*.

Simile (p. 304): A figure of speech, or metaphor, that uses the word "like" or "as" in the comparison. An example is "My love is like a red red rose."

Slant Rhyme (p. 303): An imperfect rhyme or off-rhyme, such as "heaven" rhymed with "even."

Solecism: A substandard intrusion into standard English involving errors in grammar or diction.

Sonnet (p. 298): A poem of fourteen lines.

Spenserian Stanza (p. 300): A nine-line stanza, the first eight lines of which are iambic pentameter and the last line of which is iambic hexameter. The rhyme scheme is *ababbcbcc*.

Spondee (p. 301): A poetic foot in which both of the two syllables are accented.

Spoonerism: A slip of the tongue in which the sounds of words are accidentally transposed, as in "our queer old dean" for "our dear old queen." The term is named after Dr. W. A. Spooner of Oxford, who was noted for such slips.

Sprung Rhythm: As defined by the creator of the term, Gerard Manley Hopkins, poetry whose rhythm is determined by stressed syllables only. In other words, so long as each foot has one stressed syllable, it can vary from the other feet by having from one to three unstressed syllables.

Stanza (p. 300): A section or division within a poem.

Surrealism: A post-World-War-I movement in art and literature based on the expression of the contents of the mind uncontrolled by reason. It seeks to reach the subconscious mind as revealed in fantasies or dreams through devices like "automatic writing," —that is, writing free from rational control.

Syllabic Verse (p. 302): A form employing a certain number of syllables for each line, without regard to accent.

Symbol (p. 305): An object that both carries its own meaning and suggests a meaning larger than itself. The cross is a symbol of Christianity.

Synecdoche (p. 305): Use of a part to stand for the whole, or of the whole to stand for a part.

Synesthesia: A device describing one sensation in the language usually used to describe another. An example is the use of "loud" to describe a bright color.

Syntax: The relations of words within a sentence. Syntax refers to the patterns by which words are formed into phrases and sentences and describes their functions as subject, verb, and so forth.

Tanka: A form of Japanese poetry very much like the Haiku. It consists of five lines, the first and third having five syllables and the rest having seven, for a total always of thirty-one.

Tautology: The repetition of an idea in words that add neither meaning nor emphasis, as in "the shady shade" and "repetitious refrain."

Tercet (p. 300): A three-line stanza.

Terza Rima: A technique using three-line stanzas in which the stanzas rhyme *aba/bcb/cdc*, and so forth. This rhyme scheme was used by Dante in his *Divine Comedy.*

Theme: The basic meaning(s) of the poem. The essence of the meaning is derived from the content, interpreted on a more or less philosophical level, and the form. The theme may be relatively simple or complex. For example, Sharmel Iris' poem "April" (p. 133) appears to have a single lucid theme—bereaved love; whereas Matthew Arnold's "Dover Beach" (p. 189) seems to have a multiplicity of themes in complex interaction: love; war; illusion and reality; faith, doubt, and struggle; disillusionment; the exaltation of individuality; and others.

Tone (pp. 37, 305): The expression of the speaker's attitude. Tone in poetry is comparable to a speaker's tone of voice in oral communication. The tone may be formal, pompous, ironic, sentimental, and so forth.

Transferred Epithet: The use of an adjective to modify a noun and thus create a relationship that normally would be unacceptable or objectively meaningless or contradictory. Keats uses this technique when he refers to a Grecian urn as "Thou still unravished bride of quietness." Note the similarity to Pathetic Fallacy.

Triple Meter: Meter having three syllable feet, such as anapestic and dactylic meter.

Triplet: Three rhyming lines in succession.

Trochee: A metrical foot of two syllables with the accent on the first syllable such as Monday.

Ubi Sunt: Literally, "where are they?" Poems that comment upon the transitoriness of all beautiful things and of life itself are "ubi sunt" poems because in effect they ask, "Where have all the flowers gone?" and by asking the question, imply the answer: They have withered and died. One of the most famous of "ubi sunt" poems is Villon's "Ballad of Dead Ladies," in which the poet speaks of beautiful women of the past who have died and tells where they now are by asking ". . . where are the snows of yesteryear?"

Ultima Thule: The farthest limit or point possible, often in the sense of a remote goal or a mysterious country like ancient Thule.

Understatement (p. 305): A figure of speech that says less than might be expected.

Verse: Used in three senses: (1) a single metrical line; (2) a poem of lesser merit than the term "poetry" connotes; and (3) generally, a substitute for the more accurate term—poetry. "Verse" is often colloquially used to mean "stanza."

Villanelle: A short poem of nineteen lines written in five tercets and a final quatrain with only two rhymes. Lines one and three are each repeated three times within the poem. The effect of the form is usually an idyllic lightness.

Zeugma: A joining together of two words that are in the same grammatical relationship to another word but in different senses logically:

And now a rabble rages, now a fire.
Each "rages" in a different sense.

(*Dr. Johnson*)

Index of the Approaches to Poetry

Index of Poets

Index of Poems

Index and Pronunciation Guide for Poetic Terms

ABOUT THE AUTHORS

H. EDWARD RICHARDSON, Professor of English at the University of Louisville, received his B.A. from Eastern Kentucky University and his M.A. and Ph.D. from the University of Southern California. Before going to the University of Louisville, he taught at the California State Colleges at Fullerton and Los Angeles, Eastern Kentucky University, the University of Southern California, Fullerton Junior College in California, and was chairman of the Department of English at Eastern Kentucky University from 1965 to 1967. He is the author of *William Faulkner: The Journey to Self-Discovery* (1969), *How to Think and Write* (1971), and has contributed many articles to scholarly journals.

FREDERICK B. SHROYER is currently Professor of English and American Literature at California State College, Los Angeles, where he has taught since 1950. He received his B.A., M.A., and Ph.D. from the University of Southern California and, in 1969, was Bingham Professor of Humanities at the University of Louisville. Founder and director of the Pacific Coast Writers Conference and the Idyllwild Writers Conference, he has made numerous appearances on radio and television. Professor Shroyer is literary editor for the Los Angeles *Herald-Examiner*, author of *Wall Against the Night* (1957), *It Happened in Wayland* (1963), and *There None Embrace* (1966), and coeditor of *A College Treasury* (1957), *Short Story: A Thematic Anthology* (with Dorothy Parker, 1965), and *Types of Drama* (1970).

A NOTE ON THE TYPE

This old face design, BEMBO 270, has such an up-to-date appearance that it is difficult to realize this letter was cut (the first of its line) before A.D. 1500. At Venice in 1495, ALDUS MANUTIUS ROMANUS printed a small 36 pp. tract, *Petri Bembi de Aetna ad Angelum Chabrielem liber*, written by the young humanist poet PIETRO BEMBO (later Cardinal, and secretary to Pope Leo X), using a new design of type which differed considerably from that of Jenson's. The punches were cut by FRANCESCO GRIFFO of Bologna the designer responsible six years later for the first italic types. A second roman face followed in 1499 and this type design, based on the first, and used to print the famous illustrated *Hypnerotomachia Poliphili*, was the one which, after adaptation by Garamond, Voskens and others, resulted finally in Caslon Old Face.

Printed and bound by The Haddon Craftsmen, Inc., Scranton, Pa.

Typography by Al Burkhardt

Photographs by Hal Wilson